THE AMERICAN ALPINE JOURNAL

2020

[Front Cover] **Chris Wright** during the first ascent of Link Sar in Pakistan (p.12). *Steve Swenson* [This page] **Alex Honnold** messing around on the exit moves of Passage to Freedom (p.90), a newly completed free route up El Capitan. *Austin Siadak*

[Photo] Climbing above the Yentna Glacier in the Alaska Range (see p.137). Sultana (a.k.a. Mt. Foraker, 17,402') is in the background. *Joe Stock*

2020   VOLUME 62 ISSUE 94

CONTENTS

RECON

CLIMBS & EXPEDITIONS

The American Alpine Club, 710 10th St. Suite 100, Golden, Colorado

E-mail: aaj@americanalpineclub.org
www.publications.americanalpineclub.org

ISBN (paperback): 978-0-9998556-8-3
ISBN (hardcover): 978-0-9998556-9-0
©2020 The American Alpine Club. All rights reserved.
Printed in China

[Photo] **Derek Watson** finds the way during the first ascent of Ridakh Ridge in the Karakoram (see p.289). *Cati Lladó*

2019 GREAT RANGES FELLOWSHIP

[EIGER]

Yvon & Malinda Chouinard
Francis Dean
Kevin & Leanne Duncan
Chuck & Lisa Fleischman Family
Bruce Franks

Gerald Gallwas
Shawn Kahle
Louis Kasischke
Craig McKibben & Sarah Merner
Miriam Nelson & Kinloch Earle

Steve & Paula Mae Schwartz
Cody J Smith
Steven Sorkin
Roger & Sha Sha Walker

[ALPAMAYO]

Warren Adelman
Edmund & Betsy Cabot Foundation
Philip Duff
James M. Edwards & Michele Mass
Dan Emmett
James Garrett & Franziska Garrett, M.D.
Rocky Henderson

David Landman & Marian Hawley
Randy Luskey
Brent Manning
Peter & Kathleen Metcalf
James Morrissey
Mark & Teresa Richey
David Riggs
Carey Roberts

Naoe Sakashita
Janet Schlindwein
Kent Stenderup
Pavan Surapaneni
Greg Thomsen
Lawrence True & Linda Brown

[ROBSON]

Jon Anderson
Adi Azulay
Gordon A. Benner, M.D.
Stuart & Marcella Bernstein
Sumit Bhardwaj
John Bird
Mitch Campbell
R.J. Campbell

Alpenglow Foundation & The John Hobby Catto Family
Bradford Dempsey
The Duckworth Family
Sara Gerber
David Goeddel
Pat Goodman

Todd Hoffman
Richard E. Hoffman M.D.
Thomas Hornbein, M.D.
Mark Kroese
Phil Lakin Jr.
Paul Lego
Brad McQueen
Hari Mix

Michael Morgan Family Foundation
Paul Morrow
Stephen Schofield
John & Rebecca Soebbing
Travis Spitzer Family Foundation
William & Barbara Straka

Steven Swenson & Ann Dalton
Jack & Pat Tackle
William Thompson
Maggie Walker
Robert Weggel
Nicholas Weicht
Cheryl Young

[TEEWINOT]

Lisa Abbott
Mark Aiston
Joseph Andreotti
Anonymous
Anonymous
Michael & Matthew Ashley
Mia Axon
Seavron Banus
George Basch
Bob Bechaud
Rich Beeson
Vaclav Benes
John Berry
Dimitri Bevc
Matthew Biscan
Ronald Bixby
Jim Bodenhamer
Stephen Bonowski
Steve Bott
Tanya Bradby & Martin Slovacek
Martin Brigham
Pete Brownell
Paul Brunner & Coleen Curry
Jennifer Bruursema
Deanne Buck
Thomas Burch
Will Butcher
Ailie Byers
Deirdre Byers
Jennifer Chang
Ward Chewning
Jimmy Chin
Diana Choi
Randy Christopherson
John T. Cobb
Dan & Ilene Cohen
Brendan Conway

Kevin Cooney
John Costello
Billy Cox
Lawrence Crispell
Christopher Croft
Matt & Charlotte Culberson
John Davidge
Joseph Davidson
Scott Davis
Brian Deitch
Walter Dembitsky
Stanley Dempsey
Laura Deschenes
Kit DesLauriers
John N. Donlou M.D.
Melvyn Douglas
Christopher Downs
Jeff Dozier
Richard & Martha Draves
Ken Ehrhart
Charles Eilers
Stuart Ellison
Philip Erard
Chris Falkensten
Chas Fisher
Timothy Forbes
Jared Fox
James Frank
Alexander Friedman
Jim Frush
Eiichi Fukushima
Marilyn Geninatti
Clark Gerhardt
Michael Gibbons
Jock Glidden
Russell Gray
Eric Green
Wayne & Cynthia Griffin

Robert B. Hall & Sheila Matz
Rick Hanheide
Amanda Hankison
Jeff Hanks
Roger Härtl
John Hebert
Doug Henderson
Scot Hillman
Mark Hingston
Michael Hodges
Marley & Jennifer Hodgson
Robert Hoffman
Scott Holder
Katie Huskins
John Hutchinson
Alex Intermill & Lisa McKinney
Lorraine Kan
Steven Kasoff
Arthur & Diane Kearns
Kelson Foundation
Adam Kilgus
Mark & Samskriti King
James Laugharn
Michael Lederer
John Lee
Douglas Leen
Stephen Linaweaver
Daniel Lochner
Jamie Logan
Gregory Louie
Conrad & Jenni Lowe-Anker
George Lowe III
Chris Lynch
Scott McCaffrey
John McGarry

Kwyn Alice Meagher
Richard Merritt
Scott Milliman
Halsted "Hacksaw" Morris
Mark Nagle
Hilaree Nelson
John Nicholson
Sean O'Brien
Peter O'Neil
Timothy O'Neill
Bob Palais
Mr. & Mrs. Adam Patridge
Charles Peck
Samuel Perlik
Keenan Pope
Eliza Porterfield
Mari Margaret Piva Raaf
John Rehmer
Louis Reichardt
Drummond Rennie
John Reppy
Jodi Richard
Wolf Riehle
Michael Riley
Barbara Roach
Joel Robinson
John Rudolph
Amanda Ryan-Fear
Lauren Sanders
Jeb Sanford
Ben Schifrin
Theo Schuff
Ulrika & Mark Schumacher M.D.
Stephen Scofield
Trudi Seiwald
George Shaw
Lauren Sigman

Samuel Silverstein M.D.
Fred Simmons
Hang Kei Simon Wong
John Sirois
David Skyer
George N. Smith
Jay Smith
Anne Smith & Jim Herson
James Sneeringer
Joy Souligny
Katelyn Stahley
Mark Stein
Rob & Jennifer Stephenson
Theophile Strebelle
Bob & Pamela Street
Theodore "Sam" Streibert
Duncan Stuart
Parisa Tabriz & Emerson Stewart
Steve & Krista Taylor
John Tedeschi
David Thoenen
Patrick Tolley
Dirk Tyler
Gregory van Inwegen
Raymond VJ Schrag
Dieter von Hennig
Steve Whitaker
Nathan Wilhelm
Doug Wilson
Todd Winzenried
Fred Wolfe
Masayuki Yokota

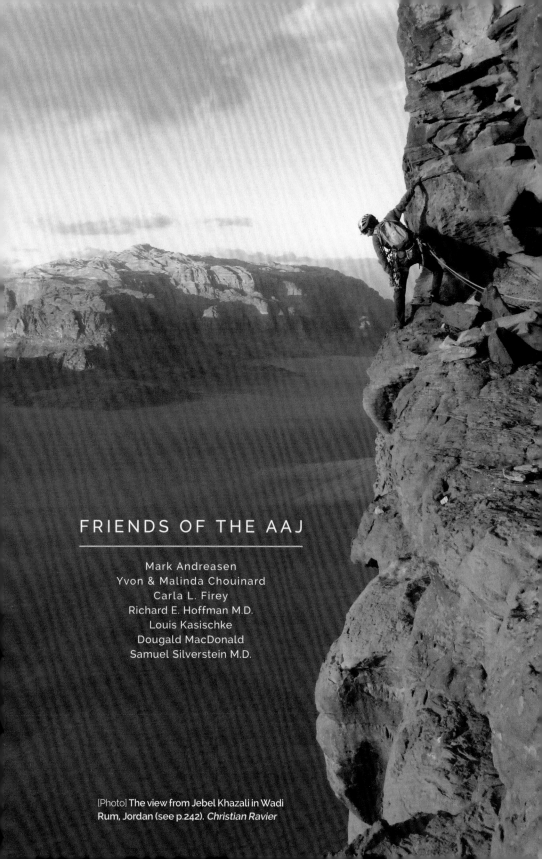

FRIENDS OF THE AAJ

Mark Andreasen
Yvon & Malinda Chouinard
Carla L. Firey
Richard E. Hoffman M.D.
Louis Kasischke
Dougald MacDonald
Samuel Silverstein M.D.

[Photo] **The view from Jebel Khazali in Wadi Rum, Jordan (see p.242).** *Christian Ravier*

THE AMERICAN ALPINE JOURNAL

EDITOR
Dougald MacDonald

ART DIRECTOR
David Boersma — Mojave Creative Lab

SENIOR EDITOR
Lindsay Griffin

ASSOCIATE EDITORS
Andy Anderson, Chris Kalman, Erik Rieger

CONTRIBUTING EDITORS
Whitney Clark, Damien Gildea, David
Stevenson (Books)

ILLUSTRATIONS AND MAPS
Tami Knight, Anna Riling

PROOFREADERS
Austin BeckDoss, Damien Gildea, Bruce
Normand, Rodolphe Popier, Simon
Richardson, Daniel Stevenson, and the
AAC headquarters crew

TRANSLATORS
Elena Dmitrenko, Zuzka Háková, Monika
Hartman, Anna Piunova, Pam Ranger
Roberts, Xia Zhongming

INDEXERS
Ralph Ferrara, Eve Tallman

REGIONAL CONTACTS
Steve Gruhn, Mark Westman, *Alaska*;
Drew Brayshaw, Ian Welsted, *Canada*;
Sevi Bohorquez, Sergio Ramírez Carrascal,
Perú; Luis Pardo, *Colombia*; Damien Gildea,
Antarctica; Rolando Garibotti, Camilo Rada,
Marcelo Scanu, *Argentina and Chile*; Robert
Rauch, Alex von Ungern, *Bolivia*; Harish
Kapadia, Nandini Purandare, *India*; Rodolphe
Popier, Richard Salisbury, *Nepal*; Tamotsu
Nakamura, Hiroshi Hagiwara, *Japan*; Peter
Jensen-Choi, Oh Young-hoon, *Korea*; Elena
Dmitrenko, Anna Piunova, *Russia, Tajikistan,
and Kyrgyzstan*; Xia Zhongming, *China*

ADVISORY BOARD
Chantel Astorga, Alison Criscitiello, Kelly
Cordes, Brody Leven (ski mountaineering),
Damien Gildea, Colin Haley, Mark Jenkins,
Simon Richardson, Graham Zimmerman

WITH SPECIAL THANKS TO...
Christine Blackmon, Kelly Cordes,
Elizabeth Cromwell, Rolando Garibotti,
Damien Gildea, Steve Gruhn, Tami Knight,
Camilo Rada, Anna Riling, members of the
American Alpine Club, and our hundreds
of authors, photographers, and donors

THE AMERICAN ALPINE CLUB

OFFICIALS FOR THE YEAR 2020

📷 *AAC member Andy Wickstrom*

You belong here.

Since 1929, the *American Alpine Journal* has stood as the world's foremost record of major long climbs. Through 91 years of publication—through the depressions, wars, recessions, and pandemics that have tested our resolve—it is the support of dedicated AAC members that has allowed the *AAJ* to continue to carry that torch. Together, we're writing the story of our sport and so much more. Are you with us?

United We Climb.

americanalpineclub.org/benefits

PREFACE

FIFTEEN YEARS AT THE AAC

BY PHIL POWERS

WHAT WONDERFUL YEARS.

Fifteen years ago, newly at the helm of the American Alpine Club, I quoted the AAJ subtitle—"the world's most significant climbs"—in my first note to members. One recipient reminded me that, "The most significant climbs are the ones we do ourselves." What we do as climbers is infinitely wilder and more varied today than I ever could have imagined when I read those words.

The central effort of these years at the AAC, as our membership has grown to over 25,000, has been to welcome the full and expanding variety of climbers and the extraordinary diversity with which we approach the vertical world. These pages tell some of those stories. But as I was reminded, the power of climbing is the role it plays in each of our lives and the ways in which we apply ourselves to the issues we face in the larger world.

Climbing has been a central force in my life since I first touched rock in Oklahoma's Wichita Mountains. It demands health and fitness and, especially for those of us who came to climbing through informal instruction, a personal commitment to competency. These years at the AAC have offered me the chance to befriend some of the early greats of our craft while, even as my own climbing slows, roping up with some of the groundbreaking talents of today. As a lifelong pursuit, climbing has anchored me in health and discipline. And, like a meditation, it draws me back when distractions steal my focus.

The most rewarding part of these years has been witnessing the growth of this discipline—that is good news for the planet and each other. In the face of existential threats like we've never seen, I'm comforted by the fact that so many are finding their way to this craft—one that demands so much of the individual while offering intimacy with and passion for the natural world. The world we depend upon.

While the AAC's membership has grown, I think the percentage of climbers who actually join the club has not. You, as a reader of this journal, are among the most engaged—leaders in efforts that benefit the entire climbing community.

Climbing has a voice on the national scene like never before. Today's climbing athletes are articulate, talented policy spokespeople. The portfolio of efforts and issues the AAC has been able to influence has expanded our horizons. National public land policy (an exceedingly broad issue) and climate change (even broader) are at the center of this agenda. Climbers open doors in these conversations, and the next generation of advocates is extremely well equipped for the job.

Given the variety we find in the climbing population, AAC membership will never be the only way this organization engages with climbers. We find ways to meet people—with knowledge and community—at every place along one's path in climbing. The AAJ has always been central to that. As one longtime editor said, "It's a book of dreams."

It is also a book of tragedy. We all know that the vertical world does not forgive mistakes; it sometimes brings hazard directly to us. Reinhold Messner described a sixth sense that practiced alpinists might use to anticipate and dodge objective hazard. In our prime, we may become expert at avoiding hazard, but we've seen it catch up with even the most skilled and aware. My personal and professional lives come together in climbing. Even having experienced great loss, I am grateful for all of it.

Tied to the great joy and clarity that climbing brings is the deep and recurring experience of loss, tragedy, and sadness. These years include nights on the phone encouraging rescue efforts, days with the families of fallen climbers, and the loss of too many friends.

In grief, climbers come with action. We respond: let's teach that skill, discuss that mistake, never let another climber rappel off the end of a rope.

Climbing allows a deep interaction with an exquisite, magical, and, as it turns out, exceedingly rare ecosystem called Planet Earth. My personal experience with fallen friends, lost partners, and grieving families leads to responses like expanding affordable climbing education and opening conversations around our mental health and loss.

Today I see a world that is being tangibly destroyed—climbers see it firsthand—by the changing climate and an economy exposed for its lack of resilience, especially for the poor, in the face of a global pandemic. But I credit climbing for helping me combine that real despair I feel with action.

I leave the AAC with what I hope is a foundation for great future. But as a climber, I also leave with a drive to turn the concern I feel for our world into the solutions I know we can find (have found) and can deploy.

As a teacher and guide I've often said that anyone can climb. But it is still not true that everyone has access to climbing. I very much hope that helping people find their way to climbing—to share this passion we are so blessed to enjoy—will remain at the very center of the AAC's work.

At each of our annual dinners, I make a point to acknowledge the support we all receive from friends and family members. My own family and friends have made it possible for me to bring my best to this job and these years—thank you for joining me in a climbing life. For me, this group overlaps thoroughly with the staff and leaders with whom I have worked: all the committee and section leaders, past presidents, board members and, importantly, the seven board presidents I have served under—thank you for your hard work, positive attitude, and dedication to climbing.

Thank you.

Phil Powers served as CEO of the American Alpine Club from 2005 to 2020.

Steve Swenson follows a corniced ridge during summit day on Link Sar. *Graham Zimmerman*

SYNERGY

THE POWER OF PARTNERSHIP ON THE FIRST ASCENT OF LINK SAR IN PAKISTAN

STEVE SWENSON AND GRAHAM ZIMMERMAN

(A) Changi Tower. (B) K6 Main. (C) Link Sar (7,041m) from the southeast, showing the line of the 2019 ascent, advanced base camp, and bivouacs. Stocking ABC at 4,700 meters (1,000 meters above base camp) with weeks of supplies was a crucial strategy behind the team's success. *Matteo Della Bordella*

G RAHAM: We had spent the night on a broad ledge at 6,800 meters. The pointy apex of Link Sar seemed to loom just above us. But as I kept climbing, it didn't appear to be getting any closer. Then the snow hardened abruptly, and I began sinking less. After many hours of thigh-deep floundering, I began to move up rapidly. Moments later, I felt an abrupt confusion: The snow in front of me seemed to be shifting, its grains moving like rice poured slowly from a bag. For an instant, I thought I was hallucinating because of the altitude. Then I realized I was standing on a slab that had been hidden amid the wind-blasted snows of the high mountain. Now, the slab had broken off, and it began to accelerate rapidly.

I tried to hang on, but I'd only set my axes with a quick punch instead of swinging them deeply into the snow. The growing stream of debris knocked the tools out of their hasty placements. "Falling!" I screamed. My partners, around a corner, couldn't see me as I tumbled backward, sliding headfirst on my back for 20 meters. I cursed loudly as I struggled to right myself, arrest my fall, and regain control. Then the avalanche swept me over a cliff, and I freefell another 15 meters until the ropes caught over a rib of snow and ice. I stopped in midair, face down, staring into 3,000 meters of void.

STEVE: Link Sar is a 7,041-meter peak in the Kondus Valley of the Pakistan Karakoram, rising above the Kaberi Glacier. By the time we arrived in June 2019, at least eight previous expeditions had failed in attempts to make the first ascent of this peak.

It wasn't just technical difficulties that prevented the mountain from being climbed. This region had an on-and-off history of opening to climbers, because of the conflict between India and Pakistan over Kashmir. In 1979, a few years after the Pakistan-administered Karakoram reopened to climbing, following a decade-long closure, a Japanese expedition made the first attempt to climb Link Sar. From the village of Kaphlu, they walked an arduous 50 kilometers to base camp, including crossings of the Shyok and Hushe rivers on flimsy bamboo rafts held afloat by goat-skin bladders and long marches up shifting, boulder-strewn glaciers. On Link Sar the Japanese found the climbing difficult and dangerous, and they turned back after reaching 5,700 meters.

Unfortunately, this part of the Karakoram would not remain open to climbers for much longer. In 1982, tensions with India caused Pakistan to close the areas to the west of the Saltoro Ridge and the passes over it that gave access onto the 47-mile-long Siachen Glacier. In the early spring of 1984, India helicoptered troops onto this ridge and the Pakistanis launched a counter-offensive. The Siachen conflict never succeeded in displacing the Indian troops, and it resulted in a standoff comparable to a modern-day version of the World War I trench warfare in the eastern Alps.

The valleys west of the Saltoro Ridge would be mostly closed to climbers for 35 years. One exception was in 2000, when Americans Dave Anderson, Jimmy Chin, Steph Davis, and Brady Robinson were allowed to climb in the Kondus Valley. They made the first ascent of a peak they named after General Tahir, the commander of the Pakistan Army Siachen Brigade, who had helped them obtain permission. Afterward, Jimmy shared with me some photos of the Kondus and pointed out the mountain dominating this valley above the village of Karmading: Link Sar, an unclimbed 7,000-meter peak. Knowing that openings to

Steve Swenson scopes the crux pitches above Camp 1. This passage, discovered in 2017, was climbed at night for safety. *Graham Zimmerman*

such restricted areas can be fickle, I applied right away and received a permit for Link Sar in 2001.

The 2001 expedition was able to drive to base camp on a narrow jeep track that in the 1980s was blasted out of the cliffs above the Kaberi Glacier to supply troops faced off with Indian soldiers. During the three weeks before I was able to arrive, Steve Larson, George Lowe, Joe Terravecchia, Andy Tuthill, and Eric Winkelman followed the 1979 Japanese route to 5,500 meters and discovered the upper part of their route was threatened by seracs. They retreated to base camp, where I finally joined them. Several of us explored a different possibility on the southeast face. We didn't have the time or resources to get much higher than about 5,200 meters, but this route seemed promising and we planned to return. Unfortunately, General Tahir rotated to a different command the following year, and the Kondus Valley was again closed to climbers.

In 2003, India and Pakistan agreed to a ceasefire in Kashmir. To test whether this would induce the Pakistanis into reopening the Kondus, I applied for and was denied a Link Sar permit in 2004, 2005, 2006, and 2007. Pakistani friends warned me that repeated applications to climb in this restricted area might arouse suspicion from the intelligence services—they might misinterpret my motives and think I was a spy. I decided to wait.

In the meantime, other climbers, most notably Jon Griffith from the U.K., started to make attempts on Link Sar from the Charakusa Valley, where it was possible to obtain climbing permits. Jon's four expeditions from 2012 to 2015 climbed up to the horseshoe-shaped ridgeline at the head of the valley, between K6 and K7, from which a spur ridge led eastward toward Link Sar. However,

[Top] Mark Richey (center) prepares porters to use a "via ferrata" the team installed for load carrying to ABC. *Steve Swenson* [Bottom] Once ABC was established, it became an ideal launch pad for the upper mountain. *Graham Zimmerman*

they discovered this spur was capped by a series of large granite towers and was nearly impossible to traverse. On their last attempt, Griffith and Andy Houseman topped the westernmost tower along the spur, naming it "Link Sar West," but illness and the obvious difficulties ahead prevented them from going further.

In 2015 and 2016, the agencies responsible for Pakistani security opened some previously closed valleys adjacent to the Kondus to climbers. By now, any suspicion of 007-style activity on my part would be forgotten, and I applied for a Link Sar permit again in 2017, along with Chris Wright and Graham Zimmerman, two much younger climbers. Our permit was granted, and my 16-year quest to return to this area had succeeded!

GRAHAM: For over two months in the summer of 2017, Steve, Chris, and I struggled to find a path up the southeast face from where Steve had left off in 2001. We clambered up ridges that wound to nowhere or ended in slopes under the threat of serac walls. We spotted a small glacier on the north side of the main ridgeline that seemed to bypass all these difficulties, but we couldn't see a way to get over the ridge and down onto the glacier. Back at ABC, we noticed that an ibex herd was crossing this complex ridge system, so we followed their tracks over "Ibex Pass" and found a way onto the little glacier and up to the site of Camp I. The route we'd discovered was relatively safe from overhead hazard, but intense storms pinned us down again and again far below the summit. When we staggered back to base camp for the last time, our expedition staff members and old friends, Hajji Rasool and his son-in-law Nadeem, embraced us. We all knew we'd be coming back.

As we negotiated for a permit for the 2019 season and discussed strategies for our next attempt, we decided to bring on a fourth partner. Like Steve, Mark Richey was in his 60s and had a family. In 2012, he and Steve had received a Piolet d'Or, with Freddie Wilkinson, for the first ascent of Saser Kangri II (7,518 meters) in the Indian Karakoram. The addition of another longtime climber, with whom Steve had such a strong partnership, seemed to create a balance between the power of youth and the wisdom of age. Mark's response to our invitation was emphatic: "Let's go do this thing!"

STEVE: The Kondus is one of the deepest valleys in the Karakoram, and our roadside base camp at 3,700 meters was 800 meters lower than base camps in the nearby Charakusa or Nangmah valleys. The 3,300 meters of relief between here and the summit was a similar distance to that found on K2 or Everest. Besides poor weather, operating out of such a low base camp was one of the main reasons we had failed in 2017. This time we had a different plan.

The idea was to establish and supply a more robust advanced base camp at 4,700 meters and live there for weeks, if necessary, with two of our hired cooks. We wouldn't need to go down to base camp every time it stormed, like we did before. There had been record snowfall in the Karakoram the previous winter, and we would have to wait for it to slide off in seasonal avalanches, melt, or consolidate before climbing. But this would give us plenty of time to carry everything we needed up to ABC.

We couldn't do all this work ourselves, and an exposed rock band above the Kaberi Glacier presented safety challenges for the low-altitude porters. Our solution was to train five experienced men from the nearby village of Karmading to use harnesses and lanyards, so they could secure themselves to a sort of via ferrata that we built through this section with old ropes.

Together with the porters, we carried all our supplies to ABC and were able to move in on July 5—it was summertime, but we still had to dig away about a meter of snow to set up our tents on the grass. The July heat triggered avalanches all around, and it wasn't until the 15th that we were able to move up to Camp I, at 5,200 meters, following the route we had established in 2017. Two days later, Chris and Graham led the team above Camp I via a mixed rock/ice gully and a snow ridge, the only safe way up a broad 600-meter-high rock wall flanked on both sides by active seracs. Climbing at night to avoid the heat, we set Camp II at 5,900 meters, which had been the high point of our previous expedition. There were no other peaks in the valley where we could readily get to this elevation to acclimatize, so we spent two nights at Camp II before descending to ABC. The top was still around 1,000 meters higher. It felt desperately far away.

Agreeing on the best weather window to make a summit attempt is one of the most stressful parts of expeditions like these. Satellite phones and internet technology enabled us to get up-to-date custom weather forecasts, but I had learned that such information doesn't completely replace gut feelings based on experience. After much debate, we finally left ABC on July 31 with a forecast for two good days followed by a couple of mild stormy days, and then what looked like a long spell of clear, calm weather. This would give us plenty of good days to reach the summit and return, as long as we carried enough food and fuel to wait out the poor weather. We were gambling that the long-term forecast wouldn't change.

GRAHAM: After waiting out the afternoon heat at Camp I and then climbing the difficult mixed pitches through the rock barrier all night (about 10 pitches, up to M6+), we were back at our second bivouac by midmorning on August 1, perched on an ice rib that was safe from all except a catastrophic collapse of the serac barrier that loomed above. We moved faster now that our bodies were more acclimatized. Still, the thought of climbing the overhanging glacial ice above us in the nearly 6,000-meter air made me wince.

The next day, Mark and Chris found a way to sneak around the seracs and onto a tabletop of ice separated from the main face. It was my turn to lead, and I hoped I could find a line that avoided the overhangs of ice rising out of the gap between us and the main face. Finally, a snow bridge spanned the chasm, and I carefully stepped onto its soft surface. It held my weight.

On the other side, I relaxed into the simple cadence of ice tool placements and crampon kicks into soft ice. I could feel moisture in the air. Clouds were starting to close in around us, but, as planned, we were prepared with enough food to wait out the short storm that was in the forecast. Soon we made it to a snowy ledge on a protruding glacial ice feature that we had seen from below and in our photographs from Changi Tower, a 6,500-meter peak that Steve and I, along with Scott

[Top Left] **Waiting out a snow squall above Camp 3.** *Graham Zimmerman* [Bottom Left] **Bypassing the enormous serac above Camp 2.** *Mark Richey* [Right] **Zimmerman leads steep ice toward the high bivouac on Link Sar's southeast face at 6,800 meters.** *Mark Richey*

Bennett, had climbed for the first ascent in 2015. We hunkered down in our tents, knowing our camp was far from any overhead hazard and for now, at least, we were safe.

Thirty-six hours later, on August 4, with the storm forecasted to end soon, we started before dawn and climbed 200 meters above our previous bivy. However, the wind and snow continued, and before long we were sitting in the dark at the edge of a bergschrund, still engulfed in a blizzard. The shoulders of my partners slumped under the pounding snow, and to maintain morale I decided that any activity was better than none, so I found our shovel and started digging. Steve immediately caught on to my plan, and then the others joined in. As I dug, I started to feel warmer. After an hour, gusts still buffeted the mountain, but now we were tucked into a snow cave, sheltered and comfortable. The mood of the team shifted quickly as our bodies warmed. Eventually, the shadowy forms of mountains around us started to emerge as the storm finally abated. Once again, we started upward.

The vertical ice directly above our snow cave was some of the best I've experienced in the mountains—with just a single swing, my axes stuck securely. Quickly, however, the firm surface gave way to seemingly endless deep snow. Hours later, I stared down between my feet at my partners, who were tied to a feeble belay anchor composed of a snow-filled stuff sack and a picket buried deep into the slope; the rope was strung out for 30 meters between us, attached to nothing. As I slowly dug upward through the drifts, I hoped for a small patch of ice into which to swing my axe or place another screw. Instead, I shoved another picket into the soft snow and continued higher, carefully crafting each step and plunging the shafts of my axes.

I looked up to a serac wall that I hoped would mark the end of the wallowing: Its ancient gray ice undulated in the flat high-mountain light. It seemed a little closer than it did the last time I'd checked, but still far away. What had drawn me to this peak? Why was I drawn to chase

Chris Wright leading awkward mixed ground with a heavy pack low on the rock band between camps 1 and 2. The team climbed all night to complete 10 pitches, up to M6+, and reach their second bivouac by midmorning, before the day's heat made lower-elevation climbing too dangerous. *Steve Swenson*

these summits, worlds away from so much that I love? I looked down again at my partners, dear friends and mentors. Chris leaned into the snow slope to rest while Mark and Steve hung off the belay and gazed out over the range, their posture demonstrating their obvious comfort in this wild and high space. I shook my head to clear my thoughts and refocused on upward progress.

From our final bivouac, our fifth night above ABC, we could see the summit 250 meters above in the fading light. Next morning, August 5, Chris led the ice wall above our tents and then started traversing up and left along the side of a steep, corniced snow ridge punctuated with a couple of rock towers. After several pitches, I took over the leading. And then snow in front of me began shifting and I was sliding headfirst toward the void.

After the avalanche sent me tumbling over the cliff, my partners were far above me and hidden around a ridge of rock and snow. I yelled toward the belay, wanting to let them know that I was conscious, but I couldn't hear a reply. I righted myself and swung into the wall to place a cam. If I could unweight the rope, they would at least know that I was awake and moving. I probed my body, expecting to find an injury, but only noticed one missing zipper pull ripped from my pants.

Steve had just arrived at the last belay station to join Chris and Mark, and now he traversed over the rock and snow ridge toward me. Finally able to communicate, we established that neither I nor they were injured. Steve placed a new anchor, and I jugged one of our ropes while Steve belayed me on the other. Two hours after the fall, I embraced him, teary-eyed. He said, "Man, I was so frightened by what might have happened to you that I'm still shaking. I think we should go down." Mark and Chris soon joined us. They were amazed that I was unscathed but remained silent, as if unsure what to do or say. Occasionally one of them would glance at the summit, less than 150 meters above us.

"Guys, I can feel myself coming down from a pretty intense adrenaline rush," I said. A chill

was creeping into my body, and my head felt light. "But I am not hurt. I'm just going to huddle into my warm jacket and sit here, but if one of you is up for leading, let's go up, because there is no way I am coming back up here after this."

Chris offered to take over the lead again, and after a short discussion he started upward. Avoiding the now-obvious section of unstable snow, he moved slowly and deliberately, trying not to waste any energy. I could tell he was tired from days of exertion at altitude, but a single-minded drive for the summit kept him moving upward.

Three pitches later, we regrouped at a stance less than a rope length below the summit. The only anchor Chris could find, a bollard constructed from a thin snow mushroom, didn't seem like enough to me, particularly given my headspace. I crawled into a hole in the snow so I could act as a deadman, another piece of the anchor.

Starting up again, hoping to reach the top, Chris placed a screw and then plunged the shafts of his ice tools into the steep slope above. They sheared through loose drifts without catching or creating any tangible pathway for upward progress. After 10 or 15 meters, he retreated.

"Is all this simply a large cornice?" Mark wondered.

"Are we on top?" Steve said as he arrived from the stance below.

"Are we failing?" I asked myself quietly.

Mark craned his neck to look up at the slate of snow that led toward the top. I knew he had a lot of experience with soft, steep snow from years of climbing in the Peruvian Andes. "Mark, I think you are the only one who knows how to deal with this," I said. "Will you have a look?"

Moving up again after an avalanche swept Zimmerman from this face, just to the right of the rocks in the foreground. Zimmerman was unharmed, and the team eventually decided to continue. *Steve Swenson*

"Yeah, I'll go see," he replied.

Up to this point, I think he'd been holding back his eagerness to lead, knowing Chris and I could go faster than he could, simply by virtue of our youth. Now his desire shone unconcealed in his eyes: the glint of a younger man.

As Mark cast off into the loose, insecure snow, with a single ice screw for protection, Steve said, "We need to be attached to the mountain better than this." He started digging into the slope in search of good ice. Above us, Mark swept his axes overhead to carve a trench in the steep wall, packing the loose snow at his

Zimmerman and Wright embrace on top of Link Sar at sunset after a hard-won summit. *Steve Swenson*

feet to support his weight and then stemming against the trench walls. Steve, with only his lower legs protruding from the tunnel he'd dug, called to me that he'd found a deep vein of ice and was building a V-thread for our anchor. After nearly an hour, Mark screamed down: "I'm on the fucking top!" The path to the summit was now clear, as was the first step back toward the safety of base camp. Thirty minutes later, we were all on the apex of Link Sar.

I arrived last and fell into a deep embrace from Chris. The sunset cast waves of purple hues over the massive breadth of the Karakoram. Some of the steepest and wildest mountains of the world surrounded us in all directions. There were no words. There was only the afterglow of depths of shared exertion and partnership. Then, I declared, "Let's get the hell off this mountain safely," and we started our descent.

STEVE: Two more days of rappelling and downclimbing brought us back to Camp I around midnight. There we had the first of several food parties, the quantity and quality of our cuisine improving the lower we got on the mountain.

Feeling comfortable and safe, I felt ready to begin reflecting on our experience. Climbing a world-class objective like Link Sar doesn't require someone to be the best climber in the world. We had survived Link Sar because of the failures we were willing to accept. We succeeded on Link Sar because we were persistent, learned from our mistakes, applied our 126 years of combined climbing experience, and understood what partnership means.

SUMMARY: First ascent of Link Sar (7,041 meters) in the Pakistan Karakoram via its 3,400-meter southeast face, by Mark Richey, Steven Swenson, Chris Wright, and Graham Zimmerman, July 31–August 8, 2019. The route gained about 2,300 meters above advanced base camp and was graded M6+ WI4 90°.

ABOUT THE AUTHORS: *Steve Swenson, a retired engineering consultant and past president of the American Alpine Club, lives in Seattle and Canmore, Alberta, with his wife, Ann Dalton. His more than 50 years of climbing includes 19 expeditions to the Greater Ranges. Graham Zimmerman lives in Bend, Oregon, with his wife, Shannon McDowell. He is co-owner of Bedrock Film Works and leader of the Protect Our Winters Climb athlete program. The two men discussed the first ascent of Link Sar in episode 22 of the AAJ's Cutting Edge podcast.*

RETURN TO THE HINDU RAJ

THREE EXPEDITIONS TO PAKISTAN'S FORGOTTEN YARKHUN VALLEY

STORIES BY: **TOM LIVINGSTONE** • **WILL SIM** • **SYMON WELFRINGER** • **PIERRE NEYRET**

Dawn at about 6,400 meters after the fourth bivouac on the northwest face of Koyo Zom, looking over the Yarkhun Valley toward the mountains of Afghanistan. *Tom Livingstone*

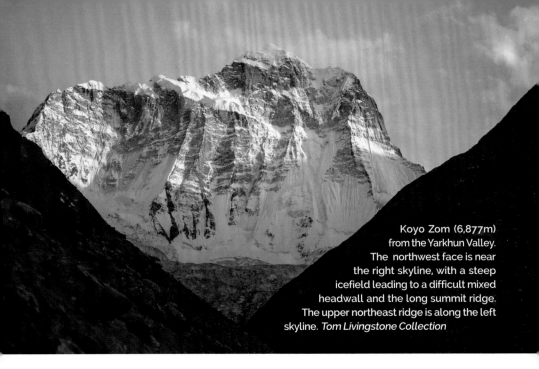

Koyo Zom (6,877m) from the Yarkhun Valley. The northwest face is near the right skyline, with a steep icefield leading to a difficult mixed headwall and the long summit ridge. The upper northeast ridge is along the left skyline. *Tom Livingstone Collection*

THE GREAT GAME

A DIFFICULT NEW ROUTE UP KOYO ZOM, 51 YEARS AFTER THE FIRST ASCENT

BY TOM LIVINGSTONE

ALLY SWINTON AND I sat in an empty hotel restaurant in Gilgit, Pakistan; the morning's silence lingered peacefully. Vaulted ceilings towered overhead. Empty tables and half-tucked chairs littered the room. The space felt overwhelming, like stepping into a cathedral, and I shifted in my seat. It reminded me of the long, cold bivies of the days before.

Just yesterday, we'd been surreally teleported to safety from one of my most intense alpine climbing experiences. Ally and I had quested up a new route, delicately pulling on flakes of rock as we picked our way through mixed ground. "Get some!" I'd shouted as we climbed overhanging granite in rock shoes, the loose stones I threw falling free for hundreds of meters. On the fifth day, bent double with heaving lungs, we slogged to the summit. The raw, pure existence of high-altitude alpinism had taken everything from us.

The day after we summited, we walked down a glacier toward base camp. *On the home straight,* I thought. *Tonight we'll be back with the rest of the lads.* But then: an accident, a helicopter rescue, and now…a hotel restaurant? Civilization was a shock: eight days in the mountains and suddenly warmth, food, water. It felt alien. The last 28 hours had been spent spooning Ally as the blood on his head dried, and I could still smell it on my clothes. Now we floated in a sea of empty restaurant tables. I thought back to where it all began.

Will Sim had "rediscovered" the Hindu Raj. Years of political instability and tension had closed big parts of this mountainous and remote area in northwestern Pakistan, immediately south of Afghanistan, to foreigners. Less than a decade earlier, the Taliban had occupied the nearby Swat Valley, just to the south. The Hindu Raj—especially the Yarkhun Valley on the north side of the range—remained submerged in mystery. [*See related story on p.31.*] But Will's curiosity and research secured a permit for the autumn, and he invited John Crook, Uisdean Hawthorn, Ally Swinton, and me to join.

Our objective was the impressive Koyo Zom (6,877 meters), the highest peak in the range. Like a medieval fortress in the wilds of Asia, its bulk looks toward the plains of Afghanistan, China, and Tajikistan. An enormous, square north face is capped by seracs, and a snowy summit pyramid sits like a crown. The seracs look terrifying, and you can immediately see why the only prior ascents have climbed the easier east face. In 1968, a team of Austrians made the first ascent; British climbers repeated this route in 1974. Since then, the mountain —and much of the range— had remained dormant.

Arriving in the heat and hustle of Islamabad on September 1, our team of five Brits was joined by four Pakistanis, who organized the logistics, cooking, and life in base camp. Imran Shigri of Jasmine Tours, along with Mohsin, Nabeem, and Eshaan, were as excited as we were to explore another region of Pakistan—most of their work was in the Karakoram.

We reached base camp on our sixth day of driving from Islamabad, two days out from the town of Chitral. From a footbridge across the Yarkhun River, it was only a 90-minute walk up a side valley to base camp at 3,500 meters. Lying on the warm, scraggy grass, surrounded by porters' loads, it was easy to forget the previous dusty, bumpy days of riding in Jeeps. As we journeyed further into the mountains, villages faded into isolated hamlets. Great fields of crops became small, precious strips of arable land. We waved to everyone and shouted the Islamic greeting *salaam alaikum!* ("peace be upon you"). Intense stares instantly cracked into friendly smiles, handshakes offered in return. Every evening we arrived at a local guesthouse. We stretched aching bodies in the sun, but when it suddenly dipped behind a ridgeline, the light and warmth were snuffed like a candle between a finger and a thumb. The hush of dusk rushed up the valley. Stars began to pinprick the sky; the moon, clear and bright, grew fatter every night. It had been a sliver when we arrived in Islamabad, and now it had swelled, glowing like a pockmarked disc.

On our final day of driving, we turned toward the east in the remote Yarkhun Valley, parallel to the border with Afghanistan's slender Wakhan Corridor. At last, we saw our mountain, instantly recognizable: Koyo Zom. We jabbered and whooped at the reality after months of anticipation. We all agreed the most attractive option was the right-hand skyline, the northwest face, which rose into a vast, pale-yellow headwall.

At sunset, as the face melted from blood-orange to gold, we knew we'd found a worthy mountain. It looked "nails for breakfast": bowing walls nearly a mile high, and that headwall glowing, alluring, daring. We couldn't stop pointing. "Maybe left from the icefield…then up and right, following a ramp line…?" It was intimidating to think of the summit being over 3,300 meters higher than our base camp. We ducked into our tents as the waxing moon shimmered over the summit. I can think of few more exciting, addictive, and dangerous things than questing onto an intimidating mountain. Koyo Zom looked just the poison.

Acclimatization is a painful necessity in alpinism. If we tried to climb straight to the summit, we'd simply grind to a halt. We had to let our bodies adapt to higher altitudes repeatedly, like a yo-yo, and we spent several days lying in tents with headaches—sudoku, chess, and the occasional meal broke the monotony. Ideally, you want to sleep 1,000 meters lower than your objec-

[Top] Pakistan vs. the U.K. at base camp. *Uisdean Hawthorn* [Bottom] During acclimatization, three team members bivouacked at 5,880 meters atop the sunlit icefield on Koyo Zom's northwest face. *Ally Swinton*

tive's summit. Since Koyo Zom was 6,877 meters and the nearby mountains reached only 5,500 meters, we decided to "crag" the start of our planned route on the northwest face. We'd sleep at the necessary altitude, get a good idea of the initial icefield, and take a closer look at the headwall.

John, Ally, and I spent a cold night at the top of the icefield, breathing heavily at 5,880 meters. We had created a ledge of snow using a purpose-built hammock to catch debris beneath us, since we quickly hit hard ice and rock. The full moon shone like a comforting beacon, and it was so bright we woke early, thinking it was dawn. Unfortunately, Will and Uisdean were ill and had stayed in base camp. It was almost inevitable that some of our team would get sick, but still we felt for them—it was unfortunate to miss out on crucial acclimatization.

After several nights away, we gorged on the luxurious, simple life of base camp. The sun warmed our stiff muscles as we stretched on mattresses, passing the intervals between food. Mohsin cooked delicious dishes of curry, dhal, vegetables, chicken, and goat. We played cricket until we lost all the balls.

The weather remained mostly settled— these were some of the best conditions I'd ever experienced on a big mountain trip. But as the leaves on stunted trees began to turn fiery red, we knew cold temperatures and autumn snows were approaching. We could now see the moon during the day, faintly arcing through the sky over Koyo Zom.

ON EXPEDITIONS YOU reach a terrible moment when you know it's time to climb. In the months before a trip, the actual climb is far in the future. During acclimatization, you're still learning the mountain's moods: You watch how clouds boil around the peak; you see where snow sticks to the face; and you stare as sunshine and shadow reveal new features. Climbing is ignored because so much can happen before then—the team, weather, and conditions all need to align. But eventually the moment arrives.

At breakfast on Sunday, September 22, a weather forecast flashed on the Garmin InReach Mini: *sunshine and good weather continues*. The carefree atmosphere slipped out the door, and long-buried thoughts of climbing surfaced. Ally and I were motivated for the northwest face, on the right. The climbing looked hard, and I reckoned a team had a 50 percent chance of climbing this line. At least the headwall looked relatively safe from objective hazards. The left-hand skyline appeared to have more moderate climbing along a complex ridge. Will, John, and Uisdean chose this line, the northeast ridge: It looked fantastic, and hopefully it would be easier—it also might be more suitable for their acclimatization. A mix of psyche and anxiety begin to bubble.

Base camp resembled a garage sale as we all packed, micro-debating the gear for hours. We clutched scraps of paper full of scribbled lists, and by evening Ally and I had two enormous rucksacks ready. I cursed the weight of our double rack of cams, set and a half of wires, set of pegs, a pair of rock shoes, double sleeping bag, a single-skin tent, food, gas stove, and fuel that might be stretched to eight days, but we couldn't trim anything more.

On Monday we all shouldered our packs and walked to advanced base camp, 1,000 meters higher. We drifted apart, lost in anticipation. *Would the weather hold? What would the climbing be like?* The crux of many alpine routes seems to be in the mind, and this is often the hardest part to control.

The following morning, after a hurried predawn "good luck!" to the others as they rushed toward the left-hand line, Ally and I slogged up the glacier to the right. We spent several painful hours kicking and punching up the icefield to our previous high point. It had been a monstrous 1,300 meters of altitude gain from ABC, but with some potential bad weather forecast at the weekend, we wanted to gain a day, and this was the only way. At the bivy, our snow ledge had retained its undercut sofa-shape from our acclimatization night. We wrapped the bivy hammock around it again and snuggled into the double sleeping bag.

On the second day, Ally led several brilliant mixed pitches up a chimney and gully system. Piece by piece, pitch by pitch, we answered more of our questions, filling in the blanks we'd noted when glassing the face. Everything climbed differently from how we'd expected—a continuing theme. Ally thrutched up granite corners, then hauled the bags, which scraped in protest and caught on every nubbin of rock. We each followed the other's leads; we carried no jumars. Although Ally and I had never climbed together before, we seemed to have an easy, relaxed partnership, based on the necessity of *up*.

Around noon I took over, aiming for a snow ridge that divides the northwest face. I unpeeled my down jacket and synthetic trousers to climb frozen-in spikes and flakes of rock. "It's like dry-tooling with your hands!" I shouted down. An icy tongue brought us to the ridge. As the sun melted into the horizon, we pitched our tent on the narrow spine, and I snapped photos of Ally in a true Greater Ranges setting. It felt like we were the only people on Earth, and in the distance, jagged 7,000-meter mountains jutted up like wonky teeth. Although I was concerned that we'd finished late and might burn out, I was too pleased with the bivy and too tired to care.

Ally took the breakfast pitches again, frontpoints screeching against the rock as we chimneyed higher. Then we bumped into the headwall's most impressive and intimidating feature: a 90-meter stretch of vertical and overhanging rock, dotted with roofs and protruding fins. Ally had dubbed it the Cathedral. It reminded me of the north face of Mt. Alberta, which I'd climbed with Uisdean a few years back. Like a fox caught in headlights, we froze. We hung on a creaking belay and craned our necks.

Without aid climbing gear or a portaledge, we'd be here all week unless we could find a way easier than this appeared. Ally urged us onward, and I was happy to have a look but doubtful it'd go. I'd only aided a couple of moves before, so several pitches of it seemed daunting. But once I'd frigged up a crack to the first belay, my confidence returned. As Ally arrived, I eagerly changed into rock shoes. I could see a line of holds leading out right, toward a groove cutting through the top of the headwall. "I think it'll go!" I shouted.

This felt like climbing at Gogarth's Main Cliff, in North Wales, a place I loved, and I began to relish our wild—yet somehow familiar—position. The sun washed over us now, and I tiptoed and smeared in my shoes—this was far better than double boots and crampons! I ripped off my gloves, crimping and pinching and bridging between giant fins, reveling at the thought of steep

[Left] Only two of the four bivouac sites on the face allowed the climbers to pitch their tent. Night two had a memorable setting. [Right] Ally Swinton on a "breakfast pitch," day three. *Tom Livingstone*

rock climbing at 6,200 meters. Before long, however, I was resting on a cam, breathing heavily, and trying to shake some warmth back into my hands and feet—my body remembered exactly where we were!

At the final belay of this difficult passage, with easier ground in sight, I whooped in delight. This was alpine climbing at its finest: I hadn't expected us to make it through the headwall, but we'd been granted a subtle and joyful passage to the upper mountain. A few hours later, we'd chopped a small snow ledge and begun to spoon as dusk overtook day. It was another long, cold night with no tent, but the stars and moon kept spinning around us, eventually fading into another day.

Ally led off and soon we popped out from the headwall. We enjoyed the easier ground, but we were still a long way from the true summit, which was well back from the subpeak we'd seen from base camp. We both checked into our altitude pain caves. A lying-down bivy in the tent (only our second so far) passed in a fatigued haze, but I remember getting up in the night to see incredible flashes of lightning from a distant storm. It was as if the sky were tearing itself apart, huge white explosions illuminating thunderheads and boiling clouds. Fortunately it didn't come our way. I watched the moon and the storm until sleep welcomed me back.

On the summit slopes, we embraced a bitter cold, cocooned in all our jackets. Hoping to see the tracks of Will, Uisdean, and John, we pushed on, but eventually figured they must've turned back. [*See report on p.30.*] Ally and I were completely alone. Sucking in all the air we could manage—and hyperventilating when we couldn't—we finally reached the summit around 1 p.m. on September 28. Our "woo-hoo!" shouts were lost to the mountains in the distance. We abseiled and down-climbed the mountain's east face, the line of the first ascent, that afternoon, finally slumping into our tent on the Pechus Glacier.

The following day we walked down the broad glacier, planning to hit the moraine and then continue downward until we could contour around on grassy slopes to base camp. Sleep-deprived, stomachs grumbling, but with all the climbing behind us and the end virtually in sight, we stomped through the snow. About 20 meters of rope separated us. I began to weave around gaping crevasses, occasionally crawling over sagging snow-bridges, reminiscent of a minefield. The snow hadn't frozen overnight. I held my breath in nervous expectation; the crevasses looked like monstrous, soulless depths.

Our zigzagging route made it difficult to keep the rope taut between us, and while checking an alternative way across a crevasse—in an unlucky instant—Ally plunged through the snow and

Ally Swinton following very steep rock at around 6,200 meters on day three. The climbers did not carry ascenders and each followed the other's leads. *Tom Livingstone*

vanished. A bridge had broken. The soft snow helped me hold the fall after 15 or 20 meters—or maybe Ally had clattered to a stop. My heart nearly beat out of my chest. I could barely move, let alone pull Ally up hand over hand, and was terrified of being dragged in after him. Unable to find ice, I set up an anchor from a buried axe and began to haul Ally using a 3:1 system. Each time I crawled back to the axe, I eyed it dubiously, praying it would hold.

For some reason, I expected Ally to be fine when he slumped over the lip of the crevasse. First came his helmet—it fell into three pieces. Then I registered the blood from his head, the grimace on his face, and the limp in his leg. I quickly put our only bandage on his head and sliced open his trousers, hoping my fingers wouldn't meet sharp bone and soft, wet flesh. Thankfully, the leg was only badly bruised.

I tried to think clearly. The only photo I'd seen of our descent route showed a long, gnarly glacier still below us—it would take all day to travel if we were fit and lucky. Ally was in shock, shivering, and bleeding from his head. We were out of gas and food, save for a few bars and nuts. I knew Ally needed more medical attention than a single bandage and painkillers. After a few minutes, I pressed the SOS button on our InReach.

I did what anyone would do in the ensuing day and a half, and cared for Ally as I'm sure he would for me. I was glad he remained conscious throughout, but in the first afternoon he seemed very faint and cold. I was really concerned, fearing the worst. Throughout the night, I spooned Ally to keep him warm, listening to his breathing, already irregular from the altitude and now perhaps his injuries. When his breath paused for seconds...and seconds...and—I'd give him a nudge, holding my own breath, waiting for his next.

At some point in the night, Ally suggested we called our new route the Great Game. This was the nickname for the rivalry and power plays between the British and Russian empires in Central Asia during the 1800s. We'd read about this history and the region during our journey into the mountains, and the name sounded fitting.

By noon the next day, Ally's condition had improved, and he even tried to hobble a few meters. As he returned to the tent, I heard the distinct *chopchopchop* of helicopter rotors—what a beautiful sound!

Back in Islamabad, a few days later, the whole team had regrouped. We shared wild stories of helicopters, hospitals, Will and John waiting in a nearby airbase for our rescue, and Uisdean packing up base camp and driving through the night. After our breakfast in the empty hotel restaurant in Gilgit, Ally and I had been driven to Islamabad. He was well on his way to recovery. We

Ally Swinton (left) and Tom Livingstone on the summit of Koyo Zom, day five of their climb via the northwest face. *Ally Swinton*

enjoyed a final meal with our Pakistani assistants and friends. As we spilled onto the street, the moon shone a bright sliver over the city, a full lunar cycle complete after a month in the mountains.

SUMMARY: First ascent of the northwest face of Koyo Zom (6,877m): The Great Game (1,500m, ED+). Ally Swinton and Tom Livingstone started up the face on September 24, summited on September 28, and descended to the Pechus Glacier, east of the mountain. After a crevasse fall the next day, a helicopter rescue was required. This was only the third ascent of Koyo Zom and the second summit route.

ABOUT THE AUTHOR: *Born in 1990, Tom Livingstone wrote about a new route on Latok I (second ascent of the peak) in AAJ 2019. A different version of this article appeared at UKClimbing.com. Livingstone spoke about this expedition in episode 24 of the AAJ's Cutting Edge podcast.*

KOYO ZOM, NORTHEAST BUTTRESS, ATTEMPT

JOHN CROOK, UISDEAN Hawthorn, and I set off for the northeast buttress of Koyo Zom on September 23 after spending the night at advanced base camp (4,500m) with Tom Livingstone and Ally Swinton, who were headed for the northwest face. After traversing a huge, messy icefall on the upper Koyo Glacier, we crossed a bergschrund and climbed the initial face to a col (ca 5,400m) in about 10 pitches of moderate but very tiring sugar snow on black ice, with some mixed sections.

At the col, we made a platform for our three-man bivy tent and enjoyed a very comfortable night. The next day we stayed on the crest of the northeast buttress and climbed around six pitches of moderate but time-consuming mixed ground, again consisting largely of exhausting powder on black ice. Upon reaching a rock pinnacle, we were forced to do a 60m rappel down the east side to bypass it. We soon decided to bivy again, as there was a rocky ledge and the next section was steep, brittle serac ice, which we didn't want to climb into the night.

The next morning we traversed a couloir and climbed the serac ice in about six pitches to a snowy spur. We continued for a further three pitches of the nasty snow on ice to reach a point where we could construct another semi-sitting bivy. We carried on the next morning, our fourth day on the route, becoming increasingly frustrated by the exhausting powder-on-ice combination. An enjoyable but loose mixed section, followed by an elegant icy gully, brought us to a point only 40m below the horizontal summit ridge, after about eight pitches that day. However, while John was leading the last stretch to the ridge, we all decided we would bail, heading down to the east to the Pechus Glacier.

This decision was due to an accumulation of factors. A storm had been forecast to arrive that evening, but since our satellite phone wasn't working, we didn't know the storm's arrival had been pushed back. We had taken two days longer than expected to climb the buttress. And Uisdean was having worrying chest pains that seemed to be getting worse. We spent the night on the Pechus Glacier and then returned to base camp six days after leaving.

– **WILL SIM**, *U.K.*

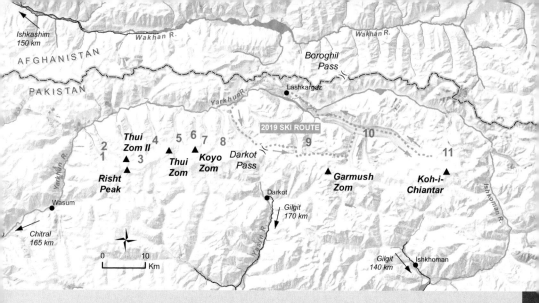

The Yarkhun Valley runs parallel to the Wakhan Corridor, just to the north in Afghanistan. The labeled glaciers are: (1) Madit, (2) Risht, (3) Shetor, (4) Ponarilio, (5) Kotalkash, (6) Koyo, (7) Pechus, (8) Chhatiboi, (9) Chikzar, (10) Chiantar, and (11) Chatiboi. The 2019 French ski loop is shown; see p.34. *Anna Riling*

EXPLORING THE YARKHUN
A BRIEF HISTORY OF THE NORTHERNMOST HINDU RAJ

BY WILL SIM

THE YARKHUN VALLEY forms the northern border of the Hindu Raj mountains, which rise in northwestern Pakistan between the Afghan Hindu Kush and the western end of the Karakoram. The valley drains southwest toward Chitral, capital of the Chitral district of Khyber Pakhtunkhwa province, and famous for its world champion polo team and a colorful British colonial history. At the Yarkhun's northeastern end is Boroghil Pass, one of the very few drivable passes over the Afghan border north of the Khyber Pass.

In 1992–93, a mostly motorable road was built all the way up the valley, giving access from the Boroghil to Chitral in a 15- to 20-hour jeep ride rather than weeks of riding and walking.

The people of the Yarkhun Valley are mostly Wakhi, originating from the neighboring Wakhan Corridor of Afghanistan. In Pakistan they are referred to as Gujali; they speak the Wakhi language and are Ismaili Muslims. They mostly follow the classic mountain-farming formula of goat and sheep herding and small-scale agriculture on irrigated terraces.

The ridge formed by the Yarkhun's northern wall forms the border between Afghanistan and Pakistan, and the mountains that create the southern and eastern walls of the valley are the largest of the Hindu Raj, including Koyo Zom (6,877m), Karol Zom (a.k.a. Thui I, 6,660m), and Thui II (6,523m). Impressive steep faces, up to 1,500m high, on numerous aspects, make these appealing as technical alpine climbing objectives. However, until 2019, the Yarkhun side of these mountains had seen no climbing activity for many decades.

The first person to visit the Hindu Raj with an eye for mountains was probably Tom Longstaff (U.K.) in 1916–17. He wrote up his findings in the *Alpine Journal* and gave a lecture in 1920, raising awareness of the Hindu Raj among climbers. A handful of German, Austrian, and Japanese expeditions visited the range through the 1960s, mostly approaching via the Yasin and Darkot valleys, by way of Gilgit.

Much of the Yarkhun Valley is inhabited by farmers and herders. *Uisdean Hawthorn*

It wasn't until 1967, when the Austrian Gerald Gruber and his team made a recce of the Yarkhun Valley as far as Boroghil, that the notion of climbing the great peaks of the Hindu Raj from the upper Yarkhun Valley was considered. This led to perhaps the most important expedition to the Yarkhun, that of Albert Stamm and his Austrian team in 1968. After getting an overview of the peaks from 5,600-meter Korum Zom on the north side of the valley, they made the first ascent of Koyo Zom and several other 6,000ers above the high plateaus of the Pechus and Chatiboi glaciers.

Other expeditions followed suit, mainly Brits and Japanese approaching the Thui peaks via the Kotalkash, Ponarilio, and Shetor glaciers. The southern side of the range also saw activity from European and Japanese teams during the 1970s, and it could be said that the '70s were the exploratory heyday of the Hindu Raj.

Much less activity was recorded through the next 30 years. Japanese teams visited and climbed Shahan Dok (6,320m) in 1987 and '88. In 1999, a large international expedition organized by the UIAA brought strong young climbers from all over the world to the south side of the main divide. Approaching from Gilgit, they made many first ascents of varying significance, mostly around the area of the Borum Bar Glacier. French and Dutch teams in 2007 and 2018, respectively, climbed a number of peaks in the Dasbar Valley, south of Koyo Zom, including the striking pyramid of Kachqiant. Since 1997, numerous Italian expeditions have explored the mountains around the upper Chiantar Glacier, which feeds the Yarkhun River, approaching this huge glacier basin via passes from the north or south. However, the main peaks and faces on the Yarkhun side of the watershed went untouched.

The relatively low volume of expeditions is due to a mix of political and practical reasons. First, the proximity of the Hindu Raj, and particularly the Yarkhun Valley, to Afghanistan means the area has been on the fringe of conflicts numerous times over the last 40 years, making climbing permits in this strategic area difficult to attain. Secondly, there are a lot of mountains in Pakistan! Climbers looking for adventurous objectives have been spoiled for choice ever since the Baltoro opened up to climbers. Thirdly, there was a time in the 1960s and '70s when a lot of European expeditions would drive to Pakistan and the Himalaya. As one of the farthest west areas of the Greater Ranges, the Hindu Raj must have felt that bit closer in the period before air travel became a more practical mode of transport.

When I asked Asghar Ali Porik of Jasmine Tours to acquire a permit for our September trip to the Yarkhun, he seemed pessimistic. Unlike that of Gilgit-Baltistan, the Khyber Pakhtunkhwa tourism office is not used to handling peak permits, and especially not for an area where none had been granted in many years. So it was with great elation and surprise that I received an email to say that he was driving back from Peshawar with the permit for Koyo Zom in his hands!

It's hard to know whether our expedition and others were able to climb in the Yarkhun Valley in 2019 as a result of sheer luck. But it is certainly the case that the current political administration in Pakistan is doing its best to make tourism more open. It is also true that the northwestern border with Afghanistan has been relatively peaceful and stable of late, compared with Pakistan's northeastern frontier with India. Hopefully, climbers will continue to have access to these remarkable mountains.

Will Sim planned the 2019 expedition to Koyo Zom described in these pages.

THE FIRST ASCENT OF RISHT PEAK

BETWEEN APRIL 26 and May 31, three friends and I, all from France, visited the remote border area between Pakistan and Afghanistan. Pierrick Fine, Antoine Rolle, Aurélien Vaissière, and I had looked on Google Earth for wild places where we could climb mixed terrain, and we found our dream spot in the Yarkhun Valley.

After driving to a base camp at 3,000m, we skied for six days up the Risht Gol (valley), finishing on the col at the head of the glacier at 5,600m. We believe we were the first mountaineers to ascend this glacier. We managed to descend the entire way back on skis in perfect snow.

After two days of rest in base camp, we learned of an upcoming window of three and a half days. In two days we raced back up the valley, reaching 5,400m—it had taken six days to gain this point before. On May 22 we were at the base of an unclimbed peak at the head of the glacier. A 500m line of rock and ice on the northwest face rose above.

Easy snow slopes led to more difficult terrain and a pitch of WI5 (90°). I led the following pitch, which proved to be the crux: tricky M6 with poor protection. Sustained

[Top] Moving up the Risht Glacier. The small pyramid at the head of the valley is Risht Peak. On the left is Thui Zom II (6,523m). Peaks to the right (ca 5,600m–5,900m) are unclimbed. [Bottom] Aurélien Vaissière on the northwest face of Risht Peak. *Symon Welfringer*

but slightly easier ice pitches then led to the southwest ridge. Here, snow conditions were awful and we had to dig deep—into our bodies, minds, and the snow—to reach the top of what we decided to call Risht Peak. We estimated the summit altitude to be 5,960m (GPS and altimeter watches). We rappelled the route in a storm and returned to base camp the following day.

After a rest, we visited a beautiful gorge southwest of our base camp, on the west side of the main valley. We opened two rock climbs: Antoine and Aurel made the first ascent of Sueurs Chaudes (150m, 6c+), while Perrick and I climbed Removable Crux (250m, 7b+). The latter had pitches of nice crack climbing, but on some pitches, especially the fifth, the rock was poor, adding spice to the day. Routes were climbed using trad gear only. This trip was by far my best expedition experience to date. 📄📷

– SYMON WELFRINGER, *FRANCE*

EDITOR'S NOTE: *The main peak of the Risht Glacier basin is Thui Zom II (6,523m), but it has not been climbed from this glacier. This mountain was first climbed in August 1978 via the southeast ridge, approached from the Qalandar Glacier to the south. During attempts on this peak in 1969 from the Shetor Glacier to the east, a British expedition climbed Pachan Zom (6,126m), a summit on the northwest ridge of Thui Zom II overlooking the Risht Glacier.*

Skiing down from Garmush Pass to the Garmush Glacier, with unclimbed summits on the north ridge of Garmush Zom behind. *Pierre Neyret*

DARKOT TO CHIANTAR GLACIER SKI TOUR

IN 2019, ON my 35th expedition since 1993, I was able to get a permit to lead a group (11 French, two Poles, and one Pakistani) to visit the upper eastern end of the Chiantar Glacier. In 1967 a German expedition penetrated the upper Chiantar, where they climbed the highest peak, Koh-i-Chiantar (6,416m). Since that time, in more than 50 years, no climbers have reached the head of the glacier. [*While it is true hat no climbers appear to have traveled up the Chiantar to its head since that era, a series of Italian expeditions, starting in 1997, climbed numerous mountains surrounding the Chiantar basin, approaching from Karambar Lake to the north or via passes from the south.*]

Traveling by road from Chitral, on April 27 we reached Chikar in the Boroghil Valley, close to the route that leads north, over Boroghil Pass, to Afghanistan. The following day we used porters to help us move to 3,500m on the Darkot Glacier. For the next 13 days we moved autonomously on skis, pulling everything we needed in pulks.

Once we reached Darkot Pass, we began exploring glacier corridors that would take us eastward to the Chiantar Glacier, the biggest glacier of either the Hindu Kush or Hindu Raj (30km in length). We crossed four passes and then descended the Garmush Glacier, arriving on the Chiantar on May 6. It had been an exciting journey but a logical route.

We then continued east and reached a point at the head of the glacier at around 5,100m, not far from Koh-i-Chiantar. From there we skied back down the glacier and out to the Boroghil Valley, reaching the village of Lashkargaz on May 11.

We found the mountains and glaciers impressive—there is still a lot to do in this area. I hope our expedition will contribute to a resurgence of interest in this remote area of Pakistan. The locals are all Wakhis—peaceful Ismaili Muslims—and the area is far from any Taliban. 📷🔍

– PIERRE NEYRET, *FRANCE*

[Top] Rest stop below unnamed and likely unclimbed Peak 5,665m on the north bank of the Chiantar Glacier, about 10 days into the 2019 team's two-week ski tour. [Bottom Left] The northeast face of Peak 6,177m, which is probably unclimbed. This is the most easterly main peak in the upper Garmush Glacier cwm. [Middle Right] Unclimbed Chiantar Central Pyramid (5,336m), which lies right in the center of the upper Chiantar Glacier basin. [Bottom Right] Looking west from the Darkot Glacier to Koyo Zom (6,877m, the highest peak in the Hindu Raj). The east ridge, the route of the first ascent (1968), faces the camera. This route was descended to the Pechus Glacier (hidden) by the 2019 team that climbed the northwest face. *Pierre Neyret (all photos)*

CHAMLANG

A COVETED NORTH FACE IN NEPAL IS FINALLY CLIMBED TO THE SUMMIT

ZDENĚK HÁK

After an expedition to Nepal in the spring of 2018 to climb a new route on Kyajo Ri, Marek Holeček and I laid plans to return to the Himalaya the following year. It would be our third high-altitude expedition together, having spent six days climbing the direct southwest face of Gasherbrum I in the summer of 2017. Our goal for 2019 was the giant unclimbed northwest face of Chamlang (7,321 meters), rising above the Hunku Valley, ten kilometers south of Baruntse.

Chamlang was first climbed in 1962 by its south ridge. The mountain's north side spans more than eight kilometers, with numerous subpeaks. Various routes had reached the ridgeline from the north, but despite attempts, no one had reached the main summit via the great northwest face or central northern spur. Marek had dreamed of climbing this face since he first saw it in 2001.

Marek and I are good friends, but back home in Europe we do not climb together at all. I have other climbing partners at home. But in the high mountains of Asia, something seems to click for us. Both of us are at about the same level, and when one of us is OK with climbing solo, the other one is too. When one of us needs a belay, the other wants a belay too. We also have similar fitness levels and acclimatization. As a result, we are able to climb fast, not having to wait for each other.

We left the Czech Republic on April 24 and spent several days waiting for all the formalities to be completed in Kathmandu. Finally, on April 29, we flew to Lukla to start our acclimatization trek. To save money, we had decided to carry the majority of our gear and food ourselves. In Lukla, we hired a Sherpa assistant

On the first pitch, Chamlang proved it would give us absolutely nothing for free.

[Top] Zdeněk Hák leading mixed ground above the first bivouac on Chamlang's northwest face. [Middle Left] Marek Holeček following the first part of the route, a long ramp of rotten rock. [Middle Right] Hák at about 5,500 meters on the first day. [Bottom] Hák descending from the summit in the afternoon of the fifth day of the climb. *Marek Holeček and Zdeněk Hák*

to carry 20 kilograms directly to Chamlang base camp while Marek and I took a longer route for acclimatization. He and I divided the remaining 40 kilograms (88 pounds), hoisted our big packs, and started walking.

We hiked through Namche Bazaar and Tengboche to Chukhung and then crossed over the Amphu Laptsa Pass (5,845 meters) to enter the Hunku Valley. Here we finally saw the northwest face of Chamlang. There was much less snow than we had expected. At base camp below Chamlang we met a Slovenian expedition who had spent a month here, climbing various routes and hoping to climb Chamlang, and they confirmed our observations: not much snow and a lot of hard water ice. Well, we would have to see....

The Slovenians were packing up to leave, and they offered us a lot of their extra expedition food. We took a little and headed to Mera Peak to continue acclimatizing. After climbing Mera (6,476 meters), we spent two days in Khare village, where we met our Sherpa and returned to base camp with the rest of our supplies. At that point I realized that my down mittens had gotten lost somewhere on the way. But at Kongma Dingma, where there is a popular campsite, I was able to borrow a pair of mittens, promising to leave an ice axe in exchange on my way home.

Marek and I spent about a week alone at base camp (elevation 4,800 meters), each of us in our own tiny bivouac tent. There was a teahouse an hour away, and we walked over there every second night for dinner. The weather was the same every day, exactly as the Slovenians had told us: beautiful in the morning and fog and drizzle in the afternoon. One day we hiked under the face of Chamlang and explored the possibilities for the first section. The face was quite "lively"—a climber would be under pressure due to falling rocks and ice from seracs in the middle of the face. We figured out that by diagonaling up to the right at the bottom, an overhang should protect us from rockfall and avalanches. We start to be optimistic and returned to base camp in a good mood.

Soon we were running out of food, so there was no more reason to wait. On May 16 we headed up toward the face again and camped at 5,300 meters, with 2,000 meters of steep mixed terrain above us. We carried a bivouac tent, one 80-meter 7mm rope, six ice screws, five pitons, five cams, food for five days, and three gas cartridges. As always, the last night before the climb was a little bit restless, with thoughts about the days to come filling our minds. We watched a massive avalanche from a collapsed serac fall in the direction of our intended climb. The wall did not sleep even at night, as we could hear the rattle of falling rocks or ice from time to time. Well, hopefully we would not be too exposed in the bottom section.

Hák on the icefield at about 6,600 meters. The two climbers ascended 800 vertical meters on this third day of the climb and bivouacked sitting on a small ledge with their tent hanging from a cam. *Marek Holeček*

We started climbing early on May 17, and on the first pitch Chamlang proved it would give us absolutely nothing for free. Under a thin layer of sugary snow there was only bad rock—very tough climbing, not to mention the lack of belay opportunities. We climbed to the right along a steep ramp that ended by a vertical rock wall, where we set up our first bivouac. It was only noon, but rock and snow avalanches were starting to fall. There was no chance to continue that day. We had done a lot of climbing and still only got to about 5,600 meters.

The second day we aimed to climb above a significant row of seracs shedding big chunks of ice. The first three pitches offered beautiful mixed climbing on high-quality ice and rock (M4). We got to a long icefield where both of us could climb simultaneously most of the time until we reached the difficult mixed section that would bring us to the level of the serac wall. These next two pitches were beautiful and exposed M5/6 with steep sections in ice. Our second bivouac, at 6,100 meters, was partially protected by a stable serac and situated on a pleasant flat spot with stunning views towards Everest and Lhotse. It was just a bit cold!

We woke to a beautiful morning and continued climbing. Above was a giant icefield, a real test of our physical and moral power. We often climbed together, trying to stay on the backs of the snake-like snow ridges between runnels, wriggling upward into the unknown. The climb felt never-ending, but slowly the next rock band seemed to get closer. The day was almost gone, however, and we still hadn't found any suitable place to bivouac.

After another three or four pitches of difficult mixed terrain, we found a small ledge where we could at least sit down. We had managed about 800 vertical meters that day! We hung the tent from a cam and spent the third night half sitting, half lying at close to 7,000 meters. We were lucky it was not as cold as the previous night. As usual, I melted snow and cooked while Marek checked the weather forecast by satellite phone. Eventually I even managed to fall asleep, considering it a little miracle, given our position.

Our goal for the fourth day was to finish the face, reach the summit, and descend at least a little down the classic route to the south. However, as the altitude was getting higher, our speed was getting slower. Our calves were on fire as the points of our crampons only just held in the hard ice, while our hands were terribly frozen. After several hours the angle eased a little and hard ice was replaced with snow. We reached the ridge about 80 meters below the main peak, late in the afternoon. Blasts of wind hit us here, so we quickly searched for a bivouac spot and set up the tent. The summit would have to wait. We checked our supplies and realized we did not have much food left, despite packing nearly everything we had at base camp. We would have to try to get down the next day!

On May 21 we woke to a beautiful cold morning. Fortunately, the wind had calmed a bit. We packed up and climbed slowly up the ridge, imperious Makalu at our backs. We stopped frequently, the altitude over 7,300 meters and overall exhaustion starting to be apparent, and didn't reach the main peak until 10 a.m.

continued on page 42...

The Czech line on the northwest face of Chamlang (7,321 meters). The climb and descent took seven nights away from base camp; the seventh bivy site is hidden. (H) marks the high point of the 2019 French attempt on Chamlang's north pillar (see next page). *Andy Houseman (autumn 2012 photo)*

The north pillar of Chamlang is the right skyline; Nicolas Jean and Benjamin Védrines crossed to the opposite side of the obvious rock buttress and climbed about two-thirds of it. On their second attempt, the pair climbed the curving ice slopes on the left to the top of the pillar at 7,240 meters. *Benjamin Védrines*

CHAMLANG: A STORY OF TWO CLIMBS
NORTH PILLAR ATTEMPT AND A CONSOLATION PRIZE NEXT DOOR

BY BENJAMIN VÉDRINES, *FRANCE*

IN THE SPRING of 2018, some friends from France attempted the north pillar of Chamlang, retreating at 6,500m (*AAJ 2019*). This feature, which really jumps out at you, separates the northeast side of this broad mountain wall from the larger northwest face, leading directly to a small top of 7,240m, east of the summit. In the autumn of 2019, this pillar was the goal for Nicolas Jean and me. On our arrival in the Hongu Valley, we could see immediately that the west flank of the pillar was far snowier than it had been during the spring 2018 attempt. Autumn had been the right choice.

For our first attempt, after acclimatizing on Meru Peak (6,470m), we started from an advanced base at 5,400m in the cirque south of Hongu Chuli. On October 10 we climbed the 300m north slope (M3/4) of Col 6,070m. This gives access to the broad upper Chamlang Glacier, flowing northeast below the various Chamlang summits. There we camped for the night at 6,050m.

Next day we reached the crest of the north pillar via the east flank, the same way our friends had in 2018. This is a much easier method than the full north ridge, which was attempted in 2016 by Jon Griffith and Andy Houseman (U.K.), and avoids the very rotten rock they reported. We encountered superb pitches of very steep snow with limited protection, 90° ice, and fortunately few sections of sugar snow.

After passing our friends' high point, and on the west flank of the crest, we could see above a succession of rock barriers separated by very steep snow. At first it seemed impossible to find a way through this vertical labyrinth. We followed ramps down to the right to avoid a scary overhanging scoop directly above and then continued upward, linking hard passages until sunset, at around 6,700m, a new high point on the pillar. Nicolas had begun to feel weaker earlier in the day, and now his condition had deteriorated markedly. Leaving one of our ropes fixed for the following day, we rappelled to a bivouac site at 6,630m, hoping things would improve during the night. But they did not. Despite fine weather and the terrain above giving us the impression we might make the summit, we had no option but to descend.

Back in Khare village, where "base camp" was in a lodge, Nicolas recovered quickly at the lower altitude and we both felt the need for revenge. We had come with the goal of climbing above 7,000m. We had an official permit for Chamlang—very expensive—so it was obvious we had to climb on this mountain. But where? Rodolphe Popier of the Himalayan Database helped us by sending more information on previous attempts, and this allowed us to see that the obvious couloir to the left of the north pillar, running directly to Point 7,240m, remained unclimbed.

On the 17th we received a forecast for a short but good weather window. We retraced our steps from Khare to a campsite at 5,540m, closer to the start of the north face of Col 6,070m. Next morning, we gained the upper Chamlang Glacier, where the cloud ceiling was much lower than expected. We erected the tent and rested until noon. Finally, keeping our fingers crossed that the snowfall forecasted for the coming night would not arrive until later, we set off just before 2 p.m. in a race against the clock.

The snow in the couloir was firm and allowed for fast progress, climbing unroped on 50–65° slopes. Gusty wind and the cold kept us from stopping much. At around 7,000m we roped up to pass an icy section. Nicolas, in front, was now in great shape. We kept going and at 7:10 p.m. reached the top—at least the top we wanted to climb.

Our headlamps lit grains of snow torn by the westerly wind. After a hug, we descended the entire route without a rappel, reaching our tent on the Chamlang Glacier a little after 10 p.m. We are proud to have lived this moment, but also to have climbed a new route in this style, typical of the Himalaya, where the effort and concentration needed for unroped climbing is greater than with the reassuring belays of more technical ascents. 📄📷

Descending the south ridge of Chamlang was more difficult than expected. *Zdeněk Hák*

...continued from page 40

We took a few photos and made a short video, but after a while we were so frozen that we started to descend as quickly as possible over the south shoulder. The ridge was exposed but not too steep, so we lost altitude quickly. It started to get warmer and we were getting tired. Clouds rose gradually from the valley, and we had to wait several times for better visibility. The terrain became steeper and steeper, and we had to abseil over several vertical rock faces. Then we strayed too far onto the southeast face. The visibility was too poor to continue. We would have to bivouac again above 7,000 meters. We had almost nothing to eat, so we just boiled water. In the evening the fog disappeared and I tried to memorize the contours of the glacier far below. It was the only possible way out.

The morning was again beautiful, and after eating our last energy bar we headed back toward the ridge we had left the day before. It was hard work, unfortunately, as we had to climb about one hundred vertical meters. Finally back on the ridge, the terrain below was very steep and we had to descend carefully, using ice screws for belays. Finally we reached the saddle and

turned right onto the glacier, heading west toward the Hunku Valley again. Yet once again the afternoon clouds rose and forced us to stop. The fog was so thick that we set up the tent and waited inside until around 7 p.m., when the visibility seemed a little better and we decided to continue. The glacier was incredibly broken, and in the dark we blindly abseiled over crevasses and ice walls. Several times we had to backtrack through the maze, losing precious energy. When the fog returned we took the opportunity to bivouac yet again under a massive ice wall. It was our sixth night on the mountain and our seventh away from base camp.

I had completely wet boots and socks, and I was afraid of frostbite, as we were very weak and dehydrated. So I used an old trick, pouring hot water into two small plastic Coke bottles we had emptied on the route. I put them into my socks and they were dry within a few minutes, then I put them into my boot liners and left them overnight in my sleeping bag. It works well! Everything was dry in the morning.

[Top] It's not over until it's over: an off-route bivouac on the southeast face during the descent. "We had nothing to eat, so we just boiled water. We thought we were going down the next day, but we were wrong—we had to make a seventh bivouac." [Bottom] Now it's over. *Hák Collection*

Clouds were approaching from the valley as in the previous days, so we set off early. I was glad I had studied the glacier from above during our unplanned bivouac. After a few more abseils we were able to start walking and soon reached the moraine. At a small lake we were finally able to drink all the water we wanted and shed the clothes that had imprisoned us for a week. An incredible feeling. As we started to descend through a meadow toward the valley, it felt like being reborn.

We reached our base camp around lunchtime, and I cooked the two dehydrated meals we had left there, the very last of our food. Marek packed his gear and began the trip back toward civilization after lunch. I preferred to stay one more night and enjoy the views of the northwest face, where we had so much adventure.

SUMMARY: First ascent of the complete northwest face of Chamlang (7,321 meters), by Zdeněk Hák and Marek Holeček, May 17–23, 2019. The two summited on the fifth day of their climb and spent two more nights out during their descent of the south ridge. They called the route UFO Line (2,000m, ABO) in honor of Doug Scott and Reinhold Messner, who saw a "box-like object, shining magnificently in the midday sun," hovering over them as they neared their high point on a climb of Chamlang's north side in 1981.

ABOUT THE AUTHOR: *Born in 1980, Zdeněk Hák is an alpinist and UIAGM mountain guide from the Czech Republic. Translated by Zuzka Háková.*

Sincronia Màgica on the west face of El Chileno
Grande. From the top of the wall, Vidal scrambled
to the closest summit in the clouds. *Felipe Andrade*

ANOTHER WORLD

THE SOLO FIRST ASCENT OF A HUGE WALL IN PATAGONIA

SÍLVIA VIDAL

When I first saw photographs of the wall, it was definitely not love at first sight; in fact, it took me some time to realize that I really wanted to give it a go. The wall is impressive, but it didn't grab my attention. And the poor weather in the Aysén Region of Chile made me cautious. The weather conditions make such a difference on a climb, and poor weather significantly reduces the likelihood of success on a solo big wall. It's true that being able to climb something depends not only on the weather but also on one's ability to cope with adverse conditions; we don't have the power to change the clouds, but we have the capability to climb in bad weather. Still, I thought it would be better to wait and see if another wall project would materialize in a more bearable place.

But a few weeks after I got those photos of the wall from two locals, Pere Vilarasau and Pancho Croxatto, the positive memories of other, similar ascents weighed more than the negatives and inspired me to give it a try. Sometimes I have the feeling that we don't choose a particular challenge, but rather there are situations, or walls, or places, that choose us. There isn't a logical explanation. It's as if life suggests each moment, and we have the option to decide whether we will make the attempt.

I decided to go to El Chileno Grande.

It ended up being a two-month trip, during which I spent a total of a month and a half climbing and hauling my gear to the wall and back. [*The west-facing granite wall called El Chileno Grande is at about 46°32'24"S, 73°05'24"W, a little over five kilometers east of the Exploradores Glacier, as the crow flies, and at least ten kilometers from the road.*] I did a total of 16 days carrying loads (round trip), through glacier, forest, and moraine, in order to transport six bags of 25kg apiece. Andrea, Marco, and Manu, who worked in the area and to whom I am profoundly grateful, offered to help, each doing one carry. The rest of the carries, and moving the equipment to the base of the wall, I did on my own, walking more than 150 kilometers going there and back.

After fixing the first 180 meters, I spent 33 days living on the wall (February 7–March 10) in order to complete the new route. It's a lot of days, but

the wall is huge and demanding—not just from pure climbing difficulty but also because of complex moves to link crack systems. Overhangs, pendulums, and traverses made hauling and rappelling complicated and slow. In fact, descending the wall took four days, having to fix pitches beforehand in order to rappel with the haul bags.

One 330-meter section of vertical terrain had a lot of vegetation, which made the climbing in this stretch hard to enjoy. I didn't really know how to grade it, so I've marked this section MT for *matojo tracción*, or "bush traction," because it involved climbing the vegetation that filled the cracks. Eventually I resorted to using crampons and an axe to make progress. The majority of this section had little to no protection, with usually only one bolt at each belay, hand-drilled, following the rules of the park.

The rest of the route (another 850 meters) was cleaner face and cracks, including some offwidths and chimneys. The slab sections had

[Top] Vidal spent 16 days carrying loads to and from the wall, covering more than 150 kilometers. [Bottom] Self-portrait above the third wall camp. *Silvia Vidal*

moss that become slippery when wet. I climbed capsule-style, with three wall camps. Two of these had two-bolt anchors, but many of my belay anchors had only a single bolt for security and hauling, and when it came time to descend, I ended up rappelling nearly the entire route, with the haul bags, from one bolt at a time.

I can't complain about the weather I had. It rained 50 percent of the days—normally it's more. There were two big storms with rain and strong wind. During one of these, the wind and rain battered the portaledge until it flipped completely over, with me inside, but it held together. I hit my head, and I couldn't get the portaledge righted. I had to crawl outside in order to flip it, but the wind spun it back as soon as I started trying to straighten it. Finally, I was able to get it righted, but before going back inside I tied the haul bags to the portaledge to weigh it down so it wouldn't happen again.

I was completely alone and without contact. I had no phone, no radio, and no GPS, because that is how I prefer to have these experiences. If I brought these things, even if I didn't use them, just the fact of knowing I had them, that I could make a call at any moment, would completely change my experience and make it that much more difficult to concentrate on the circumstances I was living. On the other hand, with no phone or radio, you don't have the ability to get a weather forecast, so deciding the best logistics for the climb depends on just going for it each day. The final attack on the summit is the most delicate moment in this regard, because there is such a great margin for error.

During this time on Chileno Grande, some circumstances happened at the perfect time, and because of that I named the route Sincronia Màgica ("magic synchronicity" in Catalán). When things—no matter how hard or difficult they can seem—are happening and flowing, and then you finally reach what you have aspired to, the experience has been worth it.

I returned happy from this experience, which for me created a distinct feeling of "before" and "after," just like every big trip. To be alone for so many weeks or months, in silence, incommunicado, in hard conditions, has an effect. However, this particular return feels different because of COVID-19, causing the before and after to feel more blurred; I have the feeling that I have not yet finished "returning." In a way, I keep feeling that synchronicity of events. Normally, when I return from an expedition, I need time to reacclimatize myself to "civilization." But in this case what has changed has been the entire planet. The world has changed, and us along with it.

SUMMARY: First ascent of the west face of El Chileno Grande, in the Aysén Region of Chile, by Sílvia Vidal, February-March 2020: Sincronia Màgica (1,180 meters, A3+ 6a+). At the top of the wall, Vidal scrambled 30 minutes to the westernmost top of the mountain, which, she discovered, was not the highest point.

ABOUT THE AUTHOR: *Sílvia Vidal lives in Catalunya, Spain. Information about her talks and presentations is at vidalsilvia.com. She would like to thank all the people who helped with this expedition, both at home and during her time in Chile. She also thanks CONAF, the administrator of Chilean national parks, "for their help and open-mindedness about this style of climb."*

Translated by Pam Ranger Roberts.

HISTORICAL AND ACCESS NOTES ON EL CHILENO GRANDE

FRANCISCO "PANCHO" CROXATTO, a Chilean mountaineer and glacier guide, was the first to scope this wall, around 2002, and was responsible for christening it. He named it after one of the early settlers of the area, a large man who was affectionately called "el Chileno Grande."

About a decade later, Croxatto showed the wall to Pascal Mao and Fabien Burlon, who in turn alerted French climber Etienne Tafary. He visited the area in 2015, with Felipe Andrade, Matias Larrain del Sante, and Enzo Oddo, but bad weather only allowed them to climb a few pitches. Tafary returned in January 2020 with Antoine Eydoux, Etienne Grosclaude, and Pierre-Jean Lallement. The French climbers spent seven days on the wall, climbing 400 meters, before heavy rain forced them to retreat. Their attempt was far to the right of the line climbed by Vidal, whom they met as they were walking out and she was just entering the valley for the first time.

The wall is located inside Laguna San Rafael National Park and is accessed via a private park (www.parquexploradores.cl). To visit, you need permission both from CONAF and from the private park; both permits are relatively easy to secure. As in any wilderness area, "leave no trace" principles should be followed. —*Rolando Garibotti*

STATE OF THE ART
EXPANDING THE COVERAGE OF WOMEN'S CLIMBING IN THE AAJ

SARAH HART

In June 2015, Chantel Astorga and Jewell Lund completed the Denali Diamond, one of the testpiece routes up North America's highest peak. When I learned of their five-day ascent I was impressed—and even more impressed upon learning it was the first time an all-female team had climbed a coveted Alaska Grade 6. So in August 2016, when I received a copy of the *American Alpine Journal*, I flipped through the feature stories at the front, expecting to see a glossy report about Chantel and Jewell's ascent. But I came up empty-handed. In the Alaska section I finally found what I was looking for—sort of. There was only a three-sentence summary of this impressive climb. This didn't feel right.

The AAJ is the world's preeminent record of each year's major ascents in the mountains and on big walls. And that record has been mostly about climbs by men. Between 2015 and 2019, the average number of reports from all-female teams in the AAJ was four, and the average number of mixed teams (female and male partners of equal strength) was 23—out of a total of more than 300 reports each year. A woman has graced the cover of the AAJ only once (Brette Harrington in 2017). With rare exceptions, a woman's climb has only been featured as a major story in the AAJ if it was groundbreaking for *all* climbers, one prominent example being Lynn Hill's first free ascent of the Nose, featured in the front of the AAJ in 1994.

Why haven't climbs like Chantel and Jewell's gotten more recognition in the AAJ? One important reason is that the AAJ has long defined the "world's most significant climbs" primarily as the first ascents of mountains, big walls, and other long routes—activities in which women have not historically participated in high numbers. As a result, years of impressive ascents by teams of women—not necessarily first ascents but "firsts" for women (some of which were, in fact, much more significant than other climbs reported in the AAJ)—have gone all but unreported. Was it time for a fresh look at the AAJ's criteria?

I recounted these observations to an international collection of friends while passing time in El Chaltén during the 2017–18 Patagonia season. Over the course of several weeks, we mulled over the topic again and again. Finally, while eating empanadas late one night, an action plan was crystalized.

In April 2018, I reached out to the AAJ editors with a proposal: Would the AAJ consider expanding its criteria and develop an objective way to elevate the most significant female accomplishments within the pages of the book, giving them more prominence than they've received

[Clockwise from top left] **Fanny Tomasi-Schmutz, Madaleine Sorkin, Silvia Vidal, Jewell Lund (left) and Chantel Astorga, Brette Harrington, Alison Hargreaves (center), Kei Taniguchi, Ines Papert (left) and Mayan Smith-Gobat, and Marina Kopteva.**

OVERLOOKED

This story and the three that follow are among those the AAJ might have included in past editions under revised guidelines.

THE DENALI DIAMOND (2015)
FIVE DAYS ON THE SOUTHWEST FACE OF DENALI

BY JEWELL LUND, *USA*

JAGGED RIDGELINES DARKEN and blur in the dim light. A palette of blues merges into thick, bland gray. I lean my head forward to rest on the rock wall in front of me and pay out slack listlessly as the rope twitches to Chantel. In the murk of early morning, we find ourselves 2,500 feet up the Denali Diamond, with another 5,500 feet of mountain above. We've taken turns belaying as we explore the "snow band" for bivy spots. So far, we've found only shallow ice over steep rock. After 30 hours of climbing, my fatigue dulls the brilliant Alaskan skyline. I forget the gift of moving in such extraordinary terrain. I might as well be checking out at the grocery store.

The rope is still. *Maybe she found something.* "Oy! How you doin', lady? What do you see?"

"I got nothing!"

Chantel returns to the belay, bleary eyed. She chops a small bench as I build another anchor and brew water. We put on all our clothing and sit—so exhausted that for almost two hours even this tiny ledge provides enough of a respite for us to sleep.

Thirty hours earlier, Chantel and I had stood at the base of the Denali Diamond at midnight. "Ready?" Chantel asked. She pulled her hood snug over her helmet, Kiwi coil over her shoulder. The darkened granite of the southwest face towered over us, impartial and still. "Can't wait," I said. "Have fun up there." Our long stay at the 14,200-foot camp on Denali's West Buttress Route, waiting through blizzards and high winds, had simplified this moment—an initiation of upward momentum. As Chantel cleared a path through the bergschrund, grains of hard snow clattered downhill with a metallic sound. Quickly, she bridged the gap and led on, steadily, efficiently. *I'm lucky to have such a solid partnership; it's straightforward to commit.* The slack dissipated, and we began to climb together, our movements sure and our minds clear.

After our two-hour nap, we continue to a better ledge, put up our tent, and sleep all through the afternoon and night. In the morning, we start up toward the crux pitches of the route, embarking on what would become another 30-hour push.

Hours blur. Our progress is marked by minute shifts in the landscape: golden granite walls merge almost imperceptibly into smoky gray. The rock steepens as picks and crampons blunt, nearing the shadow of a giant roof. Ice remains scarce.

The sun circles low, lighting Mt. Foraker in a blaze of orange before dipping briefly beneath the horizon. Chantel weaves her way through a band of fragile rock in the steep dihedral. I admire her graceful, methodical approach: never rushing, always in control. Following in muted gray light, I stem amid a cemetery of precarious blocks. "We finally found some choss," I say. "Great job." Chantel smiles when she hands me the rack. "Thanks, lady. You're up."

I step up cautiously and lean sideways on my tool, striving to get some rest while maintaining the same direction of force. I strain to find a hint of sunrise amid the shadows of an indistinct skyline. High on the face, perfectly parallel cracks require creative twisting and camming with our tools, while our crampons scum on granite dishes. Occasionally, we pull on a piece to surmount a roof, stunned to find the wall suddenly so featureless. Where did all the footholds go? Warily, I torque my tool over another small overhang, moving up. Above the roof, the angle eases, and I scramble to the snowfield above.

Chantel follows, wrapped in her belay jacket, as morning light brushes the highest peaks. Exhausted, we nearly knock our stove down the slope as we bumble to brew up. Another 4,000 feet of snow and ridge soar above toward the summit. But the giant headwall is now beneath our feet. Our prolonged efforts have felt so natural, almost magnetic: We'll continue to endeavor upward, until it makes sense to go down. What else is there to do?

Chantel Astorga and Jewell Lund climbed the Denali Diamond (7,800', Alaska Grade 6, 5.9 A3 M6 WI5+) from June 15–19, 2015. This story is adapted from an article in Alpinist 52, with permission; a longer version is available at Alpinist.com.

in the past? Along with revisiting the criteria, I proposed that benchmarks were needed to assess when a woman's climb was particularly significant *for women*. I was arguing for "equity" in reporting women's climbs versus equality in reporting. "Equity is achieved," I wrote, "when we accept that men come to the table with a complement of physiological attributes and a long history of alpine folklore that sets them on a playing field above female alpinists. Equity would mean creating space to accept these differences and taking affirmative action to bolster the historical record of women in the mountains and purposefully celebrate their accomplishment."

As a methodology for achieving these goals, I suggested creating a panel of alpinists to support the AAJ editors in selecting the most notable female ascents for a given year. The first step of this panel or task force would be an extensive data collection phase. What exactly was the state of the art for teams of women in alpinism and other forms of "AAJ style" climbing? This information did not exist in readily digestible form. By producing a document that defined the state of the art in a variety of climbing disciplines, the task force would be able to declare with some certainty when a team of women had equaled or broken through a barrier.

Secondly, when a women's team *did* reach a high mark in women's climbing, I proposed, the AAJ would offer elevated reporting in the publication, fitting to the accomplishment. To be sure, many first ascents by women in the mountains are already covered by the AAJ. But under this new proposal, the AAJ would increase its coverage of

OVERLOOKED

RIDERS ON THE STORM (2016)
FREE CLIMBING ON THE CENTRAL TOWER OF PAINE

BY MAYAN SMITH-GOBAT, *NEW ZEALAND*

As if enchanted, the tower appeared to grow bigger the higher we climbed. At 4 a.m. on February 6, 2016, after three weeks of effort, I was jumaring to the final hard pitches on the east face of Torre Central. The monotonous movement allowed me to slip into a dreamlike state. A lone condor circled past, at one with the constant winds that carried him upward. His dark eyes started straight through me as though questioning my clumsiness, my separation from the world of wind and air, from the wild freedom he enjoyed. At once, joy flooded my being and I forgot the pain. I was at peace, dangling off a tiny rope 1,000 meters above the glacier—a guest with the rare privilege to exist in this beautiful and unforgiving place.

Ines, Thomas, and I reached the top of our fixed lines as the first golden rays hit the wall. Huddled on a small snow patch, we absorbed the power of the place, watching the fireball of the sun rise over the darkened plains. Then, without words, we slipped back into our routines. It was my lead, the 31st pitch, and our time was limited. I pulled on my tight rock shoes and peeled off my thick jacket and gloves. Within seconds, my fingers and toes lost all sensation. I simply had to trust that they would hold.

The day before, Ines and I both had come close to freeing this section, so we knew what to expect: a crack barely wide enough for the fingertips. We'd have to climb it quickly before the ice above us thawed. Beneath the tape, my hands were already torn, and as I twisted them into the narrow opening, my skin ripped open in new places. I buried my fingers deeper: I knew that executing these moves required me to block out everything else and to believe in myself entirely.

"*Allez, allez, gib alles!*" Thomas and Ines shouted, mixing French and German. Their energy merged into mine, and with every remnant of strength left in my exhausted body, I lunged toward a slight widening far above. To my surprise, my numb hand landed perfectly.

I did it! Now, don't blow it. I tried to calm my breathing, to move with slow control and precision. A wave of elation swelled as I reached around the final lip and felt warm, dry rock. I heaved my body onto a ledge. Finally, I could let go. I gave an ecstatic cry. Twenty-five years had passed since Bernd Arnold and Kurt Albert first aided this crack, and I'd just free climbed it. *Was this real?* When Ines and Thomas joined me and we embraced, I felt like the happiest person in the universe.

Ahead rose a teetering stack of loose stones of every size, held in place by rapidly melting ice and snow. I admired Ines' experience as she switched between rock and ice without hesitation; she paused only to ponder our crumpled topo. For weeks we'd been confined to one side of the wall, always looking east over Argentina. On the summit, I could see for 360 degrees. Mountains stretched to the vanishing point.

The sun crept closer to the horizon and the air chilled. To save weight, we'd left our boots and warm jackets far below. Slowly, reluctantly, we coiled our ropes and gathered our jumbled gear to begin the long descent. I volunteered to go last, so I could enjoy every remaining second on the summit, with only the luminous blue sky above.

Mayan Smith-Gobat and Ines Papert (Germany) were the first women to climb Riders on the Storm (1,300m, originally 5.12d A3) on the Central Tower of Paine, Chile, with support and photography from Thomas Senf (probably the fifth ascent overall). The two women freed all but four pitches, including a couple of former aid pitches (up to 7c+), and discovered a variation that might allow the full route's first free ascent. Smith-Gobat returned in 2017 with Brette Harrington (USA), hoping to complete this project, but poor conditions and storms prevented much progress. This story is adapted from an article in Alpinist 55, with permission.

the most significant female firsts, including repeats of earlier climbs. In this way, I hoped not only to inspire other women but also to add depth and richness to climbing's historical record.

The arguments for and against the separation of gender within climbing have been hotly debated in the sport's media, and the reasoning crosses the spectrum of biological, social, and political theories. UCLA social scientist Martie Haselton argues for recognizing biological differences where they exist, but also emphasizes that there is "the misconception that as soon there is a biological explanation, there are no other factors at play, when we social scientists know that there is always an interaction, there are environmental inputs and everything occurs in a social context. It is always both." (*Making Sense,* Ep. 135, August 2018.) Indeed, environmental and social factors are at work in alpinism, but I see them as peripheral to the argument that high-level women's climbs should be recognized in new ways. Cutting-edge women's climbs should receive more recognition because there are real differences between men and women climbers, regardless of how the differences originated. The argument for these distinctions is not just a contemporary one. In the 1980s, Wanda Rutkiewicz, regarded as one of the most accomplished female high-altitude mountaineers in history, urged for the same distinctions in mountain sports (Gugglberger, 2017).

Traditional climbing remains one of the few athletic pursuits where men and women are held to the same measuring stick. The only Olympic sports in which men and women compete head to head include equestrian sports and sailing, where physical differences are secondary to a competitor's success. In competitive climbing, men and women are usually ranked separately (with the notable excep-

[Top] Yuka Endo at about 7,500 meters on the southwest face of Cho Oyu. In 1994, she and Taeko Nagao from Japan made the second ascent of the Kurtyka-Loretan-Troillet route in alpine style, pushing through chest-deep snow to reach the summit. *Taeko Nagao* [Bottom] In 2009, Kei Taniguchi (second from right) became the first woman to win a Piolet d'Or, along with Kazuya Hiraide, for the first ascent of the southeast face of Kamet in India. *Anna Piunova*

tion of the mixed climbing competition at Ouray, Colorado, where women repeatedly have placed among the top three in the overall results). Research has demonstrated biological differences between male and female athletes in a variety of capacities. A 2012 study published in the *European Journal of Applied Physiology* indicated that, "Gender differences in performance by elite endurance athletes, including runners, track cyclists and speed skaters, have been shown to be approximately 12%" (Sandbakk et. al, 2012, p. 1.) Could it be that a similar physiological performance gap exists in the alpine arena as well—perhaps more so than on pure rock climbs?

As we began talking over these ideas among a group of editors and alpinists in the summer and fall of 2018, some of the main objections came from top women climbers. Some made it clear that they wanted to be judged simply as alpinists, not as *female alpinists*. They were opposed to the real or perceived patronizing effect that might result if the AAJ changed its criteria and carved out special coverage for women or published prominent stories of women's ascents that didn't "deserve" to be included. They also worried that if the AAJ were to establish, in effect, a quota of women's climbs, ascents that were not cutting-edge might dilute the achievements of the most accomplished female alpinists. These discussions strongly guided the methodology that we ended up developing.

What we eventually agreed was that it was reasonable to rethink the AAJ criteria and account for the performance difference between men and women. And that by documenting the state of the art for women's climbing, the AAJ would have a logical way to elevate the most impressive female ascents. In partnership with the AAJ editors, we began the process of putting these ideas into action.

Through much of 2019, a task force

including 11 women and men, representing seven nationalities, began looking into the archives and history books, debating the "rules" we would follow, and selecting climbs as benchmarks. We also sought comments from various outside reviewers. The result of all this hard work is a document we call the Baseline (*see p.59*).

The Baseline examines two broad categories of women's climbing. The first is all-women teams, which we defined to include not only climbs by multiple women but also solo climbers, as well women who were supported by a man but where the accomplishment was all hers. (For example, a woman who free climbs a big wall with a man belaying her.) The second category is mixed teams where at least 50 percent of the team was female and those women contributed at least 50 percent of the "effort." (For example, an ascent where a female team member led the crux pitch or pitches.)

We then identified a variety of climbing disciplines, such as "Alpinism–High Altitude" and "Big Walls–Expeditionary," and pored over the historical record for examples of the state of the art in each discipline. We focused on the climbing styles normally reported in the AAJ (we did not examine the record for sport climbing or bouldering).

Two points are essential to understand about the Baseline. First, the example climbs in the Baseline are just that—representative examples. In most cases, other climbs are equally or nearly as significant. The goal was not to document *all* of the ground-breaking ascents in a given category, but simply to provide representative benchmarks for each, in order to guide the AAJ in future editorial decisions. (We have published some examples from the Baseline with this article; see p.59. However, to preserve a spirit of inspiration and not competition, the full Baseline will remain an internal document for use by the AAJ editors.)

Secondly, these examples represent the *current* state of the art of women's climbing, regardless of when the climb was done. A climb done in the 1990s might still be the cutting edge in one category; in a different category, the state of the art might be a climb done last year. What we are *not* doing is listing climbs that were significant "for their time."

The entire Baseline will be re-evaluated regularly. (The composition of the task force also will be updated periodically.) As climbing progresses, new ascents will replace earlier benchmarks in the baseline, and thus the bar will rise over time. In this way, we hope women will be inspired to reach new heights.

Had this process been in place in years past, many stories might have been told in greater depth in the AAJ. Consider Catherine Destivelle, who was one of the most accomplished female alpinists (and rock climbers) of all time. Between 1990 and 1995, the Frenchwoman soloed the Walker Spur in winter, the Bonatti Pillar on the Dru, and the north face of the Eiger in winter, and established solo over 11 days the Destivelle Route on the Dru. These ascents have never been surpassed by another woman in the Alps, yet they were barely mentioned in the AAJ. (The AAJ does not

IN THEIR OWN WORDS: CONVERSATIONS WITH ALPINISTS

IN CONJUNCTION WITH this project, Sarah Hart has conducted in-depth interviews with top female alpinists, past and present, about barriers, breakthroughs, unconscious bias, alpinism as a "man's sport," and the future of female climbing. "In Their Own Words: Conversations with Female Alpinists" is a podcast series based on these interviews. Find more information and episode links at americanalpineclub.org/cutting-edge-podcast.

OVERLOOKED

THE EIGER (1992)
ONE-DAY SOLO ASCENT OF THE NORTH FACE IN WINTER

BY CATHERINE DESTIVELLE, *FRANCE*

MAKING FULL USE of the remaining daylight, I traversed 40 meters to the left to a small snow-covered platform below the Exit Cracks. I looked up and was staggered to see not a cascade of ice but a large, completely vertical groove of polished rock that had a light dusting of snow. The discovery almost floored me—this was going to be far from easy. It was already 6 p.m., the night was drawing in. The idea of bivouacking crossed my mind but was instantly rejected, as I judged there was still just enough light to climb the first ten meters of the groove, which looked to be the very steepest part. I wasted no time, put my headlamp on over my helmet, and started up the giant groove.

I climbed without hesitation, spreading arms and legs to push on each side of the dihedral. I was afraid of the abyss below, but concentrating so hard that I managed to shut it out of my thoughts. As I had anticipated, after 15 meters, the gradient reduced a bit and there were better holds. However, the darkness bothered me to the extent that I found myself gripping the holds twice as hard as normal. At last I reached a small snowy ledge. There was no longer any need to hurry, as it was now dark. I would get there when I got there. So, before starting the rest of the climb, I had a drink and ate a few energy bars while trying to see what was above by sweeping the beam of my headlamp across the face.

I thought again of bivouacking, but it was risky. If I waited for daylight sitting upright or standing, dehydrated as I was, my fingers and toes risked freezing or, come the morning, I would be too dazed and sluggish with cold to leave. It was better to move on, even if it meant climbing all night. Already getting cold, I left immediately. The route was not complicated—straight on up to the top. I left no room for uncertainty, systematically checking each handhold and foothold. Each move was made with the utmost concentration.

Some meters higher, I realized I was starting to lose feeling in my fingertips, and I made myself stop, even though I did not want to interrupt my steady progress. I put on my gloves, got some feeling back into my fingers, and then conscientiously went on with the ascent. It was hard work constantly checking all my holds, and my fingers began going numb again. Once again, I needed a stop to warm up my extremities and give my mind a bit of a break.

It took a ridiculous length of time to climb just 50 meters. I could feel exhaustion setting in. After each meter I stopped, tried to relax a little, and then went on. The temptation to throw caution to the winds and power on up to the summit was great. It was a permanent struggle with myself; I needed to be sensible.

Finally I reached the ice slope. Perked up by the proximity of the summit and armed with my ice axes, I attacked the last steep section with greater cheer. Unfortunately, 20 meters higher, it was all too much and I had to stop: I needed to catch my breath. After 30 seconds, I was off again. A few moves higher, another stop. Looking up obstinately in an attempt to glimpse the summit, all I could make out was blackness.

At that point I realized I would need to concentrate on my movements again, not on reaching the summit. Climbing slowly, I would be bound to get there sooner or later. With greater determination and with my eyes fixed no more than a meter away, I set off again.

Lost in thought, I suddenly noticed I was practically crawling on a slope so gentle that I normally would walk up it. Footprints appeared in the circle of light just under my nose. I was on the summit ridge.

Catherine Destivelle onsighted the 1938 route on the Eiger's north face in 17 hours on March 9, 1992. She soloed the north face of the Grandes Jorasses in February 1993 and the north face of the Matterhorn in February 1994, all firsts for women. This passage is adapted from Destivelle's book Rock Queen *(Hayloft, 2015, originally published as* Ascensions*), with the author's permission.*

cover climbs in the Alps extensively, but there have been plenty of exceptions for male ascents.) In 1988, Lydia Bradey from New Zealand made the first female ascent of Everest without supplemental oxygen, and in 1995, Briton Alison Hargreaves did an unsupported ascent of Everest's north side, also without supplemental oxygen. The Hargreaves climb was only covered in the AAJ in a single paragraph, and coverage of the Bradey climb focused on disputes of her account later shown to be invalid.

Or consider the Russian/Ukrainian trio of Galina Chibitok, Marina Kopteva, and Anastasia Petrova, who, in 2013, climbed an extremely difficult route up the 1,900-meter northeast face of Tengkangpoche, with a 52-hour nonstop summit push. In 2009, Ines Papert from Germany teamed up with Lisi Steurer from Austria and free climbed two long 5.12+/5.13- routes in Canada's Cirque of the Unclimbables, one of them a new route—both are at least as hard as any route climbed in these mountains since the Great Canadian Knife in 1992, but that route got a feature article in the book while Papert and Steurer's climbs netted only a few paragraphs. (Papert is certainly one of the foremost ice and mixed climbers of the modern era—male or female.) In the case of the Denali Diamond, the very first ascent of the route, by two men, merited a feature article in the AAJ, in 1984, but the subsequent first all-woman's team ascent was judged a barely significant repeat, buried in the back of the book, even though Alaska climbing expert Mark Westman called it "by far the most significant [ascent] done by an all-female team in the Alaska Range" at the time.

Under the AAJ's long-held guidelines, it made sense that these climbs got limited coverage, because they weren't first ascents or weren't the standouts among all climbs that year. But they all were extraordinary ascents for women, and under revised criteria for the AAJ, their stories could have been highlighted to a greater degree.

With creation of the Baseline well under way by the time the 2019 edition of the AAJ was in production, the editors elected to highlight Chantel Astorga and Anne Gilbert Chase's ascent of the Slovak Direct (9,000', 5.9 X M6 WI6+) on Denali's south face in 2018 as a very significant moment in women's alpinism. Chase's feature article about this ascent was an important step for ensuring the history of women's climbing is thoroughly and prominently documented in the AAJ.

In an interview with Planet Mountain after completing the Slovak Direct, Chase expressed points of view we heard from other top female climbers. She was asked, "How would you like your ascent to be remembered and celebrated?" And her response was, "Honestly, I don't care too much that we were the first females to climb the route, and that was not something we thought about when we climbed it. However, if our ascent inspires women to go into the big mountains and achieve their dreams, then I am all for it."

I hope this project will lead to the AAJ providing many such examples for ambitious female climbers. As more great women's ascents are highlighted in these pages and elsewhere, I expect women's climbing will progress farther and faster than before. Furthermore, the history of alpinism and big-wall climbing will be enriched with the voices and experiences of women who pursue the sport with fervor equal to their male counterparts. Publishing their stories will provide a more complete, accurate, and colorful picture of climbing's ongoing evolution.

ABOUT THE AUTHOR: *Sarah Hart is a social worker and longtime climber who lives in Squamish, British Columbia. She wishes to thank the team of climbers who invested countless hours in this project. She also acknowledges that this project and article may contain blind spots, and it is her hope that these will be addressed as the work continues.*

A NOTE FROM THE EDITOR

THE AMERICAN ALPINE JOURNAL has committed to enhancing coverage of significant female climbs, using the guidelines and tools set out by the Women's State of the Art Project. As noted in Sarah Hart's article, the AAJ already reports many climbs by women (including dozens in this edition), and the standards outlined here will not put new hurdles in front of female climbers. Far from it. Rather, they offer a logical way to *increase* coverage of women's climbing.

We understand that many climbers, of any gender, are not interested in seeking first ascents, pursuing risky climbs, or setting new standards in climbing performance, but simply enjoy climbing for its own sake. Bravo, we say. But the AAJ's focus—our raison d'être—is documenting "firsts" of various kinds in the mountains and on big walls. The State of the Art Project gives us new tools for accomplishing these goals.

We also acknowledge that the AAJ and other publishers of climbing history may have insufficiently documented various ascents by other people who do not enjoy all the advantages of traditional, mainstream climbers. We are working to expand some of their stories as well.

Like climbing, the AAJ evolves. In some years, few changes may be noticeable in the book as a result of these initiatives—the standards for expanded coverage have deliberately been designed to encourage methodical, thoughtful evolution. But over time, we expect, the impact will be substantial. — *Dougald MacDonald, Editor*

THE WOMEN'S BASELINE
REPRESENTATIVE CLIMBS*

ALPINISM – HIGH-ALTITUDE

■ **All Female**
- North ridge of Everest (8,848m), Tibet, with no O2 and minimal support: Alison Hargreaves, 1995
- Second ascent of Kurtyka-Loretan-Troillet route on southwest face of Cho Oyu (8,188m), Tibet, in alpine style: Yuka Endo and Taeko Nagao, 1994

■ **Mixed Teams**
- First ascent of Samurai Direct (1,800m, WI5+ M5+) on southeast face of Kamet (7,756m), India: Kei Taniguchi and partner, 2008

ALPINISM – MID-ALTITUDE

■ **All Female**
- First ascent of the Battle for Love (1,900m, 6b A2) on Tengkangpoche (6,487m), Nepal: Galina Chibitok, Marina Kopteva, Anastasia Petrova, 2013
- Ascent of southwest buttress (Scottish Pillar) (1,300m, 5.10 A2) of Bhagirathi III (6,454m), India, in alpine style: Fanny Tomasi-Schmutz and Elodie LeComte, 2016
- Repeat of Slovak Direct (2,700m, WI6 M6 A2) on Denali, Alaska: Chantel Astorga and Anne Gilbert Chase, 2018

■ **Mixed Teams**
- First ascent of Lost in China (1,200m, WI5+ M6) on Kyzyl Asker (5,842m), China: Ines Papert and partner, 2016
- First ascent of Stealing Beauty (1,150m, M6 6b A2) on Kyajo Ri (6,186m), Nepal: Marina Kopteva and partner, 2013
- First ascent of Obscured Perception (1,400m, WI5 M6 A0) on Nilkanth (6,596m), India: Chantel Astorga, Anne Gilbert Chase, and partner, 2017

ALPINISM – LOWER ALTITUDE

■ **All Female**
- Winter solo ascent of the Walker Spur (1,100m, ED) on the Grandes Jorasses, France: Catherine Destivelle, 1993
- Solo ascents of six "great north faces" of the Alps in one season: Alison Hargreaves, 1993

■ **Mixed Teams**
- Ascent of No Siesta/Bonatti-Vaucher linkup (1,100m, M7) on north face of the Grandes Jorasses, France: Ines Papert and partner, 2017

ICE AND MIXED CLIMBS

- Ascent of Ritter der Kokosnuss, Kandersteg, Switzerland (165m, M12 WI5): Ines Papert, 2015
- Ascent of the Hurting, Scotland (40m, XI ,11 trad): Ines Papert, 2015
- First ascent of Saphira (50m, M15) in Vail, Colorado: Lucie Hrozová, 2016

BIG WALLS – ACCESSIBLE

■ **All Female**
- Solo ascent of Wyoming Sheep Ranch (800m, A4) on El Capitan, California: Sílvia Vidal, 2000
- Solo first ascent of the Destivelle Route on the Petit Dru (800m, 5.11 A5), Mont Blanc Massif, France: Catherine Destivelle, 1991
- Speed ascent of the Nose, El Capitan (4 hours 43 minutes): Mayan Smith-Gobat and Libby Sauter, 2014

BIG WALLS – EXPEDITIONARY

■ **All Female**
- Solo first ascent of Life is Lilac (870m, A4+ 6a+), on Shipton Spire (5,852m), Pakistan: Sílvia Vidal, 2007

■ **Mixed Teams**
- Ascent of Riders on the Storm (1,300m, free up to 5.13a) on Paine's Central Tower, Chile: Ines Papert, Mayan Smith-Gobat, and partner, 2016

LONG FREE CLIMBS

■ **All Female**
- One-day free ascent of the Nose (950m, 5.14a), El Capitan, California: Lynn Hill, 1994
- Free ascent of Die Unendliche Geschichte (350m, 5.14a) in Rätikon, Swtizerland: Nina Caprez and Barbara Zangerl (each redpointed), 2015

■ **Mixed Teams**
- Free ascent of Magic Mushroom (900m, 5.14a) on El Capitan, Yosemite, California: Barbara Zangerl and partner, 2017
- Free ascent of the Yugoslav Route (800m, 5.12) on Trango Tower (6,239m), Pakistan: Catherine Destivelle and partner, 1990

SINGLE-PITCH TRAD CLIMBS

- First ascent of Meltdown (5.14c) in Yosemite Valley, California: Beth Rodden, 2008
- First ascent of Gondo Crack (5.14b) in Cippo, Switzerland: Barbara Zangerl, 2017
- Repeat of Magic Line (5.14b) in Yosemite Valley, California: Hazel Findlay, 2019

EDITOR'S NOTE: These climbs are representative examples from the Women's Baseline. The comprehensive Baseline is an internal AAJ document.

OVERLOOKED

MAGIC MUSHROOM (2017)
A FEMALE ASCENT OF EL CAP'S SECOND-HARDEST FREE CLIMB

BY BARBARA ZANGERL, *AUSTRIA*

FORTY METERS BELOW the summit, what had seemed impossible had almost become reality. It was day nine on the wall, and Jacopo Larcher and I both were tired from the previous days. But our motivation was stronger than ever. The sun was shining, we were hanging out in our portaledge, and the weather was on our side. Although it was much too warm to try the next hard pitch in the sunshine, we kept getting perfect conditions at night. Waiting for sunset felt like an eternity, and our eyes keep wandering up the last big challenge of Magic Mushroom, the 5.14a "Seven Seas" pitch shortly before the top.

When we arrived in Yosemite on the 10th of October, 2017, we weren't sure which route we would attempt. My big dream was to climb the Nose, while Jacopo had cast an eye on Magic Mushroom, which leads up a steep wall a bit further left. Of course I was psyched to try that as well, but when I saw the topo—there were *so many* hard pitches. It sounded more like an interesting long-term project. But when we looked up El Cap the first time that fall, we quickly dropped our Nose plans. It was naïve to think it would not be overcrowded at the best time of the year.

And so, Magic Mushroom. The route began with perfect splitters and beautiful, varied climbing. This continued until we reached the first hard pitch, the sixth. We immediately knew we would not be able to just "climb" that pitch, not even with the occasional rest. We had to restore missing protection and clean the cracks, sometimes for hours, before we could attempt to redpoint. Our chosen style of climbing was ground up, without checking out pitches from above. This took a lot of time, as there is hardly any fixed protection in the route and we had little aid climbing experience—this was equally adventurous and thrilling, and we had to fight hard for every pitch. After another eight days on the wall, we finally made it to the top, our first milestone, but still far from any serious bid to free climb the whole route.

After that we invested more days working on the crux pitches, spending quite a lot of time on the last hard 5.14a pitch before the top, which turned out to be the most difficult for me. (Not so for Jacopo, who found his personal crux on pitch 20.) I was able to climb all the sequences of the Seven Seas, but hooking it all up in one go seemed impossible. My optimism quickly dwindled. In addition, our time was running out. We had already changed our flights, but we only had two weeks left, meaning we'd only get a single chance at a continuous free push. We both wanted to lead all the pitches harder than 5.12+, which would take additional time. We had stashed food and water during our previous tries, so we would be able to stay on the wall for 12 days.

On November 30 the alarm rang at 4 a.m. and off we went, climbing the first pitches in darkness. Many of the lower pitches were wet, and it was mainly luck that kept us from slipping off the holds of the first 8a pitch, but then it got better. We finally arrived at Mammoth Terraces exhausted. After some quick binge-eating there was silence and we fell asleep under a clear sky.

The next morning, I felt as if I had been run over by a train. It took a lot of effort to get out of the sleeping bag and put on my climbing shoes. Hauling the bags after each lead felt like an enormous feat, costing us half an hour per pitch. It was a battle, but we finally made it to our portaledge below pitch 20 at midnight. I felt really ill, and after two spoons of rice and a cup of tea it got worse. It was quickly clear the next day would be a rest day.

After the rest I was still weak, but as I climbed the first meters above the ledge, I realized that my head felt free. No matter how this day would end, I felt relieved to be climbing at all, and this feeling took away all the pressure. Unfortunately the day did not go that well for Jacopo—he kept slipping off the bad footholds on pitch 20 (8a+/5.13c), and he had to wait until the next day to redpoint. We still did the following 8b pitch in the evening, with Jacopo climbing the hard layback crux totally unimpressed by his previous battle.

The next day, the first 5.14a pitch waited for us. I felt recovered and fresh, and everything went smoothly. But pitch 26, which was rated 5.11, one of the easiest on the route, was soaking wet. We brushed silly amounts of chalk onto the holds and removed big soggy patches of moss—not a typical rest day! In the morning it was still completely wet, but we fought our way up, jamming wet hands and slipping off the moist footholds, relieved to know it was behind us.

Above was the Seven Seas, my personal nightmare. When we arrived it was still too hot to try this overhanging endurance monster, so we waited for evening. My first try immediately confirmed my concerns: I still was not able to maintain body tension and kept slipping off. I kept trying and trying, hoping it would start to feel easier at some point, but it didn't.

Jacopo saved that evening by fighting his way to the belay totally pumped. I felt very happy for him, but at the same time disappointed about my failure. Giving in was not yet an option. Half an hour later, the same story, again. I could not hold back my emotions and cursed and swore for at least ten minutes before I regained my composure. I knew I was too tired for another attempt, but my head wouldn't let me give in without looking yet again. And it was my head, indeed, that finally became the key! Pressing my skull against the protruding left side of the crack, under my elbow, enabled me to statically reach the crucial smeary foothold. After another rest day, I managed to climb the Seven Seas, and our cries of joy echoed from El Capitan in the first light of morning.

Barbara "Babsi" Zangerl from Austria is the only woman to free climb Magic Mushroom (VI 5.14a), generally considered the second-hardest free route on El Capitan, after the Dawn Wall. In 2019, she free climbed the Nose, her fifth El Cap free route.

High on Manaslu, just below the point where most climbers stop their ascent—a point about 20 meters before the summit. *Guy Cotter*

AN 8,000-METER MESS

THE HISTORY OF CLIMBING THE WORLD'S HIGHEST PEAKS IS NOT WHAT IT SEEMS

DAMIEN GILDEA

In recent years an international group of mountaineering researchers came to the realization that there was a major problem with the history of 8,000-meter climbing. The group, which coalesced around Eberhard Jurgalski, the leading chronicler of Himalayan and Karakoram mountaineering statistics, and his 8000ers.com website, determined that on several 8,000-meter peaks, many climbers had not been going to the summit and that this had been happening for decades. Usually this has been because of understandable ignorance or confusion about the exact nature of the summit topography. However, it has led to the remarkable situation where it is possible that no one has stood on the true highest point of all the 8,000-meter peaks.

I feel that I have to state immediately that the summit is the highest point on the mountain and there is *usually* only one. So, in this article, I don't say "main summit" or "true summit"—just "summit." Everything else is a top, a peak, a bump, or a ridge, but not the summit. You might feel that you can stop 30 meters away and 10 meters below the very highest point and still say that you have "climbed the mountain," but you have not been to the summit.

The questions that have arisen in recent years are not the well-known issues with climbers stopping at the rocky foresummit of Broad Peak or the central peak of Xixabangma (Shishapangma). They involve three other 8,000ers. It has become apparent that only around half the climbers claiming a summit of Annapurna (8,091 meters) had been to the highest point, and that almost all climbers on Manaslu (8,163 meters) had not continued to the summit. There has also been confusion on Dhaulagiri's summit (8,167 meters). The full dossiers outlining the historical and current issues with these three 8,000ers are available for free at 8000ers.com.

Many of these non-summits occurred in recent years during the boom in commercial guiding of 8,000-meter peaks, but some of the ascents in question also involve some of the biggest names and ascents in the history of Himalayan climbing. For those climbers ascending only one or two 8000ers, these missed summits may not be an issue. However, the researchers feel that these issues have significant importance for the historical record of those claiming—or attempting to climb—all 14 of the 8,000-meter peaks.

It must be stated that in the vast majority of cases the research group believes these non-summits are due to honest mistakes or justifiable ignorance, rather than willful dishonesty. Above 8,000 meters, climbers are physically and mentally extended, in no state to be conducting accurate topographical surveys or historical comparisons. Poor visibility, bad weather, fear about the descent, and concern for partners exacerbate the difficulties. The group does not want their findings to result in climbers pushing further than is safe for them at the time. There is also a long history of climbers stopping just below the summits of certain major peaks, out of respect for local beliefs and traditions (e.g., Kangchenjunga) or because the highest point is an unstable cornice; however, these concerns do not apply to the mountains under discussion here.

The researchers are also aware of the socio-economic reality that underpins modern Himalayan climbing, in that there is significant financial pressure on the Sherpas and other high-altitude guides and workers employed by so many aspirants to 8,000-meter peaks to have their clients feel they have been "successful." Depending on the company and client, this may mean a summit bonus, which can encourage Sherpas to accept tops lower than the summit (especially if other groups are stopping there), or a bonus for simply getting their client over 8,000 meters, which may reduce motivation to continue to the highest point. With a slow, tired client in a line of similar climbers all close to the top of the mountain, and with their own safety also in mind, there is tremendous pressure on Sherpas to simply "call it good" short of the summit, and a grateful but inexperienced client may not know any better or simply not care.

NEW SOURCES OF INFORMATION

These issues have surfaced only recently for several reasons. The last decade has seen a proliferation of self-propagated photos and other media from the 8,000ers, available online. This new material and other information has made it easier for researchers to compare ascents and claims, and to shed new light on the ascents of decades past. This wealth of information was not available to researchers, publishers, or climbers until very recently, a factor the research group takes into account when judging what anyone could have known previously about the summit locations.

For decades, the chronicling of mountaineering in Nepal, home to eight of the 8,000-meter peaks, was methodically done by the renowned Elizabeth Hawley. While Hawley mostly accepted

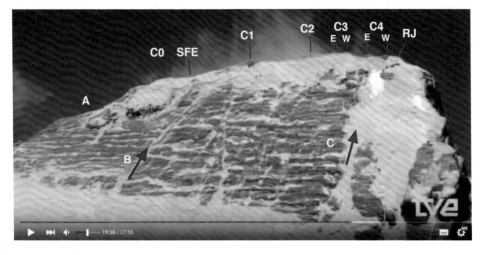

Video capture of the north side of Annapurna, showing the various tops along the summit ridge, from C0 at the east end to Ridge Junction (RJ) in the west. C2 and C3 mark the 8,091-meter summit. (A) Upper east ridge. (B) Gully leading to C1. (C) "French Couloir." (SFE) South face exit. *Joao Garcia*

climbers at their word, she grilled them mercilessly if she had doubts, particularly for bigger claims, and as one American climber attempting Everest found in 2003, she did not consider eight meters from the summit to be a successful summit. However, for information about summit topographies, Hawley relied solely on the reports of earlier climbers whom she trusted due to their experience and reputation, and from relatively scarce photos provided by climbers over the years. The research group has now realized that these climbers have been mistaken in some cases, and photos need to be carefully examined and compared to fully understand the various summit topographies of each mountain.

More than ten years ago, in 2007, Eberhard Jurgalski noticed in "summit" photos that climbers on Manaslu seemed to be stopping short of the high point that the Japanese reached on the 1956 first ascent of that mountain. After more research and discussion with a number of experienced climbers, Jurgalski was proved correct; in fact it became apparent that Manaslu claimants have been stopping at *several* different points and that this had been happening for years.

Then, in 2012 and 2015, Sherpas guiding clients on Annapurna published purported summit photos and video that did not seem to be on the highest point of the summit ridge. In ensuing discussions and research, Jurgalski approached the German Aerospace Center (DLR), which had recently published significant new satellite imagery and photographic analysis of some Himalayan regions. [One result was a book, *Mountains: Die vierte Dimension* ("Mountains: The Fourth Dimension"), published in 2016.] This imagery proved particularly interesting on Annapurna.

ANNAPURNA

The new DLR data revealed the unique topography of the long summit ridge of Annapurna, showing that *two* small tops, barely 30 meters apart, could realistically lay claim to being the highest point of the mountain—a rare situation. Since then, the examination of climbers' photos and reports by researcher Rodolphe Popier has shown that for decades many Annapurna climbers have not stood on *either* of these twin summits—some have been close, others significantly farther away.

In the photograph above of Annapurna's summit ridge, taken from the north side in 2010 from an airplane, the various points along the ridge have been labeled by Popier as C0 to C4, with "C" denoting "cornice," as this is the nature of much of the ridge. The common exit point from south face ascents (SFE), east of the summit, is also shown, as is the ridge junction (RJ) at the western end. Climbers approaching the summit of Annapurna from the north side routes, as the majority do, have ascended to the summit ridge by three variants: the upper east ridge, a thin gully leading up to C1, and the "French Couloir" at the western end of the face, meaning they end up at different places on that ridge, with different views of what appears to be the highest point. Popier's dossier on Annapurna, available on Jurgalski's 8000ers.com site, goes into much more detail about this topography, identifying key landmarks and analyzing many climbers' photos to ascertain their highest location on the summit ridge. The analysis shows that many—perhaps half—never stood on either of the two tops (C2 and C3) now shown to be the summit.

It is important to restate here that the intent of researching and publishing this information is not to denigrate any climber, nor to completely rewrite the history of 8,000-meter climbing, including landmark ascents on Annapurna and other peaks. Climbing is about much more than topographical heights—it is about people, and the history of Himalayan climbing is a tapestry of people and their exploits and experiences on and around those heights. As in other strands of alpinism, some 8,000-meter climbers have put more emphasis on a difficult or new route than the summit itself, and for such climbers reaching a summit ridge or a distinct but non-summit top, or joining a previously climbed route, may have been sufficient to claim success. These climbers' places in history are set, and questions about the precise topographical details of certain climbs should not change the cultural importance of their exploits.

DHAULAGIRI

FOR YEARS, MANY climbers on Dhaulagiri's regular northeast ridge route followed the final part of this ridge toward the summit, but some of them stopped at a point considerably down the ridge, not going to the actual summit. From the late 1980s, there was a pole placed at that lower point, which undoubtedly caused confusion. Elizabeth Hawley rejected the summit claims of an Italian pair who mistakenly stopped there in 2005, as Hawley realized even back then that the pole was not on the summit. The Italians returned in 2006 and climbed to the summit, as other climbers have done on Dhaulagiri (and for similar reasons on Xixabangma and Broad Peak), because these climbers understood that if they wanted their summit to be universally accepted or for them to be included in any definitive list of 14x8000-meter summiters, they must go to the highest point.

More recently on Dhaulagiri, most climbers have avoided the upper northeast ridge and instead traversed high and right across the top of the north

The metal pole well to the northeast of Dhaulagiri's summit. *André Georges*

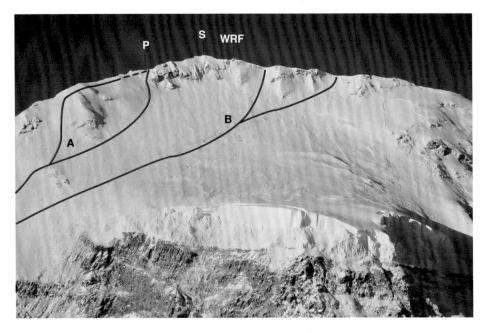

Dhaulagiri from the north, showing traditional finishes to the northeast ridge (A) and today's more common finishes (B) to the ridgeline west of the summit. (P) Metal pole east of the top. (S) Dhaulagiri's 8,167-meter summit. (WRF) Western rocky foresummit. *Boyan Petrov*

face, before cutting left up one of two shallow couloirs to reach the summit ridge. On 8000ers.com, Rodolphe Popier's Dhaulagiri dossier outlines the routes to the summit and other tops. As seen in the photograph above, climbers taking the east couloir arrive on the summit ridge to the west of a small peak, the Western Rocky Foresummit (WRF), and must continue moving east to reach the summit. If climbers take the west couloir, they hit the ridge farther away from the summit and, after turning back east, must pass an additional small top before encountering the WRF and continuing further east to the summit.

Approaching by either couloir, some climbers have been stopping at the WRF, not realizing that the point around 30 meters farther east is the summit. Several have noted that the summit is only about one or two meters higher than the WRF, and given that these tops gain considerable snow cover in the post-monsoon season, the research group has proposed that Dhaulagiri perhaps should be considered in the same way as Annapurna, having two acceptable summits that are quite close horizontally and unusually close vertically.

MANASLU

DURING THE LAST decade, Manaslu, the world's eighth-highest mountain, has become a more reliably accessible alternative to Cho Oyu (8,188 meters) for aspiring 8,000-meter climbers, many of them joining commercial expeditions and using the climb to prepare for a future attempt on Everest. However, as with Xixabangma, an otherwise straightforward climb ends with a final tricky ridge, a situation that makes Manaslu perhaps less suitable for commercially guided clients than it first appears.

At 8000ers.com, Tobias Pantel's Manaslu dossier examines this summit ridge. A climber approaching the final ridge on Manaslu cannot see the summit, but can see the prominent point C2, as shown in the accompanying photo, and some small tops before it. The summit ridge continues beyond C2, over another intermediate top, before rising to the highest point, denoted in the photos here as C4—this is the 8,163-meter summit of Manaslu. For over a decade, the majority of climbers claiming a summit of Manaslu have not reached this point, either because they did not realize that C2 was not the summit or they were not capable of the further climbing to reach the summit (C4) or unwilling to risk it.

The large numbers of climbers now on Manaslu has made this situation even more problematic. While it may be feasible for a climber, guide, or Sherpa to fix a rope from C2 to the summit even in post-monsoon snow, it is probably not feasible and certainly not safe to have dozens of people traversing such a rope back and forth within the narrow window of time they are there—and in recent years around

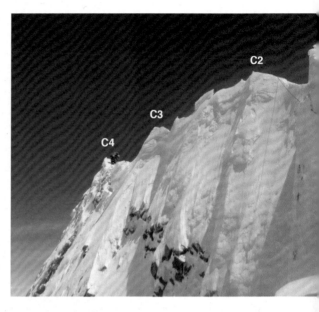

The distance between C2, where most Manaslu climbers stop their ascent, and C4, the 8,163-meter summit, is roughly 20 meters horizontally and three to six meters vertically, depending on snow conditions. *Guy Cotter*

250 to 300 people a year have claimed a summit of Manaslu, most of them having stopped around C2. This is a concrete example of one of the pitfalls, and the paradox, of mass commercial guiding: The summit is sold to clients based on its apparent achievability, and thus attracts large numbers of clients, but those large numbers end up making the summit less achievable.

The situation seems to be exacerbated in the autumn post-monsoon season on Manaslu, when deep snow and large cornices form on that final summit ridge. The spring pre-monsoon conditions of April and May usually have fewer cornices, making the final narrow traverse relatively safer, but the guiding companies are busy on Everest in the pre-monsoon spring season, so prefer to prepare clients on a lower mountain in the preceding autumn.

If climbers just want to go high over 8,000 meters on Manaslu as preparation for Everest, then following the ropes to the prayer-flag-draped "selfie spot" by C2 may suffice. But if a climber wants to be unequivocally recognized as achieving all 14 of the 8,000ers, or make any other claim based on summiting Manaslu, then it seems only fair that they must unequivocally go to the summit. This may mean going in the pre-monsoon season, prepared to fix their own rope on the final ridge.

TOLERANCE ZONES?

THE 8000ERS.COM RESEARCH group has considered and discussed the concept of a "Tolerance Zone" (TZ), a small region around the summit, usually along a ridge that includes slightly lower tops, which would be acceptable to reach for the purpose of claiming a summit and for chroniclers of mountaineering to record a successful ascent. But where should the boundaries of such a zone stop? Is 10 meters from the summit OK? Why not 20 meters? Is five meters vertically acceptable but 30 meters horizontally too far? Given the different topographies of each summit area—Manaslu is tiny and steep, Annapurna long and indistinct—there would need to be different parameters for each mountain, and that may prove to be unworkable.

For future climbers, the summit picture is clear. Given that the nature of the summit regions on these problematic peaks is now known—and has been available for a few years and covered in climbing media—the research group feels there is now no excuse for claiming a summit of these peaks without verifiably reaching the highest point, particularly for those wanting to claim all 14 of the 8,000ers. So there should be no Tolerance Zone on any of these peaks for claiming ascents after 2020. The summit is the summit.

When looking at *past* ascents, however, the research group feels it is both fair and practical to give leeway for understandable confusion or errors, and therefore summit claims should be respected for climbers who historically finished in the following zones:

Annapurna: C1 in the east to the Ridge Junction (RJ) in the west
Dhaulagiri: the Western Rocky Foresummit (WRF) as well as the summit
Manaslu: C2 to C4

It is now clear from the dossiers at 8000ers.com that a number of people previously considered to have climbed all 14 of the 8,000-meter peaks have not done so, even if you allow for the grace of a Tolerance Zone. Although the research group has attempted to acquire as many climbers' photos and accounts as possible, much of this has not been forthcoming. Moreover, some of these climbers have died and therefore cannot explain their actions (let alone consider reclimbing summits). So, with a lot of information from climbers still missing, it is impossible to make the bold claim that *no one* has climbed all 14 of the 8,000ers, but it is also possible this might be true. The most accurate and comprehensive list of 8,000-meter collectors is Jurgalski's at 8000ers. com. However, any such list is just a list of claimants—at present, there can be no definitive list of climbers that can be unequivocally verified to have reached all of the summits.

Can any list *ever* be "final"? Revision is common and ongoing in all forms of history, including the history of alpinism—facts are rarely final, and there are many aspects to stories. A definitive list for this particular matter is likely an illusion—an illusion of precision that does not exist, an illusion of control over history that can never exist.

DOES ANY OF THIS MATTER?

The research group has tried to come to conclusions that are topographically accurate, ethically fair, and socially acceptable, but this has proven extremely difficult. The group is reluctant to impose contrived rules on others or shine a harsh light on the minor missteps of inspiring climbers of the past. But they feel strongly that lines need to be drawn somewhere to clarify the historical record, to make the future chronicling of ascents workable, and to respect the efforts of those who *have* made the effort to go to the summits—particularly those who have returned to a mountain after realizing an earlier mistake, with all the risk, expense, and effort this requires.

If you want to spend your holiday doing some enjoyable climbing, you're better off going to the Sierra Nevada or Chamonix than to the Himalaya or Karakoram. If you just want to experience the Greater Ranges, you can go to any of a hundred other peaks on the permitted lists or go trekking. The 8,000ers are tough, dangerous, expensive, and rarely fun, even by the weird and masochistic standards of climbers.

On the 8,000-meter mountains, people are almost always aiming to climb to the summit. The vast majority are not exploring new terrain or pushing any boundaries in the world of alpinism. These are trophy peaks, and you don't get a trophy for stopping at 90 meters in the 100-meter

Yannick Graziani celebrates on the summit of Annapurna after an eight-day alpine-style ascent of the south face with Stéphane Benoist. The two exited the face to the east of the summit, beyond the C1 point visible in the distance along the summit ridge, then plodded to the top. To be certain he reached the highest point, Graziani continued to C3 West, then returned to this point to start the long descent. *Stéphane Benoist*

sprint. Almost all climbers attempting 8,000-meter peaks nowadays are there to achieve a singular goal—the summit—not just to have a laugh with friends or enjoy the athletic movement. So, if we climbers are honest with ourselves about why we are on these mountains, then we should maintain that honesty through the process, accepting that summit success on an 8,000-meter peak means going to the highest point.

BREATHING SPACE

As this article was completed in late April 2020, all spring and summer expeditions to the Nepal and Indian Himalaya had been canceled because of COVID-19, the Karakoram season was very likely to be a non-starter, and it was possible the post-monsoon Nepal-Tibet seasons would be canceled as well. This unique and worldwide hiatus gives the mountaineering community a rare chance to pause and draw a line under practices that have distorted our culture and its history. The community can declare that, from 2021 onward, if climbers want to be included on official summit lists and in definitive histories, we only count ascents verified to have been on the summit, not on any lower points.

This year also gives us space to think about why we do this, why we climb. Is it really for the experience, for all the intangibles we allude to in literature and social media? Or is it as simple as wanting to tick a listed item for some reason? Do we value primacy over quality, results over experience? The summit is the summit, but climbing is more than summits.

About the Author: *Damien Gildea is an Australian climber, the author of Mountaineering in Antarctica, and a contributing editor of the American Alpine Journal.*

ANGELS AND DEMONS

DRONE USE IS GROWING FAST IN THE MOUNTAINS. WHERE SHOULD THE LINES BE DRAWN?

DOUGALD MACDONALD

In the last decade, the use of remote-controlled quadcopters, a.k.a. drones, has skyrocketed. In the United States alone, more than one million unmanned aerial vehicles (UAVs) have been registered with the Federal Aviation Administration. Today's quadcopters are lighter, more reliable in the mountain environment, and can carry heavier payloads than ever before, and reports of drone use by mountaineering expeditions around the world have been filtering into pages of the AAJ—in sometimes surprising ways.

Drones infuriate many climbers with their loud whine and the general sense of invasiveness in relatively pristine environments. Many national parks and other jurisdictions around the world have banned their use. Yet creative uses of these tools continue to grow. Amid these trends, where are we headed and what guidelines should climbers follow?

PHOTOGRAPHY

DRONE USE IN the climbing world was pioneered by photographers and videographers, allowing spectacular aerial imagery at a tiny fraction of the cost of filming by helicopter. The fly-bys and vertical tracking shots of climbers in action have become so ubiquitous they almost are clichés—albeit, often very beautiful ones.

Drones are increasingly used to capture imagery in the highest mountains. Photographer Sean Haverstock operated a drone from advanced base camp below Lunag Ri in Nepal in 2018 to film the late David Lama soloing the first ascent of the nearly 7,000-meter peak, resulting in the cover shot of the 2019 *American Alpine Journal*. Lama also was one of the subjects of an early experiment in high-altitude mountaineering photography, when Corey Rich and pilot Remo Masina collaborated on drone footage of Austrians Lama and Peter Ortner making a free ascent of Trango Tower in Pakistan in 2012. In a beautiful demonstration of the power of drone photography, Renan Ozturk flew a drone from the North Col on Everest in 2019 to capture a unique 360° panorama of Everest and its surroundings.

Professional photographers aren't the only ones using these tools to capture stirring images. In a solo expedition to Greenland in 2018, the German climber Robert Jasper used a drone and other tools to photograph himself soloing a new route on an isolated granite tower. In places where drone photography remains legal and socially acceptable, it seems likely there is still enormous potential for creative image making and storytelling.

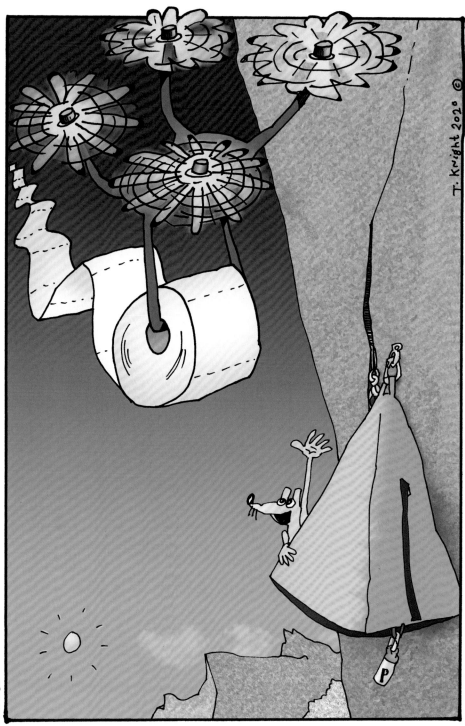

Tomi Knight

Testing a drone soon after landing on Ellesmere Island for a multi-week ski tour and research project (see p.172). The drone proved invaluable for scouting the safest route over the icefields. *Greg Horne (both)*

SCOUTING ROUTES

FROM CAPTURING AERIAL photos and video in the mountains, it's just a short step to using that imagery to plan routes and conduct reconnaissance. The first mention of such tactics in the AAJ came in 2016, when a team of Polish climbers—the first to visit the spectacular Lachit Valley in Pakistan—used a drone to photograph side arms of the glacier en route to making two first ascents.

Examples are quickly mounting of drones used to avoid exposure to dangers unseen from below. French climbers in Nepal in 2017 changed their planned attempt on an unclimbed 6,475-meter peak to the completely opposite side of the mountain after a drone reconnaissance revealed dangerous seracs above their original route. In the autumn of 2019 on Everest, several teams canceled their expeditions after a drone studied a huge serac poised above the Khumbu Icefall and determined it to be an exceptional threat.

Longtime Arctic explorer Greg Horne and his team carried drones for the first time on an expedition last spring, visiting the Prince of Wales Icefield on Ellesmere Island. Their original plan was to use the drones for studying ivory gulls, but after encountering more crevasses than Horne had seen in 10 previous expeditions, and after a crevasse fall with a 70-kilogram loaded pulk (sled), the team began deploying a drone to scout the best places to cross crevasses and meltwater river channels that were up to 50 kilometers long. "Every evening, after camp was set and supper done, we would fly a recon mission to scout ahead," Horne wrote in an email. "One evening, after I was only airborne a couple seconds, I saw that camp was right beside a multi-kilometer-long crevasse we could not see from the ground and hadn't discovered through probing. In fact, my pulk was parked right on top of it. Re-probing determined the bridge was nearly two meters thick—still, after the crevasse fall a week earlier, our senses were on high alert."

RESCUE AND AID

IN THE SUMMER of 2018, Scottish climber Rick Allen went missing during a summit bid on Broad Peak in the Karakoram. Using a telescope, a climber at base camp spotted a dark dot at around 7,000 meters that could have been the missing climber, and Polish climber and photographer Bartek Bargiel, also in base camp, agreed to fly his drone up Broad Peak for a look. Using the drone, Bargiel located Allen, still alive, marked his precise coordinates, and helped lead rescuers to him. (*The video footage can be seen with this story at the AAJ website.*)

Although their capability may be limited by weather, visibility, altitude, and payload restrictions, drones have been widely adopted by search and rescue teams; they can be equipped to detect avalanche transceiver signals and Recco reflectors or to capture thermal imagery for low-visibility searches, and increasingly they are able to deliver supplies directly to stranded or injured subjects. Bartek Bargiel, who flew his quadcopter as high as 8,500 meters to scout and film his brother Andrzej's first ski descent of K2 in 2018, also used the machine to fly medicine to Camp 3, where Andrzej's climbing partner was stranded with debilitating back pain, and to deliver a GoPro camera and batteries that Andrzej had forgotten at base camp.

Many wonder how far climbers will push the limits of this new form of aid. It's not hard to imagine powerful drones being deployed to resupply climbers at high camps with extra fuel or food, or even to deliver a spare crampon when one is dropped. In the old days, such a mistake usually would mean the end of an expedition. Now, perhaps not.

QUESTIONS OF STYLE

MANY MOUNTAIN VISITORS despise drones. Whizzing close by a crag, they may shatter the focus of a climber making delicate moves, and their persistent whine in flight breaks the silence that many seek in the mountains. They may have negative impacts on cliff-nesting birds and other wildlife. As a result of these and other concerns, drones are illegal to fly in many places, including national parks in the United States, Argentina, and many other countries; other jurisdictions require a permit for drone use.

Even climbers who have deployed drones themselves for purposes other than photography may feel misgivings. "I used a drone once while I was halfway up an unclimbed wall to scout out the terrain above, and that's one of the few stylistic regrets I have from my entire climbing career," said AAJ associate editor Chris Kalman. "It felt like cheating. But more importantly, it was antithetical to the very reason I seek out new routes. I don't want to know what's up ahead. That's why I'm up there in the first place."

Yet, many tools and technologies once decried as cheating in rock climbing and mountaineering now are used without a second thought, from cams and chalk to GPS systems and weather forecasts delivered by satellite phone. Few climbers today feel any guilt about studying Google Earth to plan an expedition. Will drone imagery soon be regarded as little different? "I'll bet that most climbers have referred to a photo of a mountain while climbing to help with route-finding," said alpinist Colin Haley. "Aerial photographers like Bradford Washburn and John Scurlock have both been celebrated for their contributions to climbing. A drone might be even more useful than their photographs—and also much quieter and more environmentally friendly than their planes—but the basic purpose is the same: using technology from afar to help decipher the route."

It seems climbers may need a new set of ethical guidelines for drone use to go along with the "rules" of clean climbing and free climbing and alpine style. Knowing and following the laws governing drone use in a given area is paramount—no climber or photographer has any excuse for flouting these rules. Avoiding negative impacts on fellow climbers' natural experience and on wild creatures is equally essential.

In remote or high-altitude areas where no impact on other climbers or wildlife is likely, and there are no regulations preventing flights, the use of drones becomes a question of style, like so many choices in climbing. What do you hope to get out of a climb? Will you adopt any technology to improve the odds of success (and return with the imagery to prove it)? Or will you eschew this new tool to maintain a sense of fair play and the allure of the unknown?

ABOUT THE AUTHOR: *Dougald MacDonald is editor of the American Alpine Journal.*

[RECON]

CORDILLERA DARWIN

THE WILD MOUNTAINS OF TIERRA DEL FUEGO

CAMILO RADA

Cerro Erguido (1,243 meters) from the south, seen from Fiordo de Agostini at the northwest end of the Cordillera Darwin. The mountain is unclimbed. *Bernard Taberlet*

The east side of Monte Sarmiento (2,207 meters). Once mistaken for a volcano because of its size and form, this peak has been the lodestone for generations of mountaineers. *Quixote Expeditions*

In today's closely connected, heavily touristed world, there are still a few places whose beauty and secrets are guarded by many barriers to entry—strata of difficulty like the layers of a pearl. One such place is the mountains of western Tierra del Fuego.

The Tierra del Fuego archipelago constitutes the southern tip of the Americas, pointing like an arrow toward Antarctica, forged by the westerlies and the bash of waves. The Isla Grande ("big island") of Tierra del Fuego is larger than Denmark, and the myriad surrounding islands and islets add an area the size of Belgium. In the southwestern corner of the Isla Grande, extending far to the west of the town of Ushuaia, a labyrinthine peninsula of fjords, channels, glaciers, and twisted fingers of land holds the 140-kilometer-long Cordillera Darwin, the southernmost fortress of the Andes.

Many aspects of the Cordillera Darwin make it unusual among the world's mountains. The most obvious, when comparing it to the rest of the Andes, is that its main axis runs east to west. Most of the South American continent belongs to a single tectonic plate, but the southern part of Tierra del Fuego is riding a completely different one: the Scotia Plate. (This plate moves eastward an average of 6.4mm per year relative to the South American Plate.) The Cordillera Darwin experiences, to a lesser extent, the same climatic gradient that characterizes Patagonia: rainy, green, and heavily glaciated in the west (where Monte Sarmiento is the dominant peak) and progressively drier and colder toward the eastern end (dominated by the mountains Frances, Bove, and Roncagli).

Uninhabited and pristine, this range looks much as it did to the first European visitors, who arrived exactly 500 years ago, or even to the people who lived here for thousands of years before. The Cordillera Darwin's rugged terrain, ferocious climate, and inherent uncertainty make it a dream world for all lovers of true adventure. Many of its valleys have not yet been explored, and many summits remain virgin, including several of the highest.

I will not say who "discovered" the Cordillera Darwin, because discovery has long been misunderstood as an event when it is, in fact, a process. In the case of Tierra del Fuego, the process began with plants and animals, which until recently included giant sloths, saber-toothed cats, and one-ton short-faced bears. As recently as 14,000 years ago, human intruders arrived, bringing extinction to these animals and others. They also brought a new age of discovery, filling the land with myths and names that were constantly mutating, rising, and dying, in languages

A view of HMS Beagle sailing past Monte Sarmiento, painted in 1838. Captain Robert Fitz Roy named the range after the ship's naturalist, a young Charles Darwin. *Henry Colburn*

that could not be written—all that is left of them is a subtle echo of their sounds. These early names of Tierra del Fuego—words like Karukinka, Ayukenk, Tkoyuská, Huisiaccui, Kojoreren, or Onasín—were written down by the second wave of intruders, the Europeans who came with vessels, guns, and germs, bringing the earlier human intruders to the brink of extinction, but also carrying pen and paper, thus leaving more than echoes between the mountains. In the following lines, we will recapitulate this modern era of discovery, and we will dream about the next.

THE FIRST MAPMAKERS

Ferdinand Magellan's expedition in 1520 was the first to leave written accounts of Tierra del Fuego. However, passing through the stormy straits to the north of the islands, Magellan's crew did not see the mountains that concern us. They just saw a coast dotted with indigenous camps and a multitude of smoke columns rising from them, eventually leading to the name Tierra del Fuego. It wasn't until 1580 that the mountains were noted on paper by Pedro Sarmiento de Gamboa, who crossed the Strait of Magellan from west to east and observed in the distance an imposing "snowy volcano;" this supposedly smoking summit would adorn the maps of Tierra del Fuego for centuries to come.

The mountain range that would come to be called the Cordillera Darwin formed a natural border between different indigenous groups: the seafaring Kaweskar in the north and west and Yámana (Yaghan) in the south, and the land-based Selk'nam in the east. Remains of indigenous shelters demonstrate these groups likely traveled over passes through the cordillera as trade routes.

As the wrecks of European ships piled up on these remote coasts, and the inter-oceanic passages of Tierra del Fuego gained strategic value, the British Admiralty sent a series of hydrographic expeditions to chart the coastline of South America's southern tip. The expedition vessels were under the command of Phillip Parker King, Pringle Stokes, and Robert Fitz Roy, who, between 1826 and 1836, mapped in detail the complex network of fjords and islands making up Tierra del Fuego. The highest portions were baptized the Darwin Mountains in commemoration of the 25th birthday of the young naturalist Charles Darwin, who was part of Captain Fitz Roy's expedition, and whose name started appearing on maps for the full cordillera about half a century later.

THE CALL OF THE MOUNTAINS

THE RANGE'S POLE of attraction during the 19th and early 20th centuries was Monte Sarmiento (2,207 meters), the "snowy volcano" spotted by Pedro Sarmiento de Gamboa and renamed by Fitz Roy after the Spanish sailor. This mountain is undoubtedly the most prominent feature of Tierra del Fuego, and its notoriety was enhanced by the growing maritime traffic passing through the Magellan Strait between the Atlantic and Pacific oceans during the age of steamships, an era that would last until the opening of the Panama Canal in 1914. Monte Sarmiento became at the time the allegory of the unreachable mountain and was portrayed in numerous works, including the novel *Twenty Thousand Leagues Under the Sea* by Jules Verne.

The first attempt to reach Sarmiento's summit was by Italian geologist Domenico Lovisato (an early champion of the theory of continental drift) in 1882. While he did not get very far, he nevertheless wrote the opening chapter for the era of mountaineering in Tierra del Fuego. Sixteen years later, British mountaineer Sir Martin Conway set his sights on Sarmiento. Conway was heading south after the first ascent of Illimani in Bolivia and getting within 50 meters of the second ascent of Aconcagua. In the Cordillera Darwin he made an honest attempt to climb Sarmiento. Still, once again, he didn't even reach the start of the main climbing problems.

Early in the 20th century, the most decisive figure in the exploration of Tierra del Fuego and the dissemination of its beauties around the world was the missionary, ethnographer, and author Alberto Maria de Agostini. After two exploratory trips to Tierra del Fuego in 1910, De Agostini completed four notable expeditions between 1913 and 1915, during which he made two bold but fruitless attempts on Monte Sarmiento. He also placed the Contraalmirante Martinez and Pigafetta fjords on maps for the first time. (Chilean authorities eventually renamed the latter as De Agostini Fjord.) His name is also given to the Chilean national park that today encompasses much of the Cordillera Darwin.

[Top] Hans Teufel, half of a two-man German expedition that made several first ascents in 1937. In back is Monte Roncagli. *Stefan Zuck* [Bottom] Eduardo Garcia, Francisco Vivanco, and Eric Shipton (clockwise from top) during their 1962 expedition. *Cedomir Marangunic*

Less known but no less daring were the adventures of the celebrated U.S. painter Rockwell Kent, who aspired to connect with the wildest and most remote expressions of nature. After a brief examination of the world map, he decided to go to Tierra del Fuego. He arrived in Punta Arenas, Chile, in 1922, and for $20 he bought the lifeboat of a shipwrecked steamer. Exchanging paintings for favors, he managed to obtain a pilothouse and a mast for his precarious vessel, and off he went to cross the Magellan Strait. He almost wrecked several times, and at one point during this trip, at the downwind end of Admiralty Sound, incessant winds pinned Kent in place for weeks. Eventually, he took the bold decision to continue by land, traveling south from Bahía Blanca with a few companions for some 40 kilometers through an unknown mountain range. Surprisingly, they managed to succeed, carrying cameras, canvases, brushes, and paintings on tumplines on the difficult journey to Yendegaia Bay. Many of these paintings are now at the Plattsburg Art Museum in New York state.

In 1937 there was a remarkable expedition to the Cordillera Darwin of which little has been written. German mountaineers Hans Teufel and Stefan Zuck became the first to reach some of the main summits, including the first ascent of Monte General Ponce (1,417 meters, later claimed as a first ascent by John Earle, who called it Cerro Caledonia) and the remarkable first ascent of Cerro Italia (2,062 meters) at the southeastern end of the range. To date, many still believe the first ascent of Cerro Italia was made in 1956 by an expedition led by De Agostini, as he indeed claimed such distinction. Such a boast would add to the many known mischiefs by De Agostini, all attributable to his need to get sponsors for his exploration. It seems that some mountaineering intricacies are older than one might think.

Despite this exaggeration, the 1956 expedition led by De Agostini was one of the most memorable ever done in the area. De Agostini was 73 years old at the time and still obsessed with Monte Sarmiento. Organizing a large expedition to besiege the Esfinge de Hielo (the "ice sphinx," as he called it), De Agostini recruited the best Italian climbers of the time. After 57 fruitless days at the foot of the mountain, they had almost lost hope, but at the last minute, Clemente Maffei and Carlo Mauri launched a bold ascent via the south ridge in alpine style. Despite bad weather, they managed to overcome the difficulties and leave their mark in history, achieving the first ascent of the "king of Tierra del Fuego."

MODERN MOUNTAINEERING

THE 1960S BROUGHT two extraordinary expeditions led by the legendary British mountaineer and explorer Eric Shipton. In 1962, Shipton, along with Chileans Eduardo Garcia, Cedomir Marangunic, and Francisco Vivanco, made the first crossing of Cordillera Darwin, from Parry Fjord to Torcido Fjord. (Rockwell Kent followed valley routes across the east end of the range; Shipton's team was the first to cross over the mountains.) During this traverse, they ascended the highest summit of the Cordillera Darwin (2,568 m), which they designated Monte Darwin, intending to honor the intention of Captain Fitz Roy. However, in Fitz Roy's time the highest peak was believed to be located farther east, over the eastern arm of Pia Fjord. This led to long-lasting confusion over the identity of the "real" Monte Darwin.

In 1970, a remarkable seven-person New Zealand expedition attempted to settle this issue. They climbed six peaks in the range, including a 2,261-meter summit in roughly the position where the British Admiralty's maps had placed Monte Darwin. They proposed this particular peak should be given the controversial name, and that the 2,568-meter summit climbed by Shipton's team should be named Monte Shipton. Later, John Shipton, son of the British explorer, formally applied to Chilean authorities to accept this name, and it has been adopted on the latest maps.

However, the confusion didn't end there. The New Zealanders also identified a summit higher than "their" Monte Darwin, which they named Cerro York Minster (2,270 meters). And this mountain corresponds to what De Agostini called Monte Darwin and also to the mountain

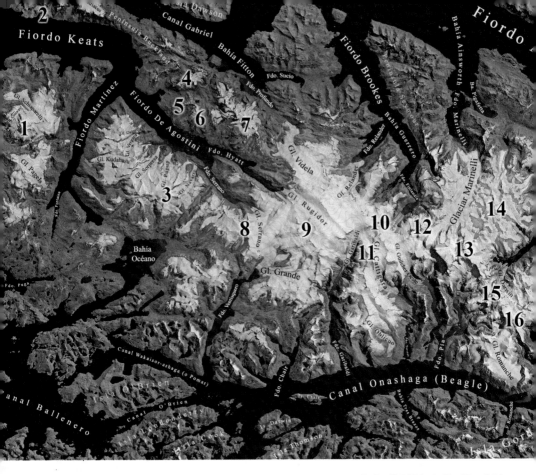

(1) Monte Sarmiento, (2) Monte Taurus (unclimbed), (3) Co. Navarro (unclimbed), (4) Monte Buckland, (5) Co. Garcia (first ascent in 2019, see p.231), (6) Co. Erguido (unclimbed), (7) Monte Giordano, (8) Co. Serrano (unclimbed), (9) Co. Mayo (unclimbed), (10) Co. Ona, (11) Co. Kaiyush, (12) Co. El Paso (unclimbed), (13) Monte Shipton (high point of range), (14) Monte Yagán, (15) Co. Jemmy Button (unclimbed), (16) Monte Darwin, (17) Monte Stoppani, (18) Monte Italia, (19) Monte Roncagli (main summit probably unclimbed, and (20) Monte Boveaccatum. A more-detailed, full-size map can be viewed or ordered at unchart.org. *UNCHARTED*

Fitz Roy most likely would have identified from his ship as the tallest peak. (The official Monte Darwin is farther back and is difficult to see from the Beagle Channel or Pia Fjord.) Thus, Cerro York Minster could be said to correspond to the "historic Monte Darwin." The first ascent of this mountain was in 1987. At the time the climbers thought they were doing the second ascent of Monte Darwin—which was right or wrong, depending on how we look at it!

Returning to Eric Shipton, he came back to Tierra del Fuego two years after his remarkable 1962 expedition, this time to climb Bove (2,279 meters) and Francés (2,261 meters) with Peter Bruchhausen, Claudio Cortéz, and John Earle. These two peaks are some of the most striking of the Cordillera Darwin, visible from the city of Ushuaia to the east.

The year 1966 was one of intense activity. A strong Italian team led by Carlo Mauri reached the summit of Monte Buckland (1,746 meters), an impressive mountain that resembles a gigantic ice tusk to the east of Monte Sarmiento. Two members of this Ragni di Lecco team eventually reached the summit via the southwest face: Cesare Giudici and a young Casimiro Ferrari. Almost simultaneously, a North American expedition led by Jack Miller conducted extensive exploration of the sector of Cordillera Darwin between Monte Sarmiento and Monte Shipton, including an

ascent of one of the highest massifs in the area, Cerro Ona (2,279 meters).

Monte Sarmiento still cast its spell, and between 1969 and 1972, the Italian Giuseppe Agnolotti led three failed attempts to reach its west summit. (At 2,145 meters, the western summit is about 60 meters lower than the main peak.) The west peak finally was climbed by the Ragni di Lecco in 1986, with the participation of Clemente Maffei, the 62-year-old veteran of the first ascent of the main summit three decades earlier.

In 1990, another of the great explorers of southern South America, the English physician David Hillebrandt, along with his team, reached the north summit of the difficult Monte Roncagli (2,226 meters). In limited visibility, they could not be certain if this was the highest of Roncagli's three tops; today it seems likely the central summit is higher, but I would never question Hillebrandt's claim to the first ascent.

Perhaps the last Tierra del Fuego adventure motivated solely by exploration was a very low-profile expedition by North Americans Douglas Krause and David Scheer during the summer of 1990 and 1991. Approaching from the south, via Torcido Fjord, they achieved formidable climbs to several of the highest peaks in the range that were still unclimbed. Three elderly Yámana women living near Puerto Williams, east of Ushuaia, were given honor of choosing these peaks' names: Eepuj (2,273 meters), Kaiyush (2,162 meters), Shakatuj (2,028 meters), and Seepain (2,004 meters).

As usual, much of the action of the last few decades has concentrated on Monte Sarmiento, of which the western summit has proved to be the most accessible. In 1996, Stephen Venables (U.K.), John Roskelley (USA), and Tim McCartney-Snape (Australia) made the second ascent by a new route on the south face. Initially, they aspired to climb both peaks, but the plan was hindered by two accidents and the usual bad weather. More recently, in the winter of 2013, Natalia Martínez (Argentina) and Camilo Rada (Chile) made the long-awaited second ascent of the main summit, by a new route on the north face—no less than 57 years after the ascent of Mauri and Maffei. Several of the many attempts on Sarmiento in the last decades have set off with the extremely challenging aim of traversing the mountain, climbing both summits along the way. When this is eventually done, it will raise the bar of Tierra del Fuego mountaineering to a new level.

Aside from Monte Sarmiento, the challenge that has motivated many attempts and successive failures in the range is the longitudinal crossing of the Cordillera Darwin. This feat was finally achieved in 2011, in just 30 days, by a French team of the GMHM (Groupe Militaire de Haute Montagne), with an extraordinary display of strength, perseverance, and technical ability. They completed their 250-kilometer route without intermediate caches, a truly remarkable achievement.

The first two decades of the 21st century have seen increasing activity, seeking to repeat some of the main summits but mostly looking to make the first ascents of the many summits that were

Unclimbed Monte Taurus, rising 1,097 meters over Canal Magdalena and Fiordo Keats. *Camilo Rada*

still unclimbed. The online version of this article (*publications.americanalpineclub.org*) has a list of the most significant recent climbs, plus links to related reports.

HIDDEN GEMS

LET US DREAM over the map and point to a few blank pages, yet to be filled, in the chronicle of mountain exploration in the Cordillera Darwin.

Starting at the west end of the range, the already mentioned west-to-east traverse of Monte Sarmiento and its two summits is a compelling objective for the most ambitious. A repetition of Sarmiento's original route, the south ridge, would also be a wonderful objective. In the Buckland peninsula, the impressive spires of Cerro Taurus (1,097 meters) rise right from the sea and have seen no climbing attempts.

Continuing to the east, the Cordón Navarro offers numerous objectives, and over a dozen ascents have been carried out in the area. Yet, surprisingly, no one has managed to reach its highest point, Cerro Navarro (1,864 meters), despite attempts by Jack Miller and his team in 1966 and a Chilean expedition in 2001. At the southeastern end of this group, Cerro Serrano (1,493 meters) remains untouched as well.

Besieged by massive glaciers on all flanks, five virgin summits of 1,800 meters-plus dominate the main glacier plateau of Cordillera Darwin. They are not tricky climbs, but they are deep into the icefield. One of them is Cerro Mayo (ca 1,900 meters), which is portrayed on some of the oldest maps of the range, yet it is still unclear to which of these summits this name corresponds.

Just north of the Beagle Channel, at the head of Oblicuo Glacier, a beautiful 1,722-meter peak attempted by James (Skip) Novak and Doug Scott in 1994 remains unclimbed, and the dreamy ski line on its south face hasn't been scratched.

The southwest faces of Cerro Kaiyush, Monte Cresta Blanca, and Monte Darwin are magnificent outcrops of Beagle Granite, but they might need to wait for a new era of cold-tolerant rock climbers. However, nearby Ovejero, El Paso, and Louhi, near the head of Finlandia Fjord, offer some of the highest and most aesthetic unclimbed summits of the range. Farther east, Monte Yagán (2,158 meters) and the rocky monolith of Cerro Selk'nam are waiting for repeats and offer numerous new lines.

At the head of Parry Fjord, the clean and direct line offered by the north ridge of Cerro Jemmy Button resisted an attempt by a strong Polish team in 2005 (they called it Monte Vavel) and is still waiting for new contestants.

Approaching the eastern end of the range, the granitic north face of Cerro Italia (2,062 meters) seems perfect for crack-seekers. Mounts Frances and Bove have appealing untrodden faces. And, as mentioned before, the main summit of the beautiful Monte Roncagli is most likely yet to be touched. To finish, we have to mention Peak 2,244m, most likely the highest unclimbed peak of the Cordillera Darwin. This mountain is just one of the many still to be climbed around the head of Stoppani Glacier.

Many of problems facing early explorers have persisted in this region, including a lack of detailed maps, ambiguous or absent geographical names, poorly documented ascents, and difficult access. But the eastern side of the range is becoming somewhat more accessible. It's already possible to drive to Lago Fagnano and Almirantazgo (Admiralty) Sound, where tours, transport, and accommodation are slowly becoming more available.

Sometime during the next decade, a road will reach Yendegaia Bay on the Beagle Channel. This easy access will open new opportunities for adventurers, in particular around the prominent and beautiful peaks of the eastern end of the range, such as Frances, Roncagli, and Bove. Already, tourist outfits offer "adventure trips" departing from Ushuaia or Puerto Williams, combining mountaineering with the navigation of the mythical Beagle Channel. In recent years, there also has been an increase in European and North American expeditions setting off in winter for ski descents on the snowy slopes above the channel.

Access to the central and west-

[Top] **Cerro Jemmy Button (2,092m, right center) was attempted in 2004 but remains unclimbed.** *GMHM.* [Middle] **Monte Giordano's left skyline (west ridge) was climbed in 2012. The spectacular prow is untouched.** *Bernard Taberlet* [Bottom] **The impressive granitic north face of Monte Italia (2,060m).** *Cristian Donoso*

ern parts of the Cordillera Darwin still requires lengthy navigation, usually two or three days on a sailboat or one day in a fast boat. Mountains near the coast can be reached in a day from the sea, often using a sailboat as a base camp. Others will require longer approaches through swampy terrain, peat bog, dense vegetation, crevassed glaciers, and unstable moraine. Together, these goodies can often turn out to be more challenging than the climbs themselves.

View to the northeast up the Grande Glacier. In the far upper left, at the head of the west (left) arm of the glacier, is a cirque of four peaks up to 1,900 meters, including unclimbed Cerro Mayo. Beyond is the isolated heart of the range, including cerros Ona and Kaiyush. *Guy Wenborne*

LESSONS FROM THE PAST

THE MANY EXPEDITIONS to the Cordillera Darwin have shown that to succeed it is essential to have a motivated and committed team. This is a place where perseverance and flexibility are more important than strength. Perhaps the essential attributes are patience, resilience, and a drive that cannot be dissolved by the rain or blown away by the wind.

The wind, in fact, is a defining characteristic of Tierra del Fuego—this is the corner of the Andes most exposed to the elements. Along the corridor between Patagonia and the Antarctic Peninsula, surface winds go round the world, free and impetuous as in no other corner of the planet, picking up speed and moisture in their endless march over the southern oceans. The Cordillera Darwin, at latitude 54° south, is the only mountain range that pokes into this windy realm, long known by sailors as the Furious Fifties. Here, clouds cling to the peaks with unmatched insistence and the westerlies dump gargantuan loads of rain and snow. This perpetual cycle sculpts rime mushrooms up to baroque exuberance.

Yet, if extreme pressure is what turns coal into diamonds, pressure cannot be a bad thing. In the same vein, I would like to emphasize the point that the severe weather of Tierra del Fuego is not *bad* weather. In fact, it is this unforgiving climate that has turned these rather small mountains into magnificent sculptures of rock and ice. It is also this climate that has kept the region magical and mysterious. Here, the mountain and the weather are so intertwined that they need to be considered as parts of one entity—the weather is a mountaineering challenge, no less than the ice and the rock. It would be pointless to sit and wait for the glaciers to melt in order to climb a mountain. Equally pointless is to sit in Tierra del Fuego to wait for "bad" weather to pass. With patience, one might finally get a sunny summer day to attempt a climb. Yet, on such a day, the whole mountain will be falling apart, rivers will rage, and avalanches will abound. Is that "good weather" then?

Given the conditions, there are a couple of skills and attributes that make a significant difference in this region. One is GPS navigation, required to move in low-visibility conditions. Another is a nose for extracting the little truth from available weather forecasts (while being prepared for the opposite). And finally, tolerance for failure is required, because even with all of the above, a fair share of luck is also needed.

The ever-present question is: When is the best time to climb in the Cordillera Darwin? And my answer is that all months are good (or bad, if you like to see glasses as half empty). While, statistically, some months could have better climbing weather than others, the inter-annual variability is large enough as to render those trends useless for plan-

The vessel Ocean Tramp in a sheltered anchorage near the far western tip of the cordillera. *Bernard Taberlet*

ning an expedition. For example, on average, December is less windy than November. However, the chances for that trend to hold on any particular year are less than 50 percent.

Nevertheless, the southern winter consistently offers a slightly more stable climate. Colder conditions also are an advantage because rain is confined to lower elevations. The main disadvantage is the short amount of daylight, which makes low temperatures and stormy weather a little harder to tolerate. While the winds are on average milder in winter, the fierce storms that have made Patagonia famous can happen at any time of the year and can last for weeks. (Occasionally, it must be admitted, there are perfect days, and experience has shown that one of these will repay months of sacrifice.) Altogether, winter's advantages outweigh the disadvantages if a climb on ice or alpine terrain is planned. Conversely, summer seems to be the best for rock climbs, and perhaps also for south-facing ice climbs.

Expeditions headed into much of the Cordillera Darwin will need a permit from Chile's Parque Nacional Alberto de Agostini, and foreign visitors may also need a permit from the Chilean Dirección de Fronteras y Límites (DIFROL). Beyond the legal requirements, climbers should produce as little impact as they can during their visit and leave nothing behind. In particular, the practice of building base camp huts is frowned upon.

The very nature of climbing in the Cordillera Darwin is isolation, uncertainty, extreme weather, and complex terrain, all spiced with the potential—very rare today—to be the first humans to set foot in a beautiful and pristine corner of the world. The area demands respect and care from those lucky enough to visit. Adventurous spirits will be rewarded with the opportunity to transform dreams into life experiences.

ABOUT THE AUTHOR: *Camilo Rada lives in Punta Arenas, Chile, his base camp for glaciological research and mountaineering. Since 2000 he has visited the Cordillera Darwin five times, along with dozens of expeditions to Patagonia and Antarctica, making 25 first ascents. Much of the information presented here is drawn from research conducted for the UNCHARTED project, a nonprofit initiative developed by Rada and Natalia Martínez, dedicated to documenting the geography and history of Patagonia and other remote, mountainous regions. Learn more at unchart.org.*

CLIMBS & EXPEDITIONS

WITH THE EXCEPTION of the lead stories in some sections, Climbs & Expeditions reports generally are arranged geographically, from north to south, and from west to east, within a country or region. Unless noted, all reports are from 2019. The complete AAJ database, from 1929 to present, can be searched at *publications.americanalpineclub.org*. Online reports frequently contain additional text, photos, maps, and topos—look for these symbols indicating additional online resources:

FULL-LENGTH REPORT ADDITIONAL PHOTOS MAPS OR TOPOS VIDEO OR MULTIMEDIA

Early morning preparation before
the first ascent of Cerro De Geer on
the Northern Patagonian Icefield,
Chile. See p.211. *Riley Rice*

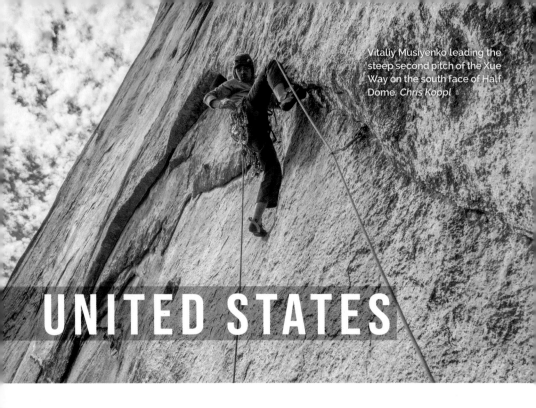

UNITED STATES

THE XUE WAY
A BRILLIANT NEW ROUTE UP HALF DOME'S HUGE SOUTH FACE

BY VITALIY MUSIYENKO

As WE QUIETLY enjoyed the waning warmth of the late fall sun on the summit of Half Dome, a breathtaking view of the Valley stretched before us. After 10 years of climbing all sorts of routes, from Alaska to the Canadian Rockies, the Sierra to the Cordillera Blanca, standing there with my good friends Chris Koppl and Brian Prince after completing a new route on the south face of Half Dome was a dream come true. All of our collective skills and gained wisdom had culminated in this route.

Yet I wasn't completely happy. I hadn't recovered since the climbing community lost the brilliant young alpinist Michelle Xue a few weeks prior. I had first met Michelle one day in Lee Vining, and we all later spent a season with her in El Chaltén, in Patagonia, sharing many meals and spectacular sunsets and rainbows in those amazing mountains.

As we descended barefoot down the exposed slabs toward our first rappel anchor, negative thoughts flooded my mind. On the same day that Michelle and her climbing partner, Jennifer Shedden, were hit by major rockfall and lost their lives in the Sierra Nevada, my grandmother also passed away. She was the person who took on the responsibility of raising me while my single mother had to work full-time. Because I see death almost daily while working in the emergency department of a trauma center, I had thought I'd become callous to the loss of life. However, this double tragedy knocked me off balance, and instead of a pleasant victory lap, our three-day push on the new route was for me a time to mourn and accept.

Two and a half years prior, we had started this climb ground up on the broad face to the right of Southern Belle. The route ascends some of the best stone any of us have touched. The dikes on the lower pitches range from ones large enough to traverse by walking to others requiring granite voodoo to climb. We found steep cracks, powerful underclings, and other wild terrain as the wall steepened to an 800' headwall.

After all kinds of battles and shenanigans on the sharp end, and a few efforts where the leader was stranded in terrain too blank to climb, we had completed about 60 percent of the route, with only two very short sections where we pulled on gear. Eventually we decided to change tactics and rappel in from the top in order to establish the best route through the steep upper headwall. We wanted to piece together a route of lasting quality, to maximize free climbing, and to make it reasonable in terms of risk for future ascensionists—and that didn't seem possible while bolting on lead without leaving trails of bathooks and rivet ladders. So we swallowed our egos and accepted the fact that some people might not pass up a chance to contribute negative remarks about our choices.

The full route's orange granite is formed into crispy incut crimps, slopers, sidepulls, intersecting bands of dikes, and a few random chickenheads positioned in just the right places to allow gymnastic free climbing—reminiscent of some of the best Shuteye Ridge pitches, but with 2,000' of exposure. The climbing is very sustained in the 5.10–5.11 range, with a few cruxes of low 5.12 and a few moves of A0. Surprisingly, the latest addition to Half Dome's south face is likely to be the most attainable. It is not as technically difficult as Growing Up or Southern Belle, and of course much better protected than the latter.

The views on top of Half Dome took me back nine years to the time when I had sat here after completing my first multi-pitch route, the super-classic Snake Dike. The night before, I had slept very little, anxious about attempting something seemingly over my head.

Now, at the culmination of our two-and-a-half-year journey on the south face, I felt some of the same sense of satisfaction that comes after completing an ambitious goal, along with climbing partners who have evolved into dear friends. Despite our feelings of sadness and loss, it felt like Michelle had been with us through the whole push, helping us heal by reminding us to keep a positive spirit and appreciate the little things—the warm rays of sun, snacking on pineapples, committing to a difficult but reasonably protected move. She reminded us to chase after big dreams while walking in the steps of kindness, joy, and generosity—to live life as she would. That is the Xue Way.

SUMMARY: *First ascent of the Xue Way (2,000', 20 pitches, VI 5.11d/12a A0) on the south face of Half Dome, completed by Chris Koppl, Vitaliy Musiyenko, and Brian Prince in fall of 2019.* 📷

[Left] The massive south face of Half Dome in Yosemite National Park, showing the line of the Xue Way (2,000', 20 pitches, VI 5.11d/12a A0). Southern Belle, Growing Up, and other routes are to the left; Karma is to the right. [Right] Michelle Xue, Chris Koppl, Brian Prince, and Jason Lakey relaxing in El Chaltén, Patagonia. *Vitaliy Musiyenko (both photos)*

PASSAGE TO FREEDOM
'SOME OF THE BEST CLIMBING ON EL CAP'

BY ALEX HONNOLD

IN OCTOBER, Tommy Caldwell and I, along with help from Austin Siadak and Kevin Jorgeson, completed a new free route on El Capitan in Yosemite Valley. We followed the old Leo Houlding route Passage to Freedom up to El Cap Tower and then pioneered an interesting traverse back right to finish on New Dawn. It was a line Tommy had considered while working on the Dawn Wall and had briefly inspected on rappel.

We knew the climbing would be fairly hard and would require some bolts on otherwise unprotectable faces, so it made sense to come in from above. We were lucky to be climbing on a relatively unpopular aid line, so we didn't have to worry about ruining anyone's climbing experience by swinging around on static lines.

The upper corners of the route were the defining features that drew Tommy to the line. Laser-cut thin-finger cracks run for hundreds of feet right through the Harding Roof, an imposingly large overhang a few hundred feet below the summit. As we began to work on them, we realized that in some ways they were the perfect difficulty—hard enough to be engaging, but not so hard that they would become a multi-year project like the neighboring Dawn Wall. As it turned out, the actual crux came on one of the final slabs above the corners, one pitch below the summit, a section of thin climbing that Tommy called "maybe one of the most unpleasant slabs I've ever climbed."

Now we just had to find a way to free climb up to the corners. Twenty years ago, Leo Houlding had pioneered Passage to Freedom, an 11-pitch 5.13d that climbed up to El Cap Tower (*see AAJ 2000*). Leo's line had one quirk—he had bolted an Alfa Romeo hood ornament onto the wall as a handhold to bypass a blank section on a 5.13d slab. But when Tommy started working on the slab, he realized it was easier for him to just climb straight up the original aid line and bypass the Alfa Romeo badge altogether. This required some extremely thin, offset laybacking/slab climbing, which also wound up in the 5.13c/d range.

That got us up to El Cap Tower, but the biggest question mark on the route remained: how to connect over to the Dawn Wall area, about 100m to the east. Tommy had done a little exploratory rappelling over the years and promised there was a big white dike that would make for easy traversing. He even joked that it would be the opposite of the crux Dawn Wall traverse: rightward on 5.10 jugs instead of leftward on 5.14c/d micro edges. We added some

bolts to the face along the most probable-look-
ing line, but we weren't able to really climb on
the pitches because their traversing nature made
it too complicated for normal Micro Traxioning.

We all put about two and half weeks of
preparation into the route between different
personal obligations drawing us out of the
Valley. Tommy found the climbing the easiest
among us (apparently, working on the Dawn
Wall for seven years really helped his granite technique), but none of us had actually
redpointed any of the hardest pitches or knew
for sure that we could do the climb. With tight
schedules for all of us, Kevin opted out of a

Tommy Caldwell makes the wild finishing moves at
El Cap's summit. *Austin Siadak*

push from the ground and Tommy and I settled on a three-day window before Halloween. Our
only firm rule was that Tommy had to be down in time to trick-or-treat with his kids.

We set out on October 28 with bivy gear pre-stashed at El Cap Tower and Austin jugging our
fixed lines, taking photos, and assisting with the general toil of big-wall life. The first crux, the
5.13+ that avoided the Alfa Romeo, took us each several tries. Two pitches higher, we were both
briefly stopped by an 8' horizontal dyno on another 5.13 pitch, but again we managed with a few
tries. We made it to El Cap Tower late that night and shared the ledge with a team of Nose climbers.

The next morning began with a big loop onto the Nose–down to the Jardine Traverse, back
up to the Lynn Hill Traverse in the Gray Bands, and then breaking right onto what I dubbed the
Tommy Traverse, the big adventure rightward, back to the Dawn Wall. When Tommy tried the
first pitch of dike traversing, which he'd originally hoped would be 5.10, he discovered it was
about mid-5.13. We both worked it out, but it was a little unnerving. I then led a 70m traverse over
to the Dawn Wall, which was the other big question mark on the route. One of the bolts wound up
being in the wrong place and I clipped into a static line in desperation to protect a few moves, but
ultimately managed to free the pitch first try. When we returned to the route later to clean our ropes
and gear, we added some bolts and an anchor to make this pitch reasonable for a ground-up ascent.

That got us to the 5.13d pitch leading to Wino Tower on the Dawn Wall, which marks the end
of that route's hard climbing. Tommy sent it that night, but I preferred to do my hard climbing in
the morning, because even though the rock was hotter and conditions weren't quite as good, at
least I could feel my fingers and see the holds.

From here we headed back left into the striking upper corners on New Dawn, spending
another two days finishing the last nine pitches. We both took many falls and at times had to aid
climb to work out gear placements. (We each top-roped the other person's leads.) It all culminated
on the final 50m 5.13d slab pitch, only 40m below the summit of El Cap. We were a day later than
planned, it was getting late, and Tommy was supposed to be down to trick-or-treat with his kids
by sunset. I fell in the middle of the pitch and wound up redpointing from a no-hands stance in
the middle of the pitch rather than re-climb the whole thing. Tommy did the same when he top-
roped the pitch. We finally summited just in time to run down and see the family.

Hopefully, someone will do the route in a day with no falls at some point. As Tommy said, it's
some of the best climbing on El Cap.

SUMMARY: *Free ascent of Passage to Freedom (27 pitches, 5.13d) on El Capitan, October 28–31, 2019.*

Hayden Kennedy ventures up the northeast face of Mt. Hooker in 2015. *John Dickey*

GAMBLING IN THE WINDS
A CLIMB FOR HAYDEN KENNEDY ON MT. HOOKER'S NORTHEAST WALL

BY WHIT MAGRO

IT'S JUST A rock climb, right? That's how it started, anyway.

In 2015, Hayden Kennedy and I planned a 10-day trip to Mt. Hooker with the goal of establishing an independent route up the large and imposing northeast face. We reeled in Jesse Huey and Mike Pennings, and in August the four of us set out for adventure. This was my third trip to Mt. Hooker, and I was super excited to share all my knowledge with three amazing friends.

That year, Hayden and I spent a total of six days climbing ground up, establishing seven entirely new pitches, and making it just over halfway up the 2,000' wall (*see AAJ 2016*). With little time left, we were not able to take our line direct to the summit and we opted for a heavy traverse right to link up with Hook, Line, and Sinker (V 5.12, *see AAJ 2015*), a route Josh Wharton and I had established the previous year. Hayden and I called our route Gambling in the Winds, but it was obvious the full line had yet to be completed—we vowed to return and add the direct finish.

Exhausted by three seasons in a row of ground-up efforts on the mountain, I opted to take a season off and did not return in 2016. That summer, Hayden fell in love with a Bozeman girl named Inge Perkins and the year flew by. Things progressed, and in 2017 I got word from HK that he was moving to Bozeman to be with Inge. I was beyond excited—one of my best climbing partners would be living just a few doors down from me.

In October 2017, Hayden and Inge headed into the backcountry with the objective of skiing off the top of Imp Peak, a majestic mountain in the Madison Range. That day tragedy struck, and Inge was buried in an avalanche. Hayden managed to dig himself out, but Inge's avalanche beacon was switched off, and he was unable to find her after hours of relentless digging.

I believe Hayden's soul left him that day at the scene of the accident, and his shell returned to Bozeman, where he ended up committing suicide that night. It was a day I will never forget, and I can't express the sorrow I felt.

Gambling in the Winds, the project that Hayden and I had started together, now took on a whole new meaning. It became a focal point of sorrow and grief. Jesse, who was also close with Hayden, and I decided that it was our collective duty to see the line finished in honor of our dear friend.

In late summer of 2018, a large group came out to Mt. Hooker: Jesse and Maury Birdwell, myself and Jason Thompson, Hayden's parents Michael and Julie Kennedy, and Hayden's friends Steve Dilk and his wife, Julia Monroe. The goal that summer was to spend time in a place Hayden loved, and to channel our grief into finishing the route. But the entire trip was plagued by terrible weather. Jason and I spent a week fixing lines up the original seven pitches, but by the end of the trip we hadn't progressed any farther. Soul-crushing defeat joined the party of heavy emotions. Jesse and Maury were a few days behind us, and with the use of our fixed ropes they were able to push the route another pitch and a half higher, but soon time was up for the season.

With a strong push from my wife, Kimberly, we decided that 2019 was going to be a family trip into the Hooker cirque. At 8 and 10 years old, my kids Eli and Mya had finally reached the age where they could handle the long approach. I let go of my ego and my personal desire to complete the route and relinquished the direct finish to Jesse and Maury. It was such a refreshing feeling to plan this trip, as I had no huge goals other than to enjoy the place with my family and establish camp for the arrival of Jesse and Maury.

With the help of horse packers, we spent 10 days back there away from the world. I showed them all the secret spots, we caught fish, battled swarms of mosquitoes, ate great food, and reveled in the alpine environment. The weather was amazing—bluebird skies and warm temps, and a completely different feel from the year before. We may have even spotted Hayden and Inge soaring around as massive golden eagles.

On our last day in camp, Jesse and Maury showed up as planned. I handed them the torch and some extra supplies, and the next morning the Magro family departed for the trailhead. Over the next week, Jesse sent me messages from camp, updating me on their progress, and the excitement continued to build. Before long Maury and Jesse had topped out Gambling in the Winds via the direct finish; they established five new difficult pitches to reach Der Major ledge and free climbed the route over two days, with a portaledge bivy halfway up (*see route line on p.122*).

Though I knew Jesse and Maury would take it to the top, I already had planned for a quick return trip before the summer shut down, just in case. Now this would be a smash-and-grab mission to complete a one-day free ascent. No horses, no toiling, and no fixed lines. I invited my good friend Harrison Teuber from the Black Hills, and after hiking in, we climbed the route to the top on day two. We swung leads, with the leader and follower both freeing every pitch, pulling the rope a few times to redpoint. The entire route took us about 10 hours. It was a moment of true bliss and provided me with a sense of closure.

Gambling in the Winds is a magnificent climb and is very sustained in the mid to upper 5.12 range, with a challenging mix of face and crack climbing on insanely good stone. It may just be a rock climb, but the route represents the team effort, friendship, and tragedy that we all shared in its establishment, and will serve as an enduring tribute to our friend Hayden for anyone who ventures out to this wild and beautiful place.

SUMMARY: *First ascent of Gambling in the Winds (2,000', 15 pitches, 5.12) on the northeast face of Mt. Hooker in the Wind River Range, by Maury Birdwell, Jesse Huey, Hayden Kennedy, and Whit Magro, 2015 to 2019.* 📷

Hayden Kennedy (left) and Whit Magro living it up on Mt. Hooker. *Whit Magro*

LIBERTY'S DARK SIDE
A MODERN TESTPIECE IN WASHINGTON PASS

BY SHANJEAN LEE

"IT'S AMAZING GRANITE and it's 20 minutes from the road, " Mikey Schaefer says emphatically, leaving no room for debate over the worthiness of climbing on the east face of Liberty Bell. Over the last decade, Mikey has freed or established multiple routes on Liberty Bell: Thin Red Line (2008), Liberty and Injustice for All (2014), and A Slave to Liberty (2016). In spring of 2018, his eye was on another line that traveled the steep and untouched northeast side of the formation.

In May that year, we climbed the neighboring Barber Pole route in somewhat alpine conditions and rappelled into the potential line, drilling anchors at 40m intervals at good stances. We were excited to find swaths of lichen-dotted, high-quality granite through steep faces, dikes, and splitter crack systems.

Mikey Schaefer bears down on Liberty Bell's hardest route. *Austin Siadak*

That summer we set to work, initially fixing lines from the top. The first four pitches held the majority of the hard climbing, and most of our attention was directed toward cleaning these pitches, figuring out moves, and discussing bolt placements. Our excitement about the route was tempered by smoke from the heavy fire season in the Pacific Northwest that year; in Washington alone, over 400,000 acres were affected. We kept showing up each day, unsure of whether the smoke would preclude our efforts. Most days, we were lucky; however, we eventually realized it would take another season to finish the route. Before leaving, we equipped all of the anchors and placed the remaining protection bolts.

In August 2019, we returned to Washington Pass, excited to simply climb now that most of the toil was behind us. We spent multiple days Micro Traxioning the first five pitches and fine-tuning our beta. The first pitch (5.12+) had a baffling and steep crux, and the second (5.13-) was one of the stunners, with face climbing on a vertical orange dike that led into a roof, followed by insecure climbing to a small stance. The third pitch (5.11) offered somewhat of a respite before the crux—a 5.13+ pitch that started with bouldery face climbing into a 5.12 corner crack and finished with a V9/V10 boulder problem. Of the remaining six pitches, three were fun and sustained 5.11 climbing, and the remainder were rompy 5.8–5.10 climbing on somewhat mediocre rock.

Pretty soon after we began lead attempts, Mikey redpointed each of the first four pitches, and I had redpointed all but the crux pitch. On Monday, August 19, we got a late start due to a work call, and our main goal was to see if I could send the crux pitch on the sharp end. When I sent it on my first try of the day, we decided to capitalize on the opportunity and take it from there to the top. The 5.11 hero climbing was extra enjoyable now that the crux pitch was behind us, and we finished the route just as it got dark.

As a nod to the darker undertones of the current political landscape, climate change, and to the aspect of the route, we dubbed our climb the Dark Side of Liberty (1,100', IV 5.13+).

Shanjean Lee laybacks the 5.12 fingers section leading into the crux boulder problem on the Dark Side of Liberty. *Austin Siadak*

MT. CLEATOR, NORTHWEST FACE, TUBBY NEEDS CHEESE

ON SEPTEMBER 1, Rolf Larson and I climbed a nine-pitch, 1,000'-plus line on the turreted massif of Mt. Cleator (7,625'), the north side of which offers many ribs and ridges that are probably unclimbed. From our campsite in the Buck Creek drainage, a beautiful area with abundant wildlife, we debated the cleanest looking line. The selected northwest rib emanates from near the main summit (not the north tower) and appears to share the granitic character of the pluton on nearby Mt. Berge, with very little of the grubby schist predominant in the area.

We approached directly from camp, passing a waterfall by jungle-pulling on alder, and then climbed nine pitches up the rib, with the technical and mental challenges concentrated in pitches two, three, eight, and nine: Tubby Needs Cheese (1,000', III 5.8+). For the descent, we enjoyed the longer but more gentlemanly and scenic return to camp via Buck Creek Pass. 📄📷

– ERIC WEHRLY

SAHALE PEAK, WEST SPUR, KLONE KALITAN

THE CONVOLUTED WEST spur of Sahale Mountain (8,681') is plainly visible in profile from the standard route up the Quien Sabe Glacier, a popular initiatory alpine climb. The spur rises from around 7,500' to 8,200', where it merges once more with the contours of the glacier below Boston-Sahale Col. I have spent many hours of my working life as a guide staring at the gendarmes, crack systems, and horrific choss intrusions of this charming little spur, and always thought it would be fun to explore.

In early July, Scott Rinckenberger and I set off to attempt the climb. An initial triangular face offered a set of clean 5.8 cracks on the right-hand side. From there we kept almost entirely to the ridge crest, which varied dramatically in character. Clouds enclosed us much of the day, alternating between greenhouse stagnation and anxiety-inducing cool currents. Scott likes to sing, as I do, and I think at one point we startled some climbers out on the Quien Sabe. At the top, the spur delivered us neatly onto the glacier, where we roped up for a white wander back down to camp.

The route included clean, solid cracks, knife edges of white Skagit gneiss, and loose blocks mortared weakly in place by garbage. The difficulty barely reached 5.8, and belay ledges presented themselves at convenient 30m intervals. Trundling the many loose blocks we found provided the real workout–humans just can't resist turning stone into projectiles.

Some years back, I named the little spire in this area after l'Aiguille de l'M, a famous escarpment in

Forest McBrian coming up the fourth pitch of Klone Kalitan as swirling fog obscures the Quien Sabe glacier and Boston Basin below. *Scott Rinckenberger*

Chamonix; the name stuck, at least among working guides. I regret that now. These mountains have beauty and history of their own, and have given life to people for thousands of years. Given the chance, I would prefer names that honor the deeper human history of this land, to which the cultures of mining, alpinism, and national parks are so far just a brief, brutal addendum.

Although I don't believe this feature on Sahale risks popularity and really doesn't need a name, I did look at an abridged dictionary of Chinook Jargon for possibilities. Chinook Jargon is a nearly extinct trade language combining words from Chinook and Nootka languages as well as English and French, and was in widespread use in the Pacific Northwest through the 19th century. (The place names Sahale and Boston both came from Chinook Jargon, meaning "high" and "American," respectively.) Klone Kalitan (roughly "three arrows," 230m, 5.8)—for the three arrowhead-shaped points along the spur—seems as good a name as any. Archaeological digs at Cascade Pass show it was a summertime hangout where, among other things, people turned stone into projectiles. 📄 📷

– FOREST MCBRIAN

WASHINGTON PASS, HIGH HORSE, UNBRIDLED ENTHUSIASM

WHEN TRAVELING UPHILL from the east on State Route 20 toward Washington Pass, several distinct granite panels are seen to the southeast after passing the Silver Star massif. They are regularly spaced along a 2/3-mile stretch of road, their bases approximately half a mile away and 1,500' above. Black Horse Rock and the regularly summited Petit Cheval are on the northeast margin of this area, while the tallest cluster of panels, which we dubbed High Horse (7,280'), lies at the southwest extent, before reaching the highway hairpin. This cluster of cliffs—though in view of popular Liberty Bell—had no recorded climbs, perhaps because of the unappealing approach slopes or nearby high-quality routes.

On August 16, Steph Williams and I approached up sparsely vegetated slopes from the hairpin, traversing to the toe of the lowest panel. Steph led the first panel by way of mostly low-fifth moves. Traversing the few meters of scree and dirt that separated us from the next panel, we arrived at a shield-splitting crack. A little more than two rope lengths led past pleasant cracks ranging from tight fingers to fists.

Upon reaching the top of the second panel, we could hardly rein in our excitement: A vertical-walled hallway less than 2m wide and 35m deep divided the big upslope panel. This other-wise hidden hall is composed of the finest-grained stone found in the Washington Pass area, abiotic-clean and graced with four vertical cracks. We dubbed it the Hall of Cracks. We chose the hand-size option, and nearly 200m of well-protected and fun climbing up corners and the left margin of the panel concluded our ascent: Unbridled Enthusiasm (550m, IV 5.10+). 📷

– SETH KEENA

Unbridled Enthusiasm (550m, IV 5.10+) generally climbs the visible left skyline. The Hall of Cracks is the vertical black shadow on the left between the middle and highest panels. *Steph Williams*

The Silver Star massif in spring conditions, showing the line of the Northwest Face (500m, IV WI4+ M6-), climbed in October. The climbers descended from the west summit to the Silver Star Glacier, then returned over Burgundy Col (visible at left). The rock route Gato Negro (2001) and the Central Couloir (2006) are farther right. *John Scurlock*

SILVER STAR MOUNTAIN, NORTHWEST FACE

THE SILVER STAR Mountain massif, just northeast of Washington Pass, contains relatively few documented snow and ice routes—like much of the Cascades, this area is normally buried under deep snow in winter. But as there is normal, there is also the abnormal. In 2019, a relatively wet autumn mixed with cold temperatures, just enough snowfall, the odd rain event, and cloud coverage to form ice and hard snow on specific aspects.

On October 30, Steph Williams and I started up a new route on the northwest face of Silver Star Mountain's west summit (8,840'), a prominent subpeak. As we climbed squeaking snow toward the initial ice couloir, timing and conditions coalesced into real opportunity. Seventy meters of perfect ice, up to 85°, led to steep snow. A high-quality ice smear, protected by rock and ice gear, gave passage to a sheltered belay above. (During an exploratory effort the previous November, Scott Johnston and I climbed a mixed corner to the left of this ice, which hadn't formed that autumn.) Above, the couloir widens to a black and gold slab. A tilted corner abuts the slab, with pleasant dry tooling past a small amount of plastered ice, leading to a hanging snow bowl. This rope length protected deceptively well and had very fine climbing on all manner of granite and ice.

A right-trending snow ramp led to an offwidth crack, which deposited us 10m below the ridge. Moving several meters southward to a mixed passage, about 80m above the Whine Spire [*AAJ 2003*], we gained the north ridge. Snow and rock along the ridge led to blocky low-fifth terrain and the west summit, as well as the twinkle of gratitude that emanates from an opportunity seized. 📷

– SETH KEENA

YOSEMITE VALLEY, SUMMARY OF 2019 ACTIVITY

OVER THE COURSE of a year and a half, Brandon Adams established a new route on the Lost Brother that quickly became a favorite among high-end free climbers. Wayward Son (13 pitches, 5.12d or 5.11 A0) features three crux pitches of 5.12 through well-protected face climbing and classic Yosemite cracks. Between attempts on his new route, Adams also managed to set two speed records on El Capitan: Genesis (VI 5.11 A4, 20:25), with Chris Gay and Steven Tata, and Lost World (VI 5.7 A3, 12:25), with Rebecca Church.

The Fifi Buttress continues to be a popular arena for new-routing. In November, Lucho Rivera and Cedar Wright established Dream Team (10 pitches, 5.13a) on the steep right side of the wall. The route weaves in and out of Vortex (IV 5.12, Russell-Zschiesche, 1982) and 9/11 (McDevitt, 2001), including a pitch previously bolted by Margaret and Trevor Shumaker. Dream Team is stout like other lines on this beautiful wall, with three pitches of 5.11, five pitches of 5.12, and one pitch of 5.13.

Chris Koppl, Vitaliy Musiyenko, and Brian Prince—all prolific Sierra Nevada first ascensionists—finished a multi-year project on the south face of Half Dome. The Xue Way is a 20-pitch route named after a friend, Michelle Xue, who had recently passed away in a climbing accident. See page 88 for a full report.

El Capitan was home to more free climbing than speed climbing in the fall, with three free ascents of the Nose (VI 5.14a), by Barbara Zangerl (Austria) and Jacopo Larcher (Italy), and Sébastien Berthe (Belgium), who was the first to send the iconic route ground-up. Nik Berry and Eric Bissell made a ground-up free ascent of El Niño via Pineapple Express (VI 5.13b). El Cap also saw two of its youngest ascents, by Selah Schneiter, 10, on the Nose and Pearl Johnson, 9, on the Triple Direct.

Undoubtedly, one of the feel-good stories of the year was Mark Hudon's "99.7% free" ascent of Freerider (VI 5.13a), aiding just 15' of the Teflon Corner pitch. One of the fathers of the "free as can be" ethos, including his 1979 nearly free ascent of the Salathé Wall with Max Jones, in which the pair freed the now-famous Enduro Corner, 63-year-old Hudon returned with partner Jordan Cannon to make a tremendous effort.

Just when it seems that all the El Cap free climbs have been found, Tommy Caldwell and Alex Honnold, with partnership from Kevin Jorgeson and Austin Siadak, finished a new route on the steep southeast face: Passage to Freedom (27 pitches, VI 5.13d). See page 90 for the full report.

One of the most notable ascents of the year happened on a single pitch: Magic Line near Vernal Falls. In November, Hazel Findlay (U.K.) made the third free ascent of the 5.14c finger crack. After a month of effort, Findlay sent the splitter crack, placing all gear on lead, on her last day in Yosemite, despite doubts caused by breaking a foothold and injuring a finger. Originally climbed by Ron Kauk in 1996, the route didn't see a second ascent until Lonnie Kauk's redpoint (also placing gear) 20 years later.

[Top] Hazel Findlay works up the ultra-thin Magic Line (5.14c) for its first female ascent and third overall. *Eliza Earle* [Bottom] Mark Hudon on Freerider. *Jordan Cannon*

Brad Gobright on a 17-hour free ascent of Golden Gate (VI 5.13a), his third in-a-day free climb on El Cap of the season. *Elliott Bernhagen*

Despite the apparent focus on hard free climbs, aid climbing is alive and well in Yosemite, with first ascents by Steve Schneider and Kevin DeWeese to prove it. Schneider enlisted a team of help for his new route on the southwest Face of El Capitan: Bellagio (VI 5.9+ R A4) follows a line between Mirage and Lurking Fear and is characterized by tiny copperheads, hooks, beaks, and rivets. In the Ribbon Falls Amphitheater, DeWeese, Steve Bosque, and Tyler Poston added Resist! (V 5.7 A2+). The route reportedly follows beak seams and thin nailing for eight pitches, with superb views of the Valley and El Capitan.

Finally, despite what most would call wet, less-than-ideal spring conditions, Brad Gobright freed El Capitan in one day three separate times, on three different routes, in the span of just six weeks. In May, with support from Maison Deschamps, Gobright climbed the Muir Wall via the Shaft (VI 5.13c) in 17.5 hours (though he would want it known that he top-roped the final 5.13c pitch). In June, he teamed up with Alex Honnold to free El Niño via Pineapple Express (VI 5.13b) in under 15 hours, and then he surprised himself by freeing Golden Gate (VI 5.13a), again with Deschamps, in under 17 hours. After leaving Yosemite in November, Gobright traveled to El Potrero Chico, Mexico, where he died in a tragic rappelling accident. For those who knew him, and for those who simply admired him, Yosemite Valley will never be the same.

– LAUREN DELAUNAY

LITTLE YOSEMITE: BUNNELL POINT, THE SALAD TOSSING DIKE; SUGARLOAF DOME, SUGAR MAMA

IN EARLY SUMMER, Chris Koppl and I hiked out to Little Yosemite Valley to check out new possibilities on walls that seemed to have a lot of potential. The first was the northwest face of Bunnell Point, approximately four trail miles east of Nevada Falls. We were unable to cross the Merced River directly to Bunnell Point, so we had to camp a couple of miles farther up the valley, by a bridge. The following morning, we backtracked on the other side, bushwhacking and scrambling over exposed moss. The wall looked large, but we assumed it wouldn't be much bigger than 1,000'. We began on a thin white dike that traversed up and left, about 200' left of the Golden Bear (5.10b R). After about 700' of sustained climbing, which required bolting, we ran out of time—still a long way from the top.

The following day, we found another bigger than expected route on Sugarloaf Dome, a south-facing formation directly above the trail, about 3.5 miles east of Nevada Fall. Beginning far to the right of existing climbs, our route began with about 600' of low fifth-class, which we soloed and simul-climbed. Above was more sustained terrain, some of which looked very improbable for free climbing. This was mostly nice cracks, with a nails-hard slab pitch that Chris did a brilliant job of bolting on lead. The crux overhang appeared unlikely to go free, but I found just enough holds and a thank-god jug (5.11a). Above that, we found about 700' of 5.9–5.10 cracks and corners, which did not let up until we pulled over the last overhang: Sugar Mama (1,600' of climbing, IV 5.11a).

In the early fall, Chris and I returned to Bunnell Point with Christian Black, hoping to finish what we'd started. This time we were able to cross the Merced with no trouble. After a day to climb and equip a few more pitches, we sent the full monster route to the top. One of the best new routes I've climbed, the Salad Tossing Dike (2,250' of climbing, IV/V 5.11a) was much bigger than it had appeared and the climbing was brilliant, ascending a huge, left-trending dike for nearly the entire wall. (The actual cliff is about 1,400' high.) The route featured some good crack climbing, but was mostly featured face climbing along a dike that was as wide as six feet in spots. 📷

– VITALIY MUSIYENKO

CALIFORNIA / EASTERN SIERRA

MAMMOTH CREST, BLUE CRAG, NEW ROUTES

BLUE CRAG IS a serene and diminutive moniker for a sizable and rowdy piece of rock. Located on the Mammoth Crest, south of Mammoth Lakes, the cliff features compact, slate-like stone and had only one previous climb, the obvious snow line slashing up the center of the north face: Why Ya Sufferin'? (Humphrey-Rhea, 2013).

In late March, Jack Cramer, Drew Smith, and I packed the spikes, janglies, and gear for an alpine slumber party and skied in from the Tamarack Cross Country Ski Center to camp on a knoll below the face. The next morning, we started up the original line, simul-climbing the first pitch and a half of snow before breaking right up an obvious steep groove. Moderate, enjoyable mixed moves and bottomless wallowing through sugary garbage snow took us several pitches up to the shoulder, before a traverse brought us to the base of the main chimney feature on the northwest face.

The north face of Blue Crag outside of Mammoth Lakes, showing established routes: (1) The McCramer (2019) , (2) Why Ya Sufferin'? (Humphrey-Rhea, 2013), and (3) Mouse Trap (Anderson-Cramer-Smith, 2019). *Jack Cramer*

From a nerve-wracking belay below a massive snow mushroom, Jack started up steep rock on the right wall of the chimney, climbing through hard stems and sketchy hooks, culminating in a difficult and poorly protected traverse back left. A short tension traverse from a fixed pin (downclimbed free by Drew on the follow) regained the main snow gully and a belay below an overhanging wall. The following rope length, dubbed the Jenga Pitch, saw Jack heroically tiptoe and trundle his way through the steep terrain.

Drew took the final pitch to the ridge, which featured a tough boulder problem around a chockstone and a glorious exit through a natural rock tunnel. We scrambled one long pitch of 4th class to reach low-angle slopes and the summit of Blue Crag: Mouse Trap (ca 1,200' climbing distance, IV M6 A1 and steep snow). We descended via Crag Couloir, north of the peak, using our rope to cut a cornice and intentionally trigger a shallow soft slab avalanche before making our way down the couloir and back to camp, about 11 hours after departing.

In mid-April, Jack returned to Blue Crag with fellow Mammoth local Ian McEleney, and they climbed another route on the far left side of the north face, the McCramer (M3 50° snow), in 12 hours car-to-car. They reported fairly solid rock and several other moderate lines still to be done. 📄 📷

– ANDY ANDERSON

The north pillar of Mt. Crocker, showing the line of Crocks 'n' Socks (IV 5.11a). *Derek Field*

MT. CROCKER, NORTH PILLAR, CROCKS 'N' SOCKS

On August 8, my wife, Giselle Field, and I established a lovely camp by Crocker Lake and the following morning started up the north pillar of Mt. Crocker (12,457'). This imposing feature sees little to no sunlight, so we were freezing cold the entire time. At the top of the second pitch, just below the hardest climbing, we cleaned an old bail anchor. The pitch above was a difficult finger crack on a steep face (5.11a). From there, continuous 5.10 cracks led to a notch in the pillar, at which point darkness forced us to retreat. On August 10, we regained our high point and continued up the pillar on 5.9 cracks to the final overhanging prow, split dramatically by a perfect two- to four-inch crack (5.10d). At last, sunshine! We called our route Crocks 'n' Socks (1,200', 11 pitches, IV 5.11a).

From the top of the pillar, we scrambled directly to the summit and descended the west ridge to the west col. Descending the north-facing couloir turned out to be the most dangerous part of the day: The ice was bulletproof and we had only sharp rocks for tools. 📷

– DEREK FIELD, *CANADA*

WHEELER CREST, NEW ROUTES

On January 26, Joel Kauffman and I made the strenuous approach up Fifth Canyon in knee-deep snow to the Rocketship, where we had been watching an ice and mixed line form throughout the month. On the right side of the formation, a north-facing snow bowl feeds an ice drip, which then funnels into a clean corner system. Well-protected mixed climbing up the snow- and ice-filled granite dihedral was enjoyable and reminiscent of Alaska. A physical 5.8+ wide crack guarding entry to the snow bowl proved to be the crux, hooking icicles deep in the crack while heel-toeing in crampons. Scottish Astronauts (700', III 5.8 WI3 M3) featured six roped pitches and a 4th-class

scramble to the summit of the Rocketship. This is the only established ice/mixed route on the Wheeler Crest.

Over the course of two trips in late April and early May, Natalie Brechtel, Brandon Thau, and I climbed an eight-pitch route up the center of Neptune Tower. Named after the only spacecraft to do a flyby of the remote planet, Voyager II (1,000', IV 5.11+) follows the first (mostly) continuous crack system to the left of Fred Beckey's Stormy Petrel route (*AAJ 1984*).

In mid-May, Vitaliy Musiyenko, Brian Prince, Brandon Thau, and I set up camp in the hanging pocket forest below Hot Tuna Tower. The four of us took turns swinging the hammer and established a seven-pitch face climb up the prow of the buttress left of the classic 1978 Harrington-Wilson route Violet Green (*AAJ 1979*). Some mystery bolts at the base to the left of our route are thought to be from a 2000s-era Mike Strassman attempt on a similar line. We poached a few of his bolts on our second pitch and continued up. Ten feet of featureless rock on pitch four prevented a completely free ascent. Nonetheless, Muy Bonito (1,050', IV 5.12 A0) is a highly recommended route on the prettiest piece of rock on the Crest; it can be rappelled with two ropes from fixed anchors. [*The online version of this report details some shorter routes, too.*] 📄 📷

— RICHARD SHORE

[Top] Joel Kauffman follows a chimney pitch on Scottish Astronauts, the first ice and mixed route on the Wheeler Crest. [Bottom] Brian Prince enjoys morning coffee below Hot Tuna Tower, with the line of Muy Bonito (1,050', IV 5.12 A0) on the left. *Richard Shore (both photos)*

SEVEN GABLES, EAST BUTTRESS

I FIRST SAW the east side of Seven Gables (13,080') several years ago, and subsequent research revealed a confusing climbing history that seemed to be focused on neighboring Seven Gables North (Peak 12,640'). It surprised me that the broad buttress that rises to the higher summit hadn't been climbed, as it's clearly visible from a number of peaks and the Sierra High Route passes nearby. In early September, Andy Stephen and I started up the east buttress just left of a broad weakness in the center. Four pitches of fun climbing on good granite led to sandy ledges just left of the ridge crest. Above this, mellow climbing interspersed with short 5.9 crack cruxes led back to the crest and to a small, chossy notch between a gendarme on the left and the main ridge on the right. We investigated several lower quality or poorly protected avenues for staying right on the ridge, but eventually ended up descending, traversing, and re-ascending low-5th-class terrain on the left side until a fun pair of pitches took us to the top (1,000', III 5.9).

— IAN MCELENEY

Piute Crag 5 on the left and Piute Crag 4 on the right, with the north couloir in center. After climbing to the notch, Richard Shore headed left to climb the west face of Crag 5 to the top. *Richard Shore*

NEW SIERRA COULOIR CLIMBS

OVER THE COURSE of 2019, solo and with several partners, I climbed three ice couloirs that were likely first ascents in the eastern Sierra.

The colorful and obscure Piute Crags, southeast of Mt. Emerson, are plainly visible along the Bishop skyline but have seen very little traffic, probably due to warnings about loose rock. No ascents have been recorded from their northern sides, even though a handful of attractive short couloirs rise between the pointy summits. In the dark hours of July 17, I drove the bumpy 4WD road to Horse Creek Spring in the Bishop Bowl. A quick approach up onto the glacial moraine led to 600' of 50° snow and alpine ice in the narrow couloir between Piute Crags 4 and 5. At the col I switched out my boots for approach shoes, which proved barely adequate for the nearly vertical 250' western headwall of Crag 5. According to the vintage summit register, the last ascent of the peak was in 1974, and mine was maybe only the fourth ever: North Couloir and West Face (850', 5.7 AI2).

South of the Piute Crags, Mt. Tom Ross (13,247') is tucked away from most vantage points, with an impressive northeast face at the head of a small cirque above Schober Lakes. There are no technical routes recorded on this peak. On September 6, sporting neckties in an effort to keep mountaineering classy, Tad McCrea and I approached from Lamarck Col, crossing over the Sierra Crest twice to drop into the base below the wall. A long, narrowing couloir rises up the left side of the face toward the peak's east ridge. After 800' of 50° snow with some narrow water-ice steps and a couple 5th-class chockstones, we reached a beautifully featured dihedral ramp that diagonaled back right for 400' of exposed 4th and easy 5th class to the summit. We climbed the route, Dress for Less (1,200', III 5.4 AI2), car to car in a long day from North Lake.

There are four couloirs to the right of the classic one on Mt. Humphreys, dropping from the half-mile-long northwest ridge; all of them have been skied in fat winter conditions, but there is no record of fall ice climbs. The third couloir from the left strikes a deep gash into a broad rock buttress and leads to the northernmost subpeak (Peak 13,440'+). Natalie Brechtel, Earl McAlister, and I climbed this line in heroic conditions on October 12, with mostly Styrofoam névé (50–70°) and swaths of exposed water ice. The rope and rack stayed in the backpack for the secure but seriously calf-burning ascent. Névé Névé Land (1,400', AI3) is one of the steeper and more sustained couloirs in the Sierra and a worthy objective. 🗎 📷

– RICHARD SHORE

BALCONY PEAK, WEST CHIMNEY

IN 1989, STEVE Porcella and I scoped out the massive climbing potential on the west side of the Middle Palisade massif, which includes peaks like Norman Clyde, Middle Palisade, and Disappointment. The obvious standout line was a massive chimney system splitting the west face of Balcony Peak (13,845+'). By then, however, Steve and I were committed to a writing project describing routes on the 14,000' peaks, so instead we struck a line directly up Middle Pal's west face.

On September 16, 2018, 29 years later, I returned to the area with Vitaliy Musiyenko and we climbed Balcony's roughly 15-pitch chimney line. The 5.10- crux came on the second pitch, which was characterized by a dihedral and then an arête. We reached the summit as the sun was setting and scrambled and rappelled down the spooky east face of the massif. ▣

– CAMERON M. BURNS

BIRCH MOUNTAIN, NORTH RIDGE, MUTUALLY ASSURED CHOSS

DESPITE ITS RESEMBLANCE to Temple Crag and position on the edge of the Palisades, Birch Mountain (13,608') has not received nearly as much attention from climbers as its geologic cousins to the northwest. In the mid-2000s there were a trio of attempts on the 2,400', Dark Star–like buttress that divides Birch's complex north face (*AAJ 2004 and 2005*). Doug Robinson and Terry Kearney topped out the face in 2004, but only after escaping off the ridge and taking an adjacent couloir to the summit.

Birch Mountain (13,608') viewed from the east. Mutually Assured Choss (V 5.10-) generally followed the right skyline (north ridge). *Jack Cramer*

In June, McKenzie Long, Chance Traub, and I set out with the goal of the complete north ridge. Unfortunately, dangerous rock and a dropped pack forced us to bail. [*The amusing full story is at the AAJ website.*] On July 7, a month after that calamity, we returned. This time we climbed a system of cracks to the right of the loose left-facing corner we had previously used, and the rock quality was substantially better. A thousand feet up we passed our previous high point, and soon after reached the top of the second prominent tower, where we rappelled into the notch that connects to the upper ridge. It was barely 3 p.m., but we settled in for the night to be fully rested for the steeper climbing above.

The next day, we agreed we had made the right choice—seven intricate pitches passed before we found another suitable bivy site. The climbing over this intimidating section was loose but spectacular, with gobs of exposure to either side. We hauled our packs up a short vertical crux (5.10-). Two more pitches took us to the terminus of the ridge and a tattered piece of webbing. This was likely the spot where in 2004 a bonking Seth Dilles and Mike Strassman retreated just 500' shy of the summit. We placed a new sling and rapped into a loose gully that appeared to connect with the summit plateau. Opting for a prouder finish, we traversed onto an adjacent buttress. Two more pitches deposited us on the summit slopes.

Inside the summit register, we found mention of another attempt from a pair of friends the week before. After at least five attempts, including that one, the complete north ridge finally goes. It awaits anyone interested in a Temple Crag–style ridge away from the crowds. Just be aware of Doug Robinson's Atomic Broom Theory: the idea that shockwaves from atomic testing used to sweep loose rock off any Sierra wall with an unobstructed view of the Nevada Test Site. Since atmospheric testing there ceased in 1962, frost wedging has been slowly returning the range to a natural state of looseness. So, don't blame us for the precarious blocks on Mutually Assured Choss (V 5.10-). Blame the anti-nuke hippies! ▤ ▣

– JACK CRAMER

TROJAN PEAK, NORTHEAST RIDGE, MAGNUM OPUS

Tad McCrea below Trojan Peak (13,947'). Magnum Opus (1,600', IV 5.8) generally followed the right skyline. *Richard Shore*

TAD MCCREA AND I made the notorious approach up rugged George Creek late on the afternoon of July 21, bivouacking near the confluence of the north and main forks of the creek. We cast off for the long northeast ridge of Trojan Peak (13,947') the following morning. This massive feature can be seen easily from Highway 395 near Lone Pine, with two large towers making up the lower two-thirds of the ridge.

Fifteen long pitches on clean granite led up and over the two towers, including a 30m rappel off the second, until we reached easy terrain and could unrope on the summit slopes. We descended the class-2 south face and hiked out the same day by headlamp. Tad had proved yet again that with endless Internet sleuthing, classic moderate rock climbs can still be found in not-so-hidden corners of the Sierra: Magnum Opus (1,600', IV 5.8). 📷

– RICHARD SHORE

MT. CARL HELLER, NORTH FACE, STAYIN' ALIVE

FOUR YEARS AGO, my friend David Pearson took a bad fall while climbing and spent a month in a coma in the Fresno hospital. Fortunately, he recovered, and every year on the anniversary of the accident we go climbing in the Sierra to celebrate David's functional brain and body. In August, we made the brutal approach up the George Creek drainage to try the likely unclimbed north face of Mt. Carl Heller (13,211').

On August 18, we started up a crack that diagonals left, a couple hundred feet to the right of the large double-crack gully that splits the face. What looked like good cracks from the ground turned out to be dirty water grooves—fun, but definitely not the splitters we were hoping for. We climbed 300' in the water grooves, encountering the 5.10+ crux of the route about 100' above the snowfield. The leader pulled on one cam while cleaning the crack on the crux move, but it was freed by the follower.

We then gained the double-crack gully and ascended it for 250'. While climbing out of the gully toward a right-facing corner system, I accidentally knocked off a large block, yelled "rock!", and watched as it crash toward David. Luckily, it only hit his hand; he had a small laceration, which bled a little and made crack climbing painful, but otherwise he was unscathed. I swear David has more lives than a cat. We continued up the corner for about 300', then up several more great pitches of arching traverses, wide cracks, and fun moves until we were on the summit—Stayin' Alive (1,100', IV 5.10+). 📷

– DAMIEN NICODEMI

TULAINYO TOWER, KIND LINE

TULAINYO TOWER (12,800'+) came into my consciousness a few years back during a masochistic phase of my life. [*Tulainyo is the first prominent tower along the ridgeline south of Mt. Carl Heller (13,211').*] I was searching out all of the classic offwidth climbs in the Sierra and learned of Tulainyo's East Face Direct (Green-Stronge, 1973, freed in 1992; *see AAJ 1993*), which has wide-crack cruxes.

In the summer of 2019, a plan finally started to come together. Ryan Evans had cached food and a rack up George Creek after an aborted climb, which would ease the arduous approach. Unfortunately, after we hiked up on July 20, we discovered Ryan's bear canister had been smashed open and all of our food was gone. Fortunately, I had hiked up with six snack bars and a package of instant mashed potatoes. Armed with optimism and a small fishing pole, we caught trout to supplement our potato dinner before the next day's climb.

Ryan had to be back at work on Monday morning, the day after our climb, so we had decided to do one of the easier looking lines on Tulainyo Tower, but when we hiked up to the base of the wall, our excitement got the best of us and we decided to follow our stoke up steep corners of golden granite, well to the left of the East Face Direct. We encountered a rappel anchor about 100' from the snow, but beyond this there were no signs of human

Approaching Tulainyo Tower, with the new route Kind Line shown. The East Face Direct (1973) is to the right. *Damien Nicodemi*

activity. Discontinuous 5.10 cracks brought us to a large golden dihedral. Much to our surprise, the climbing up the dihedral was in the 5.9 range, with lots of features around a four-inch crack that seemed to go on forever. Several incredible pitches up the dihedral led to the top of the formation. We named the route Kind Line (900', IV 5.10-) due to the incredibly giving nature of the climb: Jams, jugs, knobs, and gear placements always seemed to appear right where you wanted them. 📄 📷

– DAMIEN NICODEMI

LONE PINE PEAK, RIDGE TO TERABITHIA

IN JUNE, ANDY McQuillen and I spent nine days exploring the rock walls of the Tuttle Creek drainage. We did a variety of fun routes, the longest being a new line on the prominent right-leaning arête on the left side of the south face of Lone Pine Peak—the next arête to the left of the Direct South Face (V 5.8, Beckey-Bjornstad, 1970). Our route climbs 14 unique pitches before merging with the Direct South Face for its final pitch.

We started in the afternoon on June 17, making slow progress due to a bushwhack approach and tricky route-finding. On a short dike section, I placed two bolts using a single hook. The fifth pitch, which we called the Flying Worm, was a rare horizontal chimney, with an acrobatic exit. With darkness upon us, we retreated to camp by rappelling straight down the face.

On June 19, we arose before sunrise and regained our high point, with Andy freeing the short dike pitch at 5.10. Above, improbable traverses and downclimbs offered lucky bypasses to each apparent dead-end. Looking up from our tenth pitch, the ridge looked unappetizing, so we traversed left into a 600' third-class gully, which brought us swiftly to the upper headwall of the main south face. From here, we chose a sustained left-facing corner (5.10 hands), followed by two more pitches up and right to the final pitch of the Direct South Face. We tagged the scree plateau under a pink twilight sky and immediately began a tricky nighttime descent.

We named our route Ridge to Terabithia (2,600', 15 pitches, IV 5.10). 🖼️🔍

— DEREK FIELD, *CANADA*

PEAK 3,986, RAIDERS OF THE LOST DIKE; LONE PINE, THE SURFBOARD

IN EARLY JUNE, Jeremy Ross, Sean Sullivan, and I climbed the highly recommended Michael Strassman Memorial Route (700', III 5.10d) on the south face of Lone Pine Peak. We planned to check out the south face of nearby Peak 3,986m on the following day. I had spotted a prominent and continuous dike that seemed to go from the bottom all the way to the top. Even though we were not prepared for the extensive bolting required to climb such routes, we decided to try it.

We located the start of the Zig Zag Dihedral, and began to the left on a half-roof, half-dike feature. After piecing together the first pitch (5.10), we climbed a shorter but more difficult pitch of 5.10d/5.11a in order to reach what turned out to be the crux—thin and sustained 5.11 face climbing past three bolts to start the third pitch. More good climbing up dikes and overhangs took us to the top of a prominent tower where we joined the Zig Zag Dihedral. We rappelled from here, more or less down the route we ascended. Raiders of the Lost Dike (1,800' of climbing, IV 5.11a) is a highly recommended climb!

I don't know many people as excited about dike climbing as my friend Chris Koppl, so a few weeks later, at the end of June, we hiked back out to Lone Pine Peak to check out a potential new route I'd noticed while making the first free ascent of Streets of the Mountains (IV 5.11a; *see AAJ 2019*). These beautiful dikes and cracks looked harder than Streets and begged to be tried.

After hiking in and setting up camp, that afternoon we managed to climb two long and sustained pitches (both 5.11). We fixed our two ropes and enjoyed a calm night. The next day we kept on stacking fun, difficult leads. In all, we climbed eight long new pitches till we linked into the upper corner of Streets of the Mountains. Three more pitches led to a huge balcony with a bivy site, and from there, another 300–400' of loose fourth class guarded the slog to the scenic summit. The Surfboard (1,500', IV 5.11c) is a great addition to the south face. 🖼️

— VITALIY MUSIYENKO

[Left] Sean Sullivan and Jeremy Ross following a pitch on Raiders of the Lost Dike (1,800' of climbing, IV 5.11a) on the south face of Peak 3,986'. The Owens Valley is in the background. [Right] Chris Koppl leading a pretty pitch on the first ascent of the Surfboard (1,500', IV 5.11c) on the south face of Lone Pine Peak. *Vitaliy Musiyenko (both photos)*

CARTAGO WALL, THE REVENANT

OVER TWO SEPARATE trips—both exceptionally difficult, and for various reasons—Joey Jarrell and I completed a new route on the Cartago Wall, the second known line on the granodiorite wall (*see AAJ 2018*), and possibly the first to summit the formation.

We set off the first time on May 28. Even though the approach was bluntly described as "the most unpleasant in the Sierra," we still managed to underestimate it. Challenges included bushwhacking up a nettle- and ant-infested gorge, finding and flattening a suitable campsite among cactus, bashing through thick alders, and tiptoeing up polished slabs. We began climbing well to the left of the 2017 route, in a wide system on the next buttress uphill. We did not start until late in the afternoon of May 29 and did only one 180' pitch before retreating to camp.

On May 30, we made a 21-hour push for the summit. The endless offwidth cracks ensured slow progress. From the top of the ninth pitch, 1,300' up our route and with the sun setting, we retreated using slung blocks and single-bolt anchors. We stumbled back to camp at 2 a.m., coming in on nothing but fumes, and

The seldom-visited Cartago Wall is over 1,500 feet high. (1) The Revenant (2019). (2) Saddle Sores (2017). *Richard Shore*

were devastated to find our camp had been utterly destroyed by a bear. The two of us slept on the ground in shifts and twice had to scare away the large cinnamon black bear. When at last morning dawned, we rounded up the scattered gear and food wrappers, and limped back to the car.

Acting on the skewed judgment with which only the impassioned mountaineer can sympathize, Joey and I decided to return to Cartago Wall at the end of the season. We started the approach at 10:30 a.m. on November 14 and made it to Bear Camp just before sunset.

Our idea was to improve our chances by partitioning the ascent over two days, so we spent all of November 15 climbing the first four pitches and hauling bivouac gear up to a ledge atop the fourth. By noon the next day, we had regained our previous high point via free climbing up to 5.10, but not without event. While manteling onto a ledge on the ninth pitch, I inadvertently trundled a coffee table–size boulder, which careened down the chimney and struck Joey in the thigh. Thankfully, the only injuries were surface wounds and extensive bruising.

The subsequent 200' pitch, the Cinnamon Chimney (5.10), was probably the crux of the route. We proceeded to the summit via three pitches of moderate climbing (5.8) and bouldered onto the highest pinnacle at 3:30 p.m.

About halfway down the rappels, things started to go haywire. Both of us were becoming dangerously fatigued, and our lead rope suffered two mysterious core shots that reduced its length to 100 feet. Shortly thereafter, our tag line got hopelessly stuck and we had to cut it. When at last we touched solid ground we felt extremely lucky. Two hours later, we felt even more fortunate to discover that our camp was intact.

Given that we had gotten screwed by a bear and metaphorically came back from the dead, we named our route after a 2015 movie: The Revenant (2,000', 13 pitches, IV 5.10). 📷

– DEREK FIELD, *CANADA*

Ben Ditto on the third pitch of Wild Kingdom (IV 5.11), a new route on the north face of the Citadel (11,744'). *Julie Ellison*

THE CITADEL, WILD KINGDOM

ON AUGUST 25, Katie Lambert and I topped out a new 16-pitch route on the north face of the Citadel (11,744'). Our goal had been to free the original north face route (IV 5.7 A2, Herbert-Hennek-Lauria; *see AAJ 1969*), as it's shown in the Secor guidebook. We roughly followed the route outlined in the book—the first major dihedral system to the right of Edge of Time Arête (IV 5.10+, Howell-Nettle, 1991)—but found no trace of prior passage. Secor also shows Nothing but Time (IV 5.10+, Haden-Pennings, *AAJ 2002*) as being too far to the left, which leads us to believe the original route must be further right, in one of the other large dihedral systems. Subsequent research revealed that other parties had hiked in intending to climb the 1968 line but also wound up putting up new routes.

With supplies for two weeks, we left the South Lake Trailhead and hiked around 18 miles over Bishop Pass to our first camp alongside the Kings River. We had hired packers to take our gear, but due to a high snow year, they were unable to cross Bishop Pass, so four friends helped us porter the loads.

After finding a section of the Kings River that we could wade across, we carried loads up into Ladder Creek and established a camp there. The next day was spent climbing and fixing a few ropes. We expected to be climbing the dihedrals but instead found very clean rock on the face to the left for five pitches.

As we climbed higher, our anticipation of the guidebook's description of "hard aid climbing out a roof" dissipated and we were comfortable in the realization that we were climbing a new route. We found no trace of passage, pins, or tat anywhere on the wall. Finally we took a rest day, and the following day we climbed to the top of the wall in a push.

From our high point, we quested into some steep and heady choss, which dramatically slowed our progress. Around pitch 10, the angle of the wall and the difficulty eased, lowering our anxiety somewhat. Upon topping out the east summit, we descended to the saddle and simul-climbed to the true (west) summit. From there we raced the remaining daylight down the west ridge to Ladder Lake and our camp.

We called our route Wild Kingdom (1,700', IV 5.11) in honor of the wonderful nature we experienced while in the Ladder Creek basin. Having two weeks available meant we could take it slow and enjoy the time away from the hustle and bustle of everyday life.

– BEN DITTO

LAKE BASIN, ALEXANDRA'S ARÊTE AND OTHER ROUTES

In July, Chaz Langelier, Cam Smith, Brian Prince, and I made the long haul to Lake Basin to check out this photogenic place and attempt a large and likely unclimbed arête, photos of which had intrigued us for the last couple of years. With an abundance of possible climbing objectives in Lake Basin, the 17-mile approach over Taboose Pass and Cartridge Pass seemed like a reasonable price of admission.

The day after arriving in the basin, Brian and I climbed the attractive north-facing feature we had come for, in the drainage above Marion Lake. The sharp ridge ended up having about 1,300' of good and challenging climbing, with several nice pitches and a few 5.11 cruxes—I dubbed it Alexandra's Arête (IV 5.11b) after my grandmother, who had recently passed away. After climbing the wall, we traversed the long ridge west to the top of Marion Peak and then returned to our camp.

The scenic basin above Marion Lake, in the Lake Basin area of Kings Canyon National Park. Vitaliy Musiyenko and Brian Prince's route Alexandra's Arête (1,300', IV 5.11b) follows the obvious sharp ridge along the sun/shade line to the wall's highest point. *Vitaliy Musiyenko*

Over the next couple of days, the team climbed several other likely new routes, including two lines on an attractive wall, which we called the Hessen Wall, on the north side of an unnamed 12,091' peak: the Swish Dike (5.10+) and the Ring Finger (1,000', 5.10d). From the top of the latter, Brian and I traversed east to Mt. Ruskin, which was a great scramble! Cameron and Chaz also did a couple of routes on the east side of Lake Basin, including sBelle Arête (5.10+) on a rarely climbed mountain called Staghorn Peak (12,828'), roughly halfway between Mt. Ruskin and Vennacher Needle. [*Details of these routes are at the AAJ website.*]

The following day Cam felt sick, so Chaz joined Brian and me on a climb on a formation said to be called the Hershey's Kiss, northwest of Cartridge Pass. Our route, which may have been done before, featured one of the most continuous corner splitters I have done in the Sierra: Sugaree (1,200', IV 5.11c). 📄 📷

– VITALIY MUSIYENKO, *WITH INFO FROM CAM SMITH*

NORTH DOME, LUCID DREAM AND GREAT WHITE NORTH

North Dome is one of the most prominent formations in Kings Canyon, and Vitaliy Musiyenko, Brian Prince, and I had parked below it many times on our way to other rocks. We had looked at its big south face and discussed possibilities for years, but it wasn't until Richard "Dick" Leversee told Vitaliy of an unclimbed "king line" that we decided to finally attempt a new route on the El Cap of Kings Canyon. If Dick Leversee says a route has potential, then you have to at least check it out.

In June, Vitaliy and I walked along the base and tried to decide between a line I had scoped and the line Richard had recommended. We ended up choosing his line: the prominent slanting buttress in the center of the wall. This was my first time back on a serious climb since I broke both of my heels in a climbing accident, so I was belay slave while Vitaliy did all the work.

North Dome, near Road's End in Kings Canyon National Park, showing two lines completed in 2019. Lucid Dream (1,500', 9 pitches, V 5.11 A2) on the left and (2) Great White North (1,500', 10 pitches, V 5.11+) on the right. Other routes not shown. *Vitaliy Musiyenko*

The first few pitches had some amazing crack climbing but led into a blank section. That day ended with Vitaliy on a three-hour lead through a mixture of hooks, beaks, bolts, and free climbing. We bailed about four pitches up. It took two more visits on separate days to push through the next aid pitch and the final four free pitches to the summit. I felt a bit better on each attempt and contributed with a few leads where I could, but Vitaliy did the bulk of the work. The route follows fantastic rock up an independent line, fishing with a steep and burly corner to the summit. We took Richard's suggestion for the name: Lucid Dream (1,500', 9 pitches, V 5.11 A2).

We came back to North Dome in July, along with Brian Prince, to try the other route we had all separately considered. It had a few improbable looking roofs, but from our view on the previous climb, it looked like they might go, and go they did.

Our route went directly from toe to summit up the tallest and steepest portion of the face, in between A Tall Cool One (V 5.11 R) and North of Eden (V 5.10+). We started early, kept moving, and before we knew it were linking great cracks through the roofs. We climbed the final pitch that night by headlamp and wandered around the summit ledges before finding the top of Lucid Dream and rapping that route, making it back down to the car by 2:30 a.m. It was a fantastic adventure, going mostly at 5.10, with a few harder pitches that can likely be bypassed. Great White North (1,500', 10 pitches, V 5.11+) is a tribute to the formation and to Brian, the Alaskan rope gun. ◙

– DANIEL JEFFCOACH

BUBBS CREEK WALL, HANSHI

BUBBS CREEK, NAMED for the 19th-century prospector John Bubbs, flows 16 miles through a deep, glaciated canyon to the mighty Kings River. Equidistant from the east and west sides of the Sierra, the drainage's namesake wall rises prominently from the valley floor. Patina faces crossed by continuous dikes, a few corners, and a smattering of knobs yield passage up 2,000' of otherwise blank, steep granite.

In the fall of 2015, Taylor Lamoureaux, Nicky Dyal, and I made two attempts on a line that begins with the first pitch of the Emperor (5.12a, established in 2014 and freed in 2015). From there we struck off right, climbing free-as-can-be and drilling from stances and hooks in harder sections, until a nearby wildfire swelled to the point where the canyon was evacuated. Our high point, 1,000' above the valley floor and just shy of the final headwall, appeared to be blocked by 30' of blank rock.

In the early fall of 2019, Chris Williams and I fixed ropes to the previous high point and started to explore roofs, dikes, and cracks that could circumvent the blank section. After an initial scouting trip, we returned home demoralized: Three possible variations had not panned out, and the prospect of equipping a bolt ladder was untenable.

Later in the fall, Rob Kennedy and I hiked the eight miles to Bubbs Creek Wall to make a push for the top. With fresh eyes, Rob was able to sort out the most improbable face sequence between the previously explored features, which led to a monster knob and more featured rock. From there, we climbed the first crux of the Sensei route, then turned a corner to find a tufa-like dike on slightly overhanging rock; this continued to the horizon and over the headwall, eventually linking into the exit pitches shared by the Emperor and the Sensei/What's Up Bubb? We had a rock climb. But three of the pitches had yet to be freed.

The following week, Rob and I started at the base and climbed each pitch to the top over the course of three days, making use of our 1,500' of fixed line to commute up and down from a camp in the valley each day. Many pitches took multiple goes, some with double-digit burns before sending—we dug deep.

Hanshi (2,400', V 5.12+) is damn fun and sustained. The climb has 108 protection bolts and anchors, with fixed rap stations to pitch 12. I named the route after the top-level Kendo degree, in keeping with the Bubbs route-naming theme. But it's also named for my friend Hansi Standteiner, who always puts a big smile on my face.

– TOWNSEND BROWN

CALIFORNIA / SEQUOIA NATIONAL PARK

TOKOPAH VALLEY, WATCHTOWER, BIG TIME

A FEW YEARS ago, Richard Leversee encouraged Brian Prince and me to take over a project he had worked on for several years in the 1990s with Scott Cosgrove, Jay Smith, and Jim Zellers: an all-free line up the prow of the Watchtower, originally climbed by Greg Henzie and Galen Rowell in 1970. Brian and I had drooled over the Watchtower from Tokopah Dome, across the valley. The history of stronger climbers attempting it did not encourage much confidence, but the magic line of Sequoia was worth the time investment.

We first checked it out in 2018 and learned it would require a lot of crack cleaning, some bolts, and more trickery to avoid the sections that appear to be impossible. In July 2019, we fixed several ropes to work on the line. We weren't sure it would be free climbable until the day we redpointed it, as some of the cruxes traversed a lot and we were working on the route separately, since our days off did not align well.

On August 22, everything came together perfectly. We connected the first four pitches of the original Rowell route (Northeast Arête) with new terrain leading into All Along the Watchtower (Harrison-Long, 1985), from which we found a three-pitch independent finish up steep cracks and over big roofs. This allowed for a fully free line up the main prow, as Richard and we had dreamed. To involve him in the process a little more, we encouraged him to find a name for the route, and he dubbed it Big Time (1,200', IV 5.12a).

The Watchtower showing the line of Big Time (1,200', IV 5.12a), linking the Northeast Arête and All Along the Watchtower with much new terrain. *Vitaliy Musiyenko*

– VITALIY MUSIYENKO

CASTLE ROCKS, TEMPLAR TOWER

IN MAY, CHAZ Langelier and I checked out the largest tower in the group of rocks collectively labeled the Broken Towers in the old Sequoia guidebook. It is immediately west of Castle Rock Spire and plainly visible from many vantages around Moro Rock. We climbed 1.5 new routes.

From the gully below the west face of the tower, three pitches led to a large ledge that splits the face in half. We then walked around to the north face and climbed two long pitches of nice cracks left of an obvious chimney. A classic 5.11 thin crack, the only feasible line, split the final block. We believe we were the first to summit this formation, which we called Templar Tower. We drilled a single bolt and rapped off, continuing down the west face.

The next day, inspired by cracks we'd seen on the upper west face while descending, we repeated the same initial pitches and continued straight up. We named the full west face route Bludgeon Your Eye (III 5.11). The upper north face variation is Ring the Bell (III 5.11). ◙

– BRIAN PRINCE

SPRING LAKE WALL, NO FUN ALLOWED

IN AUGUST, ELLIOTT Bernhagen, Tad McCrea, and I hiked in to the Spring Lake Wall, tucked in to the north of Sawtooth Pass. On our first day, we completed No Fun Allowed (1,200', IV 5.10d R), which featured several top-notch cracks in the middle of the wall. The price of admission was a very chossy and not so well-protected 30-foot section on the second pitch, and another poor section on the third, which could use at least one bolt to protect a 5.10a-ish move amid long run-outs. (If anyone wants to add fixed pro to this route, you are welcome.) Three more pitches of great splitters and another pitch of typical Sierra low 5th took us to the scenic *cumbre.* [*Editor's Note: In 1975, Vern Clevenger and Galen Rowell climbed That's a Sheer Cliff (IV 5.9, see AAJ 1976), which follows one of the many dihedrals in the center portion of the wall. The exact line is unknown, but it is likely to the right of the 2019 route.*]

On the following day, Elliott and I wanted to repeat one of the good-looking established climbs on the wall while Tad went for a hike. We managed to eliminate the aid that had been used on the first pitch of the One that Got Away (1,500', IV 5.11a/b, Kalman-Siadak, 2015; see AAJ 2016). This route ascends a variety of nice splitter cracks once you're past initial 400' choss scramble (one of the worst I have encountered in the Sierra!). It appears it might be possible to traverse into the route above this initial band on a long, sloping ledge from the right.

The Spring Lake Wall, showing (1) No Fun Allowed (1,200', IV 5.10d R) and (2) The One that Got Away (1,500', IV 5.11a/b, Kalman-Siadak, 2015), which was freed in 2019. That's a Sheer Cliff (5.9, Clevenger-Rowell, 1975) is likely to the right. *Vitaliy Musiyenko*

– VITALIY MUSIYENKO

BIG FIVE LAKES, PEAK 11,880', CINCO GRANDE

IN 1985, I was managing the Bearpaw Meadows High Sierra Camp in Sequoia National Park when Claude and Nancy Fiddler passed through during a multi-week backpacking and climbing blitz. I helped them out of a pinch when their gear drop didn't materialize, and in exchange they shared some accounts of first ascents they'd made in the area. One of the most intriguing was a 5.11 line on a wall above Big Five Lakes, which in R.J. Secor's guidebook gets only a two-line teaser: "Follow a crack system up the center of the face for 17 pitches. A long and committing route on steep rock."

It wasn't until almost 35 years after I first heard about this wall, in October 2019, that I finally headed into Big Five Lakes with Clayton Helzer to check it out. We made the hike with full packs from Mineral King over Sawtooth Pass and looped around Lost Canyon and the Little Five Lakes Trail—a 15-mile grind through a spectacular and inspiring stretch of the southern Sierra.

In addition to being an impressive formation of granite, with numerous features and possible lines on its 1,000' wall, Peak 11,880' rises above a beautiful forested cirque of five lakes, which is a worthy reason alone to make the long hike in. After an easy approach and recon along the base of the wall, Clayton and I settled on a steep line that starts at the toe of the main buttress, in the center of the face. The meat of the route is in the first few pitches, where the wall is steepest. It then tapers off to a moderate and engaging midsection that leads to an airy arête and an easy, wandering finish: Cinco Grande (10 pitches, IV 5.11-). We descended east into an idyllic hidden basin then north down a gully and back to the main lake in the basin.

The northwest face of Peak 11,880' (The Wall Above Big Five), showing (1) Cinco Grande (10 pitches, 5.11-, 2019) and (2) approximate line of original route (5.11, 1985). *Dave Nettle*

Based on a conversation with Claude, it appears their 1985 route took a line just right of ours, with a short difficult passage in the center of the wall. He recalled being put to the test on their first ascent, as they only carried a 120' rope and a single rack of Friends.

– DAVE NETTLE

PLEASANT POINT, NORTHEAST BUTTRESS AND MORDWAND DIRECT

PLEASANT POINT (9,690') is two miles north of the historic mining town of Cerro Gordo in the southern Inyo Mountains, a limestone range to the east of the Owens River Valley and south of the White Mountains. When viewed from the Owens Valley, Pleasant Point is but a minor bump along the ridge crest. When seen from the Saline Valley, however, the dramatic 1,000' eastern escarpment is a bit more apparent. Attractive yet extremely loose, this complex, fluted cliff has been dubbed the "Eiger of the Inyos."

The wall is like a giant overstuffed Oreo cookie: black wafers of limestone sandwiching the soft, poor white dolomite in the middle. A few sport routes have been developed at the base of the cliff on the black limestone, but no one had attempted to push a line up the giant mountain face above.

On April 20, Natalie Brechtel and I climbed what we deemed to be the "safest" route on the far right side of the peak. Safe is a relative term on this cliff—torrents of climber-induced rockfall are inevitable, and the dolomite is so sharp that a fall by leader or follower seems likely to cut the

The east face of Pleasant Point (9,690') in the Inyo Mountains, showing (1) Mordwand Direct (1,100', IV 5.10+ R/X) and (2) Northeast Buttress (1,300', IV 5.9 R/X). *Richard Shore*

rope. Steeper technical sections were interspersed with narrow alpine ridges, and most pitches took an hour or more to lead, due to navigational and protection difficulties in the choss. Soft-iron WWII army surplus pitons proved to be most valuable—bolts were often worthless in the shattered mess, and hard steel pins would explode the rock into bits.

Eight long pitches up the Northeast Buttress (1,300', IV 5.9 R/X) provided full-value mental engagement. We descended an easy snow-filled gully back to the base, and I vowed never to return to this pile of garbage. Yet, against my better judgment, I returned with Myles Moser on September 29 to attempt a harder line directly up the wall's central buttress. Myles and I swung leads, climbing onsight through eight similarly dangerous but even more difficult pitches than the Northeast Buttress to complete the Mordwand Direct (1,100', IV 5.10+ R/X).

Pleasant Point is hardly a recommended climbing destination, due to the poor rock quality, but the peak has potential for great ice and mixed climbing in wintertime, with difficult and remote access. [*The online report has useful information on access options.*] 📄 📷

– RICHARD SHORE

FIRST CREEK CANYON, NEW ROUTES

IN EARLY 2019, I made two trips to Red Rock, where local wise man and climbing historian Larry DeAngelo had convinced me to investigate First Creek Canyon for new route opportunities. The result was three long routes.

On January 9, my wife, Giselle, and I completed a new route up a seldom-visited rock tower known as Bearclaw Spire to climbers and White Pinnacle Peak to scramblers. Dirtbag Geologist (1,040', 11 pitches, III 5.10d) was named in honor of recently retired professor and authentic dirtbag geologist Ernie Duebendorfer, who was one of my grad-school mentors and, more importantly, contributed a good chunk of his career to research in the Las Vegas region.

On April 19, Giselle and I teamed up with Larry to pursue an objective that had been in the back of his mind for years: the seemingly unclimbed Slippery Peak, a small subsidiary summit jutting out of the complex north face of Indecison Peak. Starting right of Larry's route Leviathan (III 5.9, DeAngelo-Duncan, 2009), we reached the summit via Plate Tectonics (630', 6 pitches, III 5.10a).

On April 21, Steve Stosky (Canada) and I endured the heinous three-hour approach to the Basin Wall on the southeast aspect of Mt. Wilson. Starting just right of the prominent right-leaning crack on the right side of the wall, we eventually gained this crack system via four pitches of airy arêtes and cracks up to 5.10a, and then continued up four more pitches of moderate ramp climbing. The Canadian Route (1,200, IV 5.10a) is the second known route on the Basin Wall and is a rather serious undertaking at the grade. [*More details on these routes are at the AAJ website.*] 📄 📷

– DEREK FIELD, *CANADA*

UTAH

ZION NATIONAL PARK, SUMMARY OF 2019 ACTIVITY

THE YEAR IN southwest Utah began with a wet winter and spring, swinging wildly to a record dry spell, allowing for more climbing in the summer and fall monsoon season than the average year.

In March, Derrick Fassbender and Steffan Gregory completed a five-pitch variation to Gentleman's Agreement (IV 5.13b) on the Left Mary. Forced Enthusiasm (IV 5.10+ C1) starts with a pendulum right from the top of pitch three of Gentleman's Agreement to reach the obvious wide crack system that goes to the top of the Mary.

April brought a likely first free ascent of Force Boyle on Johnson Mountain. The route, established by Robbie Colbert, Bill Ohran, and Dan Snyder at 5.11 A0, has been awaiting a free ascent for many years; only two pitches were undone. Jake Jarzyniecki and Dion Obermeyer heeded the call, and the route now goes free at III/IV 5.12a.

In May, Brent Barghahn freed Moon Patrol (V 5.8 A3), an old line on the Leaning Wall, left of Spaceshot. First ascensionist Ron Olevsky had originally reported that both Spaceshot and Moon Patrol would become popular classics due to their roadside location, great ledges, and easy descent—while that was true for Spaceshot, the latter fell into obscurity. The route shares the first three pitches of Equinox, then continues up a less than vertical seam at IV 5.12- R.

Rob Pizem, with a slew of partners, established three long face routes in the Holy Amphitheater, a wall high in the North Fork of Taylor Creek: Over Too Soon (5.11), the Water Kelpie (5.13), and Way of the Hueco (5.10). All three are five pitches and wind through the massive huecos that tend to form high up in Kolob.

In October, Ethan Newman and Steffan Gregory freed the original start to the Silmaril on the Watchman. Dave Jones and Gary Grey established this route in 1983 at V 5.11 A2, and in 2007 Mike Anderson, supported by Brian Smoot, freed the route via a three-pitch variation at the start. With permission from the first ascensionists, we added two protection bolts to the original first pitch and two more to the second pitch. The second pitch goes in the mid to upper 5.12 range.

Over three trips throughout the course of the year, Dan Stih made the first ascents of three backcountry peaks: Big Red, the Point, and Triangle Peak. Stih accessed these peaks from the Birch Creek drainage and climbed solo, encountering 1,500'–2,000' of roped climbing, with difficulties to 5.9 A2+. Later, Stih made a traverse of the Buck Pasture Amphitheater in Kolob Canyons, during which he established a six-pitch 5.7 on Death Point. The traverse took him four days, with the last reliable water being found at La Verkin Creek. [*The online report contains additional route descriptions and topos from 2019.*] 📄 📷 🔍

– STEFFAN GREGORY *AND* ETHAN NEWMAN

Dakota Walz on Way of the Hueco (5.10), one of three new five-pitch routes in the Holy Amphitheater, high in the North Fork of Taylor Creek in Kolob Canyons. *Rob Pizem*

SAN RAFAEL SWELL, GILSON BUTTE, TWO ROUTES

STEVE "CRUSHER" BARTLETT and partners climbed two routes on Gilson Butte, a formation just west of Highway 24, midway between Green River and Hanksville, with a quarter-mile plateau summit surrounded by 400' cliffs of poor rock. In late April, over three days, Bartlett and Chip Wilson climbed an outlying summit with a sturdy-looking blob top they named the Moai: Gazing Rights (240', 3 pitches, 5.7 A3). In October, Bartlett returned with Joe Shultz and Keiko Tanaka to complete Alice in Sandland (280', 5.4 A3+), again over three days. They had assumed they were making the first ascent of Gilson Butte, but on top they found a makeshift register left by an unknown soloist, "Max Supertramp," in October 2017. Bartlett's entertaining story of these climbs is at the AAJ website. 📄 📷

– INFORMATION FROM STEVE "CRUSHER" BARTLETT

MOAB AREA, MYSTERY TOWERS, NEW ROUTES

A questionable placement on the second pitch of Desert Monkeys (5.7 A4+) on Gothic Nightmare. *David Palmada*

NOT ALL OF us have the good fortune of living close to paradise, and not all of us have the luck to travel when we would like. And so we have no alternative but to adapt to the situation and travel when work permits, which often happens to be during the blistering months of July and August. But I'm going to confess to a secret. Thanks to this, I have discovered my paradise in an oven of 40°C (104°F), where the sensations experienced feel much like a mystical encounter. All that was left was to find the perfect partner and get to work. Joan Gibert was ready, and so was born our project: Three from Hell, a trio of first ascents in the Mystery Towers, a brilliant and magical place. This endeavor took place in July and August 2019, during 20 uninterrupted days of hauling and climbing.

Our first tower was Gothic Nightmare. On the south face we climbed Desert Monkeys (5.7 A4+), the longest and most intense route, featuring very hard sections that kept us absorbed and focused. Resting in our portaledge, we enjoyed an absolute calm in the desert, only disturbed by the occasional summer storm.

From there we headed to the Doric Column, a gem of nature. On this tower we were lucky because our chosen route was north-facing, thus allowing us to climb much more at ease, away from the intense heat. The first pitch was perhaps the most difficult and followed a thin crack. We then trended left to follow a very beautiful but dirty crack that we had to clean a lot. We continued up the last pitch between gigantic mud cauliflowers with an incredible location. Reaching the top at sunset, we reveled in the magnificent display it gave us, moments that will live in our memories—Empebrats from Hell (5.9 A5).

The final prize was found on the southwest face of the Fortress: Muerte Destruccion (5.11a A4), an incredible crack that ran from the bottom to the top of the wall, waiting for us with open arms. I had spotted it years ago, and I couldn't believe that it had never been climbed. We did the entire climb with no fixed anchors. Here we were not so lucky with the sun, which punished us mercilessly, almost to the point of sunstroke. But the magnificent tower gifted us with a small virgin summit. Thanks to my partner Joan for sharing it with me, and thanks to the towers for providing the good vibrations. 📷 🔍

– DAVID "PELUT" PALMADA, SPAIN, TRANSLATED BY PAM RANGER ROBERTS

THREE MYSTERY TOWERS ROUTES: *Jim Beyer (USA) reported solo ascents of three new routes in the Mystery Towers in 2019: Iron Age Master (A4) on the south face of Gothic Nightmare and Enter Sandman on the southeast face of the Citadel in April, and Two Fall Wall (A4+ R) on the north face of Gothic Nightmare in May. Brief descriptions are available at Mountain Project.*

NEW MEXICO

BEAR CANYON, NEW ROUTES

THE 800' WALLS on the west side of Bear Canyon are easily visible from the road east of the town of Questa, but perhaps due to New Mexico's lack of climbers, the steep, overgrown terrain, and dubious-looking rock, they stood unclimbed until recently. When the nearby Lion's Den—a sport crag I had thought would be choss but eventually became arguably one of the best 5.13 crags in New Mexico—was completed, I was psyched to look for more routes in the area. Bear Canyon was the obvious place to begin.

Jay Foley on the fifth pitch of Silk Road (6 pitches, 5.12a), one of several long new routes in Bear Canyon. *Troy Paff*

The canyon was overgrown and hard to access but eventually showed the potential for quality climbs on good granite. After completing many single-pitch routes in the area, I teamed up with John Kear and began exploring the bigger cliffs in November 2016. Going ground up, we swapped leads and stance-drilled the first two long routes, Beyond Stone (5 pitches, 5.10) and Loaded For Bear (6 pitches, 5.11). At first John and I had trouble envisioning the lines, but after completing the first route we were pleasantly surprised with the high quality of rock, abundance of belay ledges, and enjoyable movement.

To date, with the help of John, Joel Tinl, and a few other Taos locals, I have completed five multi-pitch routes up to 5.12a, all five or six pitches in length and all but one fully bolted. We found evidence of only one previous single-pitch route attempt. Full topos and route descriptions will be available in the forthcoming second edition of *Taos Rock*. 🖸

– JAY FOLEY

ORGAN MOUNTAINS, ORGAN SAINT SKYLINE TRAVERSE

FROM MAY 3–5, Kevin Boyko and I made a 38-hour, unsupported traverse of the Organ Mountains between Fillmore Canyon and Baylor Pass. This crossing expanded on a previous traverse of the 22 major peaks along the ridge (*see AAJ 2015*), adding eight lesser summits for a total of 30. The Organ Saint Skyline Traverse (VI 5.10 C0 R/X) features 29 pitches of technical climbing with 26 rappels and around 20,000' of elevation gain and loss. We aided a few moves on two of the pitches, both of which would likely go free at 5.12. 📄🔍

– JON TYLKA

MT. BREITENBACH, COWBOY POETRY

TWENTY-ONE YEARS AGO, I camped beneath the north face of Mt. Breitenbach (12,140'), the fifth-highest peak in Idaho, on a six-day solo backpacking trip through the Lost River Range. Of course I wanted to stand on the summit, but climbing the face was so far beyond my skill set at the time that it was really an abstraction.

Fast forward to 2010, when I began my alpine guiding track with the AMGA and learned that conditions are everything on these ephemeral alpine routes in the high desert of Idaho. Now, in my mid-40s, with a family and obligations, I don't have the free time that I had in my 20s, but I do have the skills, experience, patience, and, dare I say, wisdom that age brings.

So this year, when the stars aligned, it was time to pardon myself from day-to-day duties and try to make it happen. Always up for an adventure, Paddy McIlvoy, co-owner of Backwoods Mountain Sports in Ketchum, joined me for an after-work approach on June 21, a combination of high-clearance two-track roads, mountain biking, and hiking. We got to the base at last light, with just enough visibility to study lines.

The only completed route on the north face was the Grand Chockstone Couloir (Boyles-Olson-Weber, *AAJ 1983*), which climbs ramps, gullies, cliff bands, and a couloir to just east (looker's left) of the summit. We decided to try a new line, and after 13 hours from camp to camp, I'm proud to say we succeeded.

[Top] The north face of Mt. Breitenbach (12,140'), showing approximate lines of (1) Cowboy Poetry (2019) and (2) Grand Chockstone Couloir (1983). [Bottom] Paddy McIlvoy following a steep traverse on Cowboy Poetry. *Mark Hanselman (both)*

Cowboy Poetry (2,800', IV 5.7 R AI2 50° snow) climbs the most obvious couloir toward the lower east summit of the peak.

After soloing the first 1,000' of snow, the first crux came where the main couloir jogs left, and we found a mix of choss, thin ice, snow, and thankfully solid rock for a few dry-tool moves. The next several pitches were scenic and classy alpine pitches on snow. These led to a steep headwall, but I sniffed out a ledge that traversed left and ended in an 80' blunt arête with run-out 5.7 climbing—lots of exposure, minimal and questionable gear. Thankfully, we brought rock shoes.

The rock pitch ended on a chossy ledge below a giant headwall, disconnected from the summit couloir. Here we made a 40' rappel to connect into the final hanging summit couloir. Three more pitches of steep snow led to the east summit. In total we did eight roped pitches. We did not go to Breitenbach's true summit, as both of us had been there before via other routes. Though I had guided the east-northeast ridge of Breitenbach in summer, we found the descent this way not straightforward as anticipated and opted to do two rappels rather than downclimb.

To my knowledge, our route has been attempted before but not completed. The Grand Chockstone Couloir has only seen one known repeat. Other potential lines exist, but timing the conditions is difficult and essential—of note, the winter of 2019 was a big one, with a cool, wet spring.

— MARC HANSELMAN

OSBORN MOUNTAIN, KILLER PILLAR AND WHERE'S THE WHISKEY?

IN JULY, OLIVER Deshler and I once again returned to our old haunts of the Clear Creek region in the northern Winds. Two years prior, we had reconned the east-southeast face of Osborn Mountain (11,811'), several hundred feet right (east) of Forlorn Pinnacle (11,660'; *AAJ 2017*), and this time, in two days, we did a pair of new routes, up the two primary crack systems in the center of the wall.

Killer Pillar (350m, 5.10) had a gorgeous dihedral on pitch five, hard fingers on pitch seven, and topped out on the easternmost pinnacle of Osborn. We rapped the route, and during the descent Oliver kicked off a TV-sized block that landed atop a traincar-size pillar, which then collapsed, leaving Oliver swinging in midair in a cloud of dust—hence the name.

Where's the Whiskey? (8 pitches, 5.11) has run-out 5.10 facing climbing on pitch three, crosses Killer Pillar on pitch four, engages an overhanging thin-hands crux on pitch five, and has a gorgeous hand crack near the top, joining Killer Pillar atop the main wall. We did not take this route up the final pinnacle, having done that the previous day. Descending to our camp by Clear Lake after a second day of semi-treacherous climbing, we'd worked up a mighty thirst—hence the name. 📷

– MARK JENKINS

WOLVERINE CIRQUE, NEW ROUTES

IN AUGUST, Jon Jugenheimer, Jared Leader, Bryan Miller, Geoff Ris, and I established several new routes in the Wolverine Cirque in the northeastern Winds: Bombs Away (IV 5.9) up the right side of the Flying Buttress, which protrudes from the north face of Saddle Mountain; A-Minor (III 5.7), starting one buttress right of Ride the Lighting on Lighting Rod Spire and continuing up the spire from the saddle to its right; and Thunder Struck (III/IV, 6 pitches, 5.9) on the northeast face of Thunderbolt Spire. [*The online report provides more detail on these routes. See AAJ 2019 for additional info on this area.*] 📷

– HEATH ROWLAND

MT. HOOKER, NORTHEAST FACE, CACHE PIRATES

SOME 15 MILES of rolling forest and open grassy meadows lead from Big Sandy Opening to the boulder-strewn base of Mt. Hooker in the Wind Rivers. In August 2018, Nick Mestre and I met up to explore some crack systems on the left side of the impressive northeast face. We camped in the boulders immediately below the intimidating wall; Nick emerged every morning from his gloomy coffin-size bivy pretending to be Gollum as I brewed him coffee and hoped for a passage-way through the granite above.

Over a couple of days we climbed three fun crack pitches and hand-drilled two anchors, but then ran out of time. We retreated below an intimidating, six-inch-wide overhanging crack, which loomed in our minds over the next year as we made plans to return and see what lay above.

We shouldered our packs in August 2019 with a number 6 Camalot and hopes of pushing the route higher. The wide crack yielded wild and sporty yet surprisingly reasonable climbing at 5.10+. Over the next few days we pushed the route out a long diagonal crack and negotiated a face section with tension traversing, hooking, and a couple of bolts placed on lead. We found incredibly clean rock, amazing features, and more quality crack systems, leading up a total of

Northeast face of Mt. Hooker with (1) Cache Pirates (IV 5.11+), ending at Der Major Ledge, and (2) Gambling in the Winds (see p.92). *Austin Siadak*

eight pitches before work required us to head home. It was now clear we had found something special, so we made the committing decision to leave ropes fixed to our high point to facilitate a return.

A couple of weeks later, we marched back in for our third visit, fueled by curiosity and an odd desire for further toil. Nick led the wandering pitch nine at a snail's pace, which is a good speed when you don't know where you're going. Established at the base of a promising corner, we were poised for a push to the wall's big traverse ledge, Der Major, which heads up right to the summit plateau. Commuting up and down our fixed ropes was becoming a chore, but we used these passages to clean and equip the route, in hopes of creating a new-age classic.

I led the pitch 10 corner onsight, pawing at grainy rock and fighting for tricky gear amid lichen and discontinuous cracks. I was forced to free climb some gear-less terrain as I fought pump and uncertainty, hoping for a path higher. After nearly 60m I arrived at a ledge near Der Major, our logical ending (for now). In disbelief, we heard friendly calls from below while descending. Not many people can sniff out 1,200' of perfectly rigged fixed line on a north wall deep in the wilderness, but our friends Greg and Hans are a special breed of hound dog. The following morning, our friends enjoyed a Mini Traxion lap for the ages before Nick and I stripped the fixed lines once and for all.

We had but one more day to free the route. Battered and sore, with little skin remaining, we went for it and eventually found ourselves lying on grassy Der Major, having established Cache Pirates (10 pitches, IV 5.11+).

– PAUL KIMBROUGH

SPEARPOINT LAKE, NEW ROUTES

HAVING BOTH BEEN born within a few days of each other in mid-August, Drew Smith and I have a tradition of celebrating together with an annual backcountry getaway. This year we decided to make it a real party and invited our good buds Jack Cramer and Rob Duncan to check out some imposing walls above Spearpoint Lake, about five miles north of the Cirque of the Towers. Only one previous party had reported climbing here (*AAJ 2017*), though we discovered hardware on an unreported route or attempt up one of the steepest and cleanest lines.

On August 8, the four of us shouldered monster packs in the Big Sandy parking lot and marched 16 miles over Washakie Pass, going cross-country the last several miles and gaining the awe-inspiring cirque via a small pass to the south. The next day we explored possibilities on the farthest right wall. After identifying two possible lines, we split into pairs and left camp before dawn on August 10.

Rob and I started with a long scramble up slabs, which led to the base of an obvious cleft on the right margin. The first roped pitch headed left across this gully midway up and gained the main wall via a sneaky broken crack. After three fun pitches on this aspect, we traversed a ledge straight left and onto a steeper face. Here we encountered the crux of the route, trending up and left for several pitches to a tiered corner system that spit us out on the boulder-strewn summit plateau. ConSpearacy Theory (1,200', IV 5.10+) is fairly sustained at 5.10.

Drew and Jack began on the left side of the face, following a prominent feature that slashed up and right. They reported deceptively tricky climbing off the snow (5.10+), followed by 800' of wandering terrain in the 5.9–5.10 range. The crux materialized in the form of an ever-shrinking rail extending out of view to the right; they named their route Tomahawk Swing (1,200', IV 5.11) for the wrecking-ball potential of a fall during this wildly exposed hand traverse. One hundred feet higher, they gained the same finishing corners and followed our chalk marks for a pitch and a half to the top.

After a rest day, which included trekking pole fishing (little success), numerous games of rock bocce (varying success), and cutting Drew a stylish mullet with a dull pair of Leatherman scissors (huge success), we deemed many of the possible lines in the cirque too wet, discontinuous, or chossy-looking. Before moving on to greener pastures, we left at first light to climb the right-hand skyline ridge of the cirque, which proved to be a highly enjoyable path to the summit plateau, only requiring the rope for a half-pitch in a flared corner: the Bandito Scramble (1,200', 5.5). ▣

— ANDY ANDERSON

Approaching the 1,200-foot wall on the right side of the Spearpoint Lake cirque. (1) Tomahawk Swing (5.11, bottom not shown). (2) ConSpearacy Theory (5.10+). *Drew Smith*

CIRQUE OF THE MOON, NEW ROUTES

BETWEEN JULY 15 and 20, Chris Natalie and I explored the seldom-visited walls of the Cirque of the Moon, south of the North Fork of the Popo Agie River, between Long Lake and Papoose Lake. We began by questing up the unclimbed north face of Flattop Spire. Five pitches up, a short blank section necessitated a bolt and two pendulums rightward. Three more moderate pitches took us to the summit plateau. It may be possible to eliminate the swings on Moss on the Moon (800', III 5.9 A1) by clipping the bolt, downclimbing, and traversing on lower holds (5.11?). Bring beaks to make it reasonable.

After a rest day, we attempted another unclimbed feature: the Wombat. Like previous parties in this cirque, however, we found the southeast-facing rock to be extremely loose. We explored two possibilities but bailed after just 300'. Finally, we set our sights on a system of wide cracks on the Green Cheese Buttress. Our ascent began on Telstar then veered left into a prominent right-facing chimney, where I was forced to tiptoe past unstable blocks. Above a tight tunnel-through, I sliced two fingers while trundling a particularly precarious bastard. Chris eagerly took over and forged a surprising enjoyable line to the top on Space Aged Cheddar (700', III 5.8).

Overall, we were delighted to discover this wild place remains pristine, but after a five-day visit we're saddened to agree with Mark Dalen, one of the first to explore the cirque's climbing (in 1978) that "all the plum lines are surely plucked in the Cirque of the Moon" (*see AAJ 2017*). ▣

— JACK CRAMER

Afternoon light on the northwest face of East Temple Peak. The left margin is obscured by Lost Temple Spire (outlined), whose right side hides the classic Southwest Arête. During their enchainment of peaks around Deep Lake, Jack Cramer and Grant Kleeves climbed this route, rappelled into the notch, then snuck across a 5.7 traverse (1) to top out on East Temple. The original Northwest Face (5.9 A3, Chouinard-Gran, 1961) followed corner systems in the center, connected by a traverse ledge. (2) Drought Year (1,000', IV 5.11+, 2019) freed the lower portion of the original route then struck off on new terrain. (3) Thieves in the Temple (700', IV 5.12a, 2019). *Scott Patterson*

EAST TEMPLE PEAK, NORTHWEST FACE, DROUGHT YEAR

"WE'D BE CLIMBING 90-degree water ice right now if it were only winter," I said to a very moist Casey Elliot as he mantled onto moss on a tiered ledge system after two pitches of dripping wet offwidth chimneys. Even in summer, the northwest face of East Temple Peak is cold and streaked with runoff. It receives direct sunlight only briefly and thus rarely dries out. For the first four pitches of our climb, we had followed the incredible splitter cracks and slab traverses of the original 1961 route (Chouinard-Gran; see *AAJ 1962*). Our research had revealed no attempts to free or even repeat this route, so to encourage future ascents and possible variations, we had decided to equip the lower route with rappel stations.

As Casey hand-drilled a bolt at the halfway ledge, the sky erupted with the wettest hail either of us had ever experienced and didn't let up for a full hour. We were slowly becoming hypothermic, so we orchestrated a complex bail. On our "rest day," we then installed three more sets of anchors, using a few bolts, plentiful Chouinard relics, and good nut placements.

Day three saw us jugging back up the first two pitches, then free climbing back to the ledge, beyond which lay the tantalizing unknown. I led a traverse to the right, following the '61 route, and found myself beneath the gaping wet maw of the route's upper chimney system. It looked unclimbable in its current condition. Casey started up a thin crack to the left of the chimney, but was forced to downclimb after half a rope length. We could have aided through the muck to get to the top, but we were committed to a free route. So, instead, we reversed the traverse pitch and then I belayed, rather flinchingly, as Casey climbed a series of hollow flakes directly above the ledge.

Atop this, we traversed right on a catwalk ledge to rejoin the original line below its crux aid pitch. This wide corner was wet as well, so after an initial 20' of offwidth, we followed an impressive splitter heading right, eventually taking us to the top—Drought Year (1,000', IV 5.11+). Our line awaits a one-day free ascent, and Casey and I agreed we'd love to return for it—if Wyoming experiences a drought year! 📄 📷 🔍

– CASSADY BINDRUP

EAST TEMPLE PEAK, THIEVES IN THE TEMPLE

WITH NO REAL objectives other than finding unscripted adventure in the mountains, Matt Threlfall and I set off for the Winds in early August. We decided to start in the Deep Lake area and upon arrival we were immediately drawn to the sheer walls of the northwest face of East Temple Peak.

After several days of scouting, we discovered a few weaknesses in the wall other than the original 1961 route (Chouinard-Gran, see AAJ 1962). We decided to try what looked like a continuous 700' hand- and finger-size crack that led to the zenith of the wall. The bottom pitch was a bit grassy in sections, and although it looked like 5.9 from the ground, it turned out to be in the 5.11 R range. The next five pitches featured incredible rock quality—pitches two, three, and four were 5.10, and the fifth pitch (5.11c) saw us up a beautiful rope-stretching dihedral with perfect stone. Pitch six (5.12a) was the crux, beginning with a boulder problem out a roof, then easing up to 5.11 jamming to the top.

After two days of working out the pitches, on August 8 we climbed the route free, alternating leads with no falls. We rapped the route to the first ledge and hid under a roof as it started raining—noticing two climbers starting work on the Chouinard-Gran route far to the left—then made our way down to camp. Thieves in the Temple (700', 6 pitches, IV 5.12a) was, to our knowledge, the first free climb up the northwest face and is named after a route at the New River Gorge, our home crag. 📷

– MATT FANNING

DEEP LAKE CIRQUE ENCHAINMENT

FIFTY-EIGHT YEARS AFTER the first ascent by Art Gran and Yvon Chouinard (AAJ 1962), two parties met below the ominous northwest face of East Temple Peak in August 2019 to vie for its first free ascent, resulting in a pair of 5.11+/12- routes. Their proud efforts were unnecessary, however, because only a week prior, Grant Kleeves and I had discovered an alternative passage up this imposing wall. And at a meager 5.7!

Our discovery arose out of a goal to enchain the seven named peaks of the Deep Lake Cirque. All had existing routes suitable to our plan, except for East Temple Peak. Its two published routes from the north were grade V and VI and out of sync with our "light and fast" aspirations. We ignored this minor detail and set out in early August with a single rope and a double dose of positivity.

The north face of Haystack Mountain (II 5.6) and north ridge of Steeple Peak (III 5.8) went smoothly, and we settled in for the night below Lost Temple Spire. At dawn we cast off up the Southwest Arête (IV 5.10b). Throughout our ascent, our eyes wandered south toward East Temple and its northwest face, which appeared to overhang for nearly its entirety. But one possibility filled our fearful hearts with hope: a long, grassy ledge that traversed the upper half of the face.

After topping out Lost Temple Spire, we did two 30m rappels into the notch that separates it from East Temple. Worry grew as we searched for an upward path through daunting overhangs. As we butt-scooted further out the narrow grassy ledge, however, the wall relented and we spotted a right-arching crack system. Although it was wet, the climbing proved moderate and protectable (5.7). After 250', we shook our heads in gleeful surprise and put the rope away. The next 4.5 miles included ample fourth-class, a few rappels, and a second bivy before we had tagged the summits on the western half of the cirque (Temple Peak, À Cheval Peak, and Schiestler Peak).

Within the tight-lipped Wyoming community it is possible, and perhaps even likely, that someone has enchained these peaks before. We do not want to take anything away from these soft-spoken hardmen, but simply to encourage more folks to take up this challenge and revel in its beauty. 📷🔍

– JACK CRAMER

Bayard Russell gains the hanging ice curtain on the crux pitch of Maidenhead (165m, M8 NEI5+), a five-pitch mixed route at Lake Willoughby, Vermont. *Peter Doucette*

MT. PISGAH (LAKE WILLOUGHBY), MAIDENHEAD

In January 2020, Bayard Russell and I put in three days of work to establish and send Maidenhead (165m, 5 pitches, M8 (M6+ R) NEI5+) above Lake Willoughby. This adventurous new route explores a less-traveled section of a famous and popular wall to create a completely independent new route, something that can be hard to find in the Northeast.

The wall held some recent snow on our first day on the route, and we climbed slowly over dark rock, unearthing useful features. The pace of ground-up new-routing in winter is something we're both familiar with, but for me, having a drill in tow induced a different headspace. The possibility of better protection on seasonally ephemeral smears is new to me and requires a lot more consideration than my normal go/no-go mental wrestling. In fact, I drilled the first bolt of my 25-year climbing career on this route—I'd had a good run.

Maidenhead starts at the base of Five Musketeers (Mailhot-Morin--Mayo-Pellet-Peloquin, 2001) and slashes to the right for its first two pitches, connecting off-balance climbing on ramps with creative trad gear and two bolts. Excepting a few ice climbing sequences, it's mostly dry tooling for the first two pitches (70m). The second pitch brings an early, heady crux, at M6+ R and marked our high point on day one.

On our second attempt, arriving at the anchors above pitch two, the stage was set for the crescendo of the climb. Pitch three served up a slabby traverse leading right to a steep headwall, where the climbing follows flat edges to gain entrance to hanging ice (M8 NEI5+). I deployed Bayard, who craftily navigated and sussed out the business. With the hardware in place, on the third day, January 24, he moved with cat-like acrobatic savvy for the send. Spectacular climbing and position make this the prize pitch.

We continued up pitch four, the Adirondack Pitch, which is no gimme, with finicky gear and thin ice over slabs and overlaps. The final stretch to the top embodies what those familiar with Lake Willoughby might call its essence: brilliant columns of blue pouring forth from welcoming cedar trees. It's an oasis above the vertical, similar to many of the top-outs at the Lake—grounding, yet endlessly memorable.

The route was satisfying and in many ways unlikely—including the fact that two fathers of young kiddos could find three days in one month to work on a new project with both conditions and families permitting. Considering that Bayard and Anne Skidmore Russell, his wife, had their second child, Whit, just a week after we finished, our timing was borderline ridiculous.

– PETER DOUCETTE

Nick Aiello-Popeo leading the second pitch—a bathook traverse to a WI6 ice smear—during the third winter ascent of the Mordor Wall (WI6 M5 A2) at Cathedral Ledge. *Matt Shove*

CATHEDRAL LEDGE, MORDOR WALL, ICE CLIMBING ASCENT

THE THIN STREAK of ice seemed to defy gravity as it clung to the gently overhanging, blank granite. As I tiptoed onto the ice sheet, with a bolt still above my waist, I bounced on my feet and tools to prove the ice was adhered to the cliff face. Lacking any excuse, it was time to launch into 90 feet of the steepest ice I'd ever tried to climb.

Established by Steve Arsenault, Scott Brim, and Joe Cote over the course of several summers in the 1960s and early '70s, Cathedral Ledge's Mordor Wall (originally 5.9 A4) had a fearsome reputation for scary aid. The first winter ascent in 1979 required three days of effort by Bryan Becker and Alain Comeau. A second winter ascent of the route, 17 years later, still relied on extensive aid.

When a massive curtain of ice formed on the upper Mordor Wall in early 2019—bigger than anyone had ever seen before—Justin Guarino and I dreamed of doing the third winter ascent of this route as a wildly steep ice line. With a busy guiding schedule and an impending heat wave, I decided to fix the first A2 pitch solo by headlamp.

A few days later, Justin and I jugged the fixed line at first light. After bathooking about 75 percent of the way across the second-pitch traverse (marveling at the many "chicken bolts" that had sprouted since Arsenault's first ascent), I put on crampons and stepped down onto the ice, bounce-testing it with protection close by. I then cast off and committed to the thin smear, but after 45' of overhanging ice with no pro, I started to wonder if a fall from any higher would result in hitting the ground 125' below. Fighting back panic, I found an ancient bashie and clipped it to the rope, optimistically hoping the ice encrusting it would make it a viable piece of pro. My spirit was renewed when I found an old bolt in verglas, just below the small ice roof that would be the crux of the 200' pitch.

Higher, the equally long third pitch featured acrobatic M5 out the six-foot Mordor Roof to an upper ice curtain. We followed this straight up at WI5+, making a pleasant 195' final pitch. [*Editor's Note: The third winter ascent of the Mordor Wall (3 pitches, 560') was graded WI6 M5 A2. Both previous winter ascents relied mostly on aid with short bits of ice climbing.*] 📷

— NICK AIELLO-POPEO

Jackson Marvell leading an AI6 pitch on the first ice hose of Ruth Gorge Grinder (5,000', AI6+ M7 A1) on the east face of Mt. Dickey. *Alan Rousseau*

RUTH GORGE GRINDER
A NEW ROUTE UP THE EAST FACE OF MT. DICKEY

BY ALAN ROUSSEAU

EVERY ALPINIST HAS one peak or a mountain feature they think about more than any other. The feature acts as a compass, providing direction and motivation for one's climbing. For the past decade, my direction has come largely from the east face of Mt. Dickey (9,545') and the ephemeral white lines that streak down it.

The plan to actually climb them was hatched at a sponsor booth and over a pint at the Bozeman Ice Festival. After I handed out the last set of demo tools for the night, Jackson Marvell asked, "So, are we climbing in Alaska this year?"

A few minutes later, a gentleman's agreement had been made to fly to Anchorage on April 1. Having never roped up together before, we made a point to climb once a week back home in Utah before we left. Our days ranged from bolting new lines on local crags to big linkups, and our confidence in one another grew quickly.

Beeeeep, beep, beep. The alarm on April 3 came much too soon, as it usually does in the cold Alaskan night. Without much delay, we donned our prepacked bags and skinned across the glacier to the base of Dickey's incomparable east wall, our sights set on Blood From the Stone (5,000', WI6+ X M7+ A1, Easton-Steck, *AAJ 2003*).

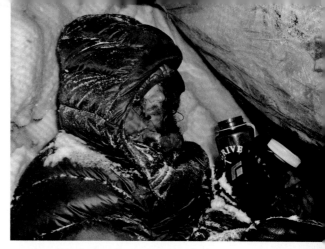

Without a cloud in the sky, we started up steepening snow slopes that led to rock. Jackson led three pitches of engaging and steep mixed climbing (M5 R, M6+, M7), which brought us to a small snowfield where the really sustained stretch of the east face begins.

Our plan was to fix 400' above and return to a bivy site on the snowfield, but a pitch and a half up it became obvious to me there was not enough ice on the route to safely continue. After looking up at a large portion of dry, unprotectable rock, I made the decision to descend back to our bivouac.

If we didn't feel defeated enough in that moment, as we rappelled back to the bivy, we saw two ravens fervently tearing through Jackson's bag of stashed food. As I approached them, they threw what was left of the 6,000 calories off the ledge and down to the base of the wall, so they could finish it in peace. The mood was somber as we finished chopping out the bivy ledge and started to talk about our next play.

From the lower glacier, we had noticed a large unclimbed cleft to the left of the Wine Bottle (Bonapace-Orgler, 1988), and it seemed we could access this by angling up to climber's right from the snowfield. After some quick math, we figured we had enough food for two more days at 1,500 calories a person, and we decided to quest off the next morning and see if we could find more ice in this unknown system.

Thankful for the wall's eastern exposure, we were greeted by the day's first rays of sun and were able to start out with dry kit. As we left the bivy, the climbing was surprisingly

[Top] Jackson Marvell enduring a spindrift-blasted bivouac partway up Ruth Gorge Grinder. "At 4 a.m., we gave up the illusion that sleep was possible and started melting water." *Alan Rousseau* [Bottom] The 5,000-foot east face of Mt. Dickey, showing (1) Blood From the Stone (Easton-Steck, 2002) and (2) Ruth Gorge Grinder (Marvell-Rousseau, 2019), with bivouacs marked. The prominent pillar to the right is the line of the Wine Bottle (Bonapace-Orgler, 1988), and the less distinct pillars to the left were climbed by Tomas Gross and Vera Komarkova in 1977. *Jackson Marvell*

The upper headwall slot had 340 meters of ice, rarely over a meter wide. *Alan Rousseau*

good, exceptional even. Shoulder-wide strips of ice with engaging mixed climbing to M6+ defined the first few rope lengths. This led us to a pendulum point that would hopefully allow us to reach the main cleft. After swinging across the face, I was relieved to stretch out and swing into supportable névé.

The chimneys above were filled with near-perfect névé—albeit really steep! Jackson led the next four pitches: 60m stretchers of AI5 to AI6+. We climbed these pitches fast, trying to beat the fading light and ominous cloud layers that had begun to spill into the gorge.

We arrived at a small area of 50° snow and decided to chop another ledge for our second night on the face. We received a forecast for four inches of snow and 0°F temps overnight, and with 2,000' of near vertical terrain overhead, we knew it would be a bivy to remember. We only had a tarp and light summer sleeping bags for shelter, so we dug in as much as we could and got ready for a cold, snowy night.

Around midnight the heavy spindrift blasts began. I assumed the position of a boxer on the defense, holding mitten-clad hands over my face so the spindrift could only land body blows. Jackson sat up with his hood cinched tight to keep the snow from going down his neck. At 4 a.m., we gave up the illusion that sleep was possible and started melting water, followed by coffee. Around 5:30 we could see a gap in the cloud layers and it looked like the weather was breaking.

By seven, after Jackson literally dumped snow out of his sleeping bag, we were bathing in sun, although the warmth came at a price—the rock rapidly shed any remaining snow clinging to the coarse granite. Snow moved over and past us like a river, and our nervous giggling was occasionally silenced as big air blasts enveloped our small perch.

Eventually the face finished shedding and we prepared to head into the final headwall. Dreamy yet almost unfathomably steep, the 340m ice-choked tube that split the headwall was rarely more than a meter wide, never easier than AI5, and at times sustained at 10° past vertical. As each pitch ended and I looked up at another perfect strip of ice above, I began to wonder if I would ever climb a better alpine route.

Soon the headwall was below us, but a new challenge awaited. We spent hours wallowing over the deceptively steep upper slopes of the mountain, managing run-out moderate mixed climbing through shale bands. In two long simul blocks, often with no real protection clipped, we finally managed to top out the east face of the mountain. I was elated to walk on the moderate, non-consequential glacial slopes for the final hundred vertical feet to the summit: Ruth Gorge Grinder (5,000', AI6+ M7 A1).

We had little time to celebrate, however, since it was already 6 p.m. and we hoped to arrive in camp before dark. Fortunately, we had excellent snow conditions and a bit of gas left in the tank. We cruised down the west face and through 747 Pass, and strolled back to camp in under 3.5 hours. In the last moments of twilight, we ripped open the food bins and feasted like pigs at the trough. 📷

MT. BRADLEY ATTEMPT: *After climbing the route described above and repeating the Trailer Park (Cordes-DeCapio, 2000) on "London Tower" to the summit ridge, Marvell and Rousseau attempted a new route on the north face of Mt. Bradley. Approximately 3,000' up their route, Rousseau was hit in the face by a piece of ice, badly injuring his left eye, and the two retreated.*

REVEALED!
FIVE NEW ROUTES ABOVE THE REVELATION GLACIER

BY JANEZ SVOLJŠAK, *SLOVENIA*

OUR TABLE FOOTBALL skills had started to improve when we finally heard "weather is good for flying, get ready." It was mid-March, and Miha Zupin and I enjoyed the beautiful views flying into the Alaska Range, passing Denali, the Kichatna Spires, and more. Our first stop was the Fish Glacier, where a Dutch team exited the plane. There was almost a meter of powder on the glacier, and as we took off again and flew over to the Revelation Glacier, we worried about conditions there. However, we were surprised to find no new snow on our glacier, and we happily began to prepare base camp.

Strong winds kept us in camp the next day, digging snow out of our kitchen and improving the wall around the tent. The wind was about the same next morning, but we decided to try the west face of Pyramid Peak anyway. We were shut down on the first pitch due to windblown snow in a corner, but from there we saw a nice ridgeline to the south, on the previously unclimbed north summit of the Four Horsemen (ca 8,450'). We immediately switched plans.

Our route followed a gully to a col, and from there we followed the east ridge. The first technical pitch in the gully was a bouldery M6 with some loose blocks. The next pitches were easier, climbing left and right to find the way to the col. Traversing the ridge was demanding due to the strong winds, which occasionally forced us to crawl on our knees. We did one short rappel from the crest of the ridge and then climbed to the summit.

We descended south to reach the couloir between the summit and the main Four Horsemen summit and headed down to the glacier from there. We were happy with the climb and thinking about dinner, but the base camp reality was not what we had hoped—collapsed snow walls and a misshapen tent covered with snow. We worked late into the night and the entire next day to dig out, and luckily our tent poles were just bent not broken. A day later we attempted a chimney system on the east face of Golgotha, but after nine pitches, in worsening conditions, we decided to go down. Spindrift made the descent demanding.

We rested for three days and then went back to Golgotha. An easier line on the right side of the east face had attracted our attention. The first half was more "walking" than climb-

[Top] **Northwest face of Apocalypse North (8,985')** showing the line of the Slovenian Route (1,300m, AI4+ R M6 85'). This was the first ascent of the peak, a distinct summit to the north of Apocalypse (9,345'). [Bottom] **Northeast face of Seraph (8,540')**, showing the line of the Last Supper for Snow Strugglers (700m, M7 80'). The climbers continued to Peak 8,650' (behind), which may have been unclimbed before. *Janez Svoljšak (both photos)*

ing, but the upper part was steeper, with perfect snow conditions. We belayed for three pitches. Clear weather at the top offered us an endless view to all directions. We downclimbed the first ascent route (*AAJ 2013*), returning to the base of the east face by a snow couloir.

After two rest days, we went to an unnamed peak above the cirque at the head of the Revelation Glacier, between Golgotha and Hydra. The 700m northeast face, which we named the Wailing Wall, had looked smaller from base camp. We followed a corner with perfect snow and ice conditions, climbing unroped for the first 350m. The crux was a corner filled with thin ice. The route then followed ice smears through a big chimney under a chockstone with an overhanging exit. From there we followed the ridge and climbed the summit block. The descent continued along the ridge and dropped to a gully, right of our route, with some downclimbing and rappelling to reach the glacier.

The weather forecast was good, so after a rest day we went down the glacier to climb a line we had checked out a few days before: a gully on the northwest face of unclimbed Apocalypse North. After 300m up to 80°, we reached a vertical, dry, and loose corner, which we bypassed to the left. The first pitch was thin ice and hard to protect. The next pitches had perfect conditions up to 85° with one pitch of M6. We then regained the main gully and followed it for 300m. We did not know what to expect in the upper part because it previously had been obscured by clouds. The climbing was sketchy, with thin ice and unconsolidated snow over rock, but not too difficult. We found an easy passage through the final rock band and then followed the ridge to the top.

We did not want to descend our route due to the steep and unconsolidated snow and hard-to-protect rock. We tried to follow the ridgeline to the northeast, but cornices made it impossible to reach a col from which we could descend to the Revelation Glacier. Instead we downclimbed and rappeled to the east and reached an unnamed glacier. We did not know if it was possible to return to the Revelation Glacier from here so we were very happy when we saw a snow gully leading to a col from which we knew we could descend. The next few days were colder and windier, so three rest days felt good.

Before we flew out, we decided to try a line on the northeast face of Seraph. Our line is an obvious gully left of the 2018 French route (*AAJ 2019*). The first 300m were easier than they looked, until we reached a chockstone and steep chimney where we started to belay. It was not easy to clear the snow, and an overhanging exit did not make it any easier, but the climbing was enjoyable for the second. The next pitch was easier with a steep, bouldery crux. Now we were standing below a chimney that we hadn't seen from the ground. The first part was narrow with ice, sometimes with barely enough room to swing an axe. The exit was, again, blown with snow, worse than the first pitch, and it took me a while to remove all the snow. The crux was thin ice followed by an overhang, and my competition experience proved very useful here. [*The author was a frequent finalist in ice climbing World Cups until 2017, when he began focusing on alpine routes.*] After an easier pitch we coiled the rope and continued to the top of Seraph. Thinking this was just a false summit, we continued southwest to a higher peak (8,650') and later learned we may have made its first ascent. Our descent followed the ridge to the east and then to a gully, which led us back to the base of the route.

SUMMARY: *First ascent of unclimbed north summit of the Four Horseman (ca 8,450') via the east ridge (600m, M6 70° A1). Father (900m, AI5 70°) on the east face of Golgotha (8,940'). First ascent of Wailing Wall (ca 8,040') via Secret (750m, AI6). First ascent of Apocalypse North (8,985') via the Slovenian Route (1,300m, AI4+ R M6 85°). The Last Supper for Snow Strugglers (700m, M7 80°) on the northeast face of Seraph (8,540') and possible first ascent of Peak 8,650'.* 📷 🔍

Tragically, a few months after this expedition, Janez Svoljšak died at base camp from unknown causes after descending from an attempt on Tahu Rutum in Pakistan. He was 25 years old.

Janez Svoljšak climbing an aesthetic ice pitch on Secret (750m, AI6), during the first ascent of a formation the climbers named the Wailing Wall. *Miha Zupin*

NEACOLA MOUNTAINS

THE CITADEL, NORTHWEST FACE, AGENT OF CHAOS

ON MARCH 29, Ryan Driscoll and I flew into the Neacola Mountains with a sustained high-pressure system in place. As soon as we landed, we went on a recon ski and decided the most inviting objective was an unfinished line on the Citadel (8,305'), attempted by a team in 2016 (*see AAJ 2017*). They had reported good climbing but challenging snow conditions on a line they called the Sliver, an obvious couloir on the right side of the northwest buttress. [*Editor's note: The 2016 party ascended about 3,000' up the couloir, reaching the corniced ridgeline atop the buttress before retreating below the upper headwall.*]

The northwest face of the Citadel, showing the line of Agent of Chaos (3,500', V M5+ AI4 A0). This line was attempted in 2016 by David Fay, Craig Muderlak, and Drew Thayer, who reached the ridgeline adjacent to the big rock tower, calling their line the Sliver. A direct route up the rock tower, the northwest buttress, was attempted in 2015 by Jon Bracey and Matt Helliker. *Elliot Gaddy*

Ryan had only been in Alaska for 24 hours and was feeling tired from travel, so we decided to get a late start, leaving camp around 10 the next morning. After a two-mile ski from base camp, we tied in and started climbing the initial snow on the Citadel. Four pitches of steep, snowy simul-climbing with occasional rock gear put us at the base of the deep couloir.

The day had warmed by this point, and spindrift avalanches were rather continuous. We found harder mixed climbing than the initial attempt reported, potentially due to lower snow levels, which made for some difficult climbing through several rock steps. Ryan had to pendulum out of one crack system to gain a snow ramp, but I was able to follow the pitch cleanly. The hardest mixed climbing we encountered was a pitch of M5+, and we climbed some pitches of water ice that would be classic at any crag.

At the top of the couloir, as the sun was setting and the winds were picking up, we were met with a double-corniced ridgeline that we had to traverse to gain the buttress above. Here we found good anchors for a bivy and set up our tent on a small snow ledge we stamped out, but we stayed tied in while sleeping.

The next morning, we did one 70' rap to access a rightward traverse on snow to the base of an upper couloir. Three pitches of ice and mixed climbing and an interesting traverse under a large cornice put us on the snowy summit cone, and we walked up to the top.

We descended the southeast ridge to a glacier that led down to the north fork of the Pitchfork Glacier, then walked back to our skis and continued to camp. Our most pressing concern on the trip back up-glacier was the state of our camp, as our cached skis and poles had been chewed by a wolverine. We were relieved to see that, despite many tracks pacing around our camp, our post-climb carnitas had been spared. We called our route Agent of Chaos (3,500', V M5+ AI4 A0). ▣

– ELLIOT GADDY

MT. TITANIC, NORTH RIDGE; TANTALUS (PEAK 8,910'), SOUTH COULOIR

AFTER SIX DAYS of sitting out bad weather and enjoying the true Alaskan lifestyle in Talkeetna, Bas Visscher and I finally got flown into the Revelation Mountains in mid-March. To our surprise, we stepped off the plane and onto the Fish Glacier in waist-deep snow. When the sound of the engine disappeared and the last snow crystals whirled down, we were surrounded by a deep and prevailing silence.

The first week brought bad weather with more fresh snow. We spent time excavating a snow cave and did a lot of reading. Occasionally fragments of the mountains surrounding us loomed out of the colorless fog. The amount of snow made us drop our initial plan of a strategic base camp on a pass to the north. Although we made numerous exploratory ski trips to this pass, our hard-fought tracks were erased every single night.

Finally a large high-pressure system came in. With the first blue skies and rays of sunlight, we skied over the pass to the north side of Jezebel (9,620'). We were amazed to see this side of the mountain was extremely dry and the glacier was icy, a huge contrast with the deep snow on the east side of the mountain. After a challenging day of skiing with heavy backpacks, we finally arrived underneath our main goal, the north face of Mt. Titanic (ca 9,350'). [*Editor's note: Titanic has only two previously recorded ascents: the first ascent of the peak via the east face (Beckey-Hogan-McCarty-Tillery, 1981; see AAJ 1983), and the west face (Helander-Zimmerman, 2014; see AAJ 2015).*] We immediately noticed the dry conditions on the face, and that night we heard the ominous thunder of a snow avalanche crashing down the only plausible line on the face.

Worried about the signals the mountain was giving us, we decided to try Titanic's unclimbed north ridge instead. At first we expected an easy climb, but arriving at the base of the ridge at dawn, a sentence from an expedition report immediately crossed my mind: "In Alaska everything is bigger than it seems." We climbed on the ridge as much as possible, but sometimes we were forced to climb the eastern flank to pass deep notches in the ridge. Straightforward climbing alter-

Niek de Jonge heading up Mt. Titanic during the first ascent of the north ridge. *Bas Visscher*

nated with challenging and demanding pitches on bad snow and high-quality granite. The money pitch was a beautiful corner leading up to a squeeze chimney surpassing a gigantic chockstone. After the knife-edge summit ridge, we arrived on top of Titanic, enjoying the arctic palette of colors and a stunning view of the Alaska Range (1,130m, M5 60˚).

After downclimbing the upper ridge and descending the east face to the glacier, our return trip to base camp was long and heavy. Whiteouts, unexpected slides, and constantly changing snow conditions made skiing a hellish yet often hilarious undertaking.

The high-pressure system was holding, so we prepared for another attempt, this time on the unclimbed northwest face of Peak 8,910'. [*Editor's note: The first ascent of Peak 8,910' was made via a col on the northeast side leading to the east ridge (III 5.4, Funsten-Gonzales-Raynor; see AAJ 1995.*] Unfortunately, we quickly climbed into a section of bare granite slabs, without ice or protection. From our high point we caught a tantalizing glimpse of a perfect line through the face—close but unreachable.

[Top] The south face of Tantalus (Peak 8,910'). The south couloir, climbed in 2019, splits the rock face just down and left of the main summit. The first ascent was by the east ridge (right), reached from the far side. [Bottom] Bas Visscher on his way to the summit of Mt. Titanic (ca 9,300') during the first ascent of the peak's north ridge. The northwest face of Tantalus (Peak 8,910'), briefly attempted by the 2019 team, is in the background. *Niek de Jonge (both)*

We tried a nice ridge to an unclimbed subpeak of the Obelisk, but this attempt was also aborted quickly, mainly due to extremely bad snow. Back in camp, we hid in our sleeping bags and behind our e-readers. I tried to put our failed attempts into perspective. An appropriate quote from Ernest Hemingway caught my attention: "The ultimate value of our lives is decided not by how we win but by how we lose."

Now a strong low-pressure system was building over the Gulf of Alaska. On the last beautiful day in the range, we left base camp in a wind chill of -22°C. Our objective was the south couloir of Peak 8,910'. The biting cold soon gave way to burning sun as we climbed the beautiful couloir, flanked by steep, red granite walls. The couloir was interrupted in two places by steep sections without snow, where we enjoyed short sections of technical climbing. Unfortunately, the final ridge consisted of bizarre unconsolidated snow, and we struggled to find any holds on the smooth granite slabs beneath. Our hard work eventually paid off and we stood on the summit of Peak 8,910' (800m, M4 60˚). We downclimbed and rappelled our line.

A beautiful mountain in a stunning mountain range deserves a name—we would like to propose Tantalus, a figure from Greek mythology that symbolizes something that's highly desirable but just out of reach. 📷 🔍

– NIEK DE JONGE, *NETHERLANDS*

YENTNA GLACIER, THREE FIRST ASCENTS

FROM JUNE 4–14, our group, which included Elliot Gaddy, James Kesterson, Paul Muscat, Matt Sanborn, Glenn Wilson, and me, climbed four peaks on the upper west lobe of the Yentna Glacier in Denali National Park. Three of them are believed to be first ascents.

We had planned on climbing in the Wrangell Mountains, but, just as we like it, plans changed at the last minute. Paul Roderick flew us from Talkeetna to our 7,700-foot base camp on the glacier northeast of Mt. Russell (11,670'). This was the popular landing zone for climbers attempting Mt. Russell before conditions changed on the north ridge. [*Editor's note: Formerly the standard*

Glenn Wilson, Paul Muscat, Elliot Gaddy, James Kesterson, and Matt Sanborn climbing Terrapin Peak (9,300'+), with the mountain they called Wandering Spirit Peak (9,200'+) in the background. *Joe Stock*

route up the peak, the north ridge has in recent years seen large crevasses open up, making the route more difficult. It seems the most popular way up the peak likely will become the recently climbed south ridge (Drummond-Wilkinson, 2017; see AAJ 2018), accessed via the east fork of the Dall Glacier.]

Our camp was surrounded by several 8,000' to 10,000' peaks with no record of ascents. We climbed four of the peaks to the north and west of our camp, which we named Wandering Spirit Peak (9,200'+), the three summits of The Boys (9,200'+), Terrapin Peak (9,300'+), and Our Man Steve (10,150'). We initially thought all four to be unclimbed, but after more research it was discovered that Our Man Steve, which is a satellite peak of Mt. Russell along its northeast ridge, had been climbed at least two times (both unreported) by parties climbing Russell. [*Editor's note: Peter Brown, John Hauck, Dick Jablonowski, Thomas Kensler, and Dan Osborne likely made this peak's first ascent en route to the first ascent of Russell's northeast ridge in 1972 (see AAJ 1973).*]

We also attempted two summits on the south side of the glacier. The September 2019 issue of *The Scree* from the Mountaineering Club of Alaska has a more detailed account of our climbs. 📷 🔍

– JOE STOCK

DALL GLACIER AREA, MT. KATHERINE, FIRST ASCENT

IN AN ERA of heightened climbing and skiing popularity, there are still many less-explored corners of the Alaska Range. Exploration can even come at moderate difficulties, which is exactly what Thomas Eaves and I found during our mid-May expedition.

The Dall Glacier is south of Mt. Russell (11,670'), ultimately flowing into the Yentna River at its terminus. We flew onto the glacier on May 16 and immediately began scouting. Acting as guide, I recommended an unnamed and likely unclimbed peak east of the Dall Glacier, located across a shallow divide and in the Yentna Glacier drainage (62°44'49"N, 151°47'04"W), that offered an amicable southwest ridge rising above a serac-laden west face. We made our climb from May 19 to May 20, after waiting a few days to let a snow-shedding cycle run its course.

Thomas Eaves looking east from the summit of Mt. Katherine (ca 8,300'). Eaves and Zach Lovell climbed at night for good conditions and summited under a bright moon. *Zach Lovell*

Given warm temperatures, we departed in the evening and used skis to ascend low-angle glacial ramps toward the southwest ridge. After 4.5 miles and 1,900' of elevation gain, we reached our proposed line, cached our skis, and donned crampons. For 2,300 vertical feet we were gifted with classic and aesthetic Alaskan ridge climbing, with snow/névé and rock up to 60°. As we neared the end of the ridge, a full moon emerged, casting a surreal glow upon the mountain's final tower. Our summit views were some of the most unique I've experienced, with the Yentna River, Mt. Russell, Mt. Foraker, and Denali all joining us in a moonlit dance party.

Moon Walk (III 60° snow) was completed in 14 hours camp to camp, including a total of 10.5 miles of travel and 4,200' of elevation gain/loss. Thomas dubbed the peak Mt. Katherine (ca 8,300') for his wife. There have been very few recorded trips to the Dall Glacier—there is much left to be explored.

– ZACH LOVELL

DENALI, WEST BUTTRESS SPEED RECORD

KARL EGLOFF (ECUADOR) broke the speed record for the West Buttress of Denali on June 20, running and climbing from Kahiltna base camp to the 20,310' summit in 7 hours 40 minutes. His round trip from base camp was 11 hours 44 minutes. Both marks were faster than the previous records, set by Catalan legend Kilian Jornet (*AAJ 2015*); Egloff's ascent time was more than two hours faster.

Unlike Jornet, who used skis on much of the route, Egloff traveled on snowshoes or foot. He cached supplies and clothing along the route and was supported by a friend. The Ecuadorian, who also holds speed records on Kilimanjaro and Aconcagua, described his Denali climb in episode 20 of the AAJ's Cutting Edge podcast.

– DOUGALD MACDONALD

DENALI, RIDGE OF NO RETURN, HOT CARS AND FAST WOMEN

IN WHAT IS becoming an annual tradition, Michael Gardner and I showed up in Alaska in the final hours of a massive high-pressure system. A few hours after flying into the west fork of the Ruth Glacier, we found ourselves partway up the north buttress of the Rooster Comb (*AAJ 1982*) under descending clouds. We bailed as the first snowflakes began to fall.

Four days later, after several feet of new snow, we took advantage of a short break in the storm to investigate a pyramid-like feature on the southeast face of the Ridge of No Return, which I scoped several years earlier. [*Editor's note: The Ridge of No Return extends generally southeast from Point 15,000' on Denali's South Buttress down to the west fork of the Ruth Glacier. It was first climbed by Italian Renato Casarotto, solo, in 1984.*] As we had hoped, the waist-deep wallowing of the snow cone gave way to firm névé as the angle steepened. After several hundred feet of snow, we roped up for a pitch of thin ice and a scary traverse on faceted snow to the base of the main weakness.

What followed was 200m of sustained mixed climbing up to M6+ on perfect rock—an excellent treat after all the sketchy snow! Several rope lengths of easy snow, a fully buried M5 pitch on which Michael did a great job of burrowing, and a few final rope lengths of attention-grabbing steep facets brought us to an arbitrary high point along the Ridge of No Return. At this point it began snowing. We chugged the rest of our water and started rappelling into the whiteout. We named our route Hot Cars and Fast Women (850m, M6+), after our friend Dominic Toretto from the movie *The Fast and the Furious*, who has inspired us for many years.

Aside from guided ascents of Denali's West Buttress, our only successful climb in the next five weeks of unsettled weather was a repeat of the Infinite Spur on Sultana (a.k.a. Mt. Foraker). We carried skis up the route, making the round-trip from base camp in 48 hours. The Spur is well suited for this style of "ski alpinism," as it is moderate enough to climb in ski boots and skiing makes the descent vastly easier, as well as eliminates the need for caches and return trips along the approach. 🔘

– SAM HENNESSEY

MT. BARRILL, EAST FACE, KING COBRA

DAN JOLL, KIM Ladiges, John Price, and I came to Alaska at the beginning of June for the Kichatna Spires, lured by a dream of El Capitan–size walls set on remote glaciers. But the Kichatnas' reputation for abysmal weather held true. After four days of sitting in Talkeetna, our patience ran dry and we hatched a new plan.

An hour later, Paul Roderick of Talkeetna Air Taxi was flying us into the Ruth Gorge. Mt. Barrill's east face and the famed Cobra Pillar (Donini-Tackle, *AAJ 1992*) appeared in view—almost 1,000m of steep, featured granite, capped with snow. The weather was perfect, so we went straight to work on a new line up the face right of Cobra Pillar. However, our attempt ended prematurely when we encountered poor rock and realized we were dangerously exposed to sluff avalanches from the top of the mountain—we had a frightening near miss.

After four days of effort, it was back to the drawing board. Between servings of bacon grease and whipped-cream coffee at camp, it became apparent the only sliver of the mountain relatively safe from avalanches was the central prow, climbed by the classic Cobra Pillar. We started up again and soon discovered a multitude of fixed gear and fun 5.10 climbing, confirming we had started on the Cobra. Determined to climb quality virgin terrain, we branched out to the right after three pitches. Kim had spied a thin face climbing traverse to access a new crack system, and from a strenuous kneebar he laboriously hand-drilled a bolt and was able to crimp his way across the steep wall.

Upon reaching the new system, Kim looked upward and discovered splitter five- and six-

Kim Ladiges jams a clean splitter during the first attempt on the east face of Mt. Barrill. *John Price*

inch cracks rocketing straight up the proudest part of the prow. He led mega pitches of glorious heel-toes and butterfly jams, as good as anything in Tasmania. Adding to the delight, Kim and John discovered a set of ledges where we could set up a comfortable camp, 350m up the wall.

After a day of hauling loads, a sickness that had been nagging John suddenly worsened. Fortunately, our five ropes strung together just reached the glacier, and Kim and Dan spent an exhausting night helping John evacuate. The next day I took over the lead and pushed the ropes higher, cleaning blocks and loose gravel from the cracks. The thought that this might become a real classic spurred us on—we genuinely thought this route contained some of the best alpine rock climbing we'd ever done, with sustained pitches of 5.10 and 5.11 cracks.

Ropes fixed high, it was time for a push to the summit. After seven new pitches, we rejoined the Cobra Pillar route. Above its sensational arching splitter, we stripped down into alpine mode and began simul-climbing. However, as Kim led through increasingly wet cracks, drenched by melt from the summit's heavy snowpack, our worst fears were confirmed: We were too early in the season to safely reach the summit. We were disappointed but still happy with our beautiful all-free route: King Cobra (550m, 5.11). 📄 📷 🔍

– ALASTAIR MCDOWELL, *NEW ZEALAND*

CHUGACH MOUNTAINS

BASHFUL PEAK, FIRST SKI DESCENT

At 8,005', Bashful Peak is the tallest peak in Chugach State Park and has long been sought as a ski descent. The northwest face rises steeply for more than 4,000' from the basin below the peak and was first climbed in July 1965 by Art Davidson and Hisazumi Nakamura.

In mid-April, the western Chugach received a series of storms over a six-day period that dropped four inches of water, resulting in an enormous snow load. Our hopes were that the week of high pressure that followed would allow for reasonable stability. Early on the morning of April 28, my brother-in-law Samuel Holmes Johnson and I began hiking from the East Fork Eklutna River Trailhead, after driving the 10.5 miles of dirt road around the reservoir on a borrowed side-by-side vehicle. After 2,500' of heavy alders and devil's club, we arrived in the basin below the face. Once in the main couloir, we switched to crampons. A hanging ramp, a snowfield, and another ramp took us to the summit snowfield. By this time we were wallowing, but, amazingly, stability was very good.

We hit the ridge just to climber's left of the rocky summit nipple, where we left our skis and scrambled the remaining 15 vertical feet to the tippy top. After a few photos, we skied the line, enjoying outstanding deep powder conditions, with massive sloughing being the only real detractor. 🖿 ⊡

– RYAN HOKANSON

PEAK 8,010', FIRST ASCENT AND SKI DESCENT

PEAK 8,010' IS LOCATED on the eastern shore of the Copper River, upstream of the Bremner River and within Wrangell-St. Elias National Park. Its southwestern flank drops from the summit at 8,010' to the Copper River, at about 300', in a single fall line, over less than two miles of horizontal distance. As one of the taller peaks in the region, Peak 8,010' is visible from many summits around the Thompson Pass area. Some heli-ski operators have informally given it the name Spirit Peak, not to be confused with Spirit Mountain, 12 miles to the north.

I am unaware of any previous ascents of 8,010', though several people have tried it, including me. [*Editor's note: On Bivouac.com, this mountain is called Dewey Peak, though it's unknown who gave it this name. It was one of the most prominent unclimbed summits in the state.*] There is an old tale of Chet Simmons landing Doug Coombs somewhere on Peak 8,010' back in the early days of Thompson Pass heli-skiing, but details are sparse. There are also rumors of a popular air taxi operator landing in the high glaciated basin to the east of 8,010 and skiing something on the eastern aspect; however, it's unknown if this party summited.

On March 5, Tobey Carman, Jon Cobb, Tim Stephens, and I launched on snowmachines down the Copper River from the town of Chitina, arriving at the base of Peak 8,010' that evening. After camping on the river ice, we began skinning up a large alluvial fan draining the northwest aspect. Amazingly, we were able to skin through 3,500' of alders without touching a single bush.

Some roped route-finding through crevasses led us to the bergschrund, where Jon elected to stay. Tim, Tobey, and I cramponed up through worsening surface conditions, staying to climber's right of a sweeping rock band and finally breaking through it 500' from the top. We changed over on top under clear, calm skies, and skied our ascent route, meeting Jon midway down. After 7,700' of skiing, we reached the river and our camp, where we spent another night and then motored back to the truck without incident.

– RYAN HOKANSON

KLUTINA PEAK ASCENT AND SKI DESCENT: *On March 31, near Thompson Pass, Ryan Hokanson and Trevor Grams made the possible first ascent and descent of Klutina Peak (ca 8,080') via its northwest face. This peak is off the toe of the Klutina Glacier about 3.2 miles northeast of Mt. Schrader (ca 7,400').*

The northwest face of Peak 8,010', above the Copper River. The skiers followed the obvious drainage into a glaciated basin, then proceeded up and right under a sweeping rock band, taking the first major break directly to the summit. They skied down their line of ascent. *Ryan Hokanson*

"Humpback Peak" from the northwest. The Humpback Arête (III 5.9) followed the right skyline, then continued up the long upper ridge (hidden) to the top. Stoned Virgins (III 5.10d) takes a steeper line to the right. *Derek Field*

TAKU RANGE, VARIOUS ASCENTS

GISELLE FIELD, JOEY Jarrell, Dave Spies, and I used an AAC Live Your Dream Grant to support an expedition to the Juneau Icefield. On July 14, after two days in Juneau, we were flown to the west side of the Taku Range by Northstar Trekking Helicopters. The four of us dug out a fine base camp in the cirque between Taku Towers and Emperor Peak where we spent the following seven days in an omnipresent mist, mostly playing board games, reading books, and tending to our ever-melting campsites.

Periodically, we ventured out into the fog to climb. Giselle and I first climbed the northernmost and smallest summit of the Dukes massif. This 500-foot tower of psychedelic-looking migmatite was attempted in 2014 by John Kelley, who thought it to be unclimbed. Our route followed a series of corners on the southwest face: Candy Cornwall (II 5.9). We found no evidence of prior ascent on the pointy top and named it the Duchess (ca 6,250').

Giselle and I also completed the west arête of the unnamed high point between the Taku Towers and Cathedral Peak. We referred to this as Humpback Peak. After climbing the steeper lower arête via four pitches (up to 5.9), we simul-climbed and belayed short pitches along the upper ridge, which was wonderfully narrow: Humpback Arête (III 5.9).

The next day it was raining lightly, so Giselle and I chose an easy looking line and were rewarded with one of the most spectacular scrambles of our lives: the West Arête (1,000', III 5.7 50°) of the north summit of Cathedral Peak. A pencil-thin ribbon of gneiss, sculpted perfectly on both sides by the active glacier, led to the peak's dwindling icecap and the top.

On July 21, the last day of our trip, good weather finally arrived. Giselle and I attempted the steep west pillar of the domelike formation immediately south of South Taku Tower but retreated after four pitches, having run into munge cracks and run-out slabs. When we returned to base camp, around midnight, we learned that Dave and Joey had succeeded on their route Stoned Virgins (III 5.10d), an impressive line that tackles thin cracks on the steep wall to the right of Humpback Arête. They continued along the upper ridge to tag the top. 📄 📷

– DEREK FIELD, *CANADA*

STIKINE ICECAP, HYDER PEAK AND OTHER SUMMITS

MARK ROBSON AND I have made several trips to the Coast Mountains of British Columbia and were keen to visit the Stikine Icecap, which straddles the USA-Canada border farther north. Our primary aim was the second ascent of Oasis Peak (7,925', *see AAJ 2001*) via a new route from the north. The plan was to visit in early May, hoping to find good snow, ice, and mixed climbing conditions. We helicoptered into the North Baird Glacier from the fishing village of Petersburg on April 30. As far as we could tell, we were the first climbing expedition to visit this glacier in over 40 years.

As soon as we arrived, it was immediately clear that any technical climbing would be unlikely. All the mountains were draped with enormous cornices and unstable snow mushrooms. More significantly, it was not freezing at night and there were (literally) hundreds of avalanches falling. After a week of this, we abandoned plans for Oasis and moved our camp down the glacier to a point where we could access the north arm of the North Baird Glacier.

Finally, on May 9, the weather improved enough for us to climb through the icefall guarding entry to the north arm. We were probably the first mountaineers ever to visit this part of the icecap and were surrounded by over a dozen unclimbed peaks. The big prize was Peak 7,180', which lay 8km away at the head of the adjacent Dawes Glacier. [*Editor' note: This mountain, located at 57.36970, -132.84810, is named Hyder Peak on Bivouac.com, though the origins of the name are unknown.*] This massive and isolated mountain, with a steep, rocky summit triangle, lies on the western edge of the Stikine Icecap. We made the 5km-long and 1,200m ascent of the northeast ridge and southeast face the following day, during a 24-hour weather window, via a combination of post-holing through deep snow, skiing where possible, and mixed climbing on the summit triangle. The view from the precarious and massively corniced summit, looking east to all the major peaks of the Stikine, was breathtaking.

Mark Robson traversing above the clouds and below the cornice during the first ascent of Peak 5,919', above the north arm of the North Baird Glacier. The high peaks on the right skyline are in Canada and include Noel Peak, Mussell Peak, and Mt. Ratz (3,090m), the highest peak in the Stikine region. *Simon Richardson*

During the trip, we ascended four other summits. Peak 5,800' and Peak 5,720' lie west of Turkey Peak (6,570') and were climbed by their south flank and east ridge, respectively, on May 1. We climbed Peak 5,910' by its long southwest ridge on May 9, and Peak 5,919' by its east ridge just before flying out on May 12. Peak 5,910' and the shapely Peak 5,919' lie on either side of the North Arm.

Alaskan climbers are notoriously modest about publicizing their achievements, but there are no records of previous ascents of any of the peaks we climbed. Hyder Peak was among the higher unclimbed summits (with over 3,000' prominence) in Southeast Alaska.

Overall, we only had three days when it was not raining and the visibility was good enough to climb. Despite the challenges, it was an extremely rewarding expedition. The climbing was rarely technical, but picking safe lines and negotiating the beautiful corniced summit ridges made it very exacting. (We had one huge cornice collapse, but fortunately both stayed upright on the solid side of the fracture line!) Above all, when the rain stopped and the fog lifted, we were treated to some of the most beautiful and pristine mountain landscapes either of us had ever seen. 📷

– **SIMON RICHARDSON**, *SCOTLAND*

Ian Welsted approaching the Northwest Summit of Mt. Waddington during his and Simon Richardson's ascent of the complete west ridge. *Simon Richardson*

WEST TO EAST ON WADDINGTON
A NEW ROUTE AND 12-KILOMETER TRAVERSE

BY SIMON RICHARDSON, *SCOTLAND*

"Hey, Simon, I'd like to go somewhere big like Waddington rather than go rock climbing on obscure spires." *Well*, I thought, *that's raised the bar*.

Ian Welsted and I were discussing climbing objectives for a Coast Mountains trip in the summer. "Well, if it's Waddington you're after, let's go for the complete west ridge," I suggested. "It's unclimbed and one of the biggest features in the range."

It may strike the reader as highly unlikely that in 2019 the central spine of this 4,019m mountain, the highest peak in the Coast Mountains, had not been climbed. But in the chase for more technical objectives across the range, it had indeed been overlooked. And there it was in the guidebook: Waddington's upper west ridge marching boldly across a double-page spread—a sharp, 1,500m pinnacled crest rising up to a fine snow arête and the summit plateau.

Don and Phyllis Munday's pioneering route up Waddington in 1928 climbed the lower 3.5km of the west ridge to 3,300m, and then followed the natural line of weakness to the left (north) of the spine, up the Angel Glacier, to reach the northwest summit. [*The full ridgeline runs west-northwest.*] It was a logical line and hugely committing for the time. Unfortunately, the Mundays did not have the firepower to continue to the main summit, which had to wait until 1936 when Bill House and Fritz Wiessner summited via the southwest face. This bold undertaking was the most difficult alpine route in North America at the time.

Our plan was to traverse Waddington starting from Fury Gap at its western end. We would follow the Munday route to the foot of the unclimbed Epaulette Ridge (the upper west ridge), climb this and continue on to bag the False Summit (3,980m), Northwest Summit (4,000m), and Main Summit Tower (4,019m) before descending the Bravo Glacier route. We would complete our 12km journey at the eastern extremity of the mountain at Rainy Knob.

Mike King dropped us off by helicopter at Fury Gap (2,500m) on August 3. We felt rather exposed to be in the heart of the Waddington Range with just light alpine packs, but the weather was excellent, and without further ado we set off up the snow slopes toward Fireworks Peak, the first minor summit on the lower west ridge. The snow was knee-deep after days of storm and it was slow going, but Ian's famous trail-breaking power saved the day. We stopped to bivouac at 2 p.m., a little past Herald Peak. It felt ridiculously early, but we were not going to make the start of the true west ridge that evening, so there was no point in pushing too hard.

The next day we traversed over the two Men At Arms summits and followed a spectacular corniced ridge over Bodyguard and Councillor peaks. The going continued to be tough in the deep snow, but we were hopeful that the upper ridge had been scoured by the wind and the snow consolidated in the sun. Once again we had a leisurely midafternoon bivouac near the start of the upper ridge.

On day three we were up and away before dawn, and sure enough conditions on the ridge were excellent, with fast climbing on hard snow and easy ice, following a ramp running below the south side of the crest. We moved together, with the occasional belayed pitch, until a hidden gully

Mt. Waddington from the northwest, with the west ridge on the right skyline and the massive icefall of the Scimitar Glacier flowing down to the right. Simon Richardson and Ian Welsted started their traverse of the mountain at Fury Gap, off-picture to the right, and passed over Fireworks and Herald peaks (not shown) and then (M) Men at Arms, (B) Bodyguard Peak, and (C) Councillor Peak. Above this, they traversed the south side (hidden) of the sharp Epaulette Ridge (E), crossed the Epaulette Glacier (also hidden), and finished with Waddington's summit towers (from right to left): False Summit, Northwest Summit, and the Summit Tower. They descended by the Bravo Glacier, hidden behind the left skyline. *John Scurlock*

Simon Richardson climbing Mt. Waddington's Summit Tower during the first ascent of the complete west ridge in August. *Ian Welsted*

led onto the previously untrodden Epaulette Glacier, astride the central section of the ridge.

It had all gone so smoothly that we couldn't believe our luck, but we were soon confronted with the sting in the tail. As we left the glacier, the ensuing snow ridge narrowed to a knife-edge draped in delicate cornices. I traversed *à cheval* along the wafer-thin crest and belayed by excavating a deep hole in the snow. Our situation was precarious, but there was no option other than to continue across the steep and heavily loaded slope on the north side of the crest.

Ian made a long and committing traverse, digging deep to find ice screw placements. I led next and plowed a sideways trench for 30m until a blind 3m jump into a bergschrund brought us back into more reasonable terrain. That afternoon we tagged the False and Northwest summits before descending established terrain on a route called the Stroll to gain a campsite on the broad terrace below the main summit.

Day four was beautiful, but we were nearly turned back on the Summit Tower due to falling rime ice. As the sun moved behind the Tooth, the onslaught abated, and we enjoyed a succession of excellent mixed pitches up the icy central chimney, reminding me of home in Scotland. On the summit we took in the 360° panorama, looking north-south along the spine of the Coast Mountains and west to the Pacific Ocean, before making a series of abseils back to our bivouac tent.

Before the trip, my friend Don Serl had warned that descending the Bravo Glacier might be the crux of the whole route. We awoke at 3 a.m. and set off down steep névé slopes to gain the Bravo Headwall. How things had changed in the 22 years since I'd last climbed Waddington! Instead of deep snow flutings it was now a broken rocky slope, which we carefully abseiled toward the Bravo Glacier icefall.

We soon became lost in a maze of huge crevasses and serac walls. After an hour we reached an impasse, trying three different routes without success. Then Ian spotted some old footsteps in the distance on the glacier below. This gave us the incentive to force a way through, and soon we were following a trail of wands left by an American team several weeks before. They had been unable to find a way up to the Bravo Headwall, but their tracks saved our day.

We reached Rainy Knob at 11 a.m., not ready to break the spell by calling for a pickup. We lounged on a huge flat slab of granite, drinking coffee and taking in the magnificence of the surroundings, enjoying the deep glow that comes when you achieve something that you set out to do. Eventually we reached for the radio, and within minutes we heard the throb of the helicopter.

I don't think it makes sense to provide an overall grade for this 12km traverse. Don Serl gives the summit tower and the route we descended TD- in *The Waddington Guide*. Our climb was clearly more involved than that but pretty much ungradable on any alpine scale.

Summary: *First ascent of the complete west ridge of Mt. Waddington in the Coast Mountains of British Columbia, August 3–7, 2019, by Simon Richardson (U.K.) and Ian Welsted (Canada).* ▢

Luka Lindič leading the crux M8 roof pitch of the Sound of Silence on the east face of Mt. Fay. Lindič first aided the roof and then, knowing he'd never be back, decided to attempt the redpoint. *Ines Papert*

THE SOUND OF SILENCE
THE DIRECT EAST FACE OF MT. FAY

BY LUKA LINDIČ, *SLOVENIA*

I FIRST STOOD below the mighty east face of Mt. Fay in early April 2016 with the late Marc-André Leclerc. The night before we intended to climb was warm, and we saw the first avalanche come down the line that Barry Blanchard, Dave Cheesmond, and Carl Tobin climbed in 1984 before we even had our breakfast. Marc and I walked away without touching that wall, but the idea of completing a direct finish to the 1984 line stayed with us.

When Ines Papert and I packed for a trip to the Canadian Rockies in late winter, a year after Marc died in Alaska, we definitely had the east face of Mt. Fay in mind. It had been extremely cold in the Rockies for a very long time, which usually doesn't promise anything good on the big faces. But two weeks before flying to Canada, we got a very friendly message from Maarten van Haeren saying that there might be some ice growing on Mt. Fay.

We arrived at the end of March and immediately approached the Valley of the Ten Peaks to check the conditions on various walls. We thought there was still too much unconsolidated snow on Mt. Fay. On our second trip into the valley, we tried two north-facing walls and got shut down for the same reason. We decided we might explore some other areas, and we carried out all our equipment.

After a few days of rest, a good weather window arrived. So did Brette Harrington, Marc's partner before he passed away. Ines and I wanted to climb something with Brette, but we weren't sure if a face like Fay would be a good idea for a first climb together. After a couple hours of catching up, though, we all felt that it was worth a try.

We moved quite fast on the approach to base camp, thanks to a track established by friends during the previous window. In the evening, there was no spindrift coming down, and it was

Sound of Silence (1,100m, M8 WI5) on the east face of Mt. Fay. The original route (1985) finished up and right from the snowfield at two-thirds height. Sans Blitz (2000) climbed the obvious ice to the left. *Jon Walsh*

quite cold. But we knew the situation could be different once the sun hit the face in the morning, so we decided to get a very early start.

We were moving again after a few hours of sleep. We quickly reached the left-trending snow ramp at the base of the wall where the 1984 route starts and climbed to the end of the ramp unroped. At this point we entered into a main fall line of avalanches and spindrift, so we tied in and simul-climbed.

We soon reached the first steep section of ice, which we also climbed quickly. Then the rising sun hit the upper headwall and brought spindrift avalanches as expected. Luckily, I was already over the steep ice when it hit us. I built an anchor and belayed Ines and Brette, who arrived at the anchor covered in snow but smiling. The terrain above was less steep and we started simul-climbing again. We were actually gaining speed until Ines slipped. Fortunately, that didn't happen too far from an ice screw, but it reminded us to take care.

At the big snow bowl in the middle of the wall, where the 1984 route traversed out right to finish, we needed to deal with some very deep snow. I climbed a rope length without finding any protection or suitable anchor. Rather than simul-climb, I decided to untie from one rope and toss it down to Ines and Brette, who tied the ropes together so that I could continue. After a long struggle to find suitable features, I was able to build a belay below a steep step.

A stripe of ice and snow that had looked very promising from the valley turned out to be horrible. After traversing left and right, searching for a route, I spotted a very steep crack system. It looked very hard—especially with our light alpine rack of one set of cams, nuts, and a few pitons—but we agreed to give it a try.

I made it through a roof with a mixture of free climbing and aid, cleaning loose rock and snow on the way. As I built the next belay, I started thinking how incredible it would be to free climb the pitch. I spent a few minutes alone, deciding what to do. Seeing the big headwall above made me want to keep moving, but I knew I would regret not trying to free the pitch. Ines sensed what I was thinking and hollered encouraging words from below. "Fuck it! It's now or never!" I said.

Brette Harrington on the first pitch above the bivouac on Fay's east face. Though the M8 roof the previous afternoon was the route's spectacular highlight, the climbing remained sustained to the top. *Luka Lindič*

They lowered me, I pulled the ropes, and after a short rest I freed the pitch at M8.

Another hard pitch brought us to terrain that was a bit easier, following dihedrals and snow ramps. However, the snow eventually became horrible and scary. After a very long pitch of digging and climbing, we reached a spot that seemed like the only reasonable place to spend the night. We ate a Spartan dinner and went to sleep with the hope of waking up with the warm rays of the morning sun.

The morning was cold and cloudy, and we got moving quickly. Brette led two pitches and then Ines led another two. The terrain got steeper again, the rock very loose, and it was really difficult to find a promising route. We didn't talk much in the next hours. We worked well as a team, everyone did what he or she could. Soon a snowstorm hit us and made everything even more intense.

We finally found ourselves about 30m from the top of the face. The summit was guarded by a final pitch of superb drytooling on overhanging rock. I pulled the last moves, rolled over onto a very windy ridge, and started screaming from happiness. Ines and Brette joined me in the fading light and we screamed together. It was a short but very intense time at the top.

We downclimbed to the big plateau on the other side of the mountain and started navigating toward the Neil Colgan Hut through intense snowfall and fog. We never would have found the hut without a GPS. As relief and fatigue set in, I felt very proud of our climb and our style—and happy that Brette had joined us. During the ascent, I could almost hear Marc talking to me. In the moments when we were totally silent because it was so serious, I could hear him saying, "Hey, dude, thanks for taking Little B on this climb." We named the route the Sound of Silence (1,100m, M8 WI5) in his memory. Brette told us that Marc had wanted to name a route after the Simon and Garfunkel song, but unfortunately he passed away too soon.

SUMMARY: *First ascent of the Sound of Silence (1,100m, WI5 M8), the direct east face of Mt. Fay in the Valley of the Ten Peaks in the Canadian Rockies, by Brette Harrington (USA), Luka Lindič (Slovenia), and Ines Papert (Germany), April 2–3, 2019.* ▣

Hansjörg Auer at 9:57 a.m. on April 16, partway up the 1,000-meter east face of Howse Peak. *Jess Roskelley*

HOWSE PEAK: NEW ROUTE AND TRAGEDY
THE LAST CLIMB OF HANSJÖRG AUER, DAVID LAMA, AND JESS ROSKELLEY

BY JOHN ROSKELLEY, *USA*

THE FOLLOWING REPORT is based on the photographic record and the equipment found with Hansjörg Auer, David Lama, and Jess Roskelley after an accident on April 16 on the east face of Howse Peak in the Canadian Rockies. Jess' iPhone was found on him at the base of the face. The phone provided exact time, altitude, and GPS locations from each of his photos, which not only proved they made the summit of the 3,295m peak, but also gave clues to the location of their new route, a significant variation of the climb M-16.

On my second trip (of three) to the accident site, on June 2, Tim Sanford, a good friend of Jess, and I found David Lama's GoPro and Hansjörg Auer's camera, both with valuable, informative photos. Using Jess's iPhone as the control for time and location, I sequenced David's and Hansjörg's photos into a time line, which enabled Grant Statham and Steve Holeczi, two of the search and recovery personnel, to determine the route they climbed pitch by pitch. The evidence shows they climbed the east face of Howse from their camp at the base to the summit, an altitude gain of 1,340m, in less than seven hours. Their ascent is a tribute to their strength, talent, and tenacity. Their deaths prove once again, though, that the mountain passes final judgment on success or failure.

The three men, all members of the North Face athlete team, arrived in Canmore the first week in April to test a new clothing system. They had a number of difficult routes on their agenda, and within a short period of time had made speedy ascents of Andromeda Strain and Nemesis, a WI6 waterfall climb in thin spring conditions.

While they were waiting out bad weather in Canmore, Jess called me numerous times to talk about their first two climbs and one final objective: the east face of Howse Peak. On April 14, he asked about descent routes off the top, as I had climbed the northeast buttress route many years before. We concluded their ascent route (which we didn't discuss) would be the logical choice for descent.

Early on the morning of April 15, the three drove to the Waterfowl Lakes parking area, put on their skis and packs, and departed at 11 a.m. for the 8km ski to camp. Within one hour they were at Chephron Lake, and by 12:40 p.m. all three had reached their campsite on the glacier below the east face. That evening, Hansjörg took several photos of small powder snow avalanches sweeping their intended route.

By 5:51 the next morning, April 16, in cold, but clear weather, with Hansjörg on foot and David and Jess on skis, they had climbed the lower snow slopes below M-16, a difficult mixed climb with only one previous ascent (Backes-Blanchard-House, 1999, completing the face but not reaching the summit). Leaving the skis, all three reached the bottom of the first difficulty, a WI6 waterfall, before 7 a.m. Hansjörg grabbed the first lead and, after waiting out a spindrift avalanche that swept over him, quickly climbed the vertical ice. Another 15 minutes saw all three climbers at the top of the pitch.

Whether seeking a new variation or finding the two routes above them—M-16 and Howse of Cards— out of condition this late in the season, David then traversed left along a snow band toward a difficult right-to-left leaning ramp. Jess followed using a Petzl Micro Traxion to self-belay, while David belayed Hansjörg. They climbed approximately 80m up the ramp before David traversed left again—it was now 8:36 a.m.— along another horizontal snow band in search of the upper pitches of the "King Line," a name given by Steve House to an unclimbed mixed route left of M-16. David led a WI6+ waterfall pitch, and

The east face of Howse Peak (3,295m), showing the line followed by Auer, Lama, and Roskelley. Their route started on M16, then traversed left to a bowl above Life By the Drop, continuing to the top with difficult mixed climbing. During their descent, an avalanche of ice and snow swept them from the upper bowl. *Parks Canada*

Jess and Hansjörg quickly followed. At the top of the waterfall, they untied and stored the ropes in their packs. Fifty minutes later, at 9:42 a.m., Hansjörg took a photo of David and Jess approaching the top of a long snow gully above the "King Line" waterfall. Blocked by difficult mixed climbing, the three traversed left, yet again, to reach a large, concave snow basin above a waterfall route known as Life By the Drop.

Ankle-deep in sun-warmed snow, Jess took the lead up the moderate snow basin to reach the southwest ridge. At 11:02 a.m., Jess, trailing a single rope, led a mixed pitch along the ridge. After 330m of difficult mixed climbing, the threesome reached the summit prior to 12:41 p.m. The sun was shining, but a few clouds were starting to move in. Both Hansjörg and Jess used the opportunity to take summit photos of the three of them in their heavy down coats.

Sometime after Jess' summit photo taken at 12:44 p.m., the three climbers began their descent. Hansjörg continued to take a few photos as they made rappel after rappel down the ridge. At 1:27 p.m., Hansjörg took the last photo found on any of the three cameras. The photo is probably of David at the bottom of their final rappel off the southwest ridge into the snow basin. Their ascent tracks can be seen reaching the ridge crest in the bottom right corner of the photo.

Just before 2 p.m., Quentin Roberts, an experienced alpinist living in Canmore, stopped his car along the Icefields Parkway to examine the routes on Howse Peak. As he and his climbing part-

Roskelley, Auer, and Lama on the summit. They climbed the east face in less than seven hours.

ner stood looking at the east face, an avalanche, possibly from a cornice break, swept the basin above the route Life by the Drop and billowed onto the glacier at the bottom of the face. They did not know that Hansjörg, David, and Jess were on the face at the time. Roberts ran to his car for his camera and took a photo of the massive snow cloud forming at the bottom of the face. It was 1:58 p.m., 31 minutes after the three climbers had entered the basin.

Allison, Jess's wife, and Joyce, his mother, spoke multiple times on the evening of April 16 and the morning of April 17. Jess always phoned in after a climb, and he had told Alli they would be out of the mountains that night. If he couldn't reach a phone, he would have texted his position to her on his InReach device. Early on April 17, I reached a Parks Canada ranger by phone. I told him where the men were climbing and that we were concerned they hadn't checked in. Parks Canada immediately dispatched a ranger to the trailhead to see if Jess' truck was still there. It was.

Subsequently, several members of a Parks Canada search and rescue team were flown by helicopter to the base of Howse's east face. Clouds now blanketed the upper slopes, and visibility was limited to the bottom half of the face. As they flew toward the avalanche cones at the bottom of the face, the rangers were drawn to bright colors in the snow. A close inspection of the scene from the helicopter indicated at least one climber, possibly two, were buried halfway up the large avalanche cone below the route Life By the Drop. Avalanche conditions were extreme, so the SAR team decided not to put anyone on the ground. They tossed two large fluorescent traffic cones and two avalanche beacons where the climber(s) were located and departed. For the next four days, bad weather prevented any search and rescue or recovery efforts.

On April 21, the weather was clear and sunny. A helicopter carrying a few SAR team members flew up and down the east face, over the summit, and around the mountain, looking for signs of survivors. Nothing was seen after a meticulous search. A recovery dog and her handler, attached to long lines and flown to the avalanche cone by helicopter, were able to locate one of the climbers. With the warming day increasing the risk of avalanche danger from the upper slopes of the face, other SAR team members were flown to the site and were able to expose all three climbers, who were buried close together, tangled in rope. The rangers quickly cut their two 50m ropes in as many as 30 places to free the climbers from the ice and each other. They were then placed in cargo netting and long-lined to the staging area and eventually to ambulances waiting on the highway.

The last photo found with the climbers' gear shows that the three of them had rappelled from the ridge above the east face of Howse Peak into the basin below using the entire lengths of their two 50m ropes. Evidence from the ropes and equipment suggests they did not rope up once they pulled the rappel ropes and that one of the climbers, probably Jess, had coiled both ropes (and possibly clipped into them) to carry them. As competent as they all were, they would have plunge-stepped quickly down the slope toward the traverse that led to the gully above the "King Line." All the evidence indicates they were swept to their deaths in that short window of 31 minutes from the time they dropped into the basin and the photo from the highway confirmed a cornice break and/or avalanche. It doesn't bring them back into our arms, but the final story of their last climb gives some closure to their families, friends, and loved ones.

Editor's note: The online version of this report provides additional analysis of the accident. 📄 📷

Believed to be the first to combine climbing and packrafting in this area, four climbers paddled tandem rafts up Pangnirtung Fjord and dragged their loaded boats about 10km up the Weasel River. On the way out, they paddled most of the way, saving about 25km of hiking with very heavy loads. *Jacob Cook*

NEVER LAUGH AT DRAGONS
NEW ROUTES—AND PACKRAFTING—ON BAFFIN ISLAND

BY BRONWYN HODGINS, *CANADA*

I CROUCHED ON a rock ledge that was barely wider than a picnic bench and sloped disconcertingly toward the abyss. Both my hands supported our little stove as the water rolled to a boil. I quickly cut the fuel and poured the water into pouches of instant rice. There was no room for Jacob on the ledge, so he kneeled on a Grade 7 inflatable portaledge beside me. My watch read 1 a.m. Dinner in ten and then we'd try to sleep.

Our free-hanging camp was halfway up an unnamed 400m tower of golden granite on Baffin Island. Above us a headwall stretched upward, immaculate, totally blank but for one striking splitter that disappeared into the sky.

Five weeks earlier, Jacob Cook (U.K.), Zack Goldberg Poch, Thor Stewart (both Canadian), and I had paddled packrafts up Pangnirtung Fjord, riding the swelling tide on a magical calm day. After towing the loaded rafts partway up the Weasel River, we deflated the boats, hoisted our packs, and slogged up valley for four days under icy rain, aiming for a cache of climbing gear, food, and fuel that had been stashed by Peter Kilabuk—our local outfitter—via snowmobile four months earlier.

We reached the cache (relieved that no polar bears had found it) and pushed on up the Caribou Glacier to make high camp under Mt. Asgard. In the morning, under a dazzling sun, Jacob and I set off to repeat the Brazeau-Walsh Route on the south face of Mt. Asgard's South Tower. But while approaching the wall, we spied a parallel crack system that deviated left after 100m and excitedly changed objectives. Twenty hours later, we were back in camp, having climbed a new route, Never Laugh At Live Dragons (600m, 5.11- R). The name quotes Bilbo Baggins from *The Hobbit,* who sneaks into the dragon Smaug's lair and steals back the sacred Arkenstone. We too felt as though we had snuck up on a beast, snatched our prize, and returned unscathed.

Jacob and I next turned our attention to the classic 1972 British route on the east side of Asgard's North Tower. Near the top we found a three-pitch free variation (likely joining the aid line Bilfrost Buttress) up an airy 5.11+ finger crack, an excellent alternative to the often wet chimney finish. Meanwhile, Thor and Zack had their own adventure on what we believe to be an unclimbed subsummit of Mt. Midgard. In a 27-hour push, they established Beach Vacation (600m, 5.10+) on the east side of the subpeak (which they called Mt. Zacky), with mostly slabby face and crack climbing on excellent rock.

Impending storm clouds forced us back to the Weasel River Valley for some much-needed rest days. Rejuvenated, we inflated our packrafts and set off downstream, running what we could of the raging and technical Arctic whitewater. Two days later, we stopped to climb Mt. Thor, simul-climbing the south ridge and succeeding in Thor's life goal to summit his namesake mountain! After several more days on the river and a failed attempt (due to poor rock) on the 600m west face of Mt. Tirokwa, we set up a final camp where the river meets the sea. We had time for one last climb—a new line on Mt. Ulu for Zack and Thor, and that unnamed golden tower for Jacob and me.

Above our portaledge camp, the alluring splitter

[Top] Thor Stewart celebrates atop his namesake peak. [Middle] Bronwyn Hodgins following a splitter on the Niv Mizzet Line. The 400-meter line had a 5.13- crux. [Bottom] Paddling the Weasel River, with Mt. Thor in the background. [Opposite Page] A Pangnirtung child on his first climb. *Jacob Cook (all photos)*

crack tapered to a seam that was nearly closed. Jacob looked like he could pop off any second, but he finished the pitch and put me on belay. I started cautiously up flakes, pulled a roof, and then desperately crimped up the seam. I arrived at the anchor totally worked. The crack continued upward and the wall steepened slightly. It was going to get harder before it got easier.

Jacob set off again. He plugged our smallest Totem cam, pulled up the rope to clip…then *whoosh*, his feet popped and he came sailing down beside me. Next go, he fell one move higher, sagging onto the cam. He looked down at me: "Do you have the brush?" I had a funny moment where I was outside my body, looking down at the two of us, watching Jacob as he scrubbed the rock. It felt comical to be in such a wild place and faffing with the minutiae of hard free climbing. Jacob swung about, testing some moves and ticking the rock with chalk. "I give myself a 20 percent chance of sending," he shrugged after lowering again.

I watched Jacob—my partner for the past seven years—dance up the wall, looking desperate but somehow in control. Then he was past the crux and into finger locks, which turned to ring locks and eventually to thin hands. I whooped as he carried on up the perfect hand crack, cruising jam after jam.

Breathe, I told myself. *It's a slab,* a *very steep slab.* I made about five moves before I was spat off. I pulled on again and fell almost instantly. I decided to yard on a few cams, thinking only, *What a crazy place to be!*

Above, I took the lead as we continued up a never-ending splitter on our tower's west face. There was a faint shout in the distance, and I looked across the cirque to see two miniature silhouettes on the summit of the neighboring Mt. Ulu, which may have been previously unclimbed. Thor and Zack had just finished the Beached Whale (600m, 5.10+ A0) on the south face. A pendulum down low was the only aid and could have been avoided if they'd started slightly to the left.

Soon Jacob and I stood on the summit of our tower, which rises to the north of the very east end of Ulu's north face. We called our route the Niv Mizzet Line (400m, 5.13-). I raised my eyes to look across at the jagged mountains, and then beyond at the fringes of the great white Penny Ice Cap. I let my gaze fall to the ocean fjord, the homestretch. I felt peaceful, deeply satisfied. This had truly been the trip of a lifetime. But my mind and body craved the safety and comforts of home.

After a long deep sleep at our seaside camp, we four friends pushed off into the fjord, aiming our bows south toward the small Inuit community of Pangnirtung. Before our flight home, we put up posters around the village inviting local kids to try rock climbing. Twenty of them showed up for an afternoon of top-roping. Sometimes we get caught up in our own stories in the mountains, but this day was for them, the children of Pangnirtung. 📷 🔍

EDITOR'S NOTE: *Two California climbers, Thomas Bukowski and Brian Knowles, repeated Never Laugh At Live Dragons on Asgard's South Tower shortly after the first ascent. They stayed in the obvious chimney up high, avoiding Hodgins and Cook's 5.11- R finish. According to Hodgins, their variation is likely wetter in early season but creates an all-free 5.10+ on excellent rock.*

The east face of Mt. Wood (15,912') in early March 2019, showing the route up the east-northeast spur climbed by Dupre and Marceau. They summited on March 10. *Pascale Marceau*

MT. WOOD, FIRST WINTER ASCENT

On March 11, at 3:10 p.m., Pascale Marceau and I reached the summit of Mt. Wood in wind chill of -45°C. Located in Kluane National Park and Reserve, Mt. Wood is Canada's sixth-highest peak at 15,912' (4,860m). This was not only the first winter ascent of the mountain, it also made Pascale the first woman to reach the summit of a major subarctic peak (50–70° north latitude) in winter.

We flew from Burwash Landing on March 4, landing on an arm of the Hodgson Glacier at 9,800' (very high for a Piper Super Cub). We skied a short way uphill from the landing and set up camp near the base of the mountain's east face. On March 7 we established Camp 1 at 11,200' after three precarious carries up the most technical section of our route (some sustained 60° ice slopes). We had supplied Camp 2 at 12,500', with two carries, by the 9th. Our first summit bid on the 10th was thwarted by high winds and driving snow just a couple of hours from the top.

On the morning of the 11th, with a poor forecast, we prepared to descend the mountain. But by 10 a.m. the weather appeared to be stabilizing, so we decided to make a fast push for the summit. With good traction over hard-packed snow, we reached the peak of Mt. Wood in just over five hours, then quickly descended, grabbing the gear at Camp 2 and scurrying on to Camp 1 in a race against darkness. The next day, we cautiously worked our way back to base camp.

Mt. Wood was first climbed in 1941 from a base camp southeast of the mountain. Since then, the east face has been climbed several times in spring/summer, though the exact lines followed are not known. We felt our 6,000' ascent was Alaska Grade III, mainly due to numerous crevasses and the initial difficulties reaching Camp I. We spent a total of nine days on the climb. 📷

— LONNIE DUPRE, *USA*

RAGGED RANGE EXPLORATION

In early August, Katie Mills, Wojtek Pagacz, Nick Pappas, and I flew in to Nahanni National Park Reserve. Inspired by aerial video footage of spectacular and little-known spires, and funded in part by the 2019 Bob Wilson Grant from the Mazamas, we planned to spend two weeks exploring a small portion of the Ragged Range, just 8km south of the well-known Cirque of the Unclimbables. We had hoped to find similarly solid granite; however, our immediate surroundings were less inspiring, with discontinuous and loose rock lines.

Base camp was above the south fork of the Fool's River (and above the area's ferocious mosquitoes) at about 1,850m (61.974110N, 127.604607W). After a week of hiking in the rain and peering through foggy binoculars, morale was low. Wojtek and I decided to hike up into the westernmost cirque from base camp to see if we could gain a ridge and press on toward Mt. Sidney Dobson, the most prominent and only named peak in the region. [*Several peaks of about 2,600m in this area have been given this same name; the mountain this group called Sidney Dobson South is actually Plymouth Peak, climbed in 1952. See note below.*]

The valley of the South Fork of the Fool's River in the Ragged Range. The Sentinel (unclimbed) is at center left. *Katie Mills*

A north-facing couloir snaked down from a high col, and the lack of rockfall encouraged us. The next day, we armed ourselves with the full team's four ice tools (two axes and two technical tools) and climbed the couloir, on ever-steepening ice (up to 65°), covering 270m in only three pitches. From the col, we first ventured up the ridge to the right, which we believed might continue toward Sidney Dobson, but decided it was too loose and rappelled back to the col. We then climbed peak that flanked the left side of our couloir, simul-climbing broken terrain (up to 5.7) up the northwest gully to reach the broad summit at 2,435m. We descended steep, loose talus on the east face. Twisting Couloir (340m, AD AI3 5.7) would be an instant classic if located closer to a major roadway instead of accessed by a chopper ride from the end of the road at a defunct tungsten mine.

During our climb, Nick and Katie had been exploring peaks lower in the valley for free climbing potential. After waiting out bad weather, they attempted a peak they called "The Chair" but were forced to turn back after 800' of climbing up to 5.11, due to inadequate protection, dirt, and vegetation. They then set sights on "The Sentinel," a commanding tower that guards the entrance to the valley below. Again, the cracks were filled with dirt and vegetation, and after circumnavigating the tower in search of a line, they returned to base camp empty-handed.

With a major storm forecast for a couple of days out, they attempted the imposing Mt. Doom, a craggy glaciated peak towering over our camp. [*This peak was climbed from the same valley by the 1952 Yale expedition; they named the mountain Die Eisspitze (ca 2,550m).*] They were once again forced to turn back, characterizing the mountain as "a pile of stacked dinner plate choss." As they descended, they decided to make a last-ditch attempt at a nearby summit (61.9702, -127.5893). Nick was able to scramble to the top at 2,201m, dubbing the line Consolation Prize (180m, 5.4). ▣

– **AMY PAGACZ,** *CANADA*

THE MT. SIDNEY DOBSON MYSTERY: *At least four peaks in the cluster of rugged mountains south of Glacier Lake, all around 2,600m in elevation, have been labeled Mt. Sidney Dobson by different maps. Several of these were climbed in 1952 by a Yale University expedition that spent two and a half months in the area, building a log raft to cross a lake and subsisting in part on game they shot and smoked. They climbed nine peaks, mostly first ascents. (A great account is in the 1953 Canadian Alpine Journal.) Forcing their way up the Fool's River from Brintnell Creek, the Yale team climbed a peak now commonly called Sidney Dobson from near the head of the west fork of the Fool's River; they called this mountain Plymouth Peak. The Yale team also climbed two mountains about 5km to the northeast, near the junction of the west and south forks of the river, calling them Marble Mountain and Snow*

View south at the head of the south fork of the Fool's River. (BC) The 2019 team's base camp. (A) An unnamed peak, likely unclimbed. (B) Plymouth Peak, climbed by Howell Martyn and Harry Nance in 1952; this peak is frequently labeled Mt. Sidney Dobson on maps. (C) Peak 2,435m, climbed by Twisting Couloir, visible above the glacier on the north face. *Amy Pagacz*

Chute Peak; the Sidney Dobson label also has been applied to this group. In between, about 2km north of Plymouth Peak, is yet another frequently labeled Sidney Dobson that apparently is unclimbed.

The original Sidney Dobson may well be a peak at the northeast end of this group, visible from the Brintnell Creek area east of Glacier Lake and also climbed by the 1952 team, via the east ridge. This peak was surveyed by the 1937 Snyder expedition to the Logan Mountains and was labeled "Amphitheater Peak (Sidney Dobson)" in their report; Sydney Dobson was general manger of the Royal Bank of Canada in that era and possibly helped sponsor the Snyder expedition. Which Sidney Dobson is highest? Map sources aren't clear, and the 2019 team could not tell which peak was highest from their vantage points. —Dougald MacDonald

BRITISH COLUMBIA / COAST MOUNTAINS – PACIFIC RANGES

WADDINGTON RANGE, MT. COMBATANT, PEACEFUL WARRIOR

PAUL CORDY, PAUL McSORLEY, and Tony Richardson climbed a new line on the rightmost buttress of the southwest face of Mt. Combatant (3,756m), left of Kshatrya (Cairns-Downs, 1982). The trio climbed six long pitches (5.11a) before joining Kshatrya and following it to the top: Peaceful Warrior (750m, TD- 5.11a). In August 2002, Conrad Anker and Jimmy Chin put up a five-pitch variation on this same buttress, but after comparing notes, the 2019 team is sure their route is new. 📄 📷

– INFORMATION FROM **PAUL MCSORLEY**, *CANADA*

TOBA INLET, SOUTH FACES OF KLITE PEAK AND KLITE E1

IN JULY, TWO climbers sailed from Washington state to the Toba Inlet, about 100 miles northwest of Vancouver. They made their way to the head of the Tahumming River and hiked a little less than four miles on logging roads before reaching a sign that read "Klahoose First Nation NO ENTRY." They disregarded the sign and hurried along to the Klite River drainage, which they ascended for 12 to 13 miles over two days until they reached a cirque of big granite walls. Over the next few days, they climbed two routes: the Southwest Cleft on the south face of Klite E1 (900m, 5.10 R) and the Southeast Ridge on the south face of Klite Peak (1,000m, 5.10+).

The *AAJ* does not support trespass on tribal (or any) land. In the past, the Klahoose have granted permission to climb in their territory to some climbers who formally requested it. To learn more, visit klahoose.org.

– CHRIS KALMAN, USA

DANIELS RIVER VALLEY: SUPER UNKNOWN, SCHNEIDER QUITS

FOR THE THIRD year in a row, I returned to the Daniels River Valley, funded in part by an AAC Live Your Dream grant. John Bolte, Josh Schuh, and I first attempted a new route on the most striking formation of the valley, Red Alert Wall, first climbed in 2017 by Travis Foster and Drew Leiterman (Jungle Is Massive, 25 pitches, VI 5.10 C2). We had scoped a more direct but far less featured line several hundred meters to the right. We started up with supplies for five days, plus 35 bolts (not nearly enough and we knew it). After three days of climbing, with difficulties up to 5.10+ and A2, we decided to bail from a pitch and a half above the Halfway Highway ledge.

John had to go back to the States, but Josh and I had time for another objective. We got in contact with Ari Schneider, who had made a trip to the Daniels early in the season and attempted a route on the Super Unknown formation. With his permission, we decided to try to push his route to the summit.

We began on August 26, starting with the first pitch of Evan Guilbault and my 2017 route Sacred Stone (1,200m, 27 pitches, 5.10 A1). We soon broke left and, for five more pitches, ascended a large right-facing corner system that we believed to be the line Ari attempted. That evening we established our portaledge camp under the massive Coastal Ledge. On day two we skirted a roof via a short bolt ladder begging to be freed, and then Josh put up two steep pitches in a deep corner just right of our 2018 route (The Prow, 26 pitches, 5.10 A1). Then we suddenly found ourselves in familiar terrain: Josh and I had explored this way in 2018, attempting a variation to Sacred Stone. We repeated a five-star pitch of free climbing and then executed a quick traverse left and into unknown terrain again.

Day three dawned sunny, and we started early, excited for the climbing ahead. On the upper north buttress of Super Unknown is a band of rock about 400m high with some of the most beautiful, continuous, and clean cracks of the southern Coast Mountains. We have named this zone La Linea Blanca. The pitches on our new line follow layback corners and splitter hand cracks, aid seams and pendulums, all on pristine white granite with minimal need for the cleaning tools.

The final pitches of our route were generally lower angle and could clean up to be fun free climbing. We joined the last 20m of the Prow and reached the summit at 1 p.m. on August 30. After several visits, this summit is still one of the most powerful, divine places I have ever been; I howled the names of my loved ones into the void. On our descent the same evening, we completed our multi-season rappel route project: Starting from the massive cairn west of the true summit, two 70m ropes will take you past 21 two-bolt stations down to the approach slabs.

We named our route Schneider Quits (1,200m, 27 pitches, 5.10+ A2+) in honor of those who quested up this line before us. We hope our friendly jab will inspire a return trip from the only other party in the Daniels this season. The vast majority of the aid on our route will clean up into stellar free climbing, at an estimated overall grade of 5.11+. 📄 📷

– COLIN LANDECK, *USA*

PRINCESS LOUISA WALL, JOURNEY TO THE CENTER OF THE EARTH

INSPIRED BY A story in the 2018 AAJ, which heralded unclimbed walls along the BC coast, I had been curing my winter blues with virtual flights through Google Earth. On the last day of 2018, I stumbled onto a low-res photo of a hulking mass of swamp and stone geotagged to Princess Louisa Inlet. Research revealed this east-facing wall to be about 1,400m tall, with only one known route: PLI Trail (17 pitches, ED1/2 V 5.10+), established by John Brodie and Peter Rowat over

The Princess Louisa Inlet Wall, rising about 1,400 meters at the head of a fjord off Jervis Inlet. (1) PLI Trail (17 pitches, ED1/2 V 5.10+, Brodie-Rowat, 2002). (2) Journey to the Center of the Earth (25 pitches, VI 5.10+ C2, Besen-Heinrich, 2019). *Noah Besen*

the course of nearly two decades, and ending on a prominent pinnacle halfway up the wall. My interest hastily morphed into a foolhardy obsession.

Eight months later, in August 2019, Noah Besen and I stood beneath that wall with our necks craning to see granite dissolving into roiling cloud far above. With only a few Yosemite trade walls between us and not a single first ascent, we had gotten so caught up in scheming and dreaming that we neglected reality until we were starkly in it. We blundered ourselves and our gear to the base over three days, openly wondering what the hell we were doing there.

The wall looked horribly uninviting from below—all we could see was moss and dirt—but the rock was actually quite solid and compact. Unfortunately, we were largely forced to avoid the cleanest stone, since our bolt kit had been seized by a ranger upon arrival in Princess Louisa Marine Provincial Park. Instead, we stuck to the few continuous cracks, which tended to be packed with dirt, mud, and flora.

Much to our delight, the first four low-angle pitches went well. We fixed 180m of rope to a large ledge and returned to the ground to wait out some rain. When we woke from triumphant dreams, we were floating. Literally. We had pitched our tent in a waterway, and now we crashed through a sudden torrent to collect our flotsam and move our tent out of the river. Cell phones and toilet paper were the only casualties.

We dried out and continued to purchase passage up the wall with toil and fret. Pitch six (5.10+) presented our first real challenge: a stemming corner split by a turfy tips flare. Intimidated, I tried to treat it like any other pitch, except it was unlike anything I'd ever done. All holds and gear placements required constant and mostly fruitless excavation with fingernails from strenuous stances.

Seven days in and halfway through our trip, we had fixed all six of our ropes up about one-third of the wall. A good forecast forbade surrender and obliged us to commit to the route with a few days of food, two gallons of water, and little confidence in success. Over the next three days we aided hand cracks running with muck, freed fingertip flares filled with filth, squirmed up an offwidth walled with moss, slurped from puddles, broke a gear loop, backflopped onto a slab, and loved every goddamn second of it. With each foot we climbed we became more confident. Eventually we found ourselves in a forest atop the right shoulder of the main wall, with 25 pitches below us, having completed our Journey to the Center of the Earth (1,000m, VI 5.10+ C2).

We hadn't thought about how to get down, as we hadn't thought we'd get up in the first place. Rappelling seemed a dangerous, expensive, and time-consuming chore that would cover the mountain with trash, so we opted to "walk off" instead. We spent the next 18 hours covering eight miles back to camp, laden like mules and negotiating a maze of granite terraces, an unexpected glacier, and a consequential hanging talus field. We reached the dock suffering only a golfball-size welt, a sprained MCL, and a misaligned patella. Next time we'd rappel.

Despite our generally poor climbing style, we left the face as we found it, placing no bolts and leaving no anchors, tat, or fixed gear behind. 📄 📷

– KEVIN HEINRICH, *USA*

BIG CLIMBS IN SQUAMISH, 2017–2019

NEW ROUTE DEVELOPMENT continued to be very popular in Squamish and the surrounding Sea to Sky corridor during 2017–2019, as local first ascensionists (a.k.a. "Scrubbers") uncovered numerous treasures under the coastal BC rainforest to produce an estimated 500 new pitches. [*This report highlights a handful of the notable long routes; the extended online version of this report also covers key cragging developments.*]

On the Stawamus Chief itself, the pace of development has slowed compared with the early 2010s. The increasing popularity of hiking, bouldering, and climbing in the forest beneath the walls makes the scrubbing and cleaning of loose blocks necessary to new routing highly problematic (that is, poten-

David Ellison following the stacked corners on pitch seven (5.12a) of the new climb Borealis. *Colin Moorhead*

tially dangerous to anyone below). Despite these limitations, some of the most dedicated Squamish scrubbers continue to establish high-quality lines. Colin Moorhead, for example, did most of the development on Borealis (5 pitches, 5.12a, 2019) at night. Borealis starts off the Astro Ledge and extends from what remains of the Calling (5.12a) after a massive 2015 rockfall. When linked with Alaska Highway (5.11d), this route produces a 14-pitch masterpiece, said to be one of the most sustained routes on the Chief.

Elsewhere in the North Walls, Stu Smith established Trad Climbing Goof: an eight-pitch excursion up the Manitou Wall featuring four 5.13 and three 5.12- pitches—the climb was seven years off and on in the making before being completed in 2019. The Chief also saw its first new aid line in a long time in 2017, with Danny Guestrin, Jon Rigg, and Chris Trull's Pantera (V A3+ 5.10).

On the Apron, Kris Wild endured days of torrential rain over three consecutive winters while excavating two very popular moderate multipitches: Long Time, No See (10 pitches, 5.9, 2017) and Read Between the Lines (5 pitches, 5.10a, 2019).

Locals Tony McLane and Jacob Cook have been particularly active on the Chief. In 2017, Cook and McLane opened a unique 5.12d on the Sheriff's Badge called Badge to the Bone, which starts at the third-pitch anchors of Daily Planet and traverses right for four pitches through super-steep terrain. In the same area, also in 2017, they opened Inner Space, a three-pitch 5.12c variation finish to the Daily Universe, continuing through some roofs up high. And in 2019, Drew Marshall joined Cook (with some help prepping the route from McLane) for Inner Fire (5 pitches, 5.12d), a highly technical slab adventure bolted on lead up a number of small traversing dikes departing from Bellygood Ledge.

One of the biggest recent developments was the announcement that some popular crags in the Murrin Park area are part of a land package that will be transferred to the Squamish First Nation

Jacob Cook leading steep terrain on Badge to the Bone (5.12d), an unusual addition to the Sheriff's Badge that mostly traverses for four pitches. *Bronwyn Hodgins*

pursuant to federal reconciliation efforts and local industrial and infrastructure development. The package includes Petrifying Wall and Up Among the Firs. It is not known if the transfer will affect access to recreational climbing areas. There is ongoing discussion within the community about collaborative efforts to maintain some level of climbing access while respecting the Squamish First Nation's land use priorities. Climbers can assist by practicing a strict Leave No Trace ethic and engaging in respectful discourse to learn more about the process. Respect for the land and for everyone involved will be crucial.

Finally, there has even been a rash of new alpine and ice climbs over the past three years, especially during the winter of 2017–2018, when the polar vortex visited the south coast of B.C. to produce ice conditions that led some locals to joke how Squamish had become "Squamonix." In February 2018, Ledge Mountain in the Sky Pilot group finally saw the second winter ascent of its north face by Brette Harrington and Marc-André Leclerc, some 47 years after the first winter ascent by Arnold Shives and Glenn Woodsworth. In 2018, on Mt. Habbrich, Jason Ammerlaan and Alistair Davis established Life on Mars (180m, WI3). Also in 2018, on the bluffs above the Papoose, Jia Condon, Paul McSorely, and Tony Richardson climbed Eagle Eye (100m, WI5). And in 2019, Josh Lavigne and Paul McSorley climbed the Mother of the Wind (250m, M5 WI6) on the lower Zodiac Wall.

The "ultimate" prize of the last few ice seasons was the Ultimate Ultimate Everything—the first bottom to top all-ice ascent of the Chief, following the popular summer route called the Ultimate Everything, by Condon, Jason Kruk, McSorley, and Richardson, in January 2017. Within a week of the first ascent, this line received a "tandem solo," linked up with the Dream, by Leclerc and Luka Lindic. 📄 📷

– **CHRIS SMALL,** *CANADA*

ELKHORN MOUNTAIN, EAST RIDGE, BULL ELK

ELKHORN MOUNTAIN (2,194M) in Strathcona Provincial Park is the second-highest peak on Vancouver Island and has a reputation for being chossy. This is especially true of the northwest and west aspects of the mountain. But, as I found out with my partner Mike Ford, the east face is a whole other story.

The east face of Elkhorn Mountain (2,194m), showing Bull Elk (900m, 5.10). Earlier routes to the left and right can be seen at the AAJ website, including Horny Elk (500m, 5.7), climbed in June 2019. *Ryan Van Horne*

The east face has seen a handful of climbs over the years, the first of which was Al Harrison's impressive solo effort from 1975, climbing a line above the East Glacier. In 1985, Tim Rippel soloed the first ascent of the northeast face (400m, 5.7), east of the east ridge. Sometime in the 1980s, the legendary Greg Foweraker attempted to climb the full east ridge. In 1993, Philip Stone and Greg Shea established Into the Sadistic (500m, 5.10b), which started on the East Glacier and ended at the upper east ridge, without summiting. Stone returned in 2016 with Ryan Van Horne and Hunter Lee and climbed about ten pitches left of the east ridge before pulling the plug. In spite of strong suitors, the longest and most prominent line on this face awaited a complete ascent.

On August 5, Mike and I bushwhacked up the Cervus Creek jungle for five hours before popping out into the alpine and getting our first view of the full east ridge. It looked huge, complex, intimidating, and probably devoid of water. We loaded our packs with 4.5 liters and started climbing around 12:30 p.m. We began at the toe of the east ridge, approximately 400m below and climber's right of the East Glacier. The first six pitches of our climb followed a huge right-facing dihedral on beautiful compact stone, with difficulties to 5.9. Midway up the ridge we found a steep headwall with a variety of crack features. We climbed the leftmost, finding the terrain steep, positive, and a bit heady. There was 500m of air under me as I pulled what turned out to be the crux pitch (5.10). The climbing above was fun and engaging, mostly falling in the 5.8 to 5.9 range. We stopped as the sun was leaving the sky around 9:15 p.m., laid out our little foam butt pads and light sleeping bags on a vegetated ledge, and fell asleep.

On the upper 300–400m of the ridge, we linked tower to tower, with difficulties up to 5.9, joining the Harrison Route a few pitches from the top. We arrived at the main summit at 10:15 a.m., then started down the infamously steep Elkhorn Trail to retrieve the cold beers we had hidden in Cervus Creek. We named the full east ridge Bull Elk (900m, 5.10), because it is the most impressive feature on the mountain. About 75 to 80 percent of our route climbed new terrain. 🖹 🖸

– MAX FISHER, *CANADA*

RUGGED MOUNTAIN, THUNDERBIRD

NEAR THE WEST coast of Vancouver Island, the Haihte Range is crowned by the aptly named Rugged Mountain (6,151'), whose south face drops dramatically for nearly 4,000'. Heavy logging in the mid-1980s brought road access nearly to the base of the wall, and the only two existing routes—the Southwest Face Route (2,200', 5.6, Briggs-Berryman, 1987) and the Johnson-Newman

The southwest face of Rugged Mountain in the Haihte Range. (The photo was taken in a dry February.) (1) Thunderbird (22 pitches, 5.10 A1). (2) Johnson-Newman Route (1,600', 5.8). (3) The original Southwest Face Route (2,200', 5.6). *Ahren Rankin*

Route (1,600', 5.8, 1989)—were established at that time.

James Rode and I were in the area in July 2017 with Garner Begeron, intent on climbing a new route linking steep features and slabs on the left side of the wall, far from the existing lines. After 400' of approach slabs, we climbed about half a dozen pitches (all 5.7 or under). We had decided to establish the route with bolted anchors for rappelling and protection bolts where absolutely necessary, so we spent the rest of the day rappelling and drilling.

Two weeks later we climbed back to our high point and continued up. The stellar-looking corner pitch we had seen cutting through the headwall was actually quite moderate (5.8), ending on a large ledge. Above, the climbing remained fairly easy to a huge, heather-covered ledge. Down to climber's left, we found a spacious ledge with a miraculous rivulet of water pouring out of the rock even late in the summer. We bivied here, watching the sun set into the Pacific Ocean. In the morning we explored another two pitches to reach the apparent crux of the route, then headed down again.

It wasn't until August 2019 that we finally returned to finish our route. We climbed the 13 pitches to the bivy in leisurely fashion, enjoying the fruits of our labor from two years earlier. In the morning we headed up into the amazing set of features that had drawn us to this face years ago. We swapped leads, drilling a few more bolts, and finally reached the top of the wall by headlamp. In the pitch black, we engineered three passable bivy spots on sloping ledges and tried to sleep. I woke several times in the most contorted shapes imaginable. It was one of the best nights of my life.

We named our route Thunderbird (ca 800m, 22 pitches, 5.10 A1) after the mythological creature celebrated by various northwestern First Nations.

– **AHREN RANKIN**, *CANADA*

CHINESE PUZZLE WALL, MANCHU WOK

IN 2008, SQUAMISH hardman Dan Tetzlaff and I made a comical botched attempt on the virgin Chinese Puzzle Wall, high on a shoulder of South Illusion Peak. A loose flake and a giant whipper onto an old Ray Jardine–model rigid Friend stopped us short. I've been thinking of a rematch ever since. Eight years later, from the east face of Slesse Mountain, I watched the headlamps of my friends Marc-André Leclerc and Brette Harrington as they worked to establish Hidden Dragon, the first route up the face. Brette later came back with Caro North and Chris Kalman and opened the route that Dan and I had attempted, calling it Crouching Tiger.

After 11 years of wondering, I finally found myself back on the Puzzle—this time with Brette, who was hungry for more. We started up steep terrain about 100m to climber's right of the two established routes in early July, and began aid climbing, cleaning, free climbing, and fixing ropes as we went. With the route primed, an iffy but somewhat optimistic weather window was motivation enough to hit the road from Squamish again. Brette made an impressive push to join me, waking at 3 a.m., flying to Seattle from Alaska, borrowing a truck, driving across the U.S.-Canada border and up to the dirt road in the Nesakwatch Valley, and hiking up to the wall with me late in the evening.

In the morning we were doubtful the route would be dry, but the opening moves looked reasonable, so the games began. Brette took the crux lead, a powerful overhanging dike pitch. I was fully expecting her to come off at the top, but she managed to stay on. We nearly blew the redpoint on the final scrappy pitch—a short, powerful Marc-André "5.10d"—but eventually we sat at the top having both freed all 13 pitches, mainly in the 5.10+ to 5.11 range, with one 12d pitch: Manchu Wok (500m, 5.12+).

Spending time on the Puzzle with Marc-André's loved one, climbing in his local area, produced a potent emotional release. His boundless energy and charisma touched me like no other. He would be pleased if you would visit this wonderful playground. 🗏 ◙

– **TONY MCLANE**, *CANADA*

BRITISH COLUMBIA / SELKIRK MOUNTAINS – VALHALLA RANGES

GIMLI PEAK, KOOTENAY CANALETA

THE VALHALLAS ARE primarily a rock climbing destination, but that doesn't mean winter-season climbing is impossible. In fact, it can be quite good, as David Lussier and I discovered in November during the first ascent of Kootenay Canaleta (350m, D+ WI4 M5) on the north face of Gimli Peak (2,774m).

We camped before our climb near the classic south ridge of Gimli. In the morning, we moved over snow, rock, ice, and moss to get to the west col, from which we did one short rappel and then contoured around via a small pocket glacier to reach the base of the north face, 1.5 hours after leaving camp.

Kootenay Canaleta on Gimli. *Douglas Noblet*

David graciously let me lead the first pitch, which had the most ice climbing on it. He then gracefully ascended classic, heady thin ice that brought us into the main weakness of the face. The crux M5 pitch climbed up through some wider cracks. Four more mixed pitches took us into the last 100m of the couloir, where we took off the rope and climbed steep snow with a couple of rock and ice steps. Each pitch had its challenges, and the climbing protected reasonably well with stubbies, nuts, and cams. We descended the route, mostly rappelling from slung horns or chockstones.

According to Lussier, a local guide, the main reason the route had escaped attention is the difficulty of access in winter. The logging road into this area is not plowed in winter, but was still open during our early season climb. To our knowledge, there haven't been other significant ice or mixed climbs in the Valhallas. Lussier thinks there may be potential on the north-facing gullies of Mt. Dag and Little Dag (up to 1,000m tall), but it is hard to see the conditions and the walls are difficult to access. ◙

– **JEN OLSON**, *CANADA*

BILL'S DOME, DELUSION DWELLER

ONE HUNDRED YEARS ago, a trapper named Bill Drinnan roamed the headwaters of Hoder Creek, in the southwest corner of what's now Valhalla Provincial Park. Drinnan Pass is named for him, and so is Bill's Dome—an imposing hulk of compact gneiss 1.5km from the Drinnan Pass trailhead. In 2019, its 500m west face had yet to be climbed.

Over the course of four years, Steve Ogle and I made four ground-up attempts on this impressive face, which is not quite so slabby as it looks. On August 28 we finally succeeded, leaving the trailhead at 5:30 a.m. and topping out at 5 p.m. We walked off via the north ridge to the Drinnan Peak–Bill's Dome col and then down a west-facing bowl to reach the trail by 9 p.m.

Delusion Dweller (500m, 5.10d/5.11a) on the west face of Bill's Dome. *David Lussier*

We believe this is the easiest and most natural line up the west face. About half the route was under 5.10, which we often ran out as the compact gneiss does not present an abundance of gear placements. The other half of the route was in the 5.10/10+realm, with bolts where needed (placed on lead with a power drill). We named our route Delusion Dweller (500m, 13–14 pitches, 5.10d/5.11a) due to a particular optical illusion that occurs when climbing the route—you'll have to do the climb to see it for yourself. 📄 📷

– DAVID LUSSIER, *CANADA*

ALBERTA / CANADIAN ROCKIES

MT. PHILLIPS, NORTH SPUR

SIMON RICHARDSON AND I branched out to new-for-us ground when, in July, we turned off the Berg Lake trail at Emperor Falls and headed toward Mt. Phillips (3,246m). I had hiked the popular trail at least a dozen times in order to attempt and climb Robson. But prior to Richardson showing me a photo of Mt. Phillips, I had scarcely known it existed. One new turn led us through the most astounding meadows of wildflowers and on to the first ascent of the obvious north spur of Mt. Phillips. It was a lesson in how even a tiny change to our usual habits can yield a beautiful experience.

We approached up the Phillips Glacier and bivied on the climber's right flank of the glacier. By sun-up we were on the north spur, simul-climbing easy 5th-class ledges and loose steps, the rockfall from shattered stone being serious enough to require judicious care. Starting on the right side of the rib up a slight gully, we then traversed out left to stay on easy 5th-class face. At one stance below

The line of the North Spur (600m, IV) on Mt. Phillips (3,246m). The high peak behind the left skyline is Whitehorn. *John Scurlock*

a steepening in the spur at mid-height, I took an hour to smash the choss down enough to tie together a few knifeblades and a nut slotted into a manufactured spot for the anchor. (I threw in my tools for good measure.) A gully cut right to left through the slight headwall until some run-out but very easy isothermal snow scrambling led to a safe ledge right on the north spur. About 200m of easy horizontal scrambling across a catwalk of choss pillars, and the summit was ours.

We called the route the North Spur and gave it a grade of IV. The climbing was never hard—it was mostly 4th class. However, we always had the rope on, as an avalanche or rockfall easily could have caused us trouble. In terms of adventure and exploration the route was very worthwhile. Simon became the second stalwart of the Scottish Mountaineering Club to establish a new route on the peak, the first ascent (via a glacier on the south side) having fallen in 1910 to Norman Collie, another proud SMC member. 📄 📷

– IAN WELSTED, *CANADA*

NORTH TWIN, COMPLETE NORTH RIDGE

ANYONE WHO WALKS over Woolley Shoulder, passing Mt. Alberta to the north and Stutfield Peak to the south, is rewarded with a fine view, but the eye is drawn inexorably to the west. There lies Twins Tower—whose huge shadowy face is the starkest of all the mythical north walls of the range—and jagged Son of Twin, off its north shoulder, with the smooth, glaciated North Twin higher still and just to the south. The complete north ridge of North Twin tags all three high points, beckoning climbers with an obvious and aesthetic line.

The complete traverse of the 4km ridge has been talked up by locals at least as far back as 2000, when I moved to the area. Many have compared it to the Peuterey Ridge of Mont Blanc in the Alps—jokingly, primarily, as the rock quality on Twin is notoriously bad. In spite of all the talk, the only actual attempt on the complete ridge that I know of is Dave Cheesmond and Sean Dougherty's effort in 1985, and they didn't make it far. Undoubtedly, most have been discouraged by the poor rock quality. Also, most who *would* be inter-

The full north ridge of the Twins, seen from Woolley Shoulder. The 4km traverse began at far right (off picture) and climbed over the prominent Son of Twin, Twins Tower (with its famous north face), and North Twin, hidden in the clouds. The adventure took five days, car to car. *Ian Welsted*

ested have probably been drawn to the bigger prizes on Twins Tower or Alberta.

On Monday, August 26, Alik Berg and I spent a day approaching over Woolley Shoulder, and the next day began soloing up the ridgeline, starting at 2,400m. When we arrived at two roughly 100m towers, Alik was eager to climb them, but I had guiding work booked for Saturday and was keen to complete this climb as rapidly as possible, in the hope of getting a day of rest. Eventually I convinced Alik to walk around the towers, so a pure ascent of the "full full" north ridge yet remains.

We camped that night below the start of the technical climbing on Son of Twin (3,260m) in windy, threatening weather. Son of Twin had only one documented previous ascent, via the northwest ridge, reached from a pocket glacier below the face, by Al Spero and Dane Waterman in 1979. We intended to follow their route but saw no signs of passage on our line. The climbing included 5.7 cracks with loose blocks, followed by run-out easy climbing on an arête. From the

Ian Welsted 150 meters below the shoulder of the Twins Tower, leading on crumbly rock. *Alik Berg*

top, Alik led approximately six rappels into the col between Son of Twin and Twins Tower. We arrived just at dark and settled in for another night.

Our fourth day started by rapping down the ice gully from the col, as we had to gain low-angled ledges on the northwest face of Twins Tower in order to link into the first and most moderate route up this aspect, climbed by Hank L. Abrons, Peter Carman, and Rick Millikan on July 17–18, 1965. Brandon Pullan and I had made the second known ascent of this route in 2014. Instead of taking the far left gully that Brandon and I climbed, Alik and I chose blockier terrain to the right, due to unclimbable melting snow in the gully. We had a few run-out stretches approximately 100m below the top shoulder, but eventually found enough marginal protection to make the climbing reasonable.

From the shoulder, Alik had to lead a traverse above the north face over wet, snow-covered terrain where protection was difficult to find, partly due to our ice rack of only two screws. Slightly after sunset, we topped out on the Twins Tower (3,627m). We descended the south ridge to a snowy col and then walked uphill in darkness to the summit of the North Twin (3,731m). Soaked by the wet snow, we chose to continue moving, walking down to the north side of Stutfield Peak, and finally camping on a shaley rock slope among glaciers at 2 a.m.

The next day, our fifth, we descended the Cromwell-Stutfield col, which proved to be more technical than we had hoped. By 4 p.m. on Friday we had crossed the Sunwapta River a few kilometers south of where we started five days earlier.

Overall, the Peuterey Integrale of Choss (1,300m-plus, V 5.7) is more a challenge of mental and physical endurance than a technical one. The climbing is never of a difficult grade, and in spite of marginal rock quality, none of the individual pitches is X- or even R-rated—if one is adept at knifeblade placements. 🖸

– IAN WELSTED, *CANADA*

PEYTO TOWER, NEW ROUTES

IN MAY 2018, Niall Hamill and I were on our way to Mt. Robson but couldn't help pulling the van over to the side of the Icefields Parkway to stare at Peyto Tower, a 300m shield of bright white quartzite jutting off Mt. Wilson. We took note of the numerous striking crack systems scarring the quartzite, envisioning a veritable buffet of unclimbed free routes.

Peyto Tower was not unclimbed, of course. In 1992, Rob Orvig and Larry Stanier climbed the prow on looker's left of Peyto's southeast face, said to be a moderate classic. In 2003, the far right side of the face was climbed. But the rest of the steep and intriguing southeast face had largely escaped the interest of the very active Bow Valley climbing community.

I needed to return stateside for work that summer in 2018, but Niall wasted no time venturing up to the face. When he couldn't find a psyched partner for the three-hour approach, he scrambled to the tower's summit and rappeled down a potential new line. After setting anchors through the upper headwall, which was littered with cracks, he equipped a sport pitch of steep, beautiful climbing through the blank white band where the lower limestone converges with the upper quartzite. Later he returned with Grant Stewart to free the line from the ground. Their route—Prairie Gold (5.11c, 280m)—was the first free route (and possibly the easiest) on the face.

Come spring of 2019, I was back in Canada, swinging tools with Niall, who couldn't stop talking about Peyto Tower. With dreams of Bugaboos splitters and Banff bolt clipping filling my head, I was having trouble matching his enthusiasm, but he wore me down with the promise of a perfect ledge (which we took to calling Summer Camp Ledge) a third of the way up the face. I was soon daydreaming of spending summer days on this miniature big wall.

In June we climbed through the lower limestone to reach this ledge, which turned out to be nothing more than an uncomfortable, uneven ramp. Niall had sandbagged me! After half-hanging in harnesses all night through intermittent rain showers, we started up a harder variation to Prairie Gold. We aided and equipped a steep corner, leaving a pin and bolt where the crack sealed shut, and climbed two more adventurous pitches before the weather turned nasty and we descended. Niall returned on the first day of July to complete the route with Cory Rogans, dubbing it Gravity's Rainbow (300m, 5.12a R).

Niall Hamill on pitch three roof of Prairie Gold (280m, 5.11c) on the east face of Peyto Tower. *Adam Gearing*

In spite of generally bad weather, we established two more routes on the upper wall that summer. The huge, crimson right-facing corner to the right of Gravity's Rainbow had pulled our eyes every time we went up to Peyto, so we started there. While the first pitch from Summer Camp Ledge was a brilliant series of bouldery 5.11 crack moves, some sections of the upper corner were coated by centuries of mud that had drained the mountain. We called this route Primordial Soup (300m, 5.11c).

For our last stint on Peyto, we made a tensioned rappel down and right from Summer Camp Ledge to reach a ledge system and a towering overhang of white quartzite. Each pitch took a few hours as I lead soloed in the aiders while Niall cleaned and bolted the pitches for free climbing. After two days, two whippers, and a strained ankle, I was spent. Niall graciously took over, freeing the pitches on the sharp end as I followed with everything I had left. On the final push, Niall led through the last 5.11 roof, then traversed poorly protected face to a final crack system. We named our route Bengal Spice Indirect (300m, 5.12c PG-13), and we believe it has all the right ingredients to be a modern classic. [*See a photo topo of all these routes at the AAJ website.*] 📷

– RYAN RICHARDSON, *USA*

Overview of the main lines at the Storm Creek Headwall in Banff National Park. Some linkups and variations are not pictured. (1) Banana Peel. (2) The Sphynx. (3) Buddha Nature. (4) Kahveology. (5) Silmarillion. All routes are in the 100- to 125-meter range. *Raphael Slawinski*

THE ROCKIES: YEAR IN REVIEW

THE SPRING SEASON in the Rockies began with a tremendous first ascent and then quickly passed into tragedy that would capture the world's attention for all the wrong reasons. At the start of April, Brette Harrington, Luka Lindic, and Ines Papert climbed the direct east face of Mt. Fay: The Sound of Silence (1,100m, WI5 M8; see report on p.147). This much-contemplated route was dedicated to the late Marc-André Leclerc, who had intended to climb it with Lindic.

Two weeks later, the community was rocked by the news that Hansjörg Auer, David Lama, and Jess Roskelley were caught in an avalanche on Howse Peak during their descent from a significant new variation to M-16 on the east face (see p. 150).

After another two weeks, with an improved snowpack, Niall Hamill returned with Ryan Richardson to his project on the north face of Mt. Lawrence Grassi and completed Canmore Swingers Party (300m, WI3 M6+ R), two and a half months after taking a gear-popping whipper from the route and fracturing his scapula. "A little older now, a little wiser," as Hamill wrote in his full report (published at the AAJ website), the two completed the third 300m line up this accessible alpine "town crag."

In June, with rock climbing season kicking into gear, Kevin Rohn opened two new routes on the numbered buttresses of Mt. Rundle, also above Canmore: Coaches Corner with Alik Berg, and the Southeast Shoulder of Fourth Buttress with Dylan Cunningham. Both were 350m 5.10-climbs. Also on Rundle, Patrick Delaney and Magda Kosior finished Supernova (13/14 pitches, 5.11), with help from Hans Eric Schnack and Brent Peters. This partly bolted route starts just right of the classic Reprobate on East End of Rundle (EEOR).

An unusually wet summer prevented much action in the high alpine. *(However, see reports from Mt. Phillips and the Twins earlier in this section.)* In September, Berg and Quentin Lindfield-Roberts climbed the east ridge of Synge Peak (600m, 5.8), approached via Cirque Lake. In the same month, Berg climbed the north couloir of Mt. Outram (500m, WI3 50°) with Maarten van Haeren.

When October came, the Rockies were at their finest, with perfect alpine mixed conditions and no snow to speak of. Hamill kicked things off with Tourist Trap (500m, 5.8 WI3). Starting directly from the left-hand shore of Moraine Lake, this obvious line had been partially climbed by Jen

Adolph and Dave Edgar. A compelling moderate, it was immediately repeated by numerous parties. On October 12, Grant Stewart teamed with Ryan Patteson for the East Chimney (4 pitches, M5 WI3) on the west buttress of Mt. Athabasca, to climber's right of the classic Slawinski-Takeda.

In a hanging valley north of Cirrus Mountain (home to Polar Circus), Kiff Alcocer, Dylan Cunningham, and Michele Pratt climbed two routes in memory of Anna Smith, who had done the first ascent of the Proposal in the same valley; she died in October 2016 during an expedition to the Indian Himalaya. The trio established Push-Up Bra (110m, WI5) and Boisterous (110m, M4 WI4).

Rohn made two trips to the east face of Boom Mountain, above Highway 93. With Carl Dowse he climbed the south-most gully through easy ground to end on a WI3 pitch, then with Cunningham he climbed I Can't Believe a Chicken Fried This Rice (325m, WI4 M5) on good quartzite. Two similar gullies, likely unclimbed, rise to the north.

Across the highway on Storm Mountain, Ethan Berman and Van Haeren added Eye of the Storm (700m, WI5 M6), which climbs through thin ice and a 60m quartzite corner to the lower north spur of Storm Mountain, right of the French Connection and Extended Mix. (*A full report is at the AAJ website*.) On the same day, upslope and on the

Maarten van Haeren moving up the monster dihedral on pitch eight of Eye of the Storm (700m, WI5 M6) on Storm Mountain in Banff National Park. *Ethan Berman*

opposite side of the valley from the Stanley Headwall, Bruno-Pierre Couture and Jordan Farquharson climbed Darwin Arch (470m, WI3 5.4), finishing at a spectacular rock arch.

On October 30, usual suspects Cunningham, Rohn, and Lindfield-Roberts teamed for Menage à Trois (190m, M4 WI4) on the obvious large ice flow 100m left of Guinevere in the Protection Valley, between Castle and Protection mountains. A week later, they climbed Roommate Romance (280m, WI4 M5) in the same valley. In November, also in Protection Valley, Kris Irwin and Mike Stuart discovered an amazing narrow chimney system lined with ice on the lower west face of Castle Mountain. Superdark (195m, 7 pitches, M5) is bound to be considered a unique classic. The concentration of recent routes in the Protection Valley has created a world-class mixed and ice venue, with over a dozen routes in a relatively avalanche-safe area.

Later in November, Raphael Slawinski was involved in two new lines at the Storm Creek Headwall, taking advantage of three discontinuous ice strips left of Buddha Nature. The Sphynx (125m, WI5 M7+) was completed with Hamill, who had started up it independently. To the left again is Banana Peel (110m, WI5 M6), which Slawinski climbed with Juan Henriquez and Maia Shumacher.

This amazing spree of early winter routes goes to show what is possible in the Rockies when a low snowpack, together with a wet summer, result in prime conditions. The year also showed that it is imperative to wait for the right conditions in the Rockies. 📄 📷

– IAN WELSTED, *CANADA*

INGLEFIELD MOUNTAINS, EXPLORATION AND IVORY GULL RESEARCH

Dave Critchley above Camp 1 in the Inglefield Mountains. *Greg Horne*

THE INGLEFIELD MOUNTAINS of southeast Ellesmere Island, north of Makinson Inlet, had been on my mind ever since I first saw them from the Manson Icefield in 2001. It took me until 2019 to finally visit, when Dave Critchley, Louise Jarry, and I chartered a Twin Otter ski plane from Kenn Borek Air out of Resolute Bay on May 14.

The 2.5-hour flight took us over familiar terrain of the Sydkap Ice Cap (*AAJ 2018*), west of Grise Fiord, then on to the Inglefield Mountains: range after range of nunataks breaking out of the icefield. The landscape is huge—70km-long glaciers up to 25km wide, with meltwater stream canyons carving trenches in the ice 50km long. Circling our intended landing area west of Easter Island, the flight crew gave us bad news: The terrain was way too crevassed to attempt a landing. A backup spot 12km southwest was picked out, 25km west-northwest of Cape Mouat.

We had come, primarily, to check for activity at ivory gull nesting sites last surveyed in 2009. The population of the gull in northern Canada has declined dramatically in the last several decades. The first seven nesting sites we had planned to survey were now too far away from our landing site, so we began skiing northwest, heading toward other nunataks occupied by gulls in 2009.

Four days into the tour, we stopped to ski up Peak 1 (1,450m) by its northwest ridge. [*Coordinates of peaks are at the AAJ website.*] Returning to camp early, we packed and descended to the 50km-long Wykeham Glacier. Until this point, crevasses had been few and far between, but on the Wykeham crevasses were ubiquitous, and a roped-up crevasse fall by Dave that sucked his 70kg pulk in behind him was a reality check.

Every evening thereafter, weather permitting, we would launch a drone to scout the next day's potential route. After crossing a low glacial divide into the head of the south branch of the Trinity Glacier, it was obvious the crevasse situation would only be getting worse. We had checked four nest sites and found zero gull activity. The next sites, only two days away by direct ski travel, were blocked by hundreds of sagging crevasses, and there was no way we could reach these nests.

The only option was a one-week detour up and across a portion of the main Prince of Wales Icefield. Ski ascents of Peak 2 (1,450m) and Peak 3 (1,410m) allowed us to see eastward to Greenland. At over 1,000m of elevation, the crevasse situation improved, but the possibility of a whiteout still gave us an uncomfortable feeling. We made one more ski ascent, climbing Peak 4 (1,580m) from camp 14, before the weather—which until then had been perfect—changed for the worse. During three days stuck in camp, 25cm of fresh snow buried all sign of the previous sagging bridges.

We retreated back west to the flat icecap, and the Twin Otter picked us up on June 6, after landing in a glacial basin to our north, out of sight. After some silence, we heard the engine revving, then spotted a tail rudder in the distance as the plane taxied uphill through deep snow, weaving around crevasses, to reach our camp. Simply amazing. 📄 📷

– GREG HORNE, *CANADA*

VALKYRIE PEAK AND OTHER ASCENTS

CULMINATING A THREE-YEAR training program for young climbers, an expedition from the Swiss Alpine Club spent nearly a month in Auyuittuq National park and climbed five routes, including two possible first ascents of peaks. The team was Pierre Bétrisey, Louis Jacques, Johannes Konrad, and Mathias Ulrich (ages 21 to 24), with Denis Burdet as lead guide, along with doctor Sebastian Zurbriggen.

Much of the activity was up the Fork Beard Glacier, which extends southward from near Mt. Thor in the Weasel River Valley. The first objective was the beautiful

Looking southeast up an arm of the Fork Beard Glacier. The Swiss team climbed the 500-meter north face of the mountain at left, calling it Valkyrie Peak. Their route was Rien á Déclarer ("Nothing to Declare," 7a A2+). The other faces are probably unclimbed. *Denis Burdet Collection*

north face of a peak on the south side of a glacier extending to the east about 6km up the Fork Beard (66.508347N, 65.202059W). The team spent a week establishing Rien á Déclarer (500m, 7a A2+), leading directly to the summit, which they called Valkyrie Peak. [*This summit would be relatively easy to reach from a glacier to the south, and it's possible it was climbed this way before.*]

On August 1, members of the team climbed two side-by-side 400m routes at the west-facing head of a nearby cirque: Game of Drone and Popcorn Finger (both 6c). They descended the ridge to the north with scrambling and several rappels.

Two days later, the team climbed the south pillar of a formation farther up the Fork Beard Glacier they called Willen Peak (66.481738N, 65.207708W), named after an injured member of the team who could not join the expedition. The route was Vigier Béton (500m, 6c); they descended by rappel.

After moving their base camp back down to the main valley, the Swiss climbers attempted two routes on Tirokwa East. On August 10 and 12, Bétrisey, Burdet, and Zurbriggen climbed a long line up the left side of the west face, first climbing about 10 pitches up the lower apron and then, two days later, regaining their high point by a ledge system and then continuing for another 18 pitches or so to a point just 30m below the summit, where unprotected rock led them to descend after about 1,400m of climbing (850m vertical gain). They called the not-quite-complete line Aya Pagula (6c+). During the same period, the team also attempted a route up the main pillar on the west face of Tirokwa East but descended after about 350m of climbing (6b+ A4). 📷

– INFORMATION FROM **DENIS BURDET** *AND* **PIERRE BÉTRISEY**, *SWITZERLAND*

Edoardo Saccaro high on the south face of Nalumasortoq Central Pillar during the first ascent of La Cura. *Federica Mingolla*

HIDING IN PLAIN SIGHT
THE FIRST ROUTE UP A BIG FACE NEAR TASERMIUT FJORD

BY FEDERICA MINGOLLA, *ITALY*

TASERMIUT IS A paradise, not only for rock climbing but also because it is possible to experience living in real wilderness. On July 19, Edoardo Saccaro and I disembarked at the fjord just two days after leaving Italy. We had passed through amazing country: immense open spaces and very little civilization; some villages we encountered were comprised of a mere 10 houses, a few boats, and, occasionally, a football field.

We quickly set our sights on a few warm-up routes, getting a feel for the granite, at first on Nalumasortoq and then on Ulamertorssuaq. We found that it is not quite as solid or clean as we'd imagined. Actually, it can be somewhat treacherous, especially on the slabs; the cracks tend to be far more solid, albeit sometimes covered in thick lichen.

One day, I went for a reconnaissance and saw the "other side" of Nalumasortoq: the south face. (Only the west face is really visible from base camp.) I took photos of what seemed to me an obvious line on the south side of the Central Pillar, zigzagging through the center of the wall. It was such a plumb line that I was sure someone must have climbed it. But after carefully examining all our topos, and those of other climbers at base camp, we came to the conclusion that I was wrong. A new route would need to be established: ours! This is how La Cura came to life.

[*Editor's note: This new route climbs the previously virgin face on the right side of the Central Pillar, between Cheese Finger at Three O'Clock (6b A3, Berthet-Brambati-Dalphin-Flugi-Vitali, 1996) on the pillar's western aspect and Conspiracy Planet (VII A3+, Fluder-Golab-Piecuch-Tomaszewski, 2000) on the neighboring Righthand Pillar.*]

At the start we had no idea what to expect. Would the rock be solid or crumbly? Were those black marks streaks of water or simply darker shades of rock? And would the weather hold? By now it was the start of August, and climbers warned us about how quickly the weather could change, forcing us off the wall.

Fortunately, it held. After eight days on the wall, split into four attempts, we managed to complete our route, admittedly with the use of aid on some sections. On our final push we started up the climb on August 14 and reached the top of the south face on the 17th. As we stood there, we could feel the air becoming crisper—bad weather was on its way. Our route had 14 pitches, but we had been unable to free four of these.

Our plan was to wait for the storm to pass and then return to the face and give it all we had. Unfortunately, after having waited in base camp almost a week, we were met by radical changes on the wall. The temperature had dropped, and there was three hours less sun on the face. The rock failed to warm, even though there was not a cloud in sight. It was depressing: We couldn't even take off our two duvet jackets and woolly socks to try to free the pitches.

After one day and two freezing nights on the portaledge, we were forced to accept defeat. It was now late August and we were in Greenland, damn it! The decision was correct.

Greenland is a place I'd love to return to. Maybe we will, maybe we won't, but I hope someone will free the route, because it is a true work of art—a masterpiece of beautiful cracks, arches, and corners. So, big-wall climbers, give it a go!

SUMMARY: *First ascent of La Cura (525m, 7b+ A2) on the south face of the Central Pillar of Nalumasortoq in South Greenland.* 🔲 🔍

[Top] **Federica Mongolla starting pitch seven (7b+) of La Cura on the south face of Nalumasortoq's Central Pillar.** *Edoardo Saccaro* [Bottom] **Nalumasortoq's Central Pillar from the south-southwest, showing La Cura, the first route up the south face. Several earlier routes climbed the left (western) side of the pillar.** *Federica Mingolla*

TASERMIUT FJORD, ULAMERTORSSUAQ, WEST FACE, QUJANAG

The 2018 Brazilian line Qujanag on the west face of Ulamertorssuaq. In the upper section the route generally ascends the right edge of the great dihedral taken by Magic Tromblon, between that route and Moby Dick. *Marcos Vinicius Todero*

AFTER THREE PLANES, two boats, and four days of travel, Marcos Costa and I (both originally from Brazil) finally arrived at base camp beside Tasermiut Fjord in July 2018. During our 40-day expedition, we only saw two other climbing parties and a few groups of tourists.

After attempting a line on Nalumasortoq and making a two-day ascent of the classic Moby Dick on Ulamertorssuaq, we started looking at our next goal, a new route left of Moby Dick. We began the climb on July 26. After three pitches we found two very old anchors; we guessed these must be rappel anchors, as there are no reported routes in this area and the lower cracks were choked with vegetation.

From the top of pitch six, no new line offered natural protection, so our pitches seven to 12 followed Moby Dick. We then moved left and for pitches 13 to 15 followed the old route Magic Tromblon (6b A2, Agier-Payrau-Vigier, 1977). Above this, the next eight pitches were new and amazing. Starting with superb face climbing, we crossed small roofs and arêtes to reach a system of cracks we had spied from the ground. These started as a finger crack, widened to hands, and finally ended with a 50m offwidth. Opening some of these pitches free was the highlight of the expedition.

For pitches 23 and 24 we again were forced to follow Magic Tromblon. Above a small ledge (where it is possible to traverse right onto Moby Dick), our pitch 25 was an impressive, difficult arête, and as there seemed no possibility for natural gear, we placed seven protection bolts. We were unable to free this pitch but estimate the difficulty at 8a. Above pitch 26 we traversed right and finished up Moby Dick. We spent a total of 12 days on the face in four different pushes. Only pitches 25 and 26 did not go free; the rest involved difficulties up to 7c+.

We planned to attempt an all-free ascent of our new route, but the weather did not permit this. Three days before we were due to depart, we were forced to take an easier route to the top and rappel in to retrieve our gear. We were joined that day by a British base jumper, who leapt from the summit into a sea of clouds covering the fjord and was back in base camp in five minutes. We, on the other hand, were about to start 1,000m of rappelling.

We named our route Qujanaq (1,000m, 7c+ and some aid), which means "thank you" in local Greenlandic. [*Confusingly, there is already a route of the same name, climbed by Argentinians in 2016, on the southeast side of Ulamertorssuaq.*] One day, a family from the closest village invited us to join them on their fishing boat for a short trip to the upper part of the fjord. There, a giant glacier enters the sea from the inland ice cap. An old lady standing on the boat opened her arms toward the huge glacier and screamed "Qujanaq!" At the time we didn't understand the exact meaning but knew instantly that she was thanking Mother Nature for her greatness. 📷 🔍

– MARCOS VINICIUS TODERO, *SPAIN*

TORSSUKATAK FJORD, Å DÆVEN!; PEAK 1,303M, ÆGIR

ON JULY 13, Andreas Widlund (Sweden), Rune Harejo Jensen (Norway), and I joined Norwegian company Ægir Expeditions in Nuuk on Greenland's west coast. For the next four weeks we sailed the 12m Sofie around the tip of southern Greenland, climbing three probable new routes before continuing to Iceland.

Gale-force southerlies initially forced us to sail north from Nuuk to near the settlement of Igdlúnguaq, where we sheltered from the storm. There we managed to climb a route on the northwest face of an unnamed peak above the fjord (64.226944°N 50.876389°W). We named it Blod på Tann (450m of roped climbing, 5.8; the name means "Blood on the Tooth" in Norwegian dialect). It was a scrappy route with very loose rock. We descended the same line, leaving a few nuts.

We then moved to Torssukatak Fjord in South Greenland, where our first route was on a summit above the west coast at 60.081682°N, 44.520083°W. [*This is a subsidiary summit of a higher peak to the north that was probably first climbed by a 1975 Scottish expedition.*] We climbed the southeast face and east ridge, naming the route Å Dæven! ("The Devil!", 5.11a). On the 280m lower wall, we followed an obvious splitter for five pitches. Above, the terrain became more broken, but the rock stayed good. We passed this section in three rope-stretching pitches of 5.9. We then unroped for a few pitches of choose your own adventure. Above, I expected to reach a big ledge—instead I found a series of gendarmes set on an extremely exposed, knife-edge arête. *Å dæven!* Thankfully, the ridge was solid, and from its end a very long pitch led to the summit. We descended the northwest ridge to a col and then back to the base. The vertical interval was around 600m, but the climbing distance was more like 1,000m.

While on this climb we observed, just across the valley to the south, our next objective: the east-northeast pillar of Peak 1,303m. The first three pitches were fun, aesthetic 5.9, with the occasional move of 5.10. Above, the headwall was mainly vertical, with the crux on pitch eight: a series of overlaps with thin cracks and stemming. In the lead, I had to aid about 8m, but Rune followed free, suggesting a grade of 5.12b. The route finished above a ledge and ice patch with an unbelievable splitter crack and a pair of dueling offwidths. We topped out, chapped by the wind, with our minds blown, having completed Ægir (450m, ca 600m of climbing, 5.11c C1). We descended the east ridge, rappelling and scrambling, until we could contour back to our high camp, where we sheltered under a tarp while the wind raged throughout the night. 🖸

– **CHARLIE LONG**, *CANADA*

On the gendarmed ridge near the top of Å Dæven!, with Pamiagdluk Island behind and the Baron (1,340m) to the right. *Charlie Long*

STAUNING ALPS, SUGARLUMP AND BJØRNSSKULDERFJELL

LEO CAREW AND I (both U.K.) climbed in the Gurreholm Dal, a valley in the southern Stauning Alps that sits just within the Northeast Greenland National Park, in May 2018. Our agent, Tangent Expeditions Ltd., first brought us by snowmobile to a hut—the Red House (a former space observatory)—about 50km north of Constable Pynt, and from there we skied unsupported northwest for 150km to reach the Gurreholm Dal. Starting on April 19, this journey took nearly 10 days with pulks, each of which initially weighed 100kg.

We first attempted Peak 1,161m and then beautiful twin-summited Peak 1,630m, but turned around not far below the top of each because of avalanche risk. At the time we believed the latter to be unclimbed, but later discovered the southerly and higher summit had been climbed in 2014 and 2016 by Tangent-supported expeditions. On the return from our attempt on Peak 1,630m, we made a slight detour to take in a summit we called Sugarlump (1,167m) by the northwest flank. The full round trip from camp was 31km.

On the evening of May 9, we set off to attempt the first ascent of Peak 1,620m. We skinned up a broad ridge, and then, after crossing a col, a steeper and more challenging ridge led to the summit plateau, where we turned southwest and skied 5km to the highest point. We named the mountain Bjørnsskulderfjell. [*Coordinates for all peaks are at the AAJ website.*] We descended by continuing south around the head of a large cwm, then east to the main valley.

– MATTHEW HAY, *U.K.*

(A) Peak 1,881m, climbed in 2019 by the west ridge. (B) Northern Sun Spire, with the unclimbed 700m east face facing the camera. The upper section of A Grand Day Out is marked. *Tom Harding*

RENLAND, FIVE FIRST ASCENTS

IN A YEAR when the rapid melting of Greenland's ice was making international news, it was surprising to find ourselves stuck at Nerlerit Inaat Airport (Constable Pynt), waiting for the sea ice to break up so we could make the 180km boat journey to Renland. Inspired by photographs of an unnamed and little-visited valley in the southeast of this icecap-covered peninsula, we had spent more than a year planning this trip—now the four-day wait seemed endless. [*Editor's note: This area has been visited three times, though only two expeditions completed anything of significance; see AAJ 2013 and AAJ 2017.*]

Finally, on July 2, boats carried Neil Cox, Niall Newport, Cameron Ree, and me across the iceberg-filled Scoresby Sund, leaving us on Renland's sandy coast. We spent the next eight days hauling food and equipment through difficult glacier terrain to establish a high camp at 1,290m. This became our home for the next 11 days and gave access to a number of unclimbed objectives.

We made first ascents of five peaks, including the huge spire that dominates the entire valley, and climbed six routes in all, three of them long rock climbs. [*A complete report is at the AAJ website.*] Among these was Skyline Peak (2,080m), which we climbed via the southwest flank and west face: the Bristol Flyer (480m, AD+). This is probably the second-highest mountain in the area; the highest, Peak 2,084m, was climbed in 2012. We also climbed Northern Sun Spire (1,527m), whose impressive 700m east face had been noted by the 2016 expedition. We found broken terrain on the west face, reaching the summit via A Grand Day Out (450m, PD+, UIAA III).

We have published the first large-scale map to this valley (available at the AAJ website). There is still huge potential for future expeditions, and the logistics are generally manageable. We flew in with all of our equipment, saving the stress and cost of advance shipping. 📄📷🔍

– TOM HARDING, *U.K.*

Looking east from Dromedary Peak to mountains north of Sermiligaaq Fjord. The sharpest summit across the valley is Peak 1,569m. "Castle Peak" is the pyramid-shaped peak to the right. *Brian Jackson*

SCHWEIZERLAND, SERMILIGAAQ FJORD, VARIOUS ASCENTS

IN AUGUST, DAVE Head, UIAGM guide John Lyall, and I traveled by boat from Kulusuk to a base camp a little above the shore of Sermiligaaq Fjord, between the termini of the Karale (Kaarale) Glacier and an unnamed glacier west of the Apuseeg (a.k.a. Knud Rasmussen) Glacier. From here we climbed four mountains, which we called Dromedary Peak, Castle Peak, Consolation Peak, and Crest Peak. We saw some evidence of past climbers on Castle Peak but not on the other summits. A full report with coordinates and descriptions of each climb is at the AAJ website. 📄📷

– BRIAN JACKSON, *EXPEDITIONWISE.COM, U.K.*

QIANARTEQ ISLAND, PEAK 620M, NORTHWEST FACE

PEAK 620M LIES on the north coast of Qianarteq Island, opposite the abandoned Bluie East Two Airfield, built by Americans during World War II. I caught sight of it while working in this area. From the water, the northwest face seemed like a "must climb" line.

I climbed this face alone in August, back-roping some sections. About 200m of delicate slabs led to a midway ledge, above which the face steepened to give five excellent pitches on immaculate rock (about E2 5c overall). I finished about 50m right of the true summit after six hours of climbing, then began an epic 7.5-hour descent of the west-facing slope over scree, boulders, and slippery grass—all in rock shoes. I couldn't walk properly for weeks. 📄📷

– DAVID GLADWIN, *FRANCE*

MÉXICO

The south pillar of La Gloria (9,688 feet), west of El Salto. The 1,500-foot route Rezando follows the prominent buttress left of the center shadow line. *Zach Clanton*

LA GLORIA
A SPECTACULAR 13-PITCH ROUTE IN THE SIERRA MADRE ORIENTAL

BY ZACH CLANTON, *USA*

THE FIRST TIME I saw La Gloria, it was just a dreamy nameless pinnacle high above the ponderosa pine country of the Sierra Madre Oriental, 30km to the west of the popular sport climbing destination of El Salto. It wasn't until we stood on the summit after two months of effort that we learned its name, from a note in a glass jar on top. Although our new route on the south face was the first rock climb up the peak, Dave Henkel (Canada) and I were the fifth party to sign in at the summit. According to the register, La Gloria was first climbed in 1981 by a group from Saltillo, who ascended the third-class west ridge, followed by three other Mexican groups in later years.

But in January 2019, when I saw the peak from the road near the small town of San José de las Boquillas, I knew none of this. To me, the southern pillar of this peak was like the Mexican Beckey-Chouinard, a line of perfect blue-orange limestone just begging to be the range's first alpine sport climb.

Of course, it wasn't all that simple. It took countless trips up the steep, cactus-riddled hill to create something resembling a trail, stock a base camp, and equip a route of this size. Starting in late 2019, Dave and I managed to haul up 96 lead bolts, 13 anchors (two bolts with chains for each), 280m of static line, cams, hooks, a drill, and an ungodly amount of food and water. For all of that effort, we were rewarded with immaculate stone from the first move to the last, and a fantastic ground-up adventure on every lead.

Although we used all sorts of trad trickery to create this sport climb, we did not simply go where gear was available—we followed the coolest looking grips. As we leapfrogged leads up the giant pillar, there was an indescribable sense of freedom and excitement every time we arrived at a new belay. Looking up at the massive expanse of rock, it was thrilling to launch into the unknown

and create the next pitch. Mexican limestone can be quite the muse.

Less inspiring were the local coatimundi, similar to ringtail cats but bigger and more dexterous. Over the course of our route development, these animals tampered with our packs and hanging food caches, stealing many meters of exposed straps, draw cords, and cordelettes, along with slings, a headlamp, scissors, and needle and thread. They unzipped bags and emptied the contents of our packs across camp. We have reason to believe the coati are working on their own route, so be on the lookout for that.

Our route, Rezando, ended up having 13 pitches in 1,500' of rock, with climbing up to 5.12b/c. All that will be required to repeat it is a 70m rope and 13 quickdraws. After the last anchor, you can take off your harness and go on a short third-class jaunt to the summit of La Gloria (9,688'). The climbing is mostly in the 5.10–5.11 range, with two 5.12 pitches in wildly exposed positions. The central pillar makes up the first nine pitches, with nothing but small stances and ledges for belays. Once you crest the summit ridge, there is an excellent bivy spot for two under a pair of giant cactus trees.

After countless nights at the base of the mountain, establishing the first nine pitches, we spent two nights at this 9,300' bivy during our final push. We reached the top on January 30, 2020, and lingered in the warm sunshine for hours, reading old accounts by fellow summiters, taking pictures, and looking into the distance at future adventures.

After six 35m rappels, we made it back to high camp just in time to build a campfire and shoot bottle rockets in celebration. During our work on the route, we had frequently signaled the villagers in Las Boquillas with our lights, and they would blast mariachi music in response. When we shot bottle rockets into the black abyss after our summit push, the whole town seemed to come out for the celebration. 📷

EDITOR'S NOTE: *While establishing this route, the climbers free climbed all but one move; they were unable to complete a single-push free ascent after high winds and frigid temperatures arrived in the area at the end of January. They intend to return in late 2020 and request that other climbers give them the privilege of completing the first free ascent.*

[Top] Dave Henkel bolting pitch four of Rezando. Each pitch on the route was established ground up. [Bottom] An exotic bivy ledge, nine pitches up the south pillar of La Gloria. *Zach Clanton (both photos)*

The north-facing wall of Cañon de la Sandía, showing (1) Karma Bonfire (11 pitches, 5.12c) and (2) Vuelo de Fortuna (9 pitches, 5.13b), both completed in 2019. *Jason Nelson*

NUEVO LEÓN / LA HUASTECA

CAÑÓN DE LA SANDÍA AND CAÑÓN DE GUITARRITAS, NEW ROUTES

CAÑÓN DE LA Sandía is situated at the southeastern end of the larger Huasteca climbing area, just outside Monterrey. This canyon can be seen from the road 2.1 km past Rompepicos Dam, with an obvious overhanging orange wall. In April, I was fortunate to complete Vuelo de Fortuna (300m, 5.13b) with Rolando Larcher from Italy.

I had my eye on this gem of a line for years—it was a bit of an obsession. The overhanging tufas, the solid rock, the northern exposure, and the easy access really make it unique. The route starts on gray rock, and the enormous cat-claw tufas at the top of the first pitch are a good land-mark. I started the route solo in January and completed four pitches ground up and mostly free, with a few removable bolts.

Rolando quickly appreciated the beauty of the line from the photos I sent him and signed up to finish it with me. The spectacular and solid rock allowed us to free climb the remaining pitches ground up, drilling off hooks. Although we had to wander back and forth, we felt incred-ibly fortunate to find an "easy" line up this very intimidating wall. The climbing was sustained, with most of the pitches in the mid to upper 5.12 range. We were even blessed with unusually cool temps for the redpoint—quite a "flight of fortune!"

I returned to Cañón de la Sandía in November and completed Karma Bonfire (330m, 5.12c) with Jay Foley from New Mexico. The route starts 20m left of Vuelo de Fortuna, with the first two and a half pitches following a vertical seam. Connie Rochelle and I had started this line in 2016, ground up off stances, but my shoulder injury stopped us dead. Jay offered to step in and finish it with me.

Jay and I continued ground up, using stances and hooks to place the bolts. We then freed the 11-pitch route in a two-day push, swapping leads. The route follows the left edge of the overhanging and north-facing wall, making it a great year-round option. There is an aid bolt that allows one to skip the 5.12c crux, allowing the route to go at 5.12a A0. This route has magnificent views, mostly comfy belays, and fun, varied climbing. There is also a nice bivy ledge after pitch seven.

Also, in January 2019, Connie Rochelle and I established Don Julio (130m, 5.10 R) in Cañon de Guitarritas. The route starts where the rock ridge on the east side of the canyon touches the road; it pretty much follows the ridge but sometimes cuts left onto the south face. This is an adventure route, with some plants and loose rock; the bolts are sparse, but the cruxes are well protected. We rappelled the north side of the ridge via four independent rap stations.

– ALEX CATLIN, *MÉXICO*

CAÑON DE GUITARRITAS, LA PARED DEL OMBLIGO DEL MUNDO

WHEN I FIRST came to La Huasteca to open the route Nayeri (500m, 12b, *AAJ 2010*) and later Pau (550m, 5.13b, *AAJ 2016*), both on the Tatewari Wall, I saw a beautiful black, north-facing wall across the valley. It was begging to be climbed.

La Pared del Ombligo del Mundo ("the wall of the world's navel") was named by indigenous people from the state of Nayarit in western México. Best known to the world as the Huichol, they refer to themselves as Wixáritari ("the people"). They frequent Cañon de Guitarritas to perform ceremonies involving the taking of peyote, which they get from La Huasteca.

On February 12 and 13, 2020, Álvaro Peiró and I, both from Spain, bolted a route up this wall ground up, gaining height by hooking and free climbing on easier sections. Marcelo González from México helped with cleaning the lower pitches and photographed the climb. On our third day we finished the eight-pitch route (250m). We then free climbed all but one pitch in a day, with difficulties up to 5.12d.

The route, Tinder Push, is just excellent, on perfect limestone. The rock on the first four pitches, up to a sweeping arch, is black and features mostly clean crimps and some pockets. The upper half is composed of gray rock with amazing friction and features a bigger variety of holds. Anchors are fixed to rappel.

– ORIOL ANGLADA, *SPAIN*

Álvaro Peiró on pitch six (5.12a) of the eight-pitch route up La Pared del Ombligo del Mundo in La Huasteca, completed in February 2020. "Every pitch is a joy for lovers of technical face climbing." *Marcelo González*

EL SALTO, IBIZA WALL, THE IBIZA CLUB WEAPON

GOOGLE MAPS SHOWS an impressive blue line when displaying the route from Calgary, Alberta, to El Salto in La Ciénaga de González, Mexico. We traced it south for five days, but not without issues: a new radiator in Salt Lake City, cracked suspension coils somewhere on the outskirts of Monterrey, and at least a dozen jugs of coolant along the way. It was unfortunate but manageable until we got in a car accident on the way into town from El Salto to buy groceries, resulting in a totaled van.

Being that we were now stuck in Ciénaga de González, we refocused our attention on El Salto. We walked the riverbed and approached walls that showed potential. One very steep north-facing wall had impressive streaks, tufa features, and seemingly good stone. After speaking with local route developers, we determined that our chosen wall had yet to be climbed.

On December 12, our team of five (all from Calgary)—Luke Dean, Nathan Hart, Tyson Martino, Ethan Somji, and I—placed the first bolt on the Ibiza Club Weapon. The route was bolted on lead. Some bolts were placed from stances, but,

Sam Tucker on the crux fifth pitch of the Ibiza Club Weapon (250m, 5.14b). *Edwin Teran*

given the consistent difficulty of the climbing, most of our upward progress was by aid tactics. Each pitch was cleaned thoroughly on rappel while the next pitch went up. The two portaledges that we brought were a nice mitigation for bruised hips and raw skin. We finished equipping the seven-pitch line on Christmas Eve.

It wasn't apparent in the bolting stages how difficult and stacked our line would be. Now, most of my time went into projecting the crux fifth pitch—I knew that with limited time I needed to be sure of that pitch.

On January 22 and 23, Luke Dean and I went back up to send the Ibiza Club Weapon. On the first day, I led pitches one through four clean, and then we spent the night in a portaledge. The next day I finished the route, leading every pitch, including the 5.14b crux. Having not rehearsed the last two pitches before my ground-up push, I fell off pitch seven on the last move below the anchor (the only time I fell during my redpoint) and lowered to the belay. After a short rest, I climbed the pitch clean. The breakdown of the route is: 13b, 13b, 12b, 13d, 14b, 12b, 13a, and it's approximately 250m.

There is potential for more lines or a variation of our line on the Ibiza Wall. The rock quality on either side of our route on the lower three pitches is less than ideal, but could be bolted and climbed with enough cleaning. The quality improves greatly on the top half of the cliff and could likely be home to similarly difficult testpieces.

– SAM TUCKER, *CANADA*

SAN ISIDRO CANYON, GATOS WALL, SEPARATION ANXIETY

SAN ISIDRO CANYON is just west of El Salto, the limestone climbing paradise in northern Mexico, and it boasts huge potential for multi-pitch routes. Over long weekends in September and October, Michael Perry and I (both from Texas) equipped the five-pitch Separation Anxiety (5.13+) on the Gatos Wall ground up and on lead. There are a couple of single-pitch routes on the right side of Gatos Wall, but ours is the first to reach the top of the climbable terrain.

We made the free push on December 19, swapping leads and redpointing all pitches, with the crux on the third pitch: 30m of epic tufa pulling out a 45° wall leading to a very bouldery section, followed by more techy block climbing and then an incredible bullet gray headwall. This wall offers big-wall adventure with just a 15-minute approach and stays in the shade until 2 p.m. during the winter months. 🗎 🔲

– CLAYTON REAGAN, *USA*

CHIAPAS

SUMIDERO CANYON, XIBALBÁ UPRISING

FOR MILLIONS OF years, the Grijalva River carved the Cañón del Sumidero, and it is now one of the most important tourist attractions in the state of Chiapas. For a few years we have been living in San Cristóbal de las Casas, which is only one hour from the canyon. Our dream was to develop a new and completely free route through the central and highest part of this natural wonder.

Previously, there was only one route climbing to the top of Cañón del Sumidero: Hombres del Pañuelo Rojo (500m, 17 pitches, V 5.11 A1+), established with aid through a very steep section of wall by a group of climbers from Chiapas in 2006 (*see AAJ 2007*). Our planned route was on the bigger walls deeper into the canyon—from the Grijalva River to the top is approximately 850m. The wall in this area is split into two parts: a steep ascent through jungle, with a few moderate rock pitches, and the main upper headwall.

We began working on this line from the ground up in June 2018, but after about 550m of climbing, we decided to retreat because we had encountered a lot of very big, loose rocks, and to continue would have been life-threatening. We came back exactly one year later, having decided to equip the route from above. To reach the top, we had to get permission from the local commune, Triunfo Agrarista. In one of their monthly meetings, we convinced them to let us cross their land and started working on the route.

The work took a couple of weeks because the two of us could only carry water and supplies for a maximum of four days. On each trip, we managed to equip three to four pitches with the necessary bolts and to clean the route while rappelling. Our aim was to establish a secure route but not overbolt the line. We used 90 bolts to protect the entire climb, using

Xibalbá Uprising in Cañón del Sumidero. The total vertical gain is about 850 meters; the upper rock wall has 13 pitches. *Ulf Fuchslueger*

Carsten Thess climbing pitch 12 (5.11b) of Xibalbá Uprising in Cañon del Sumidero. *Jan Hoebeeck*

traditional gear when we could. We waited for the rainy months to pass, and then, in December, we were able to start free climbing.

As agreed, our boatman stood at the pier in Cahuare at 6 a.m. After about half an hour, we reached the small rocky beach that marks the start of the approach. With the first step out of the boat, you enter the jungle and immediately have to be wary of possible dangers, including crocodiles, scorpions, spiders, and poisonous plants. The path leads steeply up and over a crest, gaining about 400m; this section includes several 25m rock steps (5.9).

On the first day we freed three pitches. The first 6m of the third rope length consist of brittle rock, which can be climbed free but require a little sensitivity. It took four attempts to free this pitch, and then we had achieved our daily goal. As the wall faces southeast, we only had two hours in the morning and four hours in the afternoon to climb in the shade. During the midday hours we had to protect ourselves from the heat under the portaledge.

On the second day we started at 4 a.m. and climbed a shallow ramp that leads to the crux of the route. This is an 8m section on very small crimps over a slightly overhanging plate, followed by a simple and spectacularly exposed crack. It took five attempts to solve this pitch's complex boulder problem.

On day three we were most concerned about pitch seven, because it is the longest of the route and there are several demanding passages. To our delight, it went on the first attempt. We flew through pitch eight, one of the most beautiful corners we have ever climbed, and pitch nine, which required a lot of endurance after surmounting a small roof. The most difficult climbing was now behind us.

We couldn't sleep because of the anticipation: The nicest part of the route awaited us, with three pitches of slightly overhanging stalactites over perforated plates and wavy bands of fine limestone, and then a final easier pitch. On the evening of the fourth day we reached the top and spent one more night there, at the edge of the canyon, to enjoy a campfire and the amazing surroundings. We named the route Xibalbá Uprising (850m, 5.12a/b). 📷🔍

– MARTIN SILLER, *AUSTRIA, AND* CARSTEN THESS, *GERMANY*

GUYANA

Roraima towers 2,500 meters above old-growth rainforest, creating its own weather. Despite torrential rain every day during the ascent, the overhanging wall sheltered the camps and route. *Matt "Pikey" Pycroft*

THE GREAT NORTHERN PROW
AN ANGLO-GUYANAN ADVENTURE ON MT. RORAIMA

BY LEO HOULDING, *U.K.*

"DER BE SOMTIN' in me boot, man," shouted Troy Henry in Caribbean-English creole—his primary tongue as a native Guyanan. "It gone bit me!"

Troy had just arrived on Tarantula Terrace, a vegetated ledge the size of a dinner table, three rope lengths up the northern prow of Mt. Roraima. He was wearing Waldo Etherington's jungle boots—two sizes too big for him—as he didn't want to ascend the huge, overhanging wall in his gumboots.

The mythical Roraima—which inspired Sir Arthur Conan Doyle's classic work of fiction *The Lost World* and provided the setting for the animated film *Up!*—is a huge, flat-top "tepui" on the tri-point border of Guyana, Venezuela, and Brazil. In 1973, a large Anglo-Guyanese expedition—led by Hamish MacInnes with an all-star team consisting of Joe Brown, Don Whillans, and Mo Anthoine—traveled overland through Guyana and made the first ascent of the Great Prow, relying heavily on aid climbing techniques and a small army of Amer-Indian porters. I'd seen the expedition film as a young climber, and it painted a picture of great suffering and misery but also swashbuckling adventure. Perversely, it inspired me to organize my own expedition to Roraima three decades later.

While the entire mountain is stunning, the Great Prow is without comparison. It rises above the lowland rainforest like the bow of a gigantic ship for almost 2,500m, half of which is precipitously steep, with the final 450m consisting of overhanging bulletproof quartzite estimated to be some two billion years old. The area below the cliff is an astoundingly wet and humid place, home to bizarre botanical and zoological wonders, including bird-eating spiders and scorpions whose sting can induce vomiting of blood.

The extremely remote Akawaio community of Phillipai in Guyana has the nearest air strip to the Great Prow. It is only 40km to the east as the crow flies, but the dense rainforest and the arc of the terrain result in an approach trek of precisely 100km. Wilson Cutbirth, Waldo Etherington,

Troy Henry (top) and Edward James guided the team to the wall and then became the first Guyanese to ascend Mt. Roraima, which rises above their tribal land. *Matt "Pikey" Pycroft*

Dan Howard, Matt Pycroft, Anna Taylor, and I arrived in Guyana in early November and set in motion a plan to deliver supplies to the mountain for our attempt on an all-free line somewhere on the Great Prow.

On November 8, we chartered a skytruck—an aircraft like a Mercedes Sprinter with wings and a large tailgate door—and flew from the capital, Georgetown, for around two hours. On reaching the mountain, we threw out four 125kg parachute loads into the trees below. Our self-designed aerial delivery system suspended the loads 60m below the parachutes, allowing them to penetrate the forest canopy and reach the ground before the parachutes inevitably became entangled high in the trees. A homemade locating device, featuring GPS, radio, strobe, and 120-decibel beeper, was attached to our mission-critical loads.

The seven-day trek through the jungle was far more pleasant than anticipated, and eventually we located the loads, retrieved the parachutes, and began the climb. But first we had to get to the prow itself, which meant ascending a slime forest of fantastically contorted, stunted trees and dangling icicles of transparent ooze. We emerged into the "Eldorado Swamp," an open area that looked like a decent campsite before we realized it consisted of ankle- to knee-deep white mud. In another intense downpour, we pushed through. Then came a garden of enormous tank bromeliads, capable of holding hundreds of liters of water, which could either be navigated by balancing on top of them or tunneling under, occasionally drenching one of us when the tank toppled. A final section of vertical, bamboo-like undergrowth, through which I more burrowed than climbed, eventually brought us to the bare rock of the wall.

We decided to attempt the true prow of the wall via the steepest, proudest line, mostly left of the 1973 route. Barricaded by a series of giant horizontal roofs with no continuous cracks, it looked unlikely to go free. Nevertheless, Wilson and I set to work climbing the first three rope lengths of the original route—to our surprise completely onsight—up to Tarantula Terrace, the site of Troy's run-in with the eponymous arachnid.

Troy and his uncle, Edward James, had been indispensable thus far on this adventure, cutting the trail, helping find our air-dropped gear, and ferrying loads through the slime forest to the base of the wall. So, we were pleased when they accepted our offer to join us on the wall and climb to the summit with us, while the dozen other Akawaio helpers returned to Phillipai. Neither of our Akawaio friends had ever worn a harness. Back in Phillipai, Edward works as a subsistence farmer and hunter while Troy works as a laborer in Guyana's grueling gold mining industry.

Waldo—an authority on all things related to ropes and rigging—had given them a crash course in jumaring, and they were now commencing the first Guyanese ascent of their country's highest and most iconic mountain. They quickly figured out free-hanging jumaring, rappelling, and lowering out, a constant stream of laughter accompanying their efforts as they joked and bantered with each other. They wore ear-to-ear grins in their portaledge, clearly savoring the experience as they gazed out over the forest on the few clear days to the distant smoke rising from the cooking fires in the village they call home.

While Wilson and I pushed into terra incognita through giant roofs, our youngest crew member, Anna, set to work unlocking a way to free climb the 20m of beautiful blank rock alongside a bolt ladder drilled by the 1973 team. After three days of effort, she was rewarded with a free ascent of the most technically difficult pitch (5.12+) and best of the route. By that time, Wilson and I had discovered Invisible Ledge: perfectly flat, about 10m long and 1m wide, and obscured from even just a few meters below. Halfway up the wall, it provided a comfortable perch for our eight-person team.

The frequent tropical downpours might have thwarted our efforts to free climb, but the incredible steepness of the prow kept us and the route almost completely dry. Wilson and I continued upward, both climbing onsight, swapping leads and seconding free, until I neared the end of the steepest section of wall, ten pitches up. Unfortunately, after almost two hours on lead, my onsight efforts fell short less than a meter from easier ground.

After a couple of easier pitches, our line forced us around the corner onto the left side of the mountain, and in a single step I went from dry and calm into a ferocious wind and driving rain, exposing my body to hypothermic temperatures—something I never thought I'd experience just a few degrees from the equator. Returning a day later, I opted this time to tackle the beautifully sculpted arête of the prow and managed to climb into a position where a fall would have had dire consequences; I barely hung on long enough to drape a 3mm sling over a flake the size of coin, precariously hang for a rest, and pull up the drill to place a bolt. One pitch higher, Wilson brought us to the summit.

We still needed to free the couple of pitches that had thwarted our onsight attempt, and we achieved this over the next couple of days. Finally all eight of us celebrated our excellent adventure on top with our last bottle of Guyana's celebrated El Dorado rum. This entire experience was particularly rewarding to share with our Akawaio friends, without whom we would have never made it to the base of the wall and who, without our help, could never have made it to the top. 📷

SUMMARY: *First ascent of the Great Northern Prow (600m, E6 6c or 5.12+ R), with 14 pitches, 10 of them new, November 24–December 5, 2019. Like most previous parties, the team helicoptered off the top. Leo Houlding was interviewed about this climb for episode 27 of the AAJ's Cutting Edge podcast.*

Anna Taylor leads through the mist above Tarantula Terrace on the crux fourth pitch (5.12d/ V7) of the Great Northern Prow. *Matt "Pikey" Pycroft*

The enormous granite dome of Pedra Baiana. Runnel Vision (800m, 8a A0, 2019) climbed the southeast face (left side). The 2016 route Sangre Latina ascended the center of the sunny east face. *Alun Richardson*

RUNNEL VISION
AN 800-METER SPORT CLIMB ON PEDRA BAIANA

BY MIKE "TWID" TURNER, *U.K.*

BRAZIL, LAND OF the mighty Amazon, endless sandy beaches, Caipirinha cocktails, and a big statue of Christ on a lumpy granite mountain. *Brazil must have big walls*, I thought. An internet search turned up many walls with few or no routes, and one in particular caught my eye: Pedra Baiana, a huge monolith in a lush paradise. It seemed like just the place for my summer holiday in 2018.

These days, it's difficult to assemble a group of like-minded climbers who enjoy the delights of climbing huge monoliths of vertical granite and who don't need a joint replacement or hearing aid. Miraculously, kids appeared! In the V12 outdoor shop in North Wales, I bumped into a keen young chap named Angus Killie.

Angus – "When?" Twid – "June." Angus – "Yep."

Twid – "Got a strong mate?" Angus – "Many." Twid – "See you in Rio."

Angus swaggered down Llanberis' High Street looking for a strong climber, and I chatted up my old mates Steve Long and Rob Johnston. Somehow our merry band converged on the same day on a beach in Rio de Janeiro. In the morning, we'd drive to Pedra Baiana, in the state of Minas Gervais, about 1,000km north of Rio. Luckily, Angus had brought along a burly looking partner named James Taylor. Not only was he a talented, Huber-strong climber but also, it transpired, a well-organized guy. James had taken the initiative to photocopy Google Earth maps to help us find this mythical wall.

After two days (double the Google time), we arrived below the mighty Pedra Baiana. The 800m wall looked every bit as impressive as the images we had gleaned from the internet. The next morning, as the sun rose, the team got cracking on the southeast face. Angus and James, on the early shift, unexpectedly came across a line of old bolts, which soon ended. It was apparent why previous explorers had abandoned the line: As the morning grew warmer, thousands of bees living on the rock face joined the lads, forcing a prompt retreat.

Our original plan, based on photos, had been to follow a different feature, a prominent quartz dike that runs left to right across the southeast face. [*Editor's note: The new route is to the left of the other known route on Pedra Baiana's big walls: Sangre Latina, an 800m mostly free climb (estimated at 8b/8b+) on the east face, put up in 2016 by Brazilian and Argentine climbers (see AAJ 2017).*] The next day, Steve and I started this line. Initially, we followed easy slabs then grooves to gain access to the dike. It was covered in positive edges and pockets, unlike the featureless granite walls on either side. It gave us hope for a free route of epic proportions.

Ground-up drilling was our only option, as there weren't any cracks. In the 800m of climbing, we came across a grand total of one nut placement. The angle of the rock was either just off the vertical, dead vertical, or slightly overhanging. Eventually, we got the rock boots on. Free climbing on the initial steep part of the wall, we had eight fine face climbing pitches with grades 6c upward to 7c+ and 8a (redpointed by Angus and James). In the middle of the wall, we took the line straight up through runnels until two long, blank aid pitches led to a perfect 400m runnel—we felt destined to climb this 2m-wide runnel directly to the summit.

James Taylor stemming in the upper runnel on Pedra Baiana's southeast face. *Alun Richardson*

After seven days' effort, we had climbed 18 bolted pitches to a high point about 150m vertical below the top, with many pitches freed (to 8a). We placed our last remaining bolt at our high point with the frustrating realization that we'd need a second trip to finish the climb.

A year went by. Steve and Angus couldn't make a second trip due to work, and Rob Johnson, our cameraman, was bankrupt after buying cameras. James and I asked two others to join us in June 2019: Simon Nadin, now living in Scotland, jumped at the chance of a midge-free climbing experience, and Shaun Hudson, a guide and cabinetmaker from Chamonix, fancied seeing Copacabana beach and thought big walling a fair price to pay. We were joined by Welsh photographer and guide extraordinaire Alun Richardson.

The team quickly got stuck into pushing the incomplete route toward the summit. Here, the runnel sprouted vegetation, with hanging gardens of lush plants, flowers, and hidden beasts. Shaun led the final pitch, climbing rock and lunging like Tarzan to lumps of lush vegetation. The totally flat summit was packed with amazing wildflowers. The vista was breathtaking, with the vast massif of Pedra Riscada and distant coastal cities visible beyond. However, the stark reality of the work still to come dawned on all of us—we had come to free climb.

The following day, James and Simon looked for an alternative through the blank pitches in the middle of the wall while Shaun and I cleaned the upper runnel. I soon realized that performing the splits across a 2m runnel with a new hip replacement would be risky. Eventually, Shaun and I focused on free climbing the lower sections, and James and Simon took on the runnel.

Belaying James and Simon allowed for grandstand seats. The two rubbed most of the skin from their palms while stemming the hold-free runnel and soon garnered calves worthy of the Tour de France. In all my years climbing, I'd never seen such a unique feature.

On our final night on the wall, we bivied on the towering summit. In the night, a large meteor lit up the vast sky. As the morning sun clawed through enveloping morning mists, we started the long abseil down the climb, retrieving our gear and ropes. With a couple of blank pitches remaining, we hadn't freed the whole wall, but about 90 percent of the climb had gone free: Runnel Vision (800m, 20+ pitches, 8a A0). 📖 📷

The ice roof at 5,900 meters on the first ascent of the south face of Nevado Jatunhuma's south peak. The 900-meter Via Adrenaline is now the most technical route in the Cordillera Vilcanota. *Oriol Baró Collection*

¡BONANZA!
SIX NEW ROUTES IN THE CUSCO REGION

BY NATHAN HEALD, *PERÚ*, *WITH INFORMATION FROM* **ORIOL BARÓ**, *SPAIN*

AT THE END of May, the prolific Catalan climber Oriol Baró and partners arrived in Cusco without plans or a set goal in mind, but knowing they would find a real adventure. Like Baró, his teammates Ferran Rodriguez and Guillem Sancho were fresh off a season of guiding at home in the Pyrenees. Through a mutual friend, Oriol contacted me, and we met for beers to discuss interesting objectives and logistics. [*The author runs a Cusco-based guide service and has done many first ascents in the area.*] We called my *arriero* friends in the different ranges, and the guys made their plans over a few rounds.

The first phase was to acclimatize in the sport climbing area of Chacco Huayllasca, located in Pitumarca at 4,000m, two hours southeast of Cusco. The local climbing community, led by Jorge Sirvas, has dedicated the last few years to developing this area, and it has become one of the best in Peru.

At the beginning of June, the guys drove to the village of Pacchanta, on the north side of the Cordillera Vilcanota. There they went to the house of Alejandro Crispin to get some horses for their gear; it would be three hours up to Jampa Pass at 4,900m to make their base camp.

Their first two new routes were on Concha de Caracol (5,640m) and Jatunhuma (6,127m, a.k.a. Tres Picos), which anchors the center of the Cordillera Vilcanota. First, they climbed a direct line up the south face of Concha de Caracol, which they called Via Pirenaica (TD+). The descent went west to the col with Caracol (5,625m) and down the easier slopes up which past ascents of this peak were made.

After a day of rest and time to see other possibilities, they went for the unclimbed south face of the south peak (6,070m) of the Jatunhuma, the lowest of its three summits. While this peak had seen a few ascents decades ago, it was traversed from the southeast ridge to reach the principal northern summit. Their line on this peak, Via Adrenaline (ED+ WI6 M6 R A2), is now the most technical in the entire range, with a pitch of WI6 and a run-out, mixed ice-roof crux (M6 and A2) at 5,900m elevation. However, they were just getting started.

After some rest in Cusco, the team traveled to the end of the road at Soray Pampa (3,900m) below the south face of Nevado Salkantay (6,279m) to stay in the Refugios Salkantay lodge, owned by a local friend, Edwin Espinoza. After a recon of the complex mountain, they horse-packed up to Inkachillaska Pass and made camp below the southeast ridge at 4,900m to rest for a day and study the face. After traversing over the ridge to the southeast face, they worked up a line between the Czech 1978 southeast face route and the New Zealand 1973 southeast buttress route. They descended the east ridge and returned to camp 25 hours after leaving. Manjar Rubio (1,250m, ED) is the first new line since 1986 on Salkantay, a mountain that has seen only a handful of ascents.

After the Salkantay climb, Jordi Marmolejo arrived in Cusco from Spain to join the team, replacing Rodriguez. The next peak of interest was Nevado Terijuay (5,330m), in the Cordillera Urubamba, north of Cusco. On my own ascent of Terijuay in 2017 (*see AAJ 2018*), machete-wielding locals tried to stop us from climbing the mountain. This year, the Spanish were unable to convince the community president to allow them to go up to base camp with an *arriero*, so they got back in the truck to look for something else. By chance, they ran into local climber Coqui Galvez, who told them of his recent ascent of the south peak of Nevado Chicón (AAJ 2018), and the Catalans climbed a 400m line just to the left (TD). After this, Guillem Sancho departed Perú. Since they were close by, Baro and Marmolejo repeated the normal route (D) on Nevado Veronica (5,911m) in a couple of days at the end of June.

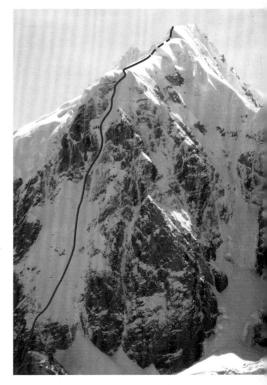

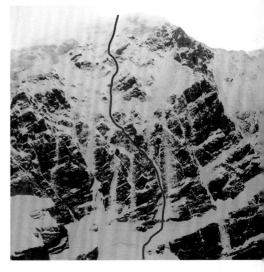

[Top] **Nevado Jatunhuma (a.k.a. Tres Picos), South Peak (6,070m), showing the route Via Adrenaline (900m, ED+ WI6 M6 R A2).** [Bottom] **Nevado Concha de Caracol (5,640m), south face, showing Via Pirenaica (550m, TD+).** *Oriol Baró Collection*

For Baró's sixth climb of the trip, he and Marmolejo teamed up with local Jorge Sirvas (Perú). They set out from Sirvas' home in Pitumarca, at the southern foot of the Cordillera Vilcanota, and in a quick sortie they climbed a new route on the south face (400m, TD) of Surimani (5,420m) on July 2.

The last climb of this incredible trip was the grand finale. Nevado Sacsarayoc (5,918m) in the Cordillera Vilcabamba lies just south of Pumasillo (5,991m) on a knife-edged ridge and had only one previous ascent, by a 1962 New Zealand expedition (*Alpine Journal 1964*). The New Zealand team spent two months in the area, using the village of Yanama as a base of operations, and made several first ascents. They first tried to traverse from Pumasillo south along the ridge to Sacsarayoc. Eventually, they circumnavigated the mountains to the east over the Lasunayoc col to reach a feasible line. After much effort, only Hermann Farrell reached the summit, following an open bivy a few hundred feet below the top.

For years, I had thought to try the second ascent of Nevado Sacsarayoc by the stunning south face, visible on the flight from Lima to Cusco. However, there are many other climbs waiting, so I shared this idea with Baró and Marmolejo. Two days later, they went to meet *arriero* Alejandro Huaman, in Yanama, which now has a decent dirt road. Alejandro took them up the grassy slopes to the south of the peak until the mule could not go further. A few hours later, they crossed an unsettled moraine to make camp on the last rock shelves before the glacier. On July 10 they climbed the south face and reached the summit at midmorning, after which they rappelled their route. They named the route after one of their favorite things in Perú between climbs: Pisco Sour (800m, TD+). 📷

[Top] **Nevado Salkantay (6,279m)**, southeast face, Manjar Rubio (1,250m, ED). [Bottom] **Nevado Sacsarayoc (5,918m)**, south face, showing Pisco Sour (800m, TD+). *Oriol Baró Collection*

SUMMARY: *New routes on Concha de Caracol, Jatunhuma, and Surimani, Cordillera Vilcanota; new routes on Salkantay and Sacsarayoc (second ascent of peak), Cordillera Vilcabamba; new route on south peak of Nevado Chicón, Cordillera Urubamba, June-July 2019.*

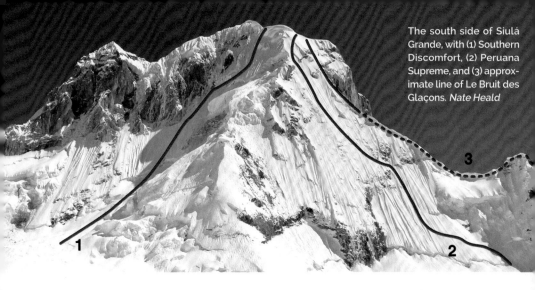

The south side of Siulá Grande, with (1) Southern Discomfort, (2) Peruana Supreme, and (3) approximate line of Le Bruit des Glaçons. *Nate Heald*

PERUANA SUPREME
A NEW ROUTE UP SIULÁ GRANDE IN THE CORDILLERA HUAYHUASH

BY NATHAN HEALD, *PERÚ*

ABOUT FIVE YEARS ago, Peruvian climbing expert Sergio Ramirez Carrascal told me about a beautiful unclimbed ramp on the south side of Siulá Grande (6,344m map height) in the Cordillera Huayhuash. Of the peak's three main faces, the south is the least frequented, due to difficult access through an icefall to a cirque below the face.

A 2001 route ascended the left side of this aspect, directly under the summit, but only reached the ridge at 6,250m (*see "Southern Discomfort," AAJ 2002*). The entire southeast pillar and ridge on the right side of the face was climbed more recently, in 2016 (*"Le Bruit des Glaçons," AAJ 2017*). I studied Google Earth imagery of the ramp between these two lines: It seemed like one of the cleanest routes on the mountain, with minimal exposure to objective dangers—if you could get through the icefall. I tucked the idea away to ripen until called to it.

On July 22, 2017, my friends Aaron and Jeanne Zimmerman (USA) summited Siulá Grande by the Catalan route on the east face, where they recorded summit elevations of 6,368m on the southern top and 6,366m on the northern (the summits are about 150m apart). I felt called to attempt the Catalan route one year later. We were not so lucky with the weather.

In May 2019, one of our team members from that climb, Benjamin Billet (France), was able to take some key photos of the south face while acclimatizing on the Huayhuash trek. These images revealed that the ramp on the south face gained the upper southeast ridge without any overhanging cornices. Thus, we decided to try this route. Arttu Pylkkanen (Finland), Billet, and I would form one rope team, while Luis Crispin and Thomas Schilter (both from Perú) would form the other.

On June 22, we traveled to Queropalca on the east side of the range, where we met our *arriero*, Cesar, at his house in the pastures below Carhuacocha. On the 23rd we hiked with the donkeys to the lagoons at the foot of Yerupaja and Siulá Grande. We had hoped to camp at the last lagoon, Quesillococha, but the locals forbade it, so we continued 2km further.

On the 24th, we dove into the labyrinth of seracs that tumble down from the basin above. We hoped to make it through in one day, but at 4 p.m. we decided to camp under a huge wave of ice that protected us from falling debris. Early the next day, we reached a camp at 5,400m on the glacial plateau. The only true obstacle we encountered was a wide crevasse at the base of the

Luis Crispin on the upper shoulder of the southeast ridge of Siulá Grande. *Nate Heald*

north face of Carnicero (5,960m), though the whole area is exposed to rockfall.

At midnight on the 26th, we started our climb. Once on the ramp proper, we climbed straightforward 60–70° snow and ice for 800m to reach the southeast ridge at 6,200m by late morning. Clouds blanketed the east, while the Cordillera Raura provided an unreal backdrop to Carnicero's unclimbed north face. A large, hidden crevasse cut through the east face, denying us an easy ridge traverse. Once past this, one last technical obstacle remained, where the shoulder steepens for 100m (WI3) to gain the snowy summit ridge. A 10-minute traverse of the broad upper ridge brought us to the summit at 4:30 p.m.; our GPS showed a height of 6,380m. We stayed for a half hour in the fading light and enjoyed our moment on top of this elusive summit.

We used a snow stake as a dead-man anchor to descend the upper ridge and reached the top of the ramp again as darkness set in. Halfway through our 17 rappels, I became very dehydrated and started to throw up bile. Eating snow provided much-needed relief for my parched throat. When we finally got to the bergschrund, I hammered in our best snow stake to descend the 10m overhang to the glacier below. We reached our high camp at 3:30 a.m., 27 hours after leaving.

Everyone was on high alert while descending the spider web of snow bridges through the icefall the following morning, this time with more rockfall. We reached our base camp at 7:30 p.m. on the 28th. Cesar arrived the next morning, cracking his whip over the donkeys. The weather had changed for the worst, as it normally does when a principal Apu has been climbed.

We called our route Peruana Supreme (1,000m, TD AI4). This ascent was special for all of us, but especially for Luis and Thomas (16 years old), both from Cusco, who became the first Peruvians to summit this famous mountain.

I met Luis in 2011 on my way back to Cusco after a climb; he lives in a village at 4,300m below Ausangate and began assisting his uncle with tourist treks when he was 12 years old. He worked with me as I established my guiding agency, and since then we have done many climbs together. From my observations, Luis did not start climbing for any other reason than curiosity and camaraderie. He loves the natural world and has vast knowledge of it, and, at first, I think he just wanted to know what it would be like up there in the snow and ice. Luis and Thomas roped up together on Siulá Grande so no one could suggest they hadn't made a purely Peruvian ascent of the peak.

For me, this was the eighth summit and last difficult peak on my personal quest to climb the 10 highest mountain massifs in Perú. ◙

CORDILLERA BLANCA

PUTKA CHICO, SOUTH FACE, JUSTO EN LAS GANAS!

FROM AUGUST 23–27, we (Simon Bustamante and Felipe Proaño) ventured to the Parón Valley, north of Huaraz. On August 25, after summiting La Esfinge by the 1985 route in about four hours, we spent the afternoon scouting a line up an interesting formation to the northeast. We later realized this was Putka Chico (5,380m). [*Editor's note: This a western satellite of Nevado Putka (5,585m), which also has been called Putaca and may have been called Aguja Nevada Chica by past parties (see AAJ 1975 and 1978). It is part of a chain of peaks that extends northeast from La Esfinge (Cerro Parón, 5,300m) through several Putka and Aguja peaks to the Caraz group.*]

That same day we opened six pitches on the south face, reaching a col along a knife-edge ridge below the upper wall. Our ascent was stalled by a snowstorm and we descended. The next morning, after hiking up the moraine, we reclimbed the six pitches and then climbed five additional pitches of low technical difficulty on good granite, via a system of dihedrals, to reach the very loose summit.

Our 11-pitch route, Justo en las Ganas! (350m, 5.10-), climbs the most prominent line on the south face up its eastern rib. This was likely the first ascent of this face. This route is also most likely the easiest route in the Parón Valley—a great warm-up line for La Esfinge. We rappeled from slings around blocks backed up with nuts. ▣

– FELIPE PROAÑO *AND* SIMON BUSTAMANTE, *ECUADOR*

HUANDOY NORTE, EAST FACE, BOYS 1970

As I LEAVE for this year's expedition to Peru, my body is ready, but my mind is tired. It is no surprise to me, as I have just returned from an expedition to Nepal (*the first ascent of Chamlang's northwest face—see p.36*). I could have stayed at home in the hot summer, but winter in the other hemisphere was calling. Such sacrifices often offer a valuable and transforming experience.

Radoslav "Radek" Groh and I have followed conditions, which point us to the eastern face of Huandoy Norte (6,360m). There is a beautiful and natural line that follows the middle of the mountain face from the glacier all the way to the summit. We simply cannot resist.

We bivouac at the base of the face, below a cascade of crevasses that provide us with at least some protection against possible stone or snow

The east face of Huandoy Norte (6,360m) showing the route BOYS 1970 (1,200m, ED+). The middle of this line shared ground with a 2003 route (Adam Kovacs, solo), which continued up the rocky section where the 2019 route angled right. Earlier routes to the left are not shown. *Tomáš Galásek*

Marek Holeček rock climbing on day one on the east face of Huandoy Norte. *Radoslav Groh*

avalanches. We start climbing at dawn. I feel a bit stiff, but the steep ascent soon warms me. Step by step, the wall gets more vertical. The firm snow turns into ice, then mixed with large rock steps. After two hours of simul-climbing, we stop at a 150m rock barrier, an obligatory section to reach the next thousand meters. I climb as quickly as possible to minimize the risk of getting hit by stones sent by the mountain. Forcing my way under each overhang, the rock provides at least some shelter from the never-ending shower. The height and terror press hard on my lungs. Fortunately, the rock is quite compact. Once past, it's too dangerous to consider retreat, so our only option is up anyway.

The next challenge is a long traverse across an icefield, which in its top left corner continues with some mixed climbing. This part looks like an "S" and starts with a tricky rock step followed by a narrow corner. The corner is well-armed with massive columns of loose ice that look like majestic organ pipes. Normally, I would just plunge my axe into the ice as deep as possible, but this is more like frost. The rock doesn't offer many holds either. Let's not even talk about possible protection. The rope is now more of a fashion statement.

Fortunately, the setting sun freezes all movement on the wall. We're in the upper third of the route, which is strictly steep. I know we won't make it to the ridge before dark, so I hope that a miracle will happen and we don't have to spend the night on a tiny ledge like two icicles. We manage to find two ledges as big as a chair, situated two meters apart. What luxury! I tell Radek, "We have to bivouac here." Our smiles are literally frozen to our faces.

We breathe cool air through the tiny holes of our sleeping bags, watching the theater of never-ending blood-red light from the setting sun. Minutes after the burning sun's gone below the horizon, the mountains stay on fire. Rocks, ice, sky—everything is burning. This unique spectacle can happen only in the Cordillera Blanca, which is situated close to the shores of the Pacific Ocean.

In the morning Radek starts to boil water. He screams. Somehow, he has poured half of the water right into the boots hung by his side. A moment later, an ice block hits my back, winding me—a friendly reminder that we should start as soon as possible. About 300m of elevation stand between us and Huandoy's final ridge. The climbing is now easier but not "easy." After one section with mixed climbing, firm snow alternates with passages of ice. Three hours later, we make our way through the last snowy part. Below us, the whole wall is exposed. Twenty minutes later, just before noon, we stand smiling at the summit of Huandoy Norte.

A six-hour rappel descent gets us back to the refugio, 55 hours after leaving (August 7–9). Our route bears the name BOYS 1970 (1,200m, ED+ WI6 M6). The name is dedicated to the group of 14 Czech climbers who died in the massive earthquake and avalanche at the foot of Huascarán in 1970. Their dreams faded together with their lives. A few minutes later, another 70,000 lives were lost in the valley below. Let's think about them for a while now.

– **MAREK HOLEČEK**, *CZECH REPUBLIC*

HISTORICAL NOTES ON HUANDOY NORTE'S EAST FACE: The main east wall of Huandoy Norte has seen at least five ascents. The 2019 Czech route, BOYS 1970, was mostly to the right of the line followed by Adam Kovacs (Sweden) in an impressive solo ascent in 2003, but shared one significant portion through the rock band in the middle of the wall. In 1979, the late Tobin Sorenson (USA) reported a solo ascent of the east face that was very likely near the 1976 Polish route (Stryczynski-Waligora) and 1996 Slovenian variation (Meglic-Soklic), both of which were left of the Kovacs and Czech routes. Snow and ice coverage on the east face has reduced dramatically in the past half-century. Most ascents today would hardly reflect the conditions found during these earlier ascents.

HUANDOY ESTE, NORTHEAST FACE, COME MOCO SPUR

ALESSANDRO FRACCHETTI, ANDREA Spezialli (both Italy), and Renato Rodriguez (Chile) climbed a line up the northeast face of Huandoy Este (5,950m) on July 19. Fracchetti and Rodriguez had attempted a similar line in 2017, stopping about 200m from the summit ridge due to poor snow. Their ascent in 2019 generally followed the rocky central buttress on the face to reach the north ridge: Come Moco Spur (650m, MD+ 75° M4/5 UIAA 5+). In poor weather, they descended the north ridge without going to the summit. [*Editor's note: The climbers' full report and a photo of the 2019 line are at the AAJ website. Several parties have climbed this face before, as far back as 1952, and parts of the central spur may have been ascended previously. Conditions on the face are much drier than in the past.*] 📄 📷

– *INFORMATION FROM* **RENATO RODRIGUEZ**, *CHILE*

PONGOS NORTE, SOUTH FACE (NOT TO SUMMIT)

ON JULY 3, David Mateo (Spain), Beto Pinto (Perú), and I climbed a possible new route on the snowy southern face of Pongos Norte (5,680m), reaching a western subsummit. Although the main summit was first reached by its north face in 1964 and has been climbed at least a few times since, we believe this face remained unclimbed. [*Editor's note: The climbers also referred to Pongos Norte as Jatunllacsha, but Jatunllacsha is the 5,646m peak just to the east. It was first climbed by Germans in 1971 (see AAJ 1972 and a naming correction in AAJ 1973).*]

We approached up the Quebrada Quesque, close to the town of Catac, in the southern Cordillera Blanca. It took about four hours to reach our base camp below the north face of Mururaju, also called Pongos Sur (5,688m). Along the way, we passed beautiful lakes and many Puya raimondii, a rare plant that does not flower until it is 100 years old.

From our camp, it took about 3.5 hours to reach the south face of Pongos Norte. The 300m climb took about three hours on predominately snowy but somewhat mixed terrain. The sixth and final pitch ascended unconsolidated powder snow, which made progress slow and dangerous.

On the same day, Max Alvarez and Cesar Vicuña attempted the west ridge of Pongos Norte but were unable to finish it.

– **ALVARO LAFUENTE**, *SPAIN, WITH INFORMATION FROM BETO PINTO, PERÚ*

[Top] Huanka Punta (left) and Cerro Tornillo, showing the 2019 routes. [Middle] The drone angle exaggerates the steepness on Huanka Punta but not the incredible limestone quality. [Bottom] The line of Andean Kingdom on the northeast face of Cashan West. *Pou Collection*

CERRO TORNILLO AND HUANKA PUNTA; CASHAN WEST, NORTHEAST FACE

OUR ANDEAN JOURNEY with Manu Ponce in June began south and east of the main Cordillera Blanca in a previously underexplored limestone area east of San Marcos and just west of the huge Antamina copper and zinc mine.

First, we opened Burrito Chin de los Andes (700m, 6b) on Cerro Tornillo (4,900m, 9°32′7.5444″S, 77°4′43.662″W), making the first ascent of its northwest face. Then, in the same area, to the northwest, we opened Cabeza Clava (470m, 6c+), the first ascent of the cold southwest face of the Huanka Punta (4,670m). Both climbs were on limestone of great quality, and this place may become an important area for rock climbing.

After these climbs, we returned to Huaraz and then traveled to Cashan West (5,686m). (*Editor's note: This is the westernmost peak on the jagged ridge south of the Quebrada Rajucolta and north of Quebrada Rurec.*) With four days of hard activity, we were able to climb Andean Kingdom (800m, 7a+), the first ascent of the peak's northeast face. The route took one day of approach from the Quebrada Rajucolta, two days of nearly continuous climbing, separated by a painful bivouac in the middle of the wall, and one day of descent. It's one of the best routes of our career. [*Editor's note: The team also climbed a shorter rock route, Aupa Gasteiz (160m, 7c+), near the entrance to Quebrada Llaca—see the AAJ website for details.*] 📷

– ENEKO POU *AND* IKER POU, *SPAIN*

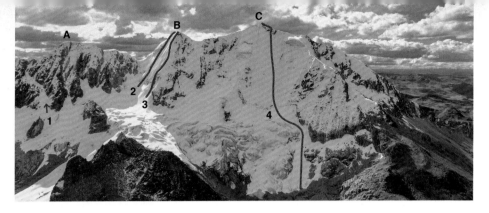

The Tunsho group showing: (A) Tunsho Sur, (1) Southeast face (2018, not to summit); (B) Tunsho Central (2) Chinita (2011) and (3) Nómadas del Kangia (2019), and (C) Tunsho main summit (4) Southeast face (2005/2019; the more recent ascent was slightly to the right of the original line). *Octavio Salazar Obregón*

TUKUMACH'AY AND TUNSHO CENTRAL, NEW ROUTES

AT THE BEGINNING of May, Pablo Rosagro and I visited the Pariacacca subrange in the Cordillera Central. We accessed the area from Canchayllo and installed our base camp at Lago Tembladera (4,480m). On May 9 we ascended the southwest face of Tukumach'ay (a.k.a. Tucumachay, Tata-tunsu, or Runshu), 5,357m on the IGN map. Our altimeters showed heights of 5,333m and 5,334m, respectively. The climb took approximately 12 hours round-trip, descending by the same route. We called our ascent Open Arms (300m, AD- 55°). The name is in honor of the rescue organization Proactiva Open Arms, which is dedicated to saving the lives of migrants who try to reach Europe across the Mediterranean and who very often die at sea. Our ascent was likely the fourth overall, with the three main ridges (west, south, east-southeast) climbed previously.

On May 18 we climbed Tunsho Central (often spelled Tunshu) via a new line on the south side. Historically, the height has been reported as 5,565m; however, our measurements of 5,679m by GPS and 5,645m by altimeter show it may be 100m taller. The height of 5,565m may correspond with the lower, southern summit climbed by Guy Fonck and Beto Pinto in 2014.

Our route began in an aesthetic goulotte on the southwest face, to the right of the route Chinita (Pinto-Morales, 2011). We climbed four pitches on the steep section to gain the more moderately angled southeast ridge, on which four more pitches led to the summit. We call our route Nómadas del Kangia (500m, MD+ 90° A1). We mostly descended the same route, downclimbing the upper ridge and rappelling the face, for a 24-hour round-trip. Ours was probably the fourth ascent of the mountain, after two ascents by Germans in 1967 and the 2011 climb. 📷 🔍

– SERGI RICART IBARS, *SPAIN*

NEVADO TUNSHO, SOUTHEAST FACE, ASCENT AND CORRECTION

IN MAY, PERUVIAN guides Octavio Salazar Obregón and Eloy Salazar Obregón, along with Erick Llantoy, climbed the southeast face of Nevado Tunsho (5,730m), believing this face to be unclimbed. [*Editor's note: The main summit of Tunsho (often spelled Tunshu) was first reached by the northeast ridge in 1958 (AAJ 1959). In November 2005, Axel Loayza, Guillermo Mejía, and Jenny Postillos climbed a new route (650m, AI3) on the main peak, reported in AAJ 2006 as the northeast face. However, it's clear this climb was actually on the southeast face and slightly to the left of the ascent described here.*] From a bivouac in the moraine, we began our ascent at 11 p.m.

on May 28. We moved first through a rocky bit until we reached the main wall. The first part was about 400m of compact snow (65–80°), which we simul-climbed. The last part is the steepest, with 80–90° mixed terrain. Here we encountered a lot of loose, fresh snow leading directly to the ridge. We thought we'd be able to simply walk along the ridge, but the snow there was in terrible condition, and so the last stretch was more mixed than expected. We arrived on the summit of Tunsho at 11:30 a.m.

We started back down the ridge, but the snow became even worse, so we decided to finish our descent via the north face, which is about 65°. We did four 60m rappels. In all, the ascent took 13 hours, with an eight-hour descent. We felt the difficulty was 600m, TD 60–90°. 📄 📷

– OCTAVIO SALAZAR OBREGÓN, *PERÚ*

ANTACHAIRE III, SOUTHWEST FACE, WAITING FOR AXELLE

Pico Americo (left) and the southwest face of Antachaire III, showing the route Waiting for Axelle (630m, D+). *Beto Pinto*

IN MAY, Malu Espinoza, Beto Pinto Toledo (both from Perú), and I climbed the southwest face of Antachaire III (ca 5,700m), the westernmost of the three Antachaire peaks. Antachaire III was first climbed in 1966 during a DAV expedition. The Germans referred to the Antachaire peaks as Yarumaria and approached from the north side (*AAJ 1967*). No further ascents of Antachaire III have been reported. The striking southwest face, with its distinctly shaped summit ridge, remained unclimbed. For Beto and me, it was our third attempt. In September 2015, dry conditions prevented access to the wall, and in May 2018 we retreated halfway up the face.

Approaching up the Quebrada Yuracmayo, we acclimatized with several camps, establishing base camp at Laguna Rinconada (4,600m) on May 8. We also scouted a possible descent route from the col between Sullcon (5,650m) and Pico Americo (5,600m). On May 9, we set up camp on the flat glacier plateau (4,900m) below Antachaire. Shortly after, intense afternoon storms settled in, with warm temperatures persisting overnight. Since seracs threatened our route, we decided to wait and observe for an extra day.

We started our summit attempt at 11:30 p.m. on May 10, approaching by the second from left-most mixed gully. We traversed under the serac zone and arrived at the base of Antachaire's southwest face after about 40 minutes. As expected, the crux of the route was the first pitch (a mixed and unconsolidated snow runnel to 90°). After this, we climbed rapidly for the next four pitches (70°) in order to escape the looming serac left of us. The sixth pitch, which passes along the rock band high on the wall, contained more ice. After this, we trended left, ending with gradual snow climbing (45°) to the summit. We were on top around 8 a.m.; the GPS read 5,677m.

We descended the north-facing slopes in two rappels followed by downclimbing. From the glacial basin beneath, we plodded up the snow slope between Sullcon and Pico Americo, then made three rappels down the west side of Americo. An hour of walking got us off the glacier around 1 p.m. The route was named for my (at the time) expected daughter: Waiting for Axelle (630m, D+). 📷

– GUY FONCK, *BELGIUM*

Chachacomani (ice peak in center) and Jakoceri (just left) from Himaciña, with the impressive Chachacomani Glacier flowing southeast from the massif. The 2019 ascent of Chachacomani's south face took a plumb line just left of the summit. The online version of this report shows all routes on this face. *Alex von Ungern*

CHACHACOMANI-AREA CLIMBS
THREE LIKELY NEW ROUTES ON THREE DIFFERENT PEAKS

BY ALEXANDER VON UNGERN, *ANDEAN ASCENTS, BOLIVIA*

FOR A LONG time, starting in the 1980s, access to the western side of the Chachacomani and Chearoco group in the Cordillera Real was difficult or impossible, because local residents did not allow travelers to pass through the area. Mountaineers instead followed a complex approach from the east. In the last decade, the relationship between tourists and residents has much improved, aided by respectful employment of local people as muleteers and cooks. As a result, climbing in this area has picked up significantly.

On May 18, under a full moon, Hari Mix (USA) and I left a camp at around 4,800m on the normal route up the west side of Chachacomani (6,074m). We followed that route for a while, then left it to cross the col (ca 5,850m) between Chachacomani and Jakoceri. On the far side, we down-climbed a little more than 100m to reach the base of Chachacomani's south face. We roped up and simul-climbed until I crossed the bergschrund and set up a belay 20m above. We then climbed five pitches in increasingly steep terrain. The crux was the exit from a runnel at an almost vertical section, on loose snow and less than firm granite. We topped out 20m left of the summit.

The south face of Chachacomani is very seldom done, and it's likely that previous parties chose a different runnel line than we did. Later in the season, more consolidated snow and underlying ice might have made our climb easier and safer, but then some crevasses might not be crossable. [*Editor's note: Most ascents of the south face, including the original ascent of the peak in 1947, followed*

[Top] Alex von Ungern on Surapatilla's western ridge. *Chris Knight* [Bottom] The 2019 route up Himaciña's south side. *Alex von Ungern*

lines much farther left, which now sport serac barriers. In 1998, Branco Ivanek, a Slovenian guide living in La Paz, and Marco Soria, a Bolivian guide, climbed the South Face Direct at D- (60°). Their route appears to lie to the right of the line reported here.]

In October, I returned to this area with Chris Knight to attempt two peaks to the south of Chachacomani. We camped at 4,700m in the valley on the west-side approach, and at dawn on October 15, we left to climb the western ridge of Cerro Surapatilla (as defined by IGM map 5945-IV). After hiking up 300m, we started climbing on the western aspect of the first satellite summit. We were hidden in shade, which made for some humid and cold cracks. Once on the northwestern aspect of the ridge, the sunny granite was dry and we enjoyed excellent ridge climbing. At the col between the first summit and the rest of the ridge, we found a short overhanging section, probably 6a. We continued along the west ridge to the main summit, which my GPS recorded as 5,472m.

From the top we scrambled down the northeast ridge toward the col at its foot and then hiked back to camp, regaining it after a round trip of 9 hours and 45 minutes. I used a 40m rope and carried a set of nuts and four Tricams. We are pretty sure we were the first persons to follow this ridge.

The next day we left our camp at 4 a.m. to climb Himaciña (5,458m). We were lucky to find a small track made by Andean deer, which allowed us to cross the steep, unstable moraine from the main glacier flowing down from Chachacomani. We reached a plateau around 5,000m from which we could easily access the glacier below Himaciña's south flanks. Almost immediately this was steep, and we pitched three rope lengths up to 55° before reaching a col close to 5,250m. (This steep section was avoided on the descent by following slopes much further to the southeast.)

We continued up Himaciña's southeast ridge, which involved interesting mixed sections. The second half of the ridge was fully snow-covered and not as steep, but it was exposed on both sides. On top my GPS recorded 5,482m. This mountain has probably been climbed at some point, as it is pretty obvious when hiking into the huge glacial valley toward Chachacomani. However, we have found no information about a previous ascent. [*Editor's note: The IGM 5945-IV map shows three tops in this vicinity. On the map, the highest appears to be an unnamed summit, with two other tops to the northwest and northeast both named Cerro Himaciña. Knight and von Ungern climbed the northwest top and felt it was of a similar height to the unnamed top. In 1983, Udo Knittel and Reinhold Siegel from a Bavarian expedition reached the northeast top, marked as 5,252m, from the north, but it is unclear whether they continued to the unnamed summit.]* ▣

NEGRUNI RANGE: KATATANI AND PURAPURANI THOJO ASCENTS

IN MID-MARCH, DANIELE Assolari, Louise Aucquier, and I climbed Katatani (5,468m, Cerro Catatani on the IGM Lago Khara Kkota map) by the glaciated southwest face and southeast ridge, with a very nice final ridge (PD+). A week later, Assolari and I, along with seven students from Peñas Adventure School, climbed the south face of Purapurani Thojo (5,440m), immediately northwest of the Palcoco mine. Both peaks had been climbed before, by similar routes, but these ascents demonstrate the early season potential of the Negruni Range, which is now too dry in the normal climbing season to be of much interest. See the AAJ website for more information and history. 📄🔍

– DAVIDE VITALE, *BOLIVIA*

CONDORIRI GROUP, PICO AUSTRIA, SOUTHEAST FACE

IN 2009, ON the Fortaleza Buttress of Pico Austria (5,320m), Gerry Galligan (Ireland) and Rob MacCallum (U.K.) climbed a line up the east ridge to give Caporales Celtica (350m, AD, British V-Diff), a good route on sound rock. Ten years later, in March 2019, Reynaldo Choque, Erandeni Nava, Davide Vitale, and Jonnatan Zapata (all from Bolivia) climbed a route some 20m to the left but found it disappointing, being mostly on easy but unsound rock.

– *INFORMATION FROM* DAVID VITALE, *BOLIVIA*

ICEFALLS BELOW HUAYNA POTOSÍ

IN JULY 2018, U.S. climbers Matt Hopkins and Matt Ward found several ephemeral ice lines on cliffs below Huayna Potosí. Approaching from the hostel at Zongo Pass, they climbed three steep one- to three-pitch routes. Hopkins' story about these climbs is at the AAJ website. 📄📷

– *INFORMATION FROM* MATT HOPKINS, *USA*

HUAYNA POTOSÍ, DOUBLE TRAVERSE, SKI DESCENTS

SEEKING NEW WAYS to explore familiar Huayna Potosí, on which I often guide, I planned an extended ski tour over the 6,088m mountain in April. After spending the night in the Anselme Baud Hut at 5,270m, the highest hut on the south side, I started up the normal route at 4 a.m. At the summit I met Sergio Condori, who wanted to ski the Pala Grande, the 45–50° east-facing slope leading to the summit. We waited an hour on top, and at 9.30 a.m. deemed the snow soft enough to start our descent. Once down this 170m slope, we parted ways and I headed down alone on the northern slopes. I'd looked at this descent many times while guiding the mountain. The first third was quite steep, then it eased and I let the skis take me. I headed down toward the small village of Botijlaca, and eventually, when the skiing ran out, reached a beautiful glacier lake.

Unfortunately, there was not one square meter of flatness on which to pitch my lightweight tent. I had no option but to start right back up again. Although the forecast had been favorable, the weather turned bad. The slopes here are vast, and with no visibility I realized I was going round in circles, so I stopped and chopped a tent platform out of steep snow. The night was miserable, but by morning the sky was clear. I quickly found my ski tracks from the day before and continued upward, climbing with axes and crampons.

I reached the summit again at 12.30 p.m. and then skied the normal route in perfect snow back to the Anselme Baud Hut. The next day I ascended the normal route once more but broke off left to reach Huayna Potosí's south summit (ca 5,960m), from the top of which I skied back to the Anselme Baud and returned to La Paz the same day.

My three-day "Haute Route" covered 3,600m of ascent and demanding descent, mostly on skis. It is a route of two strongly contrasting halves: the absolute loneliness and silence on the huge northern slopes, and the tourist hot spot of the normal route. 🔍

– ROBERT RAUCH, BOLIVIAN TOURS, RAUCHROBERT@HOTMAIL.COM

CHARQUINI, SOUTHEAST FACE, LE CHAT

ON APRIL 28, Davide Vitale and I decided to try a line on the southeast face of Charquini (5,392m), well to the left of the existing routes on the east face. Our route began with two hard pitches, the first probably 6b. At the end of the fourth pitch, Davide reached the crest of the south-southeast ridge. We continued by simul-climbing on easy but loose ground. From the summit, we descended the glacier flowing north and reached the car in the middle of the afternoon. I called the route Le Chat, not only to keep the feline theme of most other route names on this side of the mountain but also after a Belgian comic strip— Davide is a Belgian national and has a good sense of humor. 📷

– ALEXANDER VON UNGERN, ANDEAN ASCENTS, BOLIVIA

PICACHO KASIRI, SOUTH FACE, SUPAY PACHA

The southeast face of Charquini with the line of Le Chat (2019). The east face (cleaner rock on the right side of this aspect) has three known routes; see AAJ 2019. *Alex von Ungern*

AFTER THE FIRST ascent of Picacho Kasiri's south face with Juan Gabriel Estellano (*AAJ 2019*), I went back several times in early 2019 to explore its neighboring subpeak. Picacho Kasiri is comprised of twin summits reaching more or less the same altitude; I wanted to climb the south face of the easterly peak. My first three attempts failed due to bad weather or a tired climbing partner. On April 6, the day we finally succeeded, Marcelo Gomez and I parked at the *narcotráfico* control post on Ruta Nacional 3 and hiked two hours to reach the face at close to 4,700m.

We first climbed three pitches to a big terrace, along which we walked left (west) to reach the foot of an obvious dihedral. With Marcelo in front, we simul-climbed toward steeper terrain, where I took the lead and, unfortunately, found areas of quite loose rock. On the sixth pitch I was confronted with a slightly overhanging thin seam, where I used aid for around 10–15m. As we climbed out of the dihedral into the sun, we had to negotiate two pitches up a slab that offered little protection. The free climbing difficulty reached about 6a+ and felt harder given the conditions.

We ended the climb on the summit ridge, at around 5,050m, in order to start descending before nightfall. (The eastern summit height is approximately 5,160m.) We were able to walk down the other side without rappels. As we climbed approximately half the route in shadow, we called the route Supay Pacha (the underground world). The previous year, I had called the airy route on the westerly summit Araj Pacha (the world from above). 📷

– ALEXANDER VON UNGERN, ANDEAN ASCENTS, BOLIVIA

CORDILLERA QUIMSA CRUZ

CUERNOS DEL DIABLO, LOWER BUTTRESS

DURING THE FIRST weekend in May, Daniele Assolari and I, with a group of Peñas Adventure School students, climbed five pitches (200m, UIAA V) on the nice granite buttress (sometimes mossy) below the northwest face of Cuernos del Diablo, reaching the huge terrace from which most routes begin. 🖻

– DAVIDE VITALE, *BOLIVIA*

CERRO CORICAMPANA, SOUTH FACE ASCENT

JEFF SANDIFORT (a guide with Climbing South America), my wife Dagmar, and I visited the southern Quimsa Cruz in August, reaching the Huallatani Valley by 4WD from the Konani-Quime road, via Rodeo. About 100m above the northwest tip of Lake Huallatani is another tiny lake, and there we established base camp at 5,050m. On August 25, Jeff and I climbed the south face of a peak at the head of the valley, at the end of the east ridge of Huayna Cuno Collo.

We reached the Huallatani Glacier via a narrow gully and followed it to a col at its head, four hours from camp. On the south face, Jeff led two 60m pitches (55° and 50°) to the ridge, close to the summit. On top our altimeter recorded 5,550m; the overall ascent had been AD-. There has been considerable glacier retreat in this area in recent years, as shown in photos with this report at the AAJ website. 🖹🖻

– ROMAN SIEGL, *CZECH REPUBLIC*

CORICAMPANA HISTORY: *After discussion with climbing historian Evelio Echevarria, it is most likely the peak described here is Cerro Coricampana (a.k.a. Coricampana Alto). The peak's name is a hybrid: "cori" is Aymara for golden, and "campana" is Spanish for bell. This peak was climbed in 1926 by Dr. Friedrich Ahlfeld, a celebrated geologist, explorer of Bolivia, and founder of the Club Andino Boliviano, together with L. Partmuss and Robert Gerstmann, a well-known Austrian photographer of that era. Photos indicate they climbed from the Huallatani Glacier, as did the 2019 party.*

In May 1991, Echevarria attempted the peak from the mining community of Bajaderias in the valley to the northeast, but did not find snow, only very steep, rotten rock. He retreated 200m from the summit. Echevarria went on to climb Huayna Cuno Collo East, a.k.a. Huallatani (5,620m), from the north.

The upper Huallatani Valley in an image thought to have been made in 1926 by the well-known Austrian photographer Robert Gerstmann and reproduced in Evelio Echevarria's book *The Andes*. (A) Foresummit of Huayna Cuno Collo. (B) Huallatani (Huayna Cuno Collo East). (C) Cerro Coricampana (ca 5,550m), climbed in 1926 via this glacier and then in 2019 by the glacier and the south face, directly above the col. (D) Anco Collo. The Huallatani Glacier has since retreated nearly to the rocky feet of Huallatani and Anco Collo. *Evelio Echevarria Collection*

ARGENTINA-CHILE

Perfect rock, perfect hands, perfect weather. Max Didier is all smiles high on Pared De La Plata after spending more than a week in base camp waiting out torrential rain. *Austin Siadak*

PARED DE LA PLATA
A BIG-WALL FIRST ASCENT IN NORTHERN PATAGONIA

BY SIEBE VANHEE, *BELGIUM*

MAX DIDIER (CHILE), Austin Siadak, Ian Siadak (both USA), and I had met the year before in El Chaltén and talked about doing an expedition together. In February 2020, it happened: We got ambitious, formed a team of friends, and set out to explore granite walls in Northern Patagonia. The result was a challenging expedition to Valle de la Plata, near Chaitén in Chile's Palena Province.

Using Google Earth, Max had scouted some little-explored walls in a valley called Valle Alerce. We were searching for the full adventure: an unclimbed wall and time among friends in portaledges. Once there, we found Valle Alerce was wild and had lots of rock (*see AAJ 2018*). But it didn't awaken the big-wall vibes in us, with too much jungle and maybe just not enough vertical. With a plan B in the back of our minds, we returned to civilization.

South of Valle Alerce is the Valle de la Plata, which leads up to a big wall called Serrania Avalancha, above Laguna de la Plata (43°10'07"S, 72°33'08"W). This wall was climbed by Mariana Gallego, Martin Molina, and Luis Molina in 2007 and by Sílvia Vidal in 2012. We committed to a look at this mythical face, which is reached from the small village Puerto Cárdenas. Just west of Puerto Cárdenas, it is possible to cross Río Frio, then hike cross country to the Río de la Plata and follow this to Laguna de la Plata. In all, the lake is located about 10km west of Puerto Cárdenas.

Gaucho Pierre Angelo helped us cross the Río Frio by horse on our first day. Reading Sílvia's reports, we knew the approach wasn't long, though through pure jungle and along wild rivers.

After only one hour we encountered dense jungle and a steep river with lots of waterfalls. It was often impossible to walk in the riverbed. Five more challenging days followed. We spent days swinging our Bear Grylls–brand machetes, crawling on hands and knees, and wading through the river, sometimes deep and often with strong currents. Our original seven-day weather window vanished as we conquered more bamboo and river crossings. Simply reaching Laguna de la Plata seemed like a great aim in itself.

Six days into our trip, we reached the lake. To our surprise, there was more than one wall rising there. Opposite the east-facing Serrania was a beautiful, white wall full of obvious crack systems. We called this west-facing wall Pared de la Plata. Though smaller, it was more appealing, and also looked less likely to turn into a raging waterfall in the rain. In 2014, Mike Sanchez, Juan Señoret, Tola Señoret, and Sebastian Schmidt attempted a route on this wall, and our route shares the first couple of pitches before branching left.

We first spent eight days camping below the wall, and, over three climbing days (using aid and fixed ropes to make progress and return to base camp), we managed to reach the summit in very gray and unstable weather. Pitches 10 through 12 didn't go free because of wetness, mud, and moss in the cracks (A2). Descending, we spotted a cleaner variation to the left

[Top] Siebe Vanhee struggles to stay afloat while carrying a 25–30kg load into base camp at Laguna de La Plata. Though only about 7km from the road as the crow flies, it took the team six grueling days to carry 350kg of gear, food, and supplies to the lake. A machete was absolutely necessary. [Bottom] The final free line of Bailando con la Lluvia (700m, 16 pitches, 7a). The route shared the initial pitches with a 2014 attempt by Chilean climbers Mike Sanchez, Juan Señoret, Tola Señoret, and Sebastian Schmidt and then branched left. The 2019 team carried an inflatable boat up the dense jungle approach in order to cross the lake below the wall. The Chileans chose to swim the lake in 2014 and nearly suffered hypothermia. *Austin Siadak (both)*

Max Didier climbing pitch eight (5.11) of Bailando con la Lluvia on Pared de la Plata. *Austin Siadak*

of those pitches. We decided to leave static ropes fixed to pitch eight, an amazing pillar jammed into a big dihedral, hoping to try for an all-free ascent.

After one day of rain and waterfalls, we received a real five-day weather window. We quickly moved our camp onto the wall, to the top of what we called Puerto Pilar. These final two nights on the wall were for sure the high point of the trip—the contrast between the heavy rain and stable weather made us savor this wild place even more! Over one and a half days, we team-freed the new variation. Just one hand-drilled bolt was necessary to traverse left into another corner system on pitch 10. This was the beautiful free climbing we had been looking for.

Unfortunately, even with the nice weather, our weather window was closing. The long hike out of the valley would be made impossible by new rain and rising rivers. From our base camp below the wall, it took two full days—knowing the river crossings, the jungle path, and every single trick—to bring our loads back down to our starting point across the Río Frio.

This was a very committing expedition that I am happy to have shared with friends among whom I feel at ease and secure. The name of our route, Bailando con la Lluvia ("Dancing with the Rain," 700m, 16 pitches, 7a), refers to the difficulty of climbing between the curtains of rain that turn these walls into raging waterfalls. ◙

Skiing toward the northwest face of Cerro De Geer for the first ascent of the peak. *Riley Rice*

ACROSS THE NORTHERN ICEFIELD
FIRST ASCENT OF CERRO DE GEER, HIGH POINT OF CORDÓN AYSÉN

BY BEN WILCOX, *USA*

IN THE AUSTRAL winter of 2016, I worked as a caretaker on a remote ranch in the Colonia Valley, outside of Cochrane. On bluebird days, I'd walk to the shores of Lago Colonia and look across at the Northern Patagonian Icefield. Cerro Arenales dominated the skyline, but in the distance, I could make out the white summits of the Cordón Aysén (Aysén Range) on the west side of the icefield, impossibly remote and tantalizingly unknown.

Inspired by those memories and by Camilo Rada's wonderful articles in AAJ 2018 on the icefield's climbing potential, I began lobbying potential climbing partners to come south. Riley Rice and Ciarán Willis, both fellow NOLS instructors, gamely answered the call. They arrived with about 400 pounds of equipment in Puerto Guadal on December 2, 2019, and we made final preparations for a roughly 25-day expedition to the Aysén Range.

On December 4, we traveled by jet boat up the Leones River and ferried loads to the shore of Lago Leones, which we then crossed by motorboat. It took four days of heavy carries to reach the flat "pancake" of the icefield itself, crossing the low pass between Cerro Cristal and Cerro Mocho. We were aided by perfect weather—sadly, this would be the only good weather of the trip.

Over the next seven days, we skied in whiteout conditions to reach the base of Cerro De Geer (2,520m), the tallest summit in the Aysén Range and our primary objective. The precipitation was nearly constant, though more bearable when it came as snow rather than rain. Temperatures hovered around freezing. One memorable night included a pounding rainstorm that sounded like thousands of drummers rehearsing on our tent. When it seemed impossible that it could rain

[Top] The unclimbed south face of Cerro Fiero. [Bottom] Breaking camp below Cerro De Geer, preparing to ski toward the exit from the icefield following heavy snow. *Riley Rice (both photos)*

any harder, a ferocious lightning storm arrived, and the rain seemed to double in strength. This was the first of three unusual lightning events we witnessed on the icefield.

By December 14, we were at the base of De Geer, glad to have completed our ten-day approach. The only glimmer of hope in the bleak weather forecast was a brief pause in precipitation during the predawn hours of December 16. We set alarms for midnight and, after several hours of excavating equipment from snowdrifts, began to ski to the broad amphitheater that separates De Geer and Cerro Margarita. After days of opaque white vistas, it was thrilling to see De Geer and its neighboring peaks for the first time. Howling winds sent wild snow plumes from De Geer's summit ridge.

With conditions deteriorating rapidly, we cached our skis at the base of a rock rib on De Geer's northwest face and began climbing moderate snow slopes, which then steepened into ice. Two pitches of AI3, led by Riley, deposited us on the summit for the peak's first ascent. We could see only each other and the rime we stood on, and we did not linger. On our roped descent through the whiteout, we became acquainted with the interiors of several crevasses.

We had plenty of food remaining, not to mention our untouched rock climbing equipment, but the forecast offered no hope. After two days of hunkering down, we skied eastward and, over the course of five long days, exited the icefield via the "Keyhole," which uses the Nef Glacier to access the upper Soler Valley. The weather was unrelentingly wet. A notable low point involved getting benighted on a maze of dry glacier while crossing the Nef.

On December 22, we reached El Palomar, a remote outpost where we rendezvoused with the legendary gauchos Don Ramón and Don Luis, who took much of our equipment and horse-packed it to the shore of Lago Plomo. Meanwhile, we descended the swollen Soler River in pack-rafts. We made it to Puerto Guadal, on the shores of Lago General Carrera, for Christmas dinner. Though we found challenging conditions on the icefield, it is an enchanting place and there was much to be grateful for. I already look forward to going back. 🖥 🔍 ▶

Nico Favresse climbing El Flechazo on the southeast pillar of Agjua Standhardt, with Cerro Torre's rime-covered top in back. *Sean Villanueva*

BELGIANS' BANQUET
TWO NEW ROUTES AND A FIRST FREE ASCENT IN THE CHALTÉN MASSIF

BY SEAN VILLANUEVA, *BELGIUM*

NICO FAVRESSE AND I came to El Chaltén this past season without a plan. Other climbers, seemingly discontent with this explanation, would ask, "Are you keeping it a secret?" It seems to be in vogue to have a big project and focus all of your energy on it. Nevertheless, it is natural to let your feeling guide you in the mountains. Very often, for Nico and myself, our best moments in the mountains arise from having no objective and no expectations. We go up to enjoy the moment, to make the next step, the next move—the top far from thought, without importance, and maybe beyond possibility.

On our first trip into the mountains, we left Rolo Garibotti's home with five potential climbs in mind. In the end, we did something else.

While walking the glacier, Nico spotted a nice, clean, and dry line on the east side of Aguja Standhardt. "We might as well try that!" As is often the case, we didn't analyze it too much. We had borrowed two single, inflatable G7 portaledges from our friend Roger Schäli. With a weight under 4kg for two people, fly included, this gave us huge flexibility. We were relatively light but could set up camp pretty much anywhere. No need to find a ledge before nightfall.

Rock, paper, scissors. I set off on the first pitch, harder than expected. An overhanging bulge followed by a difficult-to-protect traverse on a slab gained the crack system we were aiming for. With the weight of the full rack, my camera, and layers of clothes, I was unprepared for difficult climbing. I put up a good fight but was unable decipher the slab. A few falls later, I gained a ledge, built an anchor, and lowered back down to the ground to redpoint the pitch.

Maybe it doesn't make sense to redpoint the first pitch of an 800m wall without knowing what's above, but we like to play the free climbing game. With our lightweight portaledges and three days of food, our destination was unbound.

On the sixth pitch, Nico fought hard on an overhanging, wet crack. As he let out grunts of despair, I prepared myself to give a dynamic belay. It seemed certain he would fall. All of a

The ultralight G7 inflatable portaledge (less than four kilograms, with fly, for two people) has opened new possibilities for alpine climbers. *Sean Villanueva*

sudden, he threw a blind dyno around an arête and, miraculously, reached a jug to hold on! Seconding, I was in total disbelief. How did he find the inspiration to jump out from such a blank position? "I was in total desperation," he answered. Another great pitch followed, with a dyno worthy of a modern, Olympic-style bouldering competition, which brought us to a great camp in the vertical void.

The next day was my birthday. For a present, Nico offered me a beautiful over-hanging splitter crack! Unfortunately, half-way up, I found myself unable to commit to the 35m of fists and offwidth climbing with a single number 4. I guess that's what the age of 39 does to you. With apologies to Nico, I retreated and found a variation to bypass this incredible splitter.

We installed our portaledges underneath the classic Exocet chimney. I was ready for a little birthday party with a freeze-dried meal. "Can you pass me your lighter?" Nico asked me. "Where is *your* lighter?" I barked back at him. "It must be in the bottom of my bag," he answered. Suddenly, he pulled out a gluten-free cake, with candle lit, as he sang "Happy Birthday." I felt like a fool for snapping at him!

To avoid Exocet's daytime waterfall of melting ice, we got up in the middle of the night to climb the chimney to the summit. With only five ice screws, it was important to use them sparingly, and 10m above my last screw, I nearly took a large fall while extracting an ice axe. As I started to fall backward, I desperately stretched out my right arm. The axe hooked itself right back into the ice! "Did you just almost fall?" Nico asked me.

We were the first of the season to attempt the summit mushroom of Standhardt. Although it is not as big or difficult as the ones on Torre Egger or Cerro Torre, we have little to no experience on this vertical rime stuff. Manteling onto the final blob of slush, I wondered if the whole thing might fall off. "All-you-can-eat ice cream for my birthday!" I yelled.

We named the route El Flechazo ("Cupid's Arrow," 600m, 7b M3 60˚; finishing on Exocet, it's 850m, 7b M3 WI5+). The name is an anti-missile, make love not war kind of thing, in response to the nearby Exocet and Tomahawk. However, some seem to think cupid's arrow has caused more damage than any missile in history.

LOOKING AT SOME pictures, we had envisioned a new line on the south face of Aguja Poincenot. After the long approach, standing at the base on Col Susat, the cracks seemed closed and the line a lot less obvious. "We're not going to go very far with our two Peckers and one piton," Nico pointed out. We continued on to the closest and most obvious line, Historia Interminable, climbed in 1989 by a Spanish team. This route on the southwest face had not been repeated or free climbed.

The wall was steep and offered some large cracks. On one pitch, Nico engaged in a memorable two-hour battle with a 60m offwidth (6c). At the crux of this lead, with only one completely tipped out number 6 for protection, things got really spicy. Often, this peculiar style of climbing is difficult to comprehend. With dubious protection it's difficult to commit. Nico reached the end without a fall but not without his pants stained in blood. In the following weeks, he'd complain about his scabs sticking to his pants or sleeping bag and proudly insist on showing the state of his knees to anybody asking about our climb. I made sure to announce that his knees were proof of bad technique. To be fair, the war on the sharp end is different than seconding.

Without portaledges this time, there was pressure to find a bivouac ledge around nightfall. Luckily, we stumbled upon a beautiful snowy ledge and dug out our nest for the night. The next morning, we climbed a couple of new pitches before joining easier ground to the summit (800m, 6c). There was a small setback when we arrived on the western summit, which is a little lower. So we downclimbed a pitch and a half to scramble back up to the real top!

GENERALLY, THE APPROACH from El Chaltén to an advanced base camp is about six to seven hours. At the beginning of our season, we chose Niponino in the Torre Valley for our advanced base. The downside of this strategy is it's hard to adapt. With a short and windy weather window approaching, we wanted to climb an east face, protected from the wind. However, in the Torre Valley, the east faces were covered in

Beggars Banquet on the east face of Aguja Poincenot, starting on the Whillans-Cochrane ramp. *Damian Llabres*

rime. We spotted an obvious line on the east face of Poincenot, but it was not accessible from our base camp, and the only gear we had brought down to town were our climbing shoes and chalk bag.

The climbing community, though, is extremely generous. We soon managed to gather ropes, gear, harnesses, sleeping bags, stove, and a tent. I remarked, "It's great to know that I can come to El Chaltén completely naked and find all the gear that I need to climb in the mountains!"

We started up the Whillans-Cochrane ramp on Poincenot and soon reached an evident line just left of Patagónicos Desesperados. We were coldly welcomed by wet and icy chimneys. A number 6 with crampon points welded onto it would have been handy protection! We almost always alternate leads, but it was music to my ears when Nico shared, "If there are any difficult offwidths, I might allow you to take the sharp end. You know, to spare my knees!" "Yes, for your knees!" I laughed. In the end, he managed to avoid some icy elevator shafts by venturing onto the slabs. On two occasions, we used an ice axe to mantel over icy, overhanging cracks.

It was windy, and few climbers managed to climb that day. Our decision was prescient: We were well protected from the infamous Patagonian gale. Nico built an anchor 5m below the summit, still protected, from which we prepared our assault to touch the summit. "It was a great climb, but I'm not sure if it will become an instant classic," Nico declared, referring to all the wide, icy cracks. We rappelled Patagónicos Desesperados, reaching the glacier by nightfall. We called the route Beggars Banquet (400m, 7a), after a Rolling Stones album and to show our appreciation to generous friends, without whom we would never have been able to attempt this line. 📷

ATACAMA DESERT, VOLCÁN PALPANA, SOUTH FACE

A FEW YEARS ago, I took a picture of the south face of Volcán Palpana (6,023m). It was a distant photo in which no details were distinguished other than its verticality. This is unusual in the Atacama Desert of northern Chile, where the high peaks are characterized by slopes of sand and stones rather than vertical rock or ice walls. I showed the photo to my friend Alejandro "Jimmy" Mora, and in March 2019 we decide to check it out.

The south face of Volcán Palpana (6,023m) in northern Chile's Atacama Desert. The waterfall ice attempted in 2019 splits the right side of the 300m rock headwall; the climbers eventually summited by easier slopes to the right. *Armando Montero*

After acclimatizing near San Pedro de Atacama, we drive to the northern slope of Palpana. To reach the elusive south face, we continue by truck along a precarious road to the northwest ridge and set up our first camp at 4,400m, were we leave the truck. The next day is a long walk along the west slope of the volcano. After several hours, with a magnificent view of the desert, we finally have before us the objective, the south face, and we set up a second camp at 4,900m.

The cold sunset illuminates our climbing options. The 1,000m face is divided into two sections: the first part of snow and ice couloirs, 40–60° and approximately 700m tall, and, the second part, a vertical headwall, 300m tall. The headwall is complex and crossed by ice cascades cut by overhangs, all at an elevation above 5,700m.

On March 28, we start climbing the couloir on the right side of the south face. As we gain height, the slope increases. Our plan is to sleep just below the headwall and a long ice waterfall. The day passes step by step, the mind wanders, memories drifting, the flow of consciousness begins. The sun hides as the altimeter reads 5,700m. We look for a terrace to put up our small tent. Ice ramps and vertical rock ridges surround us. Finally, we carve a terrace in the broken rock. It's cold. This desert freezes more deeply than my home mountains in Patagonia.

At last, the sun rises. The rock on the headwall is compact and decomposed and does not offer many possibilities. The frozen waterfall looks more vertical than it had from below. With many overhanging sections, the progress is slow and difficult. The ice is fragile. Overhead, the huge stalactites and ice roofs remain in the air, levitating. The route is very difficult. Great stones suddenly fall from above. The hill helps us make the decision: We decide to rappel, get off the waterfall, and continue another way.

We still have hours of light remaining as we climb unroped by 60–70° ice and snow ramps to the right of the headwall. The afternoon progresses, clouds form, and it starts to snow. Approaching the summit crater, the slope declines but the ridge plateau is covered with penitentes that slow our advance. The wind and cold increase. At sunset, with the last light, we reach the summit. Happiness is short. To get down, we have to cross the crater, more than a kilometer in diameter, and descend numerous slopes to the west. Several hours later, we arrive back at the truck, having made the first ascent of the south face of Palpana. 🖸

– ARMANDO MONTERO, *CHILE*

CERRO DE LA RAMADA, SOUTH-SOUTHEAST RIDGE

CERRO DE LA Ramada (6,384m) had just two routes, both from the north via the Río Colorado, prior to my ascent over March 24–26. The mountain is in a glacial cirque about 10km southeast of Cerro Mercedario (6,720m) and about 100km north of Aconcagua. My idea was to climb the first route from the south. Finding a suitable approach to the south side took some investigation on Google Earth and onsite reconnaissance in November 2018.

In March 2019, I approached with horses via the Valle de las Leñas, close to Portezuelo de Espinacito, in perfect weather. Starting from a base camp at 4,350m, I set one additional high camp at 5,200m. The next day, March 25, I followed the south-southeast ridge to the summit. Overall, it was an easy climb, with some scrambling on rotten rock, snow, and ice; however, it was long and time-consuming, with about 2,000m of vertical gain. 🔍

– CHRISTIAN STANGL, *AUSTRIA*

CERRO DE LOS DIABLOS, FIRST ASCENT

FROM OCTOBER 21–27, Argentines Ezequiel Dassie and Glauco Muratti made the first ascent of an interesting 5,000m peak in the remote northern section of the Cordón del Potrero Escondido. They began the expedition in Penitentes, at 2,400m on the road that connects Argentina and Chile, then headed southward by the Quebrada de Vargas, camping at 3,800m at the Portezuelo Serrata. The next day they descended to the Río Blanco valley (3,300m) and continued into the Cajón Norte del Potrero Escondido. They camped at 3,800m and the next day at 4,100m in a place they called La Cancha. They had good weather during the mornings and snowfall in the afternoons.

It was not possible to climb the mountain by its north face, as planned, because of rotten rock. So, during the fourth day, they ascended 30° snow slopes, class III rock sections, and scree to a 4,790m col east of the summit. From here, the ridge was guarded by large rock towers, so they traversed along the east-southeast face and then climbed directly to the summit up 40° snow with easy but exposed mixed passages. The official height of the summit is 5,007m; their GPS showed 5,090m (32°58′30″S, 69°55′48″W). They rated their route PD and suggest the name Cerro de los Diablos for the mountain, since the curious-looking rock towers on the summit ridge appeared like dancing devils. Their exit from the mountains took two days under heavy snowfall. 📷

– MARCELO SCANU, *ARGENTINA*

AGUJAS DEL SOSNEADO, NEW ROUTES

DURING 2019, THREE different expeditions achieved new routes in the interesting climbing zone of Sosneado, located on the east flank of Cerro de los Pantanos, southeast of Cerro el Palomo (4,850m). Together, there are some 20 granitic needles here, with up to 500m routes. Since the initial reports in *AAJ 2015* and *2016*, it has become a classic spot for climbing in Argentina.

During March, Lucas Alzamora and Juan Girolamo opened a new route on a needle called Pilar Roja; the route is Perro Chivato (150m, 6c). Afterward, in April, Alzamora joined Matías Korten and Andrés Tula, ascending a new route on Aguja Preñada (145m, 6c+). Also during April, Alzamora teamed up with Carloncho Guerra and Diego Nakamura to finish a route on Aguja Ectelion (a.k.a. Torre Blanca de Ectelion), which they had attempted twice in the preceding years. They rated it (450m, 6c). [*Editor's Note: This is the same "unfinished" route indicated in AAJ 2015. Earlier routes on this spire, Jumanji and Chaparral, begin to the right of the 2019 climb.*] 🔍

– MARCELO SCANU, *ARGENTINA*

Dana Hawlish climbing the Cosmic Corner (5.12-) of La Pluma del Cóndor on Cerro Laguna. *Brandon Hill.*

CERRO LAGUNA, LA PLUMA DEL CÓNDOR

In February, on a rainy day in Valle Trinidad, Billy Barghahn, Dana Hawlish, and I set out to look for a new line on this valley's seldom-climbed walls. On the north face of Cerro Laguna, we stumbled upon a pair of beautiful left- and then right-facing corners and a stunning splitter crack high on the headwall. Once the weather cleared, we returned and started up the route, which begins in the gully between Cerro Laguna and Tetris Wall.

After aiding the steep, thin second-pitch corner (which would eventually be dubbed the Cosmic Corner, the route's free climbing crux) we found fixed gear and decided to bail. Upon returning to base camp and asking about the line, however, we discovered that another team had scoped the route on rappel but had not climbed it.

We returned to Cerro Laguna and climbed to the top of the wall using a mix of free and aid climbing tactics. Over the several following days, we cleaned the route, equipped it for future ascents, and established a higher quality version of pitch five, which we bolted on rappel. (The route has a total of seven protection bolts plus rappel stations.) We finished the process with a team-free ascent: La Pluma del Cóndor (7 pitches, 600', 5.12-). 📷🔍

– BRANDON HILL, *USA*

ARRAYAN FREE CLIMBED: *On Trinidad Sur, Clinton Leung and Drew Marshall succeeding in free climbing the route Arrayan (AAJ 2017), which Leung and four others had established in early 2017. The free climb has nine pitches to 5.12d.*

VALLE COCHAMÓ, CERRO LA SOMBRA AND TWO FREE ASCENTS

Upon arrival in Cochamó in December 2019, I partnered up with local climber Diego Diazaguilera, who pointed out the route Sundance, which goes up the northwest face of Cerro Trinidad, as a potential free climb. Established in 1998 by Grant Farquhar and Simon Nadin (22 pitches, 7a+ A2+), the route hadn't seen any repeats. It was perfection to my ears!

Sundance climbs the center of the steepest part of Cerro Trinidad. The five aid pitches are steep and challenging, and the first two of these each took me two tries to free climb. Pitch nine was a big fight through dirty, flared, and steep cracks, and sending this pitch required overhanging chimney and stemming skills to avoid the closed, dirty cracks. My legs and lower back burned from the body tension necessary to stay on the wall. After this, three similar but less steep pitches led us to easier ground. I led all the pitches free while Diego gave me all his confidence, patience, and support. We reached the summit of Trinidad in 16 hours. Although this ascent felt incredibly hard to me, the crux pitch may only be 7c if cleaned; as it is now, it could easily be 8a.

In the beginning of January 2020, Max Didier (Chile) and I tried what is supposed to be the hardest established free climb in Cochamó, El Cóndor Pasa (20 pitches, 8b) on Trinidad Central. We arrived at the crux pitch very quickly. I was not able to onsight the pitch, though we did continue to the summit just to have a look.

We returned in mid-January and were able to make the full free ascent. We switched leads up to pitch 14 (the 8b crux pitch), with me leading most of the hard pitches. Thankfully, we arrived early at the crux, which gave me enough time for two tries before the sun hit the wall at 1 p.m. Max didn't try to free this pitch and offered to support me. On my first try a handhold broke at the very end of this technical 50m crux pitch. After a 15-minute rest, I tried it again, racing

Jardines de Piedra (16 pitches, 7b+ A2), the first ascent of Cerro la Sombra. *Siebe Vanhee*

with the sun and nearly bonking. This time, it worked: no misplacements, no stress, and no broken holds! Easier pitches lead to the summit in the burning sun, reaching the top in about nine hours.

El Cóndor Pasa was put up in 2016 by Slovakian climbers Martin Krasnansky, Jozef Kristoffy, and Vladimír Linek, and free climbed in six days after their ground-up first ascent. The route is almost entirely slab and face climbing and is well protected by bolts.

At the end of my stay in Cochamó, the desire for an unclimbed wall was high. Valle de la Luz is wild and full of rock. Max Didier, Ian Siadak (USA), and I walked into the valley past Cerro Capicua and scoped the unnamed and unclimbed peak to the north. One hour of dense, sometimes vertical, jungle hiking brought us to the base. In the gully on the left side of the wall, we found something akin to Japanese rock gardens: an amazing 20-square-meter platform surrounded by cascades, pools, and flowers. It was one of the best bivouacs any of us had ever seen.

The next day, we managed to climb our new route Jardines de Piedra (16 pitches, 7b+ A2) in 16 hours. Although the start of this west-facing wall looked easy, the ledge systems alternated with interesting vertical and technical climbing. On pitch four, I was challenged by a very thin crack in a dihedral. The first 30m went all free at 7b+, but the next 30m were very dirty and steep, and I was forced to aid through (A2, with technical piton placements).

In the middle of the wall, we chose the main dihedral (three pitches), which went almost free except for a few dirty and wet meters. Above this, where it looks like the climbing is almost over, there are still six pitches to the summit. Pitch 11 was a big challenge, with slab run-outs and a steep, flared, and dirty crack; I made a big effort but, again, aided the last few meters because of the dirt. On pitch 12, Max made a proud lead: a sea of slabs with little to no protection. When he ran out of rope, we climbed 20m simultaneously until he was able to make an anchor. The final four pitches had smooth climbing to the summit.

We descended on the north side of the wall into the gully, making six rappels and zigzagging our way down to base camp. We propose the name Cerro la Sombra for this summit.

– SIEBE VANHEE, *BELGIUM*

The granite spire of Cerro Picacho, with the route up the south face (600m, 5.10+ A0). *Armando Monterro*

CERRO PICACHO, SOUTH FACE

CERRO PICACHO (1,883m, 44°54'32"S, 72°13'11", labeled incorrectly as Cerro Punti-agudo on the IGM map), rises above dense forests along the Carretera Austral highway between Mañihuales and Villa Amengual. On January 31, 2019, Armando Montero (Chile) and I left Coyhaique to attempt a new route on the south face. From the road, we followed a steep stream to the west and passed around the north side of the mountain until we reached a col below the west face, where we bivied.

The next morning we traversed below the entire west face and passed over the southwest ridge. After crossing a small snowfield, we started up the south face. We swung leads up sustained vertical to slightly less than vertical rock, mostly in the 5.9–5.10b range, with two 5.10+ crux pitches. There was only one 80m of class 4, which we climbed unroped. The rock is beautiful alpine granite but with loose and dirty sections, and at time we resorted to aid to avoid knocking off large blocks.

We reached the summit at 6 p.m. Amazingly, there wasn't a cloud in the sky, and we had incredible views of Cerro Elefantes, the Queulat Glacier, and Volcán Melimoyu to the north and the Mañihuales Valley to the south. We rappelled toward the col between the southern (true summit) and northern summits, and then continued rappelling the west face back to our bivy. We believe our route (600m, 5.10+ A0) was the first ascent of the south side of the mountain.

The history of Cerro Picacho is very interesting, as its first ascent was done in a style that has yet to be repeated. In March 1987, Claudio Hopperdietzel, a local mountaineer from Puyuhuapi, climbed to the summit alone in a single push, going car to car in a day (around 1,700m of verti-cal gain). He climbed and downclimbed the technical southwest ridge, using a 20m rope to make rappels off natural features for a few steeper sections during the descent, though he didn't bring any harness or rappel device. Claudio has said in conversations that he never became accustomed to climbing with a rope and that his route was just 4th class. However, subsequent parties have verified that the route includes multiple sections of technical climbing, with a crux in the 5.8–5.9 range! 📷

– DUNCAN MCDANIEL, *USA*

EARLIER ROUTES ON CERRO PICACHO: *In the 1990s, after Claudio Hopperdietzel's solo first ascent of the peak, Peter Hartmann (Chile) and John Hauf (US) climbed the northwest face to the north summit then traversed to the south summit. In February 2011, Franco Cayupi, Joos Ilsbroux, and Armando Montero climbed another new route on the northwest face, west of the Hartmann-Hauf route, which they called Lost in Melimoyu (800m, 5.10a). The northeast wall is believed to be unclimbed. — From information on andeshandbook.org*

On the northwest face of Cerro Cachet, finishing the new route Gaucho Muy Complicado. *Marcos Goldin*

CERRO CACHET, GAUCHO MUY COMPLICADO, AND OTHER ASCENTS

OUR EXPEDITION TO the Northern Patagonian Icefield in Chile's Aysén region was comprised of a team of five: two French (Norbert Talazac and Pierrick Saint Martin) and three Argentines (Bruno Falco, Juan Falco, and Marcos Goldin). We put aside a month on our calendar during November and December.

We met at Coyhaique and packed three to four weeks worth of food, fuel, and equipment, and a pair of skis each. Each of us also carried a packraft, which doubled as a sledge to carry our gear on the ice and as means of transportation to descend the Soler River and cross small glacial lakes along our journey. In Puerto Bertrand, we met Ramón and Hector, the local guides who would carry our loads by horse to El Palomar, the last hut before the icefield. Finally, the expedition had begun. We shuffled gear to the boat and started to sail the Bertrand and Plomo lakes.

While the horses were taking our gear to El Palomar, we began our 20km walk inside green valleys with dense woods of lengas that made progress difficult. After two full days of bushwhacking, crossing swamps, and rivers that reached our bellies, we reached El Palomar. We spent two more days reaching the western side of the Nef Glacier, two days in tents under unstoppable rain, and two days (with abundant rain) carrying and pulling our gear into the icefield. After this eight-day approach, we finally established our camp on the ice below an unnamed nunatak on November 22.

November 23 was the only day with weather good enough for climbing, and Norbert, Pierrick, and Marcos used this window to establish a new line on Cerro Cachet (2,632m) for its second ascent. [*The peak was first climbed in 1971 by a New Zealand and Chilean trio, starting from a col to the west.*] We called the route Gaucho Muy Complicado (600m, D 90°), recalling a funny event from the first few days of expedition. The line starts on the northeast face up a 70° couloir then traverses rightward through easier ground to the north side of the mountain. Here, we climbed a steep chute, averaging 65° with occasional steeper sections; this was mainly ice and could be protected with screws. A couple of pitches on snow led to the final pitch: vertical rime ice and very difficult to protect.

The descent was made in very poor visibility and strong winds via the original route, which winds down the southwest ridge. This included a couple of hundred meters of tricky climbing along rime-covered pinnacles (up to 75°). It wasn't necessary to rappel (and it would have been very time consuming to build proper anchors), so we downclimbed.

On the same day, Bruno and Juan summited one of the spires of the unclimbed nunatak above camp: Porotos y Cerdo (200m, 6b M3). The route begins on a snow ramp then follows easy mixed climbing to reach a perfect 20m crack; after that, the climbing is on easy terrain. The following day provided another small weather window, so Bruno and Juan took the opportunity to climb another small tower immediately south of the unnamed nunatak: Siete Años De Espera (180m, 6a). The brothers named this spire Punta Roco.

[Top] **The northeast side of Cerro Cachet, showing (1)** Homenaje a los Amigos Perdidos (M7+) and (2) the first part of Gaucho Muy Complicado (D 90°), both climbed in late 2019. [Bottom] **The upper section of Gaucho Muy Complicado on the northwest face.** *Marcos Goldin (both)*

The following days were spent in base camp under copious snowfall, but, interestingly, with very little wind. The trip's main objective, the first ascent of Cerro Nora, remained undone. After descending the glacier to El Palomar, we had to content ourselves with a fun ride in packrafts down the Soler River to Plomo Lake, where we met Ramón and his boat to return to civilization. In just six hours, we rafted through jungle that we had spent two days walking. 📷 🔍

– JUAN FALCO *AND* MARCOS GOLDIN, *ARGENTINA*

CERRO CACHET, NORTHEAST FACE, HOMENAJE A LOS AMIGOS PERDIDOS

In November, I began my 19th expedition to Patagonia but my first to the Northern Icefield. Joining me were Lukas Hinterberger and Nicolas Hojac. We spent three weeks at a base camp in the forest below the Nef Glacier. On our second week, November 22, we climbed Cerro Largo (2,799m) by the northeast ridge: similar to a demanding ski tour, but with a short passage of ice at the very end.

In the days following, we traveled to the northeast side of Cerro Cachet (2,632m) and set up advanced base camp on the Nef Glacier. On December 3, we left camp after a raging storm, sinking into wet snow and navigating crevasses. Cachet now looked considerably larger and more impressive than we'd realized while looking through binoculars. There's one thing you basically never have on the mountain in Patagonia: time. In our case, it was a mere day. The weather forecast predicts wind speeds of 100 km/h for the following morning.

After about four hours of approach from camp, we reached a steep headwall rising into the blue Patagonian sky. I led the first 80m, which went quickly, even though it was just a thin sheet of ice on rock slabs. Nico surpassed a 60m ice ramp with water running under it. We followed his leads, the ragged Nef Glacier below us. Eventually, Lukas took over. Crampons crunching on rock, he made his way forward, centimeter by centimeter in a tight chimney. After a while, we finally heard the liberating "off belay." It was the hardest pitch on our route.

After another 120m of easy climbing, we stood on the summit ridge and untied to move swiftly across rime ice and snow to the main peak. Our route is an Homenaje a los Amigos Perdidos ("Homage to Lost Friends," M7+). [*The route is left (east) of Gaucho Muy Complicado, climbed just 10 days earlier; see report above.*]

We began our descent at 7 p.m., rappelling an efficient, direct line. Falling rime caused a few critical moments, but we remained unscathed, reaching our advanced base camp shortly after midnight. Back at our jungle base camp, which lay protected in a small forest, we spent the next days recovering from the strains of the summit and enjoying our last "liquid chicken"—the last beer.

– STEPHAN SIEGRIST, *SWITZERLAND*

CERRO PUÑO, FIRST ASCENT

CERRO PUÑO (2,108M) is an attractive summit at the top of the Colonia Valley, on the eastern flank of the Northern Patagonian Icefield (Campo de Hielo Norte). Puño Este (ca 2,050m), the eastern summit of the Puño massif, has been climbed by previous parties, including Jim Donini and Tad McCrea's 2016 ascent of the imposing eastern face (*AAJ 2018*). The taller western summit of the massif remained unclimbed.

On January 10, 2019, Ben Barron, David Carel, and I (all USA) began our drive up the Colonia Valley, first crossing the Baker River on a beautiful, antiquated *balsa* (car ferry). Dirt roads turned to muddy two-track, and, as the path faded, we stashed our truck in the bushes and proceeded on foot.

I had attempted Puño two years prior, in 2017, with a different team, and the faint

Approaching Cerro Puño (2,108m) through thick Patagonian brush. The south face of Puño is in view. The team ascended the glacier around the right (east) side of the nunatak visible on the right side of the photo and then climbed the rock pitches on the opposite north face. *Ben Wilcox*

machete path we'd left on that expedition appeared intermittently over the course of our approach. The bushwhack was still formidable and involved occasional fifth-class maneuvers up trees or mud walls. After six hours of painfully slow progress, we threw our sleeping bags on a granite slab near a small lake and watched the evening colors settle over the landscape.

The next day we quickly moved through the remaining forest and brush to emerge onto a series of high granite slabs leading to the Puño Glacier. At the base of the glacier we built a high camp and then roped up to scout the terrain; we found it considerably more crevassed than two years prior.

At dawn we crossed the glacier and made a few tricky steps over the bergschrund, then followed steep snow around the eastern side of a small nunatak. This brought us onto a plateau where we could see for the first time the north face of Cerro Puño. A narrow snow bridge over an otherwise impassable moat and some steep snowfields led to the rock. Ben led five pitches of moderate climbing, three of which were surprisingly aesthetic, high-quality granite. We lingered on top for 30 minutes, taking in sweeping views of Cerro Arenales, the Colonia Glacier, and the Cordón Aysén.

After two 70m rappels, we retraced our route to high camp and then descended to the Colonia Valley in howling winds and sleet over the course of two days. 📷

– BEN WILCOX, *USA*

SOUTHERN PATAGONIA / CHALTÉN MASSIF

AGUJA ST. EXUPERY, SOUTH FACE, MIR

LUKA LINDIČ AND I arrived in El Chaltén in the middle of January and planned for a six-week visit. Since we'd both visited Patagonia a few times, we knew there was no point in having fixed goals, as Mother Nature sets the rules anyways. We decided it was better to approach the walls with good ideas, strong motivation, and open minds.

Since the Torre Valley looked crowded and the walls covered with snow, we found our goal on the south face of Aguja St. Exupery, where, in 1998, Argentines Marcelo Galghera and Horacio Gratton attempted a new line to the left of Le Petit Prince (*AAJ 1995*), retreating after six pitches.

On our first try, at the end of January, we climbed nine pitches, the first six of which had been climbed by the Argentines, and found a good bivy ledge to spend the night. The next day, we climbed a traversing pitch before deciding that continuing on an overhanging traverse with minimal equipment and no option for retreat felt too committing. We rappelled and took all our gear with us to the valley. At that moment, we realized why almost no one climbs this sort of steep wall in alpine style, and why most first ascents of this magnitude use rope-fixing tactics to provide security.

After a few rest days in town, our muscles were refueled, but we couldn't sleep in peace. Our minds couldn't give up the thought of the passage we sensed through the overhangs, the one we hadn't dared to commit to trying. With the right gear and the knowledge of the wall that we had now, this story could have unwound differently.

Curiosity got the best of us. We borrowed more equipment from our friends in the valley and returned to the wall in the middle of February. With a good weather forecast, our goal was to have fun and give it our best. The climbing result would just be a consequence of the actions taken to reach that goal. Since there was no one else on the wall, we could enjoy our challenge in peace, which is becoming a more and more important factor for the quality of our experiences in the mountains.

The first day went by without many problems. The weather was warmer and knowing the pitches made the climbing more fluid and less stressful. We enjoyed the good bivy, knowing we would face reality the next day. As the wall leaned back overhead, we moved upward slowly, not knowing what to expect but accepting whatever was offered. At first, we left the rope attached on the overhanging crux pitch. After climbing further, we sensed a passage through the last part of the overhang. We decided to take up the rope. It felt committing but also liberating. From that moment on, we knew the only way was up. Luck accompanies the brave, right? The passage we had sensed, we soon discovered. It proved to be the only crack leading out of the overhanging terrain.

Tired but happy, we bivouacked on a small snowfield where our route joins Le Petit Prince.

Luka Lindič leads through icy overhangs on Mir, south face of Aguja St. Exupery. *Luka Krajnc*

The third day, we enjoyed the good climbing on that route, which led to a col and then to the summit of St. Exupery. We rappelled the Italian route on the east face and found ourselves back below the wall at sunset.

What more could we ask? We had climbed the steepest alpine wall of our lives in good style and had an amazing time. Altogether, combined with the top of Le Petit Prince, the climb was 700m, 7a+ A3 70°. We named our new line Mir (500m, 6c+ A3 70°), which means "peace" in Slovene and strongly connects to the inner and outer experience we encountered both during and after our climb. 📷🔍

– LUKA KRAJNC, *SLOVENIA*

AGUJA STANDHARDT, IL DADO E' TRATTO; AGUJA POINCENOT, 40° GRUPPO RAGNI, FREE ASCENT; EL MOCHO, JURASSIC PARK

I LEFT ITALY at the end of January 2020 with two longtime partners, Matteo Bernasconi and Matteo Pasquetto, heading south for an annual visit to the mountains that, for me, are simply the most beautiful in the world. We had a clear goal in mind: a line on Cerro Torre that I had attempted with Matteo Pasquetto the previous season.

Alpinists in Chaltén had waited weeks for the good weather to arrive. However, once it finally did, the final portion of our objective lay buried in a thick layer of ice. Adapting quickly, we decided to try a new route on Aguja Standhardt, one that I had imagined on previous visits to the Torre Valley. On February 5, we began by climbing the lower "slabs," starting about 60m down and left from the bergschrund leading to Col Standhardt and 100m left of Festerville (Martin-O'Neill, 2000). After the first seven pitches, the quality of the climb was already very good and harder than expected; however, the best had yet to come.

The following day, we began with some technical crack action, and, after a boulder-like crux, reached a crazy-overhanging hand- and fist-jam corner. Due to the sustained physical effort, we decided to split the 100m corner into three separate pitches. Unfortunately, the last meters were filled with ice. Instead of abandoning our only number 4 cam, we placed one bail bolt, lowered to our anchor, and decided to aid a thin seam 6m to the right.

Afterward was another tricky pitch, followed by some easier ones along the left arête of

Battling exciting wind and climbing on Jurassic Park (320m, 7b C1). This relatively short but stout route on the north face of El Mocho took two seasons to complete. *Della Bordella Collection*

Standhardt's north face until the first summit. Reaching this point at 6 p.m., and knowing we could count on perfect weather, we opted for a luxurious bivy. We completed the route to the summit the next day, following the upper pitches of Festerville.

In retrospect, our bivouac was a bad choice. The descent down Exocet proved to be quite scary in high daytime temperatures. Nonetheless, from an objective point of view, the rock quality, climbing style, and position on our new route are tremendous—plus it's waiting

Aguja Standhardt's final steps. *Della Bordella Collection*

for a complete free ascent: Il Dado e' Tratto ("The Die is Cast," 600m, 7b A1).

A couple of weeks later, we were blessed with another window of good weather. This time we headed for the north face of Aguja Poincenot. The first route on this wall was opened in 1986 by fellow Ragni di Lecco climbers Daniele Bosisio, Mario Panzeri, Marco Della Santa, and Paolo Vitali. They called it 40° Gruppo Ragni (550m, 6a+ C2). After climbing and fixing our two ropes on the first pitches, we slept at the base of the route. On February 21, we were able to climb the whole route in a day. Both Matteo Pasquetto and I achieved our objective to free climb the route onsight. It's a really good climb that could become popular, as it's always in the 5.10 and 5.11 range.

Our third and last climb this season involved unfinished business on the north face of El Mocho. One year prior, Matteo Pasquetto and I had teamed up with Brette Harrington (USA) to attempt the very aesthetic lower pillar, left of the route Morbito (Nagato-Sato, 2017). The climb proved to be much harder than expected, and we didn't have a large cam for the final offwidth cracks.

On February 28, Matteo Pasquetto and I managed to climb the route in very high winds. After the first four pitches (up to 7b), we chose a slightly different line than the prior year. So, for pitch five, there are now two options: a sketchy string of Peckers aided by Brette in 2019 (A2+) or a mellower, but still tricky, flared crack and slab (C1). The final, 40m offwidth was the real killer of the route. After 25m of Yosemite-like climbing, I exploded, exhausted, with bleeding ankles and without a shred of energy left (C1).

Jurassic Park (320m, 7b C1) is an excellent climb, with some really cool, sustained overhanging crack pitches in the range of 5.11+/5.12. We finished our line as planned atop the pinnacle, however, one can continue to the top of El Mocho by other routes. 📷 🔍

– MATTEO DELLA BORDELLA, ITALY

CHALTÉN AND TORRES DEL PAINE: 2019–2020 SEASON SUMMARY

THIS WAS THE fourth consecutive season with fairly poor weather and conditions. After several anomalously dry seasons in a row, when climbing success in this area was quite straightforward, it has come as a bit of a shock to go back to the Patagonia weather of old. The only extended windows of good weather were in February, but the conditions were challenging, with much snow, ice, and rime on the walls. Not enough is known about the area's climate to know if the recent changes relate to inter-annual or decadal variability. Panos Athanasiadis, a European climber and climatologist, points out, "It is perfectly normal that multi-annual climate variations are very strong, and periods of one extreme are followed by years of the opposite extreme."

A recently published paper in the journal *Nature* shows that the poleward trend of the jet stream and the ring of low pressure that circle Antarctica—the two biggest influences upon Patagonian weather—paused around the year 2000 (Banerjee et al., 2020). This poleward trend had contributed to drier, more stable weather. The authors attribute this pause to the healing of the ozone hole, as a result of the Montreal protocol, the treaty designed to phase out the production of substances responsible for ozone depletion. Over the long term, climate models predict that increasing greenhouse gases will continue the poleward pull, but as this paper suggests, for some time the effect will be dampened by the ozone hole recovery. (*See also "Sunny Patagonia?" in AAJ 2018.*)

Despierta y Lucha on the west face of Cerro Peineta. *Rolando Garibotti*

Despite the difficult conditions, many climbs were completed (*see also other reports in this section*). In the Torres del Paine Massif, in late January, Sebastian Pelletti (Austria) and Cristobal Vielma Sepulveda (Chile) opened Despierta y Lucha (400m, 5.11 A1) on the west face of Cerro Peineta, to the left of Capicúa Pastor (Arancibia-Fica, 2005). The red granite was of superb quality, with long clean corners, finger to fist cracks, and a couple of difficult slab sections to connect cracks. They found a few short sections of aid—some thin, requiring pitons and micro-nuts. They rappelled Billy the Kid (Garber-Lloyd, 1993), leaving their line completely clean.

In February, Pelletti and Javier Reyes (Chile) climbed El Tambor (230m, 5.10+), a new route on the west face of the Colmillo Oeste. Late in the month, Christophe Ogier (France) and Gašper Pintar (Slovenia) did the fifth ascent of the "W" traverse of the three Paine Towers. Steve Schneider (USA) did the first ascent of this traverse in February 2002, completing it solo in 51 hours round trip from base camp.

In the Chaltén Massif, there were a few ascents in early December, but then the weather did not allow for much until early February. On Cerro Torre, a number of parties climbed the Ragni Route during two good weather windows. Ten days later, the first rime mushroom above the upper headwall collapsed, causing a massive avalanche that would have killed anyone on the route. The factors that influence rime mushrooms to break off are not known, but it seems plausible they behave in part like a snowpack, and that the combination of gravity, heat, and moisture can result in events like this. Avoiding periods when the freezing line is above the base of the route (2,300m) would be wise.

On Torre Egger, in January 2019, Brette Harrington (USA) and Quentin Roberts (U.K.) climbed a new variation on the lower east pillar, a line first scoped by the late Marc-André Leclerc. After the first four pitches of Titanic, their line headed left, climbing nine pitches (350m, 5.12b) to rejoin Titanic. Bad weather prevented these two from reaching the summit in 2019, and so they returned this season along with Horacio Gratton (Argentina). Ice-filled cracks prevented free climbing the crux and forced them to make a three-pitch variation to their 2019 line. Eventually, they joined Titanic to reach the summit (950m altogether). They spent four days on the climb—two full climbing days, one waiting for conditions to improve at the half-height snowfield, and one descending.

Torre Egger and Aguja Standhardt from the southeast. (1) Titanic (Giarolli-Orlandi, 1987). (1a) MA's Visión (Harrington-Roberts, 2019, climbed free but not to summit). In 2020, MA's Visión was climbed again with a variation (blue line, Gratton-Harrington-Roberts), and the climbers summited via Titanic. (2) El Flechazo (Favresse-Villanueva, 2020) on the southeast pillar (see p.213). (3) Il Dado e' Tratto (Bernasconi-Bordella-Pasquetto, 2020), finishing on the north face (see p.226). Other routes not shown. *Rolando Garibotti*

In late February, Colin Haley and Alex Honnold (USA) traversed Cerro Pollone, Cerro Piergiorgio, and Cerro Domo Blanco. They first climbed Cara Sur (400m, 65° 5) on the south side of Pollone, a warmup of sorts, bivouacking at the col before Piergiorgio. They then climbed Esperando la Cumbre (400m, 70° M5) to the north top of Piergiorgio. The tricky traverse of the summit ridge was the crux (300m, WI4 M5 A0). From the main summit, they descended to the southeast (many rappels and some traversing), bivouacking before Cerro Domo Blanco. They then ascended the last portion of Filo Norte (250m, 60° 3) on Domo Blanco, making their final descent northwest to the Marconi Glacier. They named their linkup the Crystal Castles Traverse. A week later, Haley and Honnold did the first ascent of Cerro Electrico Oeste, the jagged peak to the north of Paso del Cuadrado.

On the east face of Cerro Piergiorgio, Alessandro Bau and Giovanni Zaccaria (Italy) climbed Scrumble de Manzana (WI5 M6), a stunning four-pitch, ice-filled corner that connects Cara Este to Esperando la Cumbre. Just to the west, Agustín Burgos (Argentina) and Tad McCrea (USA) climbed Muñecos de Barro (300m, 5.8 75° M3), a new route on the east face of Colmillo Este. They followed the couloir between Colmillo Este and Norte until 50m below the col, then moved left onto the north face until the summit.

In the Fitz Roy group, over February 20–21, Kiff Alcocer and Jordon Griffler (USA) climbed GBU-57A (6b+ C1), a 15-pitch new route on the south side of the west ridge of Aguja Rafael Juarez. After 12 pitches, their route briefly joins Filo Oeste, then heads left, climbing three more pitches to join the Anglo-American. The rock is of decent quality, although at times a bit gritty. They left no gear but found a few bolts at the belays of the first pitches from an earlier attempt

(Raselli-Brun, 2013). Just to the south and on the west face of Aguja de l'S, Matías Korten and Agustín Mailing (Argentina) climbed Linea Roja (350m, 5.10), a new route on the upper headwall, following the obvious red streak to the right of Thaw's Not Houlding Wright.

Among the big news this season were many paraglider flights and BASE jumps. After climbing the Ragni Route, Fabian Buhl (Germany) became the first person to fly off the summit of Cerro Torre after climbing up it. He landed on the Torre Glacier after a 17-minute flight. The history of flying here started in 1988, when Matthias and Michael Pinn (Germany) climbed the Supercanaleta and flew off the summit of Cerro Fitz Roy. Four days later, together with Uwe Passler, they climbed the Compressor Route up Cerro Torre, carrying their paragliders, but poor weather prevented them from flying. A week later, they hitchhiked a ride back to the summit in a helicopter and all three flew off. In 1991, Roman Tschurtschenthaler (Italy) also hitchhiked a ride to the summit in a helicopter and flew off.

Also on Cerro Torre, Boris Egorov, Vladimir Murzaev, and Konstantin Yaermurd (Russia) BASE jumped from the "Valery Rozov" exit, in the vicinity of the Banana Crack on the seventh pitch of the Southeast Ridge. (Rozov jumped from here in 2008.) Across the valley, Alban Alozy, Arnaud Bayol, and Pierre Sancier (France) from the Groupe Militaire de Haute Montagne BASE jumped the west face of Mojón Rojo and the west face of Aguja de l'S, both times flying around 1,300m. Later in the season, Pablo Pontoriero (Argentina) paraglided from the summit of Cerro Fitz Roy after climbing the Supercanaleta, the third person ever to do so, after the Pinn brothers. In early December, Fabrizio Maffoni (Argentina) paraglided from the summit of Aguja Guillaumet; the feat was repeated in February by Claudia Molestina and José Cobo (Ecuador).

It is important to note that although there is no specific regulation prohibiting BASE jumping or paragliding in the national park, any new activity in the park has to be specifically authorized before it is permitted. Since it poses no environmental impact, and since it's an activity practiced in the area since the late 1980s, it could eventually be legalized.

There were few accidents this season, but one was fatal. In mid-March, Johan Millacahuin Vivar, a promising, 18-year-old climber from Puerto Natales, Chile, died while descending from Torre Norte, in Torres del Paine. He may have rappelled off the end of his ropes. There is no organized rescue in the area, so a large group of friends spontaneously went to move his body to a place where he could be picked up by helicopter. Earlier in the season, Johan and two friends had done the second ascent of the British route on Cerro Cathedral.

– ROLANDO GARIBOTTI

CORDILLERA DARWIN

CERRO GARCIA AND OTHER ASCENTS

STARTING IN LATE October, the French climbers Laurent Bibolet, Antoine Cayrol, Emmanuel Chance, Merhal Desay, Gaylord Dugué, Julien Ravanello, and David Vigouroux made a 26-day expedition to the Cordillera de Darwin. Using the sailboat Podorange as a base, they moved from west to east along the range and made a number of ascents. A total of six days of good weather prevented many would-be climbing opportunities.

Starting from Fiordo De Agostini on the northwest side of the range, they completed two significant climbs. On October 28, Cayrol and Dugué ascended the south face of an unnamed 1,036m peak located west along the ridgeline from Monte Buckland: the South Face Direct (500m, TD WI4 M5).

On October 29, Chance, Desay, Bibolet, Ravanello, and Vigouroux made the first ascent of Cerro Garcia (1,244m), southwest of Monte Buckland, calling their route on the south side Sky Fish (600m, TD M5). Both routes involved considerable snow, ice, and mixed climbing. The climbers rappelled the routes.

Further east, the climbers entered Fiordo Parry. On the west side of the fjord's inlet and across from Bahía Blanca, they made an ascent of Cerro 1,123m by easy terrain. They also made an unsuccessful attempt to climb the north face of Cerro Selk'nam (1,837m), with two bivouacs to reach the base.

Lastly, further to the south, the climbers visited the zone near Monte Darwin (2,261m), accessing it from Brazo Pia Este off the Beagle Channel. They then traveled to the far southeastern part of the range to reach Bahía Yendegaia, where Dugue and Vigouroux ascended Cerro Serka (1,366m), the westernmost 1,300m peak in the Cerros Pirámides chain (AD, 50° IV). 📷 🔍

– ERIK RIEGER, *WITH INFORMATION FROM* DAVID VIGOUROUX, *FRANCE*

CERRO MAA KIPA

ON JANUARY 18, 2020, Marine Israel (France), Jeffrey Buckley, August Uribe, and Oscar Uribe (USA), and I departed via the maritime vessel Alakush from Caleta María (Azopardo Bay) in Chile, headed for the eastern Cordillera Darwin. We sailed southwest into Parry Fjord then veered into Cuevas Fjord and disembarked on the west shore where the Valley of Queen Isabel II starts. Our quintet trekked to Lake Queen Isabel II and continued on to the terminus of the glacier, where we set up base camp.

The initial objective was to ascend Cerro Tridente (1,324m), northwest of Monte Darwin (2,261m). However, foul weather forced a change of plans. We tried for a nearby peak, north of Tridente. As we climbed, we found a great couloir with perfect powder on the east face, and then made our way along the summit ridge to the top. We christened the mountain Cerro Maa Kipa, which translates to "progeny" in the indigenous Yagán language of southern Patagonia. By GPS, the elevation was 979m. 📷

– SEBASTIAN BELTRAME, *ARGENTINA*

[Top] Cerro Garcia (1,244m), seen from Fiordo de Agostini, is southwest of Monte Buckland. The French climbers linked snow ramps on the right side of the wall, calling their route Sky Fish (600m, TD M5). [Middle] Unnamed 1,036-meter peak to the west of and along the same ridgeline as Monte Buckland. The South Face Direct (500m, TD WI4 M5) followed the obvious, central gash. [Bottom] Cerro 1,123m, near the mouth of Fiordo Parry, on the west side of the inlet and across from Bahía Blanca. The French summited by easy terrain on the left side of the peak. *David Vigouroux*

ANTARCTICA

ANTARCTIC PENINSULA, ZEISS NEEDLE SUBPEAK AND GATEWAY RIDGE, TERZO PARADISO

GIAN LUCA CAVALLI, Manrico Dell'Agnola, and I spent January 2020 on the Peninsula in largely poor weather. We traveled aboard Icebird, captained by Oliver Grant.

On January 10, we climbed a steep mixed route to a subpeak (unofficially dubbed Cima Cocoon) of Zeiss Needle (696m), on the northwest Arctowski Peninsula. The 600m route, Via della Seta, ascended the rocky southwest face and, unusually for a climb on the Peninsula, climbed M4 terrain as well as more moderate snow and ice to AI4. The rock was of typically poor quality and hard to protect, but the unusually warm temperatures of this season also resulted in bad snow and ice conditions, which we found as we visited all the popular climbing and ski areas of the region. [*Zeiss Needle itself was climbed and skied by an American team in February 2000.*]

After sailing to Anvers Island and into Börgen Bay, we noticed a beautiful ice/mixed line on the south side of the end of Gateway Ridge, a southern extension of Mt. Rennie (1,555m). On January 16, in improved weather, we were dropped off at a weak point in the seracs hundreds of meters east of this wall. A circuitous and difficult route led in four hours to the bergschrund. After steep snow, ice, and mixed pitches heading right, we reached a second bergschrund and then climbed multiple

steep pitches—one vertical pitch with sections of 95°, and others at 60–85°, all with generally good ice screw protection. Before the top, we negotiated almost vertical pitches with mushrooms and cornices, reminiscent of Peru and Patagonia, which were poorly protected with deadmen and stakes. We reached the top 12 hours after drop-off to complete the 700m Terzo Paradiso (AI5 M5).

[Above] **Manrico Dell'Agnola on the upper section of Terzo Paradiso on Anvers Island, above Börgen Bay on the south face of Gateway Ridge.** [Left] **Terzo Paradiso (700m, AI5 M5) on the south side of Gateway Ridge.** *Marcello Sanguineti (both photos)*

Due to the poor ice conditions, we decided to descend the back of the ridge rather than rappel the route, traversing the Hooper Glacier and eventually rappelling a serac to the shore, a long way west of our drop-off point, where Icebird's Zodiac retrieved us.

During the expedition we conducted snow sampling as part of a research project in collaboration between myself from the DIBRIS Department of Genova University and the Institute of Polar Sciences of the Italian National Research Council. 📷

– MARCELLO SANGUINETI, *CAAI, ITALY*

HERITAGE RANGE, SEVERAL FIRST ASCENTS

FRENCH GUIDES Sam Beaugey and Manu Pellissier, with their client François Calvarin, left ALE's Union Glacier camp on November 27 with loaded sleds for the 170km journey north to Mt. Vinson. Their aim was to make first ascents in the Heritage Range along the way. Ski journeys between Vinson and ALE's bases at Patriot Hills or Union Glacier had been done before, but only in 2017 had ascents been made along the way, and that was in the reverse direction.

The French team skied north up the Driscoll Glacier, crossed into the Schneider Glacier, and camped near Rogers Peak (1,521m), first climbed in 2017. On the 29th, the trio climbed a striking, leftward-slanting gully on the southwest face of a 1,729m summit to the southeast of Rogers, which they named Calvarin Peak (79°21.409'S, 84°08.716'W). They climbed ten 60m pitches of generally steep snow with difficult belays. Traversing the very sharp summit crest, they descended the north ridge and returned to camp after 10 hours.

Over the next five days they continued north, across the Minnesota Glacier and then into the Nimitz Glacier, which drains the southern reaches of the Ellsworth Mountains. They camped on the eastern side of the southern Bastien Range. On December 5 they set off up the east ridge of a nearby peak, climbing 500m of snow and mixed terrain to a summit they named Bogets Peak (78°55.965'S, 85°24.481'W, 1,567m GPS). Descending to the west (with one rappel) they continued on to another summit, recorded as 1,468m and named Peliss Peak (mostly rock to French 3). They descended the north ridge to a col and continued up the easy south face of a third summit, Suzanne Peak (1,381m), completing the trilogy of ascents in 10 hours.

Leaving the Bastien Range, the team continued up the Nimitz, turning into the Zapol Glacier to make their way across into the lower Branscomb Glacier and to Vinson Base Camp. Beaugey and Pellissier made one foray onto Vinson's normal route but retreated in the face of unusually high avalanche danger (higher than average snowfall being a feature of the season). After waiting for weather and conditions to improve, all three returned and ascended the rocky ridge left of the steep snow face that forms this part of the normal route. This feature had first been climbed in the late 1980s but very rarely since. After a 12-hour climb from Low Camp, they reached the summit at midnight on Christmas Day and were in base camp eight hours later. 📷

– DAMIEN GILDEA, *WITH INFORMATION FROM* MANU PELLISSIER, *FRANCE*

The elegant pyramid of Bogets Peak in the southern Bastien Range. *Manu Pellissier*

NORWAY

BOLD AND BEAUTIFUL
ADVENTUROUS NEW ROUTES IN LOFOTEN

BY GERBER CUCURELL, *SPAIN*

JORDI ESTEVE AND I returned to the island of Moskenesøya in May, this time with Bernat Bilarrassa, and we climbed a couple of new routes in the Kirkefjord area. We first tried the north face of Brasrastinden, but Bernat received a direct hit from rockfall, which broke his helmet, and we retreated.

On the 24th, with tails somewhat between our legs, we went to look for something less committing and found the north face of an unnamed 672m peak northwest of Moltbaertinden (700m) and south of Breiflogtinden (750m). The first obstacle was a large slab with disconnected thin cracks, which made it difficult to protect. On the slab's second pitch, Bernat, almost recovered from his accident, made a fine zigzagging lead; he discovered the best line by opening his field of vision—if he had only looked up, he would have been stuck. Although the cracks toward the top of the wall were technically harder, this second pitch was the key to unlocking the route.

We climbed a total of 13 pitches to the summit, named our route Diamantfinner (400m, Norwegian 7/5.11 with one section of A2), and labeled the summit "Moltbaertinden North Peak." We made two rappels to reach the north-northwest ridge and then followed this to the start of a large gully, which led down east to the main valley running south to Kirkefjord.

The following day we headed south along the fjord and then back northwest up the Vesterdalen (valley) to reach the remains of a glaciated cirque below the east face of the south summit of Stamprevtinden (748m). We carried five bottles of water and a little food for the next 20 hours.

After climbing unroped up initial easy-angled slabs, we weaved a route up the face above in 19 pitches, several of them bold. One hundred or so meters below the top, with no clear route visible, the sky told us that precipitation was not long in coming. We didn't have enough gear to descend, so the only escape was up. The stress this caused was precisely why we had come to this corner of the Arctic, seeking adventure and the essence of trad climbing.

From the summit we followed the south-southeast ridge as far as the pass before Helvetestiden, then descended a gully to Kirkefjord. We named our route the Human Timeline (600m, 7/7+). There is one other route on the east side of Stamprevtinden: Sweet Dreams then Beautiful Nightmares (480m, 13 pitches, 7, Svihalek-Svihalek, 2012).

We climbed both routes with trad gear and left nothing in place. We took Camalots up to number 4 but not enough micronuts. On Diamantfinner we had to use the nut tool as a placement in the A2 section, so we recommend future parties bring a lot of micronuts. 🔲 🔍

Catalan climbers Cucurell and Esteve, along with various partners, have made near-annual visits to Moskenesøya since 2015, establishing many new routes, always without using bolts, pitons, or fixed ropes. See AAJ 2018 and 2016.

[Top] On the vast upper slabs of the Human Timeline, east face of Stamprevtinden's south peak. [Bottom Left] Diamantfinner on the north face of "Moltbaertinden North." [Bottom Right] The wide crack on pitch five of the Human Timeline, east face of Stamprevtinden's south peak. *Gerber Cucurell (three photos)*

LOFOTEN

FIVE LONG ICE AND MIXED ROUTES

In *AAJ 2019*, Chris Wright reported new routes on Stortinden and Brettviktinden, climbed with Jon Bracey (U.K.) and Luka Krajnc (Slovenia), and we noted—without details—that these two had authored several other new routes in early 2018. Here is additional information on this impressive series of climbs.

On February 28, 2018, Bracey and Krajnc climbed Jebanje Jeza (700m, M7) on the northeast face of Vågakallen (942m) in southern Austvågøy. In the lower section this route follows a line similar to the 2001 Scottish Route (Benson-Robertson), left of the Storpillaren, but once the headwall is reached it climbs a thin line on the right to finish on the southeast top (816m). The climb took 12 hours.

On March 3 they traveled to Moskenesøya and climbed the obvious depression on the north face of the 740m north top of Solbjørn (742m), the peak rising more or less out of the sea above the Fjosdalen Tunnel on the E10 highway. The route was named Insured by the Mafia (600m, WI5) and took six hours.

On March 5 the two traveled to Himmeltindan (965m), the highest mountain on the island of Vestvågøy. On the north face of the northeast summit (883m), directly above the sea, they took eight hours to climb Anaconda (750m, M5+ AI4).

Two days later they climbed the west face to the 1,035m west top of Rulten (1,062m), northeast of Svolvaer on Austvågøy. They took five hours to complete Nora's Gully (M5 AI4) on the left side of the face. The line has been tried several times in the past, and this side of the

[Top] **Happy Ending Gully** on the east face of Haveren. This line lies between Shekina (500m, AI7 M4, Årtun-Nesheim, 2009) on the left and Arctic Mousaka (AI4, Daskalakis-Daskalakis, 2009). [Middle Top] **Nora's Gully** on the west face of Rulten. See AAJ 2010 for other routes to the right on this face. [Middle Bottom] **Insured by the Mafia (600m, WI5)** on the north face of Solbjørn. [Bottom] **Jebanje Jeza (700m, M7)** on the northeast face of Vågakallen. *Luka Krajnc (all photos)*

mountain was used to make the historic first ascent in 1903 (Collie-Slingsby-Slingsby).

Finally, in three hours on March 8, the pair climbed Happy Ending Gully (400m, AI4) on the east face of Haveren (808m), on the north side of Vestvågøy. The route lies to the right of Shekina (AI7 M4), put up during the 2009 International Winter Meet by Norwegians Bjørn Eivind-Årtun and Sjur Nesheim.

– INFORMATION PROVIDED BY **LUKA KRAJNC**, *SLOVENIA*

VESTVÅGØY, KRIKKTINDAN, NORTH FACE, VAFFELVIKA

ON MARCH 17, a strong, young Lofoten local named Stian Bruvoll and I took advantage of a rare day off work to poke around the fjords. We had a million ideas, as usual, but as Stian lived very close to one objective we both had been curious about, we decided to visit the north side of Krikktindan (620m), which lies south of Bjørnsand and the head of the Steinsfjorden.

The day started typically with nearly getting a vehicle stuck in snow, followed by a long walk along some ludicrously scenic coastline and a snowy plod up a valley that felt far more remote than it was. Our efforts were rewarded when, after soloing an easy gully, we reached a five-star pitch of steep water ice. Stian dispatched it in good style, and the rest of the route followed thin ice, interesting mixed climbing, and the usual frozen moss to a spectacular belay off a conveniently placed summit cairn. We descended to the southeast and hitchhiked back to the car, counting ourselves lucky that both the day and the few passersby happened to be going our way. We called the route Vaffelvika ("Waffle Bay," 300m, WI4+ M4). ▣

– **CHRIS WRIGHT**, *USA*

KUGELHORN, NORTH FACE, VIND FÖR VÅG

THE KUGELHORN IN the Efjorden region, just to the east of Lofoten, is perhaps best known for its classic east ridge (Ostkammen, Norwegian 5-/5). The north face is steep and extensive, and to date there have been only a few routes: the North Slope (5 pitches, VI-, 2007), which slants up left to join the east ridge; Solskensdiederet (5 pitches, 7, 2007); Torskfiskaren (6 pitches, 7-, 1980); and Ogat (6 pitches, A2, 1981). In 2019 two new routes were added.

Krister Jonsson, who made the first ascent of Solskensdiederet in 2007, returned on August 26 to climb Vind för Våg (six pitches, 7+), starting to the left of his previous route. The line was climbed roped solo; it begins 30m to the left of an obvious left-slanting corner. The climb has a few fixed pegs and requires a normal rack of trad gear.

Also in August, and farther right (between Torskfiskaren and Ogat), Stian Bruvoll and Philip Curry (Norway) climbed the nine-pitch Nordwestpassasjen (7-, with sections of hard, bold climbing).

– INFORMATION FROM **KRISTER JONSSON**, *SWEDEN*

The north face of Kugelhorn and the line of Vind för Våg (2019). Other routes, mostly to the right, are not shown. Beyond is the Efjorden. *Krister Jonsson*

The east face of Bautaen and the line of Origo Heights. *Krister Jonsson*

BAUTAEN, ORIGO NIGHTS

THE FJORD OF Hornsund lies in southern Spitzbergen (Svalbard), and on the south coast of its inner waters is the small peak called Bautaen (76.97086°N, 16.38613°E). This is a remote summit, and I am not aware of any routes being climbed there. I climbed the east face on June 3, during a long night snatched between days of work and skiing. My route began more or less from the sea. After a short ski ascent, I walked to the base of the steep rock wall, which I rope soloed in six pitches. The route followed cracks and corners of surprisingly good rock (gneiss): Origo Nights (7a). Protection was mostly good except on the second to last pitch, which was wide. (Camalots number 5 and 6 would have been useful.) I rappelled the route from single-point anchors. 📷

– **KRISTER JONSSON,** *SWEDEN*

BLÅTINDEN, EAST FACE

ON JULY 23 we completed the first rock route on the east face of Blåtinden, which we named Uløya, Welcome to (360m, Norwegian VI+). Our ascent took seven hours, during which we used neither bolts nor pitons. The rock is sharp, shattered, and loose in places, and big cams are useful. Before and after this ascent, we repeated Arctandria and Bongo Bar on Blåmann (Tromsø region). On August 3 and 4, in 37 hours, we climbed the 1,200m Norwegian Route on the Troll Wall in Romsdal at VII A0 (the crux pitch was climbed A0). This route is dangerous because of unstable rock. 📷 🔍

– **GOSIA JUREWICZ** *AND* **JOZEK SOSZYNSKI,** *POLAND*

NORTH FACE OF SKJELETTINDEN: *Elsewhere on Uløya, Artur Paszczak and friends climbed the first rock route on the very steep north wall of Skjelettinden (952m). They zigzagged through overhanging sections at III /IV, then came back and tried to force a direct line, retreating when meeting blank slabs.*

GOKSØYRA AND SNOVASSKJERDINGAN CENTRALTIND: FOUR NEW ROUTES

GOKSØYRA (1,330M) LIES close to the village of Eresfjord, northeast of Andelsnes and Romsdal. On February 26, Michal Czech and Kacper Tekieli (Poland) climbed the west face to the right of Midnattsol (600m, VII, Ibanez-Metal-Oie-Pie, May 1988) to create Winter in Norway like

[Top left] The west face of Goksøyra and the lines of (1) Midnattsol, (2) Winter in Norway like Summer in Tatry, (3) Ice Forest, (4) Vertical Garden, and (5) No Wet, No Fun. [Bottom Left] Jan Kuczera starting the second pitch of Tordenruta on Snovasskjerdingan Centraltind. [Right] On the approach to Tordenruta on the southwest face of Snovasskjerdingan Centraltind. The Diamond Wall is clearly visible up and right. At the top of the approach snow slopes, Grotterruta (2019) and Alpine Kjesler ascend thin ice smears just left of the leftward-slanting corner leading to the obvious snow patch. Tordenruta (also from 2019) branches right before this. *Kacper Tekieli (three photos)*

Summer in Tatry. According to the calendar, this was a winter ascent, but they climbed it in rock shoes, hence the name.

The Polish line joined Midnattsol after around 600m of climbing, with two pitches of Norwegian VII-. A further 400m of unroped climbing and scrambling led to the summit. They descended the opposite side of the mountain, completing a 15-hour round trip from the valley. Czech is a 23-year-old rock climber with routes such as Freerider on El Capitan already under his belt.

Tekieli returned to Goksøyra on March 1 with Jan Kuczera. The far right side of the west face is much lower and has its own "summit." This sector has two parallel routes on its left side: Ice Forest (450m, WI4 M5+, Kuczera-Ksiezak, 2013) and Vertical Garden (450m, WI4 M6+, Cholewa-Soszynski, 2013). To the right of these routes, Kuczera and Tekieli climbed No Wet, No Fun (500m, M7+). Each pitch was onsighted, the ascent took 12 hours, and descent by the south face took another three hours. Conditions were far from ideal, with ubiquitous wetness. However, the climbing is top quality, with relatively good belays; Camalots number 4 and 5 are useful. Kuczera feels that if this line were in the Tatras it would be a (difficult) megaclassic.

Earlier, on February 25, Kuczera, Wadim Jablonski, and Tekieli put up Tordenruta on the southwest face of Snovasskjerdingan Centraltind (1,520m) in the Sunndalen region. The 450m route climbs under a formation known as the Diamond Wall, slants up left, then makes a hard and run-out leftward traverse (70m) to gain a final couloir. The difficulties were M7 WI3 R, and all pitches were climbed onsight. The team returned to the valley after a 16.5-hour day.

On the same day, Prezmek Cholewa, Tomasz Kujawski, and Lukasz Stempek climbed a partial new route left of the previous line, following the 2018 route Alpine Kjensler (700m, WI5 M4 50° snow, Hugaas-Nierinck), then branching right to reach the upper couloir of Tordenruta directly. Their route, Grotterruta (M6+ WI4), was completed in 11 hours.

There are a number of existing lines on this face of Snovasskjerdingan Centraltind, generally put up by Norwegian climbers in the period 2011–2014. The two new Polish routes lie left of Forskerforbundet (600m, WI5 M7+, Grynning-Mosti, 2014), and Tordenruta appears to share common ground with this for the first three pitches. 🔲

– *INFORMATION FROM* **KACPER TEKIELI**, *POLAND*

The line of Kilian Jornet's ski descent of the Fiva Route on Store Trolltind. The huge Troll Wall is to the left, across the broad snow gully. *Kilian Jornet*

STORE TROLLTIND, FIVA ROUTE, FIRST SKI DESCENT

ON AUGUST 16, 1931, the legendary Norwegian mountaineer Arne Randers Heen, with his cousin Eirik Heen, became the first to climb any of the Trolltind summits directly from the Romsdalen valley, when the pair completed the 1,550m Fiva Route to Store Trolltind (1,788m). This peak is just to the north of Trollryggen, on which lies the enormous Troll Wall. The Fiva route, named after a farm in the valley below, was first climbed in winter in 1972, over four days, by a Polish quartet. On February 17, 2018, the Catalan Kilian Jornet, who has lived in Romsdal since 2016, made the first ski descent, after waiting two years for the right conditions.

Jornet climbed the route and skied down in a total of five hours and 40 minutes (about three hours for the ascent). From the summit he skied a couloir on the south flank, climbed down a bit, and then tacked to the southeast ridge, reaching the point where the Fiva Route drops dramatically down the northeast face. After a 40m rappel into the route, the first 200m of skiing averaged 60°—Jornet said it was probably the steepest terrain he'd ever skied. This section ended with another 40m rappel. Then came a long narrow couloir (500m, 50–55°) that finished in an icefall, which he circumvented with a short climb to reach a ramp. The lower 900m were less steep (45°) and wider, with short steep sections and some blue ice. The total descent to the car was 1,688m. ▶

– **LINDSAY GRIFFIN**

ROMSDAL ULTRA-MARATHON: *In June 2018, Kilian Jornet completed a marathon tour of the Romsdal mountains. In 56 hours, with just one and a half hours of sleep, he traveled 168km with a vertical gain of 22,000m along a convoluted ridge line south of the Romsdalfjord, starting at Voll and ending at Isfjorden. Jornet started with a 3.5kg pack, including food. Portions of the ridge involved technical climbing and descents; he carried an ultralight ice axe, and a light harness and 5mm Dyneema rope for rappels.* ▶

THE ALPS

THE FOLLOWING CLIMBS appeared on the "Big List" of notable 2019 ascents prepared in advance of Piolets d'Or nominations by Lindsay Griffin, with assistance from Rodolphe Popier (FFCAM) and the AAJ.

Simon Chatelan on pitch 15 (M6) of L'Accidentelle et l'Accidenté on Aiguille de l'Amone. *Silvan Schüpbach*

VANOISE, POINTE ORIENTALE DE L'ÉPÉNA (3,348M), NORTHWEST SPUR. First winter ascent of the north face, by the 765m northwest spur route (summer TD 5c), by Léo Billon, Julien Ravanello, and Benjamin Védrines (France), in one day in February.

ECRINS, RATEAU WEST SUMMIT (3,769M), NORTH FACE. First ascent of Bonne Pioche (500m, ED M6 6a A1) by Mathieu Détrie and Octave Garbolino (France), in one February day. Second ascent with direct finish (M7 6a) by Sébastien Ratel and Benjamin Védrines (France) in March.

MONT BLANC RANGE, AIGUILLE DE L'AMONE (3,584M), EAST FACE. First ascent of L'Accidentelle et l'Accidenté (850m, M7) in February by Simon Chatelan and Silvan Schüpbach (Switzerland), with one bivouac.

BREGAGLIA, PIZ BADILE (3,305M), NORTHEAST FACE. First free ascent of the Nardella Route (900m, 7b+ 7a R) by David Hefti and Marcus Schenk (Switzerland) in September, with one bivouac. Two ancient belay bolts were replaced.

DOLOMITES, PUNTA CIVETTA (2,920M), NORTHWEST FACE. First ascent of Capitani di Ventura (700m, VIII- A1) by Davide Cassol and Luca Vallata (Italy), over four separate days, with a one-day final ascent in September.

DOLOMITES, SASS DLA CRUSC (2,907M), NORTHWEST FACE. First ascent of Rapunzel: a long snow face followed by four steep pitches (120m), graded M8 WI6+, by Manuel Baumgartner and Simon Messner (Italy) during one day in December.

In addition, there were several notable ascents in the Alps using bolts. (The Piolets d'Or considers only alpine-style routes without drilled gear placements.) These other climbs included:

- **DÉJÁ** (400m, 12 pitches, 8c+) in the Rätikon massif (Switzerland), redpointed by Fabian Buhl (Germany) in late November. Originally bolted in 1992, the route had been tried by many climbers, including four years of work by Buhl.
- **SILBERRÜCKEN** (350m, 8a+) on the Rotbrätt (Jungfrau), by Swiss climbers Roger Schäli and Stephan Siegrist. The route was put up in 2018 and redpointed in June 2019.
- **LA VIDA ES SILBER** (900m, 8a) on the north face of the Eiger (Switzerland), first one-day redpoint (July 23), by Swiss climber Roger Schäli, after several years of attempts.

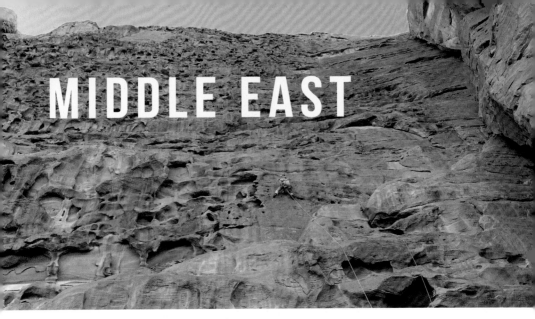

MIDDLE EAST

Climbing the incredible honeycombed sandstone of Zalabia Route (300m, 6c) on the north face of Jebel Khazali in Wadi Rum. *Christian Ravier Collection*

JORDAN / WADI RUM

JEBEL KHAZALI, VARIOUS ROUTES

JEBEL KHAZALI IS clearly visible 8km south of the village of Rum. It's a vast mountain with climbing on all sides. In 2008, Xavier Giraudet and I started a route on the west face, but it was not until 2014 that I completed it with Rémi Laborde and Rémi Thivel. The Atayek Hamad Route (300m, 6c+) is very beautiful with excellent rock—it has quickly become one of the classics of Khazali. We descended by rappelling Le Couchant (Remy-Remy, 1986).

In the fall of 2019, after accompanying some clients for a week in the heart of the magical Rum sandstone, Rémi Laborde, Stéphane Marigot, and I found ourselves at the foot of the north face of Khazali, where two very nice surprises awaited us. As we climbed a large honeycombed wall to establish Zalabia Route (300m, 6c), we were already dreaming of the incredible cracks we would encounter on Au Grès du Vent (200m, 6c+/7a), ascending the big red pillar not far to the right. [*Exceptionally beautiful topos of these routes are at the AAJ website.*] 📷 🔍

— CHRISTIAN RAVIER, *FRANCE*

OMAN / WESTERN HAJAR

WESTERN HAJAR, NEW ROUTES AND EXPLORATION

IN DECEMBER I traveled to Oman's Western Hajar Mountains to climb long new routes with Lee Burbery. We felt welcomed as always, and despite continued infrastructure development in Oman, the areas we visited remain quiet.

First, on Jebel Kawr's extensive southwest face, we climbed the Honey Hunter (520m, UIAA VI-) on the pillar right of the imposing Kawr Towers. From the apex of the pillar, we rappelled and scrambled a gully on the right.

The Kawr Pillar (a separate formation from the Kawr Towers) had one existing route, the Full Qaboos (Chaudry-Eastwood-Hornby-Ramsden, 1999). Having scouted this area on previous visits, I thought there could be an easier line to the left. From a bivy below the pillar, we followed gray, water-worn rock up the face and across to a straightforward arête, producing the Camel Hunter (700m, V+). We continued unroped up the arête for a further 500m to the top of the pillar. From the plateau, we descended farther left than previous parties via an abseil-free gully.

Moving to Jebel Misht, we climbed the previously untouched tower on the south face between Rock Vulture and Madam Butterfly. On the main upper wall, a shallow arête with consistently superb climbing took us to the col just right of Rock Vulture: Call of the Bellbird (345m, V).

Across Wadi al Ayn on the northwest face of Jabal M'Saw, we found a route that breaches long lines of overhangs to access the untouched upper face: Archimedes' Passage (270m of climbing, VI-).

At the end of the trip, we explored more remote areas about 70km to the northwest. Recent heavy rain had left access to the wadis rough but mostly passable by a 4WD vehicle. In Wadi Bani Omer, we made a reconnaissance of towers above Sheseb hamlet and its striking fortification, finding sound metamorphic limestone on the Watchtower (125m, V), on an outlier of the main jebel. After the New Year, we did the first route on the smaller northeast-facing wall left of the Jebel Nakhus Gorge, finding superlative climbing on Hawasinah Window (100m, VI). [*The online version of this report has more details and photos for each route.*] 📄 📷

– PAUL KNOTT, *NEW ZEALAND*

JEBEL MISHT AND WADI AL ALA, NEW ROUTES AND EXPLORATION

WHEN TIME OFF for climbing is limited, it makes sense to choose a destination with guaranteed good weather. With interesting culture and plenty of climbing potential, Oman fit the bill perfectly.

After familiarizing ourselves with the fossil-infused limestone by climbing the classic Shukran (1,000m, 5.10+) on Jebel Misht, we turned our attention to a southeast-facing wall on the Organ Pipes, which is about 1km wide and features numerous towers (*see "Recon," AAJ 2018*). Saule Simute and I first climbed an enjoyable route we called Camel in Distress on the left side, with some excellent pitches topped with a few squeeze chimneys. Cyrill Boesch and I then climbed the Smell of Cheese on the right side of the Organ Pipes, with continuously enjoyable climbing only slightly marred by a short traverse through loose rock. Both routes are around 400m and 6b.

While flicking through the *Field Guide to the Geology of Northeastern Oman*, we spotted a good-looking wall facing northeast in the Wadi al Ala, southeast of Jebel Kawr and between the towns of Al Ala and Sint. After figuring out a quick way to descend into the wadi (a few abseils and downclimbing, about 500m upstream from the main lookout), Cyrill and I climbed an elegant line up a red groove capped by a roof on the opposite side of the canyon, calling it Once Upon a Time in a Wadi (250m, 6a). We found no prior evidence or reports of climbers visiting this canyon. 📷

– GEDIMINAS SIMUTIS, *LITHUANIA*

JEBEL KAWR, NORTH FACE, MANY NEW ROUTES

THE FIRST TIME I visited Oman was in 2011, together with the very strong "seniors" Sigi Brachmayer, Horst Fankhauser, Oswald Oelz, and Albert Precht. This trip was really important to me for understanding the area. I returned in 2013, 2014, and most recently in 2020. This time we were four: Martin Sieberer (Austria), Manuel Baumgartner, Dietmar "Diddi" Niederbrunner, and myself (all Italy). It was all of the others' first time climbing in the desert.

We arrived at the end of January and camped near the same acacia as I did in years before. (We used its shadow as a kind of fridge and for hanging up our gear and food.) As the temperatures were high, we mostly climbed on the north side of Jebel Kawr, across the valley from the well-known south face of Jebel Misht. It's in the shade all day and offers mostly good rock.

We immediately started climbing, never repeating a route but always climbing new lines in two parties of two. The second day, Diddi took a long fall when a hold broke; he was very lucky that a small nut held, and he got away with only a scrape on his thigh. We climbed 16 new routes, which, as always, we left as clean as possible. We did not use any bolts but left several pitons and threads fixed for future ascents. More info on these routes is available at my website: simon-messner.com.

We also stopped to climb in Wadi Bani Awf and at Hadash, where we were lucky to meet *all* of Oman's "local climbers" at once—no more than 10 people! Again we were pleased with the hospitality of the Omanis. Thanks to them we will definitely come again. 📷 🔍

— SIMON MESSNER, *ITALY*

MAJLIS AL JINN CAVE, OUT OF THE DARK, AND OTHER ROUTES

In December I returned to Oman, where I had lived from 2008 until 2017, to reunite with my longtime climbing partner Jakob Oberhauser, who has been guiding in Oman since 2003, wrote the *Climbing in Oman* guidebook, and has done untold new routes. Also joining us were Alexander Huber (Germany), Aleksandra Taistra (Poland), and Guido Unterwerzacher (Austria).

For Jakob and me, the primary objective was a ground-up free line out of the Majlis al Jinn cave. Majlis means "seating place of the spirits," and the cave is the second-largest chamber in the world by surface area. It is only accessed from above, and the only exit is to ascend fixed ropes for 165m—or climb out. It is remote, too, atop the lunar landscapes of the Selma Plateau at 2,000m, requiring an exposed off-road drive to access it. The crux, however, was acquiring a permit.

Jakob and I had requested permission in December 2012 with the same idea; however, we were denied access in favor of a permit for a Red Bull filming project, which led to the route Into the Light (13 pitches, 5.14a), climbed by Chris Sharma with Stefan Glowacz in February 2014 (*see AAJ 2015*). At the time, we instead opted to climb in the 7th Hole Cave, 2km away, opening three naturally protected lines out of the cave. Finally, in 2019, a permit was granted to Jakob.

Aleksandra and I arrived in Muscat at 2 a.m. on December 13. When we met Jakob, he said that we had just two days on our permit, including *that* day—a relaxed trip now became an urgent mission! After a very brief nap, we united the team and rallied toward the cave, which in normal conditions takes about three hours to reach. Recent heavy rains, however, had washed out the main track. After seven hours of driving, we stood over the main entrance of the Majlis to rig our static lines down the sheer drop.

With two hours of daylight remaining, Jakob and I opted to scout potential exits and prepare our gear for a one-day attempt. Early the following morning, we found ourselves at the base of the cave. The excitement and awe of descending into the blackness, hooting and hollering as our eyes slowly adjusted to the grand scale, was slowly overtaken by anxiety.

At the base of our chosen line, Jakob stooped to collect a pebble for our traditional who-goes-first game. "Which hand is it in?" he asked. Honestly, at that moment I hoped to choose the wrong hand—Jakob is a master on the delicate, loose, and often scary Omani limestone. I swallowed and stammered "that one," pointing.

Two hours later, I was still on lead. The initial wall was overhanging, and the stone was really rotten. I went up and downclimbed inside a chimney multiple times, clearing loose blocks, sometimes by choice, too frequently not. With Alexander and Guido shouting encouragement, while Jakob hid away from the bombardment, I pushed onward. My only option, as Alex yelled from below, was a horizontal traverse around a flakey green pillar. When your idol speaks, you move, and so I did the traverse and found myself on a sloping shelf about 20m up, unable to continue because of rope drag. I lowered one of my ropes and hauled up the drill to place the one and only bolt on our route for an anchor.

From then on the rock improved drastically. We followed a series of dry waterfalls, laughing at the fact that we were climbing underground. Jakob and I swapped leads while Alex and Guido followed hot on our heels. After six pitches our Austrian-German-Canadian team emerged, giddy, into the brilliant afternoon sun. A campfire dream ticked: Out of the Dark (165m, 6 pitches, 6a+).

Our cave alpinism was not finished. The next day we drove a few kilometers along the plateau to 7th Hole Cave, where Guido and Alex opened a new route, Tunnel Vision (120m, 4 pitches, 7a), and Aleksandra and Jakob repeated one of our routes from 2012, the Traverse of the Gods (120m, 6a+).

Moving base camp to the beach, we celebrated and rested a day before opening two new routes in alpine style in Wadi Tiwi, just above the village of Mibam. Alex and Guido climbed the Wadi Racer (500m, 6c+), and Jakob, Aleksandra, and I climbed Mibam Roundtrip (450m, 6a+). A few days later, Guido and Alex went to Jebel Kawr to open the sustained and exposed Rihlat Saeida above Al Khumeirah village (400m, 6c+), while Jakob and I finished a short variation to a route Jakob had climbed earlier in the year on the Hamra Towers of Jebel Fokha: Central Chimney (195m, UIAA VI+).

Even after nearly 10 years living in Oman, I am still impressed with the adventure to be found. There is also a vibrant sport climbing scene. Guides to those climbs by Larry Michienzi are available through the Rakkup app. 📷 🔍

– READ MACADAM, *CANADA*

[Top] Jakob Oberhauser (leading) and Aleksandra Taistra about to top out Traverse of the Gods (6a+) in the 7th Hole Cave. [Bottom] The massive free-hanging descent into the Majlis Al Jinn cave. *Read Macadam (both)*

AFRICA

Mark Thomas leading a 7b pitch above the bivy ledge, halfway up No Rest For the Wicked (850m, 7c+) on the north face of Tagoujimt n'Tsouiannt in Taghia Gorge. *Mike Hutton*

TAGHIA GORGE, NO REST FOR THE WICKED

Four climbers and two Moroccan Berber friends sat with feet dangling over a dizzying precipice, slaking our thirst with a Flag beer and finally resting our shredded hands. Mohammed's beat box chanted melodic Berber tunes, which competed with the screeching of a bearded vulture soaring overhead. A juniper-wood fire threw up high flames, warming freezing hands as the cold, clear night encroached atop the 850m north face of Tagoujimt n'Tsouiannt (2,982m), which we had just climbed.

This was my ninth trip to Taghia. Fifteen years earlier, in 2004, I had visited for the first time and marveled at the twisting rivers carving deep gorges and clean limestone walls, the biggest and most impressive of which is the north wall of Tsouiannt. Rising directly above the tiny village, its challenge and difficulty were all too obvious. It had to be climbed!

Climbing ground-up in 2007, Stéphanie Bodet, Fred Gentet, Nicolas Kalisz, and Arnaud Petit established Babel (800m, 7c+) on the left side of the wall. Featuring a mix of trad gear and bolts, the route rightly gained notoriety for quality and seriously run-out pitches. I had previously spotted the long tapering pillar that ran the full height of the wall 50m to the right of Babel, and mused at creating a modern, safer route for many climbers to enjoy.

In 2018, fellow mountain guide Mark Thomas, sculptor Simon Hitchens, and I spent 12 days establishing the route, each day starting and finishing in the dark, drilling and climbing from the ground up. After placing over 300 bolts, we eventually reached the summit but failed to finish the climb during this two-week trip.

We returned in October 2019, and this time photographer Mike Hutton joined the crew to help and document the climb. After 20 eventful days of bolting, cleaning, and climbing, the four of us climbed the final 6c pitch and scrambled 500m to the summit of Tsouiannt.

At 850m, No Rest for the Wicked (7c+) is the longest sport route in the Taghia Gorge and in Morocco, and arguably the whole of continent of Africa: 25 pitches of fully bolted climbing from the riverbed to the summit plateau. The route has 13 pitches above 7a, with most pitches worthy of three stars at any sport climbing destination. Aficionados of big-wall free climbing will love the challenge of a one-day ascent or climbing over two days and enjoying the luxurious cave bivy at half height.

Atop the summit we met our Berber friends Mohammed and Abdur, with a strong donkey carrying provisions, and a memorable night unfolded with stories, banter, and laughs under a huge Moroccan sky. To return again is inevitable. *Inshallah!* 📷

– MIKE "TWID" TURNER, *U.K.*

LIBERTÀ BERBER: *In October 2019, an Italian party climbed a new line on the right side of the north face of Tagoujimt n'Tsouiannt. Over eight days, Lorenzo Gadda, Vincenzo Mascara, and Alessio Miori established Libertà Berber with a mixture of bolts and removable gear. They then returned to free the entire route (17 pitches, 7b+) in a day.*

Mike "Twid" Turner leading a 7a pitch about two-thirds of the way up No Rest For the Wicked. The 25-pitch route is completely bolt-protected and took Turner, Simon Hitchens, and Mark Thomas two trips to Morocco to complete. *Mike Hutton*

SUDAN

TAKA MOUNTAINS, NEW ROUTES

IN EASTERN SUDAN there lies a great collection of large granite domes situated above the town of Kassala, with a few existing routes and plenty of impressive lines and potential first ascents (*see AAJ 2014*). Jonny Baker (U.K.) and I arrived in Kassala on December 25 for a 20-day stay.

Previous information about climbs in the area was patchy and confusing; the domes don't appear to have individual names but are grouped under two names, Jebel Totil and Jebel Taka. The first climbing here was done in 1939 by some Brits, gaining the main summit of Jebel Taka. Czechs visited in 1981 and put up a few routes; French climbers came in 2003 and put up about three lines; and two Americans did a new route in 2013. Later some Brits came for a few visits, establishing several shorter lines and boulder problems.

Our first new route was up the north face of Middle Jebel, a previously unnamed dome in the center of the massif, and the only dome one can walk up. We established the route Jebel Rebel (320m, 6a+). We climbed ground up, and bolts were placed on lead. The route offers some great climbing and only gets a few hours of morning sun.

We then went to climb the south face of Jebel Totil, thinking we were doing a new route but finding bolts on the second pitch. This was not surprising, as it's by far the easiest way to the summit. We climbed three pitches separated by some scrambling and made the summit in about two hours, rappelling the same way. The route gets full sun, so an early start is essential.

From the summit of Jebel Totil, we spied a dike line on the west face, and we spent the next four days bolting and cleaning this line from the top down. False Prophet (340m, 7c) gives some amazing climbing on steep terrain, following a continuous feature the whole way, with outstanding rock on the higher pitches. After finishing the route, we flew our paragliders from the summit and were greeted by hundreds of children from the small village where we landed.

After this, we climbed the existing routes Khawadja (300m, 6b+, *see AAJ 2003*) on Jebel Taka North and the original 1939 route on Jebel Taka. We flew again from both summits.

The last new route we established was on the north face of Jebel Totil. We climbed Bat Shit Crazy (230m, 6c) ground up with bolts placed on lead. It starts with several slab pitches to gain a higher crack system that leads to the summit.

Kassala offers potential for many more new routes. The heat makes it very difficult to climb on the south faces, but most of the best rock faces more to the north. We were fortunate to get many days with temperatures in the mid-20s Celsius, giving pleasant conditions in the shade. There are many cracks, but most are discontinuous and will require bolts to link them. We found the local people to be most friendly and helpful; they didn't seem to be bothered by our climbing on the rocks but were naturally puzzled as to why we had come so far to do this.

– CHRIS WARNER, *AUSTRALIA*

[Top] Chris Warner following a featured slab pitch during the first ascent of Bat Shit Crazy (230m, 6c) on Jebel Totil, with part of the town of Kassala far below. [Middle] The Jebel Taka massif above Kassala in eastern Sudan. [Bottom] **The west face of Jebel Totil.** False Prophet (340m, 7c) follows the prominent central dike system the whole way. *Jonny Baker (three photos)*

RUSSIA

SIBERIAN WALLS
FIRST ASCENTS EAST OF LAKE BAIKAL

BY ELENA DMITRENKO, *RUSSIA, WITH INFORMATION FROM EVGENY GLAZUNOV*

THE SOUTH MUYSKY Ridge (also spelled Muiski) is a range of granite peaks in the Bauntovsky region of Buryatia. The highest point, Muysky Giant (3,067m), has seen a number of ascents and is located in the northeastern part of the range, around 280km east of the northern tip of Lake Baikal. But the southwestern part, some 125km distant from the Giant, is little known to rock climbers. It was to these mountains that Evgeny Glazunov, Nadezhda Oleneva, and Pavel Tkachenko traveled in July. The expedition was organized by the Impossible is Not Forever Foundation, inaugurated to honor Glazunov's younger brother, Sergey, who was killed on Latok I in 2018.

The trio started from the remote village of Baunt (55°15′0″N, 113°7′0″E) to the southeast of the peaks they had targeted. After a 20km drive in an all-terrain vehicle, the team walked 40km to reach these mountains, crossing four passes and meeting two bears. (The total distance covered on foot from beginning to end of the expedition was around 120km.) After reconnoitering the area, they climbed three walls. On each of the new routes, 95 percent of the climbing was free.

The team first climbed the west face of Pik Kart ("Map Peak," 2,661m). This summit has an easy route to its top and therefore had been climbed several times previously. The new route is very aesthetic, following a logical system of clean cracks. Apart from one wet section, the climbing went free at up to 6c. The 700m route was Russian 5B overall.

[Above] **The northeast face of Sergey Glazunov Peak (2,400m). Evgeny Glazunov's solo first ascent was near the right skyline.** [Right] **Glazunov, Tkachenko, and Oleneva (left to right).** *Evgeny Glazunov (both)*

The second route led to a previously unclimbed summit. Glazunov soloed the northeast face of this formation in one day and named it Sergey Glazunov Peak (2,400m). The 450m route was climbed free (6b) apart from a few places where the cracks were clogged with mud.

All three then made the first ascent of Pik Mechta ("Dream Peak," 2,590m, 55°30'35.4"N, 112°39'16.7"E) via the 800m west face. Several teams had tried to climb this wall previously. Oleneva led the first section of the route, using a little aid. In the middle, Glazunov took over and climbed mostly clean to the top. This was a great route, and the team reported that 20 logical routes could be opened on the various flanks of this impressive mountain. Moreover, they found an easy descent: four rappels and then walking. The difficulty was 5B/6A (roughly 6c+/7a), with a little aid.

The team also climbed Pik Admiral Makarov, Polar Explorers' Peak, Pik Olg, and Pik Valery Popov, the last three previously unclimbed. This area has great potential, but it is very inaccessible, and future parties may seek to approach by helicopter or with the help of other people to transport food and gear. 🖼️🔍

[Top] The 800-meter route on the west face of Pik Mechta (2,590m). The Russian climbers estimated that 20 "logical routes" could be done on this mountain. [Bottom] The 700-meter route on the west face of Pik Kart. *Evgeny Glazunov (both photos)*

EDITOR'S NOTE: *See "East of Lake Baikal" in AAJ 2006 for photos from other areas of the South Muysky Ridge.*

PIK ZAIDLER, NORTH COULOIR AND WEST RIDGE

ALEXANDER ZAIDLER (1931–2018) was an honorary member of the UIAA Youth Commission. In August, a team of alpine veterans led by Alexander Turtukov did the first ascent of a peak (3,772m) in the Central Caucasus and named it after Zaidler. The summit is on the long east ridge of Pik Shevchenko (4,161m). This area is about 10km north of the main divide and rarely visited by climbers. Turtukov's team climbed the north couloir (30-45°) and west ridge at 2A. 🖼️

– *INFORMATION PROVIDED BY* **ANNA PIUNOVA**, *MOUNTAIN.RU, RUSSIA*

ZVEZDNIY, NORTHEAST FACE, NEW ROUTE

IN EARLY DECEMBER 2015, Nicolay Matyushin and Alexander Zhigalov climbed a new route, in full winter conditions, on the northeast face of Zvezdniy (2,265m), in the Ergaki massif of the Western Sayan (AAJ 2016). Zhigalov returned with Timofey Ivanov in October 2019 to add a fifth line to the face, to the right of the 1997 Balezin Route.

In the autumn of 2019, the area was blessed with unusually warm weather, which meant they did not need the anticipated snowshoes to reach the face. It took two days to approach the wall with heavy packs. Alarmingly, they saw many bear tracks: Bears should be hibernating at this time of year, but the temperature simply wasn't low enough.

The pair began their climb at 7:45 a.m. on October 11 and reached the summit at 11:20 a.m. on the 14th. This route is perhaps the last logical line on the wall without recourse to extensive drilling. Unfortunately, there were several blank sections where they were forced to drill a total of 15 bathooks and placed two 8mm bolts. The difficulties were mainly A2 and A3, and all nights were spent in a tent on convenient ledges.

The pair descended the 2013 Temerev Route, reinforcing the anchors so this line now provides a secure direct descent down the wall (rappels 55–60m). The overall grade of the 590m new route (26 pitches, 955m of climbing) was 6A.

– INFORMATION PROVIDED BY **ANNA PIUNOVA,** *MOUNTAIN.RU, RUSSIA*

DRAGON TOOTH, SOUTHWEST FACE, WATER ROUTE

THERE ARE NOW nine routes on the broad southwest face of Dragon Tooth (2,170m), a well-traveled peak of the Ergaki Massif, located at about 52°50'31.60"N, 93°26'5.21"E in the Western Sayan. The latest, which climbs the southwest face of the western tower, was put up on August 31 by the team of Igor Loginov and Alexander Zhigalov. They belayed 12 pitches, of which five required aid (up to A2), to reach the west ridge. From there, the two climbed for around one hour along the 400m crest to the summit, return-ing to their camp a little after midnight. Their new line, Water Route (550m of elevation but 945m of climbing, 5B) is the longest on the wall to reach the Dragon Tooth summit.

Autumn in Ergaki normally comes with unpre-dictable weather. On the day of the climb, Loginov and Zhigalov experienced light rain and mist from 11 a.m. to 4 p.m. and a maximum temperature of 10°C. The climb follows a steep slab (average angle 66°) and is generally solid granite. However, on pitches nine through 11 there are large loose blocks that need extreme care.

– INFORMATION PROVIDED BY **ANNA PIUNOVA,** *RUSSIA*

The southwest face of Dragon Tooth showing the new line Water Route. *Alexander Zhigalov*

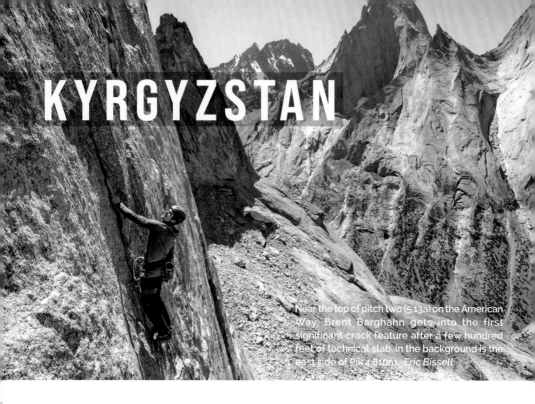

KYRGYZSTAN

THE AMERICAN WAY
THE FIRST FREE ASCENT OF PIK SLESOVA'S NORTHWEST FACE

BY ERIC BISSELL, *USA*

PIK SLESOVA (4,240M, a.k.a. Russian Tower) is an El Cap–size granite tower in the Ak-su Valley. Its southern aspect is home to one of the world's great granite free routes, Perestroika Crack (5.12b), free climbed in 1995 by Greg Child and Lynn Hill. To the left, the steeper northwest face, first climbed in 1988, holds many Grade V aid routes, but had never received a free ascent. In 1995, on the same North Face expedition mentioned above, Conrad Anker and Alex Lowe climbed the face by a new route they named the Russian Shield. [*This line was a substantial variation to the Moroz Route (1988), the original route up this face.*] Subsequently, legend grew around the possibility of a magnificent and difficult free route up this very steep wall.

Following a week of travel, David Allfrey, Brent Barghahn, Nick Berry, and I arrived in the valley with a quadruple rack, 460m of rope (inclusive of lead lines), and 75 bolts. We brought a substantial number of bolts, knowing that the first couple of hundred feet of the wall is a blank slab, with minimal natural features. Our plan was to climb the aid line of the Moroz Route, the original route of the face, fixing lines as we went and sussing free passage. We planned to come back to base camp each day until we reached the halfway point on the wall, where a convenient ledge (the White Block Bivouac) was visible from the ground. We would then redpoint the pitches team-free, in order, and to our high point, before committing to the wall and climbing to the summit.

The first couple of pitches were a major question mark but revealed incredible face climbing. Pitch two (5.13a) didn't have anything harder than V5, but was long and sustained. The next two pitches were unreal 5.12+, with pitch four in particular exemplifying the brilliant climbing of the route. At one point it was necessary to transfer from chimneying to compression climbing on a hanging arête, using toe hooks for a final crack transfer. Aside from the bolt ladders on pitches one and two, only a few additional bolts were needed to link features higher on the wall. Bolts also were added at belays.

Above the lower slab was a large feature with an ominous gaping crack on its right side. The Kyrgyz Monster, named after the Monster Offwidth on El Cap, had looked like fists from the ground, but we were happy to have brought our big green number 6 cam. The Russians had drilled a bolt ladder alongside this entire formation, so from our offwidth comfort we could push our number 6 and clip "bomber" 35-year-old Russian bolts.

The Kyrgyz Monster was the fork in the road where we thought the Russian Shield and the original route diverged. Tensioning to a mystery bolt right of our line, I looked up at the Shield cracks, hoping for a perfect challenge. Yet the seams were undeniably small and steep. At this point, there was plenty of engaging and excellent climbing below us and a massive amount of terrain still above, so we opted to seek out the line of least resistance by following the Moroz Route to the summit.

After four days of aid climbing and three of free climbing, with trips back to base camp in between, we were established at the White Block Bivouac. Just above was some terrifying climbing, the loosest of the route. It treated us to nightmare sleeps while the wind whipped, and we imagined house-of-cards flakes slicing through our down sleeping bags. To avoid one major hazard 60m above the bivouac, we did a downward traverse along a dike of bone-white stone. Funky 5.12+ hand-foot down-mantels slanted to a ledge out right, from which we could finally access the lower-angled upper wall.

On our last climbing day, we redpointed the downclimb and then started sprinting up 70m pitches. The wall went on and on, and just as it got dark and started to snow, we pulled onto the broken summit. Tired and cold, we took a dark summit selfie and rappelled to White Block Bivouac. The next day we pulled all our ropes and gear off the wall (leaving rappel anchors) and descended the familiar ankle-busting talus to base camp. All told, we spent 18 days of August in the Ak-su.

Early on, we realized the climbing was quite special, and we decided to leave a route that others could enjoy repeating. So we were delighted to hear a few weeks after leaving the valley that a French party, our neighbors in base camp, had repeated the line and said it was one of the best routes they had ever done, with inspiring free climbing. Our team would certainly agree.

The nearly 1,000-meter northwest face of Pik Slesova. (1) The Moroz Route (1988). Yellow lines show the American Way variations for the first all-free ascent of the face. (2) The Russian Shield (1995). The classic Perestroika Crack ascends the angled face near the right skyline. Other routes not shown. *Eric Bissell*

Summary: *First free ascent of the northwest face of Pik Slesova via the American Way (950m, VI 5.13a), in the Ak-Su Valley of the Karavshin region in the Pamir Alai, following the original Moroz Route (1988) with several variations. Nik Berry and Eric Bissell spoke about this climb in episode 25 of the Cutting Edge podcast.* 📷 🔍

Max Ten on the east ridge of Chon-turasu, close to where he and Kirill Belotserkovskiy reached the ridge after climbing the north face. *Kirill Belotserkovskiy*

NORTH FACE OF CHON-TURASU
A BIG PRIZE IN A LITTLE-KNOWN RANGE

BY KIRILL BELOTSERKOVSKIY, *KAZAKHSTAN*

THE CHON-TURASU VALLEY is the limestone region at the eastern end of the Western Kokshaal-too, and unlike the well-known granite monoliths in the west, the rock here is either compact or very brittle. Zakir Abduraimov, Kolya Ovchinnikov, Grisha Schukin, Max Ten, and I spent the month of August here.

The first exploration of the Chon-turasu took place in 1932, when I. Maron and A. Mash-kov from August Letavet's expedition climbed Pik Marona (4,902m). Most of the mountains here were climbed from 1957–'60, when all the lower peaks received ascents and were named. Dankova (5,982m), the highest in the range, was climbed in 1970 from the Grigoryev Glacier by Yuri Popenko and team. Pik Koroleva (5,816m) was climbed in 1969 via the west face and north ridge, while Pik Chon-turasu (5,728m) was not climbed until 1997, by the icy south face at 5A (F. Ahmatov and team). Foreign visits were impossible in the Soviet era due to the proximity of the Chinese border, so it wasn't until 1996 that the first Western climbers entered the area, in the form of a joint French-Russian team.

Using the agency called Pro Hunt, we drove to the Chon-turasu Valley from Bishkek, via Naryn and Akmuz. Max and I began by climbing Pik 4,685m while our three friends climbed Gorelik. An International School of Mountaineering (ISM) expedition led by Pat Littlejohn climbed Gorelik in 1997 and called it Sababah (4,785m), thinking it was a first ascent; however, it was climbed by Russians in the late 1950s.

The next step in our acclimatization was Pik Marona, where we spent a night just below the summit. On our return, base camp looked raped. Two of the three tents were ripped, food chewed, and tins bent. Well, it was our fault—we had left camp fully stocked and a bear had raided it. The bear returned the next night, dragging a corner of Max's tent! Eventually it disappeared. We spent the next morning moving our camp to the biggest bear-proof boulder we could find.

On August 9, Max and I went for our main objective, the unclimbed north face of Chon-turasu. [*Russian climbers attempted a line on or near the north face in 1996 but were prevented by a corniced ridge from reaching the summit. Further details are not available.*] Our three friends went for the north ridge of Pik Trapez (5,240m, first climbed from the southeast in 1996).

The central part of the north face of Chon-turasu is defended by a frighteningly active icefall, in the middle of which is a 15m-wide groove. This was the route taken by falling seracs—and, unfortunately, also by us. We climbed as fast as possible to a vertical ice wall, which led to an icy couloir that collects all the debris from the central part of the face. Once up this we crossed a gently sloping hanging glacier to the right and put our tent in a safe place on rocks. During the night it snowed 5cm.

Next day, five pitches of steep ice runnels, full of spindrift, incorrectly led to us thinking we had reached the wide snow slope in the upper third of the face. We slanted left for five more pitches until I dead-ended at steep rock walls. An Abalakov thread allowed me to descend to thick ice, where we hacked out two ledges and settled down for another night, me in a bivouac bag and Max wrapped in the tent, looking like a nylon-covered maggot.

On the third day we made a rising rightward traverse to get to the actual snow slope on the upper face. Somewhere above was a depression cutting through the rock barrier directly below the summit. That morning, the screws had only penetrated a few centimeters, but I wasn't too worried as the climbing was easy. Now I was faced with a 70° corner comprised of strange rock—monolithic with very thin cracks. Rock pitons crumbled the limestone. In front of my face I saw a beautiful shell imprinted into the rock. But I didn't need shells, I needed a crack. When I reached a snow-covered slab without protection, I searched for a piece of ice thick enough for an Abalakov so I could bail. As Max didn't want to try it, we started on what eventually became a 400m traverse to the left to reach a couloir of thick ice. Five pitches, where even 22cm screws didn't bottom out, led us to the ridge. At 8 p.m. we set up our third bivouac.

On the 12th we started long before dawn in cold, windy weather. The east ridge was gently angled but corniced, and we had to traverse the southern flank, not without incident, to arrive on the summit cone at 8:30 a.m. To descend, we went down the west ridge and northwest flank, easy at first until we turned northwest, where the terrain became steeper. Eleven rappels over loose terrain down the west side of the north face brought us to the hanging glacier we had left a couple of days ago. In just one hour we rappelled and downclimbed as fast as we could through the icefall to reach the glacier below. Three hours later we were in base camp.

In the meantime, our friends had climbed over the minor summit of Pik Skala at the end of the north ridge of Trapez, but then found the continuation much more complex than anticipated, and retreated. After this, bad weather prevented anything more than a couple of easy summits near base camp. 📷

Looking south at (A) Pik Koroleva (5,816m), (B) Pik de l'Entre Aide (5,030m), (C) Pik Zhenith (5,148m), (D) Pik Alpinist (5,492m), (E) Pik Trapez (5,240m), and (F) Chon-turasu (5,728m), showing the 2019 route up the north face. Some of these names were given by climbing teams in the mid-1990s; it is very likely many of these peaks were climbed earlier and have other names. *Kirill Belotserkovskiy*

LAYLAK VALLEY, PIK ALEXANDER BLOK, REREADING CLASSICS

FROM AUGUST 6 to 10, Alexander Parfenov, Alexey Sukharev, and Vjacheslav Timofeev, from Krasnoyarsk and Novosibirsk, Siberia, climbed a new mixed route on the north face of Pik Alexander Blok (5,239m). The climbers started up the rounded pillar between the Efimov and Lavrinenko routes, with around eight pitches of difficult free and aid climbing leading to an almost vertical ice-filled chimney. Two pitches up this, with an exit to the right, brought the pair to a junction with the Efimov Route. However, they soon left it and slanted up left for several pitches on a steep, narrow ice ramp, until more rock climbing led to the east ridge. Around 200m of vertical gain along the ridge (II–IV) brought them to the summit. The total height of the route is 890m.

The Siberian trio named their new route Rereading Classics (25 pitches, 6A, 6a A3+ WI5/6). About 430 aid points were used. After the first part of the wall, there are small ledges for semi-sitting bivouacs, so a team climbing fast could dispense with a portaledge. The Siberians bivouacked at the top of pitches five, eight, 17, and 23.

Unlike nearby Rocky Ak-su (Ak-su North, 5,217m), whose famous 1,500m north face is topped by a snow and ice cap that produces considerable objective danger, Pik Alexander Blok does not have such a feature and is considered safe in summer. ◙

– ANNA PIUNOVA, *WWW.MOUNTAIN.RU, RUSSIA*

KARA-SU VALLEY, VARIOUS ROUTES

WOLFGANG FELDERER, MARTIN Haid, Christian Mauracher, Sebastian Posch, Christoph Schranz, and I, all from the Alpine Bande Tirol (club) of Austria, visited Kyrgyzstan from July 8 to 25.

Silver and Green walls seen from the east. (1) East Ridge (2014) to Silver Wall South Summit (3,850m). (2) Ternerev Route on southeast face of Silver Wall Main Summit (2011). Not shown: Rocket Donkey (2019). (3) Opposite to Asan (2006). (4) Tyrolean (2019). (5) Eaßtbegeung (2019) on Green Wall. *Marcello Sanguineti*

After a three-day approach to the Kara-su Valley, Christoph and I focused on establishing new routes.

On July 13 we climbed a small peak that we called Green Wall. If you walk up the valley past Yellow Wall and continue toward Silver Wall, just before you reach the foot of the latter, a path leads up right (west). Half an hour of walking up this path takes you to the base of a steep, north-facing wall. As our new line climbed sections of compact slab, we placed a total of 10 bolts, including belays. We named the 400m route Eaßt-begeung. There are seven pitches up to 7a to reach the summit ridge, and then easier climbing (up to 5a) to the 3,600m top.

Our next plan was to establish a new route on the east face of the main summit of Silver Wall (4,010m), and, as the climb would be around 1,200m, we planned to bivouac in the middle of the face. We climbed the new route at 6c+ and named it Tyro-lean, as to reach this wall you need to make a Tyrolean traverse over the river. This route climbs the prominent east-facing pillar to the right of the 2006 route Opposite to Asan and its 2015 Italian variant Bye bye, Globo de Gas! (*AAJ 2017*).

Our last climb was a new route on the west face of Kotina (a.k.a. Shaitan Khana, 4,521m). The route lies to the left of the 2006 Polish route Czarna Wolga, and gave around 2,000m of climbing. We named it Krukonogi and climbed it without bolts, free, onsight, and at 7a+. We bivouacked 100m below the summit and rappelled to the valley the next day. Two Russians, Evgeny Corulin and Vasily Terekhin, were camping near us and wanted to repeat our route. We gave them information before leaving the area, but in the end they followed a parallel line to the right (*see below*).

– **GEBHARD BENDLER,** *AUSTRIA*

ITALIAN ROUTE ON SILVER WALL: *On August 11, Dmitry Anghileri, Mirco Grasso, and Matteo Motta from Italy began down and right from the start of the Ternerev Route on the southeast face of Silver Wall, climbed through the overhangs, crossed the Ternerev where it traverses right, then followed the crest of the pillar to the left to reach the summit ridge. The route is called Rocket Donkey (700m, about 14 pitches, UIAA VIII).*

KARA-SU VALLEY, KOTINA, WEST FACE, KRASNOYARSK ROUTE

Kotina from the west, showing the 2019 ascents. (1) Operation KIK. This is a direct finish to a route from 2012 that angled up left to the ridge where Operation KIK goes sharply right. (2) Krukonogi. (3) Krasnoyarsk Route. Other routes not shown; see the AAJ website for a comprehensive route diagram. *Supplied by Anna Piunova*

A FOUR-MAN TEAM from Krasnoyarsk, Siberia, operated in the Ak-su and Kara-su valleys over the summer, repeating various routes. On July 23, Evgeny Corulin and Vasily Terekhin established a long free route on the west face and upper southwest face of Kotina (a.k.a. Shaitan Khana, 4,521m). [*This route starts at the same place as Krukonogi, established by an Austrian pair a few days earlier, and continues up a mostly parallel line to the right; see report above.*]

Although this is a big wall, the two wanted to climb as quickly as possible, both climbing free, the second with a rucksack. They took a very lightweight tent, stove, food, and a walkie-talkie. Setting out at 7 a.m., they climbed 12 pitches from V to 6b, followed by almost 200m of III to reach the central terrace, where they left all their bivouac equipment. To that point, the second had carried 13kg and was glad to get rid of the pack for the steeper part of the climb.

Leaving the central terrace at 2 p.m., the pair climbed the second and crux barrier, which was consistently steep and sported cracks from 3mm to offwidth. Pitch 18 was the most difficult at 7a.

Three pitches on the third buttress (6a and 6b) led to the summit ridge, up which they scrambled rapidly (III with a few steps of V) to the top, arriving just before 8 p.m. They regained the central terrace and bivouac gear by 11:30 p.m., and the following day spent three hours descending to the valley.

The route is very long: 1,200m of vertical gain, 1,800m of climbing. The team felt the overall grade was 5B, similar to other Karavshin classics such as Perestroika Crack on Pik Slesova or Alperina on Pik Asan.

– ANNA PIUNOVA, *WWW.MOUNTAIN.RU, RUSSIA*

KARA-SU VALLEY, KOTINA, OPERATION KIK

AMONG THE VARIOUS parties in the Karavshin in the summer were Nikolai Lebedev, Nikolai Stepanov, and Ivan Temerev. Although these three had read about each other on the internet, they were not personally acquainted, but they made contact and decided to climb together. In 2018, Temerev and two friends had climbed the central buttress of the northwest face of Kotina (a.k.a. Shaitan Khana, 4,521m), making a very significant direct variant to Dreaming Spires (7a, Codrington-Cooper-Faulkner, 2012). During this ascent they had noticed several interesting possibilities to the right.

After waiting out several days of showers, the three left their base camp on August 4, and at 6 a.m. were at the base of the large corner system taken by Awesome Fucking Dihedral (6c, Habel-Wisssmeier, 2012). Despite rain and hail in the middle of the day, the three climbed 13 excellent pitches up to 6c to reach the ridge that AFD follows up left toward the top of the northwest face. Here, the three Russians moved right instead to reach the headwall of the southwest face, descending at first, then climbing four pitches to a large terrace below a steep headwall. Here they bivouacked, traversing 200m to the right, off route, to find a semi-sheltered spot.

The next day, leaving all their overnight gear on the terrace, they climbed more or less directly toward the summit. Five pitches (to 6b, with one crux aid pitch of A1 that would probably go free in the 7s) took them to the final terrace. They traversed 40m left to a wet corner, but were unable to climb it, so they moved left again. After two pitches free of free climbing and a third (A2, skyhooks), which took one and a half hours with one pendulum, they regained the wet corner near its top. More taxing climbing (6b and A2) led to easier ground and the summit at 8:30 p.m.

The three made a difficult descent down an existing line of rappel anchors equipped with lengths of black rope. (Trying to find black slings by the light of a headlamp was a real test, especially having woken at 4 a.m.) Finally, at exactly the time the alarm had gone off the previous day, they arrived back at their bivouac site. They slept until 11 a.m. and then descended to base camp by 6 p.m. the same day. The route has been named Operation KIK (1,174m, 1,450m of climbing, 30 pitches, 6c A2).

– ANNA PIUNOVA, *WWW.MOUNTAIN.RU, RUSSIA*

PAMIR ALAI

MINTEKE VALLEY: ACHU, SOUTH FACE, AND OTHER ASCENTS

A GROUP OF seven Swiss female alpinists (Anne Flechsig, Florence Nikles, Lisa Pfalgraz, Rahel Schönauer, Ramona Volken, Caroline Ware George, and I) accompanied by Swiss Alpine Club coordinator Silvan Schüpbach, cameraman Thomas Senf, and his safety officer, Martin Rerrer, climbed in the Minteke Valley during September. The Minteke is the next valley west of the Jiptek

Valley, and we found very little information on the area in English. Although most of the peaks have been climbed in the past, it was difficult to know by which routes.

We established base camp (ca 3,145m) in the east branch of the valley and from there climbed Kyzyl-Muz, Pik 3, and Pik Minteke, and opened a new traditionally protected rock route on Achu.

Our first summit, which also acted as an acclimatization ascent, was Kyzyl-Muz (5,127m, formerly known as Harturtay). We climbed a couloir to a plateau at 4,200m, where we camped. Next day we reached the east ridge of Kyzyl-Muz, followed it over rock and ice to the summit, and descended the same way. All expedition members reached the top. This peak was first climbed by non-Soviets in 1996 and almost summited again from the north 12 years later (*see AAJ 1997 and 2009*).

The full group then climbed Pik Minteke (5,482m) at the head of the Kara Tur, the right branch of the Minteke Valley. We climbed the northwest ridge (mainly rock and ice) in a four-day round trip from base camp.

Anne, Ramona, Thomas, and Martin then left to climb Pik 3 (5,070m, 39°37'44.00"N, 70°30'24.68"E), which they achieved via the northeast spur and northwest ridge (rock and ice) in a two-day round trip from base. In the meantime, Caroline, Florence, Rahel, and I climbed a new rock route on the south face of Achu (4,300m), a western outlier of Pik 4,708m, as shown on the Soviet military map. We named the route Djöruk sol jak (350m, TD- 6c) and climbed it in seven pitches, including a final pitch along the crest of the east ridge to the summit.

There is still much potential in this valley for new routes. During our stay we had no precipitation, the temperature was optimal, ice conditions were good, and there was little rockfall. [*Coordinates for the peaks climbed are at the AAJ website.*] 🖸

– LYDIANE VIKOL, *SWITZERLAND*

[Top] Spectacular "Pik Stalin" above the head of the left branch of the Minteke Glacier, as seen from Kyzyl-Muz to the north. This peak is approximately 5,190m. It likely has been climbed, but its history is not known; this name was the one used by a local shepherd who visited the Swiss base camp. [Bottom] Looking southwest at Pik 3 (5,070m, the right-hand of the two pointed peaks) from the glacier below Achu. The route of ascent more or less followed the right skyline: the northeast spur to the northwest ridge. *Silvan Schüpbach (both photos)*

JIPTIK VALLEY: PIK 4,482M, WEST FACE; RED LABYRINTH, WEST-NORTHWEST RIDGE

In May and June, Rainhard Fuchs, Lisa Kranebitter, Christian Poglitsch, Nina Poxleitner, and I visited the Jiptik Valley, hoping to try the virgin northwest face of Muz Tok (5,066m), previously attempted in July 2016 by John Proctor and Robert Taylor (*AAJ 2017*). We established base camp at 3,350m, below the Schurovsky Glacier, after a three-day trek from the last shepherds' settlement of Sary Zhaz. There were no political problems gaining access—in fact the military was pleasantly interested in what we were doing and where we lived.

Unfortunately, heavy snowfall a few days before our planned attempt on Muz Tok, combined with high temperatures during our stay, caused falling rock and ice and avalanches, and at 3 a.m. we were still breaking through a thin, hard crust on the glacier at 4,000m, turning what would normally be a three-hour approach into an eight-hour, hip-deep ordeal. These conditions made the northwest face of the mountain impractical.

Prior to the snowfall, we climbed Pik 4,482m (named Piramida on OpenStreetMap). There were no major difficulties on the ascent, with superb conditions at the time.

[Top] **Looking south up the Jiptik Valley. The highest summit (at the back) is Pik Schurosky (5,490m). To its right is Muz Tok (5,066m).** [Bottom] **During the ascent of the east-southeast ridge of Kyzyl Labyrinth (Pik 4,690m). The big peak on the right is Pik Skalistiy (5,621m), while the fine pyramid to the left is Pik Boets (5,398m).** *Project Kyrgyzstan*

We climbed the west face (AD- 60°) to reach the northern and highest of the two rock towers on top.

Later we focused on Pik 4,690m, which we named Kyzyl Labyrinth (39°41'17.16"N, 70°36'18.04"E on Google Earth) due to its majestic southwest face of red rock and a myriad of narrow snow and ice gullies. We made a relatively straightforward three-hour approach to the saddle between the mountain and Pik Kiroksan, and then followed the east-southeast ridge to the summit (AD+). There were many ups and downs and large cornices on the ridge, and it took five hours to complete; for most of the journey we were unsure we would reach the top.

We also attempted a peak near base camp on the west side of the valley, with a fine icy gully (two pitches of WI3 and 4+/5). Icefall early in the day, as well as hip-deep snow, forced a retreat. 📷

– PHILIP SCHREINER, *AUSTRIA*

SURMETASH VALLEY, SAUK DZHAYLYAU CENTRAL, NORTHEAST FACE

The development of the Sauk Dzhaylyau Cirque began in 1977 with a visit by climbers from Leningrad. Expeditions then came regularly: in 1978, 1980, 1984, and 1986. In the post-Soviet period, there are known to have been visits in 1992 and 1995, then nothing for many years. Recent history has only two expeditions, both in 2015, and both organized by Alexey Tyulyupo. The first, with the Glazunov brothers, climbed two new routes in the summertime (*AAJ 2016*). The second, in mid-September of that year, and comprising just Tyulyupo and Anton Kashevnik, attempted the northeast face of Sauk Dzhaylyau Central (5,227m) but was unsuccessful.

Kashevnik and Tyulyupo returned in September 2019 for the same objective. The idea was to complete the obvious ice line through the headwall between two large rock buttresses that had existing routes. They also wanted to climb as clean as possible, in alpine style, with no aid, and with both members free climbing each pitch.

The two left camp at 7 a.m. on September 6 and ascended the lower glaciated slopes (850m), negotiating several steep ice walls, to a bivouac in a bergschrund at 4,480m. Next day they surmounted the short, overhanging bergschrund wall and climbed ice slopes up to 75° to reach the mixed entry to the steep ice ramp splitting the headwall. This was the crux of the route, and there was no possibility to bivouac properly until they reached a traverse out left to a rocky terrace at around 4,965m.

On the 8th they climbed more steep ice and a little mixed to reach the summit at

The northeast face of Sauk Dzhaylyau Central (5,227m). (1) Moskaltsov Route (pre-1984). (2) Kashevnik-Tyulyupo Route (2019). (3) Kovtun Route (1978). The summit on the right is Sauk Dzhaylyau West II. *Supplied by Anna Piunova*

4:30 p.m. They descended to their bivouac at 4,480m and the following day reached the glacier, and their camp, around midday. The total amount of climbing was 1,750m, and the route was graded Russian 6A (ED) WI5 M5. 📷 🔍 ▶

– ANNA PIUNOVA, WWW.MOUNTAIN.RU, RUSSIA

KINDIK VALLEY AND KYZYL ALAI VALLEY, THREE ASCENTS

IN JUNE a team led by Michal Kleslo climbed two peaks east of Kindik Pass in the Central Alai. Jakub Moravik and Michal Sranc climbed the steep, rocky northwest rib of Pik Kindik (4,927m), which in June was mostly snow and ice, to just below the top section of the southwest ridge. Here, they slanted up left over snow to the summit (Russian 2B). Other members of the team climbed the 45° northern snow slopes of Pik 4,760m more or less directly to the summit, where they discovered a cairn. They have been unable to find a name for this peak. Kindik's northwest rib may have been unclimbed.

This area of the Alai, immediately north of Pik Lenin, is probably the most popular of the entire range, due to easy access from both south and north. The two peaks climbed in 2019 lie approximately 4km east of the highest mountain in this area, Pik Skobelev (5,051m).

Kleslo ventured in July to an area farther east in the Alai, north of Sary Tash and the Pamir Highway (M41). Starting from the small settlement of Kyzyl Alai (ca 2,650m), his team walked northwest up a valley to place a base camp on the highest green terraces. From here it was one hour's walk to reach the glacier on the north side of a double-summited peak, which they named Kyzyl Alai (Kyzyl Alai East, 4,360m; Kyzyl Alai West, 4,440m), as it dominates the view from the nearby settlement.

Conditions were icier here than during their June ascents farther west. The team slanted left up the icy north face of the eastern peak and into a couloir that led to the upper section of the north rib. The final stretch to the east summit was sharp and steep ice. The grade was 2A. 🖸

– LINDSAY GRIFFIN, *WITH INFO FROM* MICHAL KLESLO, *CZECH, AND* HENRI LEVEQUE, *FRANCE*

PAMIR

ZAALAYSKIY (KOOK KIIK VALLEY) AND ALAY RANGES, MANY ASCENTS

THE ZAALAYSKIY RANGE, which includes Peak Lenin (7,134m), forms a border between Kyrgyzstan in the north and Tajikistan to the south. The Western Zaalayskiy runs from the confluence of the Kyzyl-su and Muk-su rivers to Ters-Agar Pass. Its highest point is Sat Peak (5,900m), and it contains many unclimbed summits of 4,000–5,000m. Our expedition, organized by the International School of Mountaineering (ISM) and led by Adrian Nelhams, aimed to explore unclimbed summits in this range.

We initially visited the Altyn Dara valley on the way to Ters-Agar Pass. However, we were prevented by the Kyrgyz military from accessing our climbing objectives because these were very close to the Tajikistan border. We had the required special permits, but our expedition coincided with political tensions between the countries.

We therefore relocated further east to the Kook Kiik Valley (about 40km west of Pik Lenin) and established a base camp at 3,178m. From here we summited Piks 3,884m and 3,993m. From an advanced base at 4,056m, we summited Piks 4,655m and 4,250m. [*Coordinates for all these locations are at the AAJ website.*]

We then drove north to the Turkistan range and the Alay Mountains, where we made our second base camp at 3,143m (39°37.755N, 72°15.628E). From here we climbed eight summits and tops with a height range of 3,999m to 4,500m.

There were no signs of previous ascents on 11 of our 12 summits, and we believe these had not been climbed before. There was a trigonometry point on the summit of Pik 4,491m, but we are confident that our two routes to this summit had not been climbed before. Details of each ascent are at the AAJ website; additional information and photos are at the ISM website. 🗒🖸

Telephoto view of Pik 4,240m West, seen from Hidden Big Peak (Pik 4,485m), with Pik Lenin (7,134m) in the background. *Mark Aitken*

– MARK AITKEN *AND* ADRIAN NELHAMS, *U.K.*

ZAALAYSKIY RANGE, BEL ULUU VALLEY, PIK ESPÉRANCE

IN SEPTEMBER, NIKOLAY Totmianin, a climber and guide from Russia, and I explored the Bel Uluu Glacier in the western part of the Trans Alai. We had previously visited the eastern section of the same range (*AAJ 2015*). The Bel Uluu Valley flows east into the Altyn Daria Valley, which rises to the south for 50km to the border with Tajikistan. On the far side lies the great Fedchenko Glacier. I could find no information describing previous exploration.

Looking southeast to unclimbed Pik 5,080m. Pik Espérance is the rocky top at far lower left. *Henry Bizot*

From Osh we traveled to the village of Daroot Korgon and then drove south, passing a frontier post, until after three hours we reached the confluence of the Altyn Daria and Bel Uluu rivers. From here we moved into the Bel Uluu and made our base camp at 3,300m. A little later we established a high camp at 4,420m, a 6km walk from base camp.

The receding Bel Uluu Glacier is 3km long and around 700m wide. We were flanked by virgin 4,000m and 5,000m peaks, but disappointingly the conditions were poor at the end of summer. We wanted to climb Pik 5,080m by a steep couloir, but the ice was too thin and black. Instead we almost climbed Peak 4,782m, to the northeast of Pik 5,080m, following a northeast-facing spur of hard ice to the rocky east ridge, where we stopped on a foresummit. The 50m continuation to the top was rotten and uninspiring, so we reversed our route of ascent (D/D+, 60°). We named the peak Espérance. 🗎 📷 🔍

– HENRY BIZOT, *FRANCE*

TIEN SHAN

ALA ARCHA, KORONA, FIRST TOWER, NORTH PILLAR

IN THE SUMMER of 2018, Dmitriy Pavlenko (Russia) soloed a new, independent route on the First Tower of Korona (4,810m). He had previously attempted this line in the summer of 2016, stopping halfway up. A second attempt, in the winter of 2017, got no further than the glacier in temperatures down to -30°C.

On July 9, 2018, Pavlenko began a third attempt, skiing to the bottom of the face and then climbing 11 rope lengths of snow and ice in the approach couloir to reach the start of the pillar. The previous three days of fine weather had left the rock in good condition, and the first couple of pitches (IV/V) went without incident. After overcoming two more pitches at Russian VI A2, Pavlenko set up a single-point hammock for a bivouac.

Next day the wall became more difficult and he progressed at "turtle speed." Pitch five was the crux (VI A3), involving several roofs and some difficulty getting solid protection. At the top of pitch six (VI A2), he was surprised to find the summit ridge just above. This was providential, as a thunderstorm was now threatening. The last pitch (V) was still steep and involved large loose blocks. The storm caught Pavlenko partway down the 3A descent couloir, where he found it difficult to move down through the slushy snow.

Pavlenko named his route Sport Marathon (900–950m total length, 400–450m for the rock section, Russian 5B VI A3). Because Pavlenko has soloed all the other 5B routes on this face, he can say with some conviction that this new route is the hardest. It is also the steepest route on the north face of Korona's First Tower. 📷

– INFORMATION PROVIDED BY **ELENA DMITRENKO,** *RUSSIA*

DJANGART RANGE, PIK KASPAROV AND PIK DOSTUK

IN THE SUMMER of 2015, Christoph Wolter and I visited the Djangart Range in the Central Kokshaal-too, driving from Bishkek to the western end of the range. Using three horses, we crossed Djangart Pass and on August 11 reached a base camp on the south side of the main river. Although we had planned to attempt difficult mixed routes, we quickly realized that the mountains were very dry.

On August 12 we went up the Akunguz Valley, immediately south of our base camp, and spent the night just before the glacier. On the 14th, after an acclimatization day at our high camp, we climbed a new route on Pik Kasparov (4,822m). This summit was first climbed by George Cave, Clay Conlon, Ross Davidson, and Harry Kingston from a 2013 British expedition (*AAJ 2014*). The four climbed the right side of the north face to reach the west ridge, then traversed the mountain, descending the northeast ridge and far left side of the north flank back to the glacier.

We climbed a direct route up the north face of Kasparov. Above the bergschrund was a section of 70°, then it was comfortable 60° névé to reach the last section of the west ridge. We called the route Now We Have the Salad (500m, 70°), from a German saying which for us meant, "Now we are really here and have done our first route, let's see what will happen next." We regained base camp the same day.

The peak immediately to the north-northeast of Pik Kasparov, called Pik Dostuk (4,911m), was unclimbed. We approached it via the next valley to the east, which holds the N1 Glacier. From here, on August 18, we climbed the north spur and upper east ridge, beginning at around 4,300m. The route had sections of 80° ice. We rappelled from Abalakov anchors down the huge snow/ice face to the right of our line, and named our route Is There Anybody Out There?

There are still a few unclimbed peaks in this area, particularly in the eastern section. As conditions were super-dry during our stay, we didn't see many striking ice lines, but there would be potential in different conditions. The rock was generally good on our climbs, but if you are after a pure rock route, only the flanks of Pik After You looked interesting to us. Temperatures at base camp were around 30°C in the day but dropped as low as -10°C at night. 📷

Looking south up the Akunguz Glacier at the north face of Pik Kasparov, with the line of Now We Have the Salad. *Christoph Wolter*

– **LORIN ETZEL,** *GERMANY*

2019 ASCENT OF PIK DOSTUK: *The elegant German line on the north spur of Pik Dostuk was repeated in September 2019 by the Dutch team of Frank Chargois, Mike van Berkel, and Cas van de Gevel, believing they were making the first ascent of the mountain. They descended the northwest ridge and northeast slope. The range was much snowier than in 2015, and conditions in the 80° couloir were perfect, with good placements in soft ice and black ice underneath in which to place solid screws. On the summit ridge they had to negotiate a tricky rock slab covered with powder. On top, their Garmin recorded 4,947m, and they rated their 600m ascent IV/4 3a.*

Looking south across the upper N1 Glacier to Pik Dostuk and the 2015 German route. The descent was by the ridge and slope to the right. *Christoph Wolter*

USHAT-TOO, PIK USHAT, HISTORICAL CORRECTION

IN AAJ 2019, we reported the presumed first ascent of Pik Ushat by an Australian team. However, this was not the first ascent, nor even the second, as noted in the following report from an expedition in 2002.

After an almost six-week-long cartographic expedition to the region of the South Inylchek Glacier, Paul Sass and I had a few days to spare before leaving for home. We took this opportunity to make a quick reconnaissance trip to the Ushat-too, the small range of peaks a few kilometers south of Inylchek village.

On September 3, 2002, we used horses to move south from Inylchek on a dirt road, then cross a bridge over the Kayindy (Kaindy) River. We camped where the Sarydjaz River enters a canyon, then continued alone, along the east bank of the valley, until we turned left into the Ushat (Taldybulak) Valley. The lower Ushat is idyllic, with flowers and birch trees. A little path led up the valley, and when it turned right in the direction of Ushat Pass (a.k.a. Kumar Pass, 3,775m), we continued straight ahead and camped on moraine. The next day we reached the heart of the horseshoe-shaped range.

We had no information about prior ascents in the range, except for Pik Ushat (5,142m), the highest summit, which local mountain guides told us had been climbed from the north. However, they had no details. We decided to attempt this stunning pyramid. We headed east across the lower slopes and halfway up the mountain reached a campsite on a short rocky ridge. After a cold night we crossed a snow plateau to reach the icy headwall, then climbed three pitches (50–60°) to gain the crest of the sharp and sometimes corniced west ridge. It took us almost an hour to traverse the few hundred meters to the highest point, which we reached at around 10 a.m.

To our surprise, we saw fresh tracks in the snow coming up the east ridge on the opposite side of the mountain. Even more surprising, the summit sported a framed picture, showing the portrait of a man. What had at first seemed a lonely and isolated peak turned out to have been climbed just a day or two previously! Therefore, to our knowledge there were at least two ascents prior to ours, up the east and north sides, the latter route likely the same as ours. [*The 2018 Australian team approached the upper north face on snow to the right of the rock ridge followed by the Germans in 2002, then probably climbed a similar route up the icy headwall and summit ridge.*] 📄 📷

– MARKUS KAUTZ, *GERMANY*

Rubtsak Koh (5,227m) seen from the northeast. The first ascent slanted up to the right across snow and mixed ground, parallel to the sun-shade line, to reach the north ridge and then the summit. *Sergi Ricart*

TAJIKISTAN

PAMIR

RIVAK AND OKTALIOK VALLEYS: RUBTSAK KOH, EAST FACE TO NORTH RIDGE, AND OTHER ASCENTS

In May and June 2018, I made a 1,000km solo bicycle ride from Khorog, Tajikistan, to Osh, Kyrgyzstan, following the Gund River, traversing the Pamir Highlands via Murghab and Karakol Lake, and finally crossing the border to reach Osh. I saw huge potential for exploratory mountaineering.

With none of my usual partners available, I returned to Khorog alone in early September to climb in nearby valleys. With the help of two porters, I walked up the Rivak Dara (Rivak Valley) to establish base camp next to a lake at 3,870m. I remained there alone for the next 10 days. I climbed Pik 4,820m by its southeast ridge (1,000m, F+) and then made an attempt on Pik 5,428m. I was stopped by a crevasse at 5,225m on the north ridge of the subsidiary summit, Pik 5,363m, the climbing to that point having been 700m, AD 55°. The reversal of my route was delicate. [*The previous climbing history of these accessible peaks is not known; coordinates are at the AAJ website.*]

On the 19th I returned to Khorog and after a few days hitchhiked about 130km to the village of Jelondy (3,500m). Here, I hired a couple of porters to reach the smaller village of Oktaliok, transferred gear to donkeys, and trekked 15km up the Oktaliok Dara to install base camp.

Two days later I climbed a 5,227m peak at 37°37'32"N, 72°39'54"E. It took me two hours from base camp to reach the foot of the east face at 4,900m, above which introductory 35–40° slopes led to the base of a couloir splitting the face. Soft snow over loose, slabby terrain at 50° led to a steeper section at 5,050m (65° and III). Above, I self-belayed a 15m section of IV+, then continued up 50–55° snow/mixed to reach the north ridge. On the crest I had to outflank a highly decomposed rock pinnacle by a 10m diagonal rappel on the flank, followed by a section of II and 55° to regain the ridge. The final 50m along the crest had 65° ice. I returned to base camp the same way, with four rappels and some delicate downclimbing. There was no trace of any previous ascent.

After consulting local shepherds, I decided to call this unnamed peak Rubtsak Koh (Fox Peak), and my route Dies Que Duraran Anys ("Days That Will Last for Years," 450m, D- IV+ 65°). ◙

– SERGI RICART, *SPAIN*

BADAKHSHAN NATIONAL PARK, LAKE YASHILKUL REGION, VARIOUS ASCENTS

IN LATE JUNE we flew from Switzerland to Osh, a lively town in southern Kyrgyzstan that provides the most convenient starting point for trips to the eastern Pamir. Two days on the Pamir Highway brought us to the village of Murghab, Tajikistan, from which another four hours saw us to the Yashilkul Dam. From here, two friendly local men and their donkeys helped us carry our gear and supplies in a single long day to a base camp at 4,235m (37.90611°N, 72.68291°E). One of us had discovered this place on a previous hiking traverse of the area, and according to our contact from the Pamir Alpine Club, it had never been visited by mountaineers.

The region is generally very dry during summer, with only sparse vegetation along streams that are fed by glaciers. Only a few yaks and their herders visit the valleys.

After acclimatizing around base camp, we started to explore the surrounding peaks. The rock consists of some sort of gneiss that is generally OK. At the time of our expedition, there was still plenty of snow and névé above base camp. This allowed us to move efficiently in the cold morning hours, but often made for challenging conditions and some spontaneous avalanches later in the day. In total, we managed to summit four major peaks over the course of two weeks. We climbed all of them as day trips from base camp, after we had scouted the approaches and established gear caches at the foot of the climbs.

Three of the peaks required rappelling from the top, and since we didn't find anchors or any other signs of previous attempts, we strongly believe they had never been climbed. We named them Pik Elo (4,872m), Pik Anto (5,343m), and Pik Wolfi (5,104m)—the latter two in memory of our missing friends Angi, Tobi, and Wolfi.

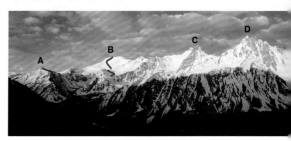

[Top] Southeast face of Pik Anto (5,343m, AD+). *Moritz Waelde* [Middle] The northwest face of Pik Elo (4,872m, AD+). *Moritz Waelde* [Bottom] Looking south from Pik Wolfi. (A) Northwest face of Pik Elo. (B) Northeast flank of Gora Riri. (C) Peak of about 5,450m. (D) Pik Anto (the southeast flank, climbed in 2019, is not visible). *Marc Andri Riedi*

All three climbs followed snow couloirs (up to 50°) that led to rocky sections, with the last two or three pitches to the tops being a bit more technical (AD with rock/mixed climbing up to UIAA IV).

The fourth peak we called Gora Riri (5,291 m). It is a long but rather easy glacier/snow hike all the way to the top, and it's possible it had been climbed in the past.

The climate here can be pretty harsh, with cold nights, high solar irradiation during the day, and strong, dry winds. Nevertheless, we recommend the region to climbers. Most peaks are still unclimbed, and they provide plenty of possibilities, with a wide variety of styles and difficulties and relatively quick access, thanks to the Pamir Highway. 📷

– MARC ANDRI RIEDI *AND* MORITZ WAELDE, *SWITZERLAND*

PIK BELETSKIY, SOUTHEAST FACE

Pik Beletskiy from the southeast, showing the 2019 route and high camp. *Michal Kleslo*

AFTER AN ACCLIMATIZATION ascent of Kyzyl Alai East in the Pamir Alai (*see Kyrgyzstan section*), my team headed for the Pamir in July. From the M41 (the Sary Tash to Karakol Lake road) in the Markansu Valley, we walked west up the Uysu Valley for two days to place a base camp at 4,800m on the northern bank of the Uysu Glacier.

Our original plan was to continue up the valley to Piks VFM (Voenno Morskogo Flota, 5,842m) and Korzhenevskiy (6,005m), but we found the glacier ahead impassable. After climbing a rocky pinnacle, which we named Pik Panorama (5,250m), to the north of base camp, we saw a feasible ascent route to Pik Beletskiy (6,050m). This summit, on the ridge that defines the Kyrgyzstan-Tajikistan frontier, had never been climbed from the south; the few known ascents all were made during traverses of the Northern Pamirs.

We climbed the broken glacier to the west of Pik Panorama to a large plateau on a hanging glacier, where we set up a high camp at 5,360m. From there we climbed the glaciated southeast face to the upper south spur, followed that onto the main watershed ridge, and continued over easy but tiring ground to the summit (3B overall). In a register on top, the last entry was in 1963 by a team from Kyrgyzstan. 📷 🔍

– MICHAL KLESLO, *CZECH REPUBLIC*

KARACHIM AND KARAJILGA RANGES, VARIOUS ASCENTS

SOUTH OF KYZYL Art Pass and immediately west of the great Karakul Lake lie the Zulumart subranges of Karachim and Karajilga. This is a fine area for traveling, with many wild animals and no people. In August, Vilnis Barons, Ronalds Feldmanis, Andrey Sichov, and I climbed three peaks in these ranges by easy slopes: Pik 5,439m, Pik 5,312m, and Pik 5,411m. We approached around the southern shores of Lake Karakul and into the valley between the Karajilga to the west and the Karachim to the east. Our first and third peaks lie in the Karachim, while our second peak lies in the Karajilga. There is no evidence of these having been climbed before. 📄 📷

– OLEG SILIN, *LATVIA*

MUZKOL RANGE, PIK AGAMAU

In 2017, from the vicinity of Ak Baital Pass on the Pamir Highway, I photographed a peak to the west with an altitude of 5,553m, according to the Soviet military map. This area in the southeast part of the North Muzkol Range has been very rarely visited by climbers. After studying all available literature, it seemed almost certain Pik 5,553m had never been climbed.

On August 24, 2019, Jerzy Kędra and I entered Tajikistan by car, having driven from Poland. Time was tight for climbing; the immigration authorities had only given us a 15-day permit for the car. On the 31st we parked near a shepherd's hut in the lower Ak Baital Valley and then walked west alongside an unnamed stream to reconnoiter the peak. This excursion showed a broad couloir on the left side of the north face to be the best option.

On September 2 we walked back up to the glacier and bivouacked on the moraine. We rested and acclimatized on the 3rd, and on the 4th woke at 4 a.m. and started to climb the ice couloir at 8 a.m. The ice was hard and the first few pitches up to 60°. It then became easier (40°) until a large crevasse that slanted up right across the face; we simul-climbed below this to reach the upper northeast ridge at 6 p.m. This was not as easy as expected (40–50° with short steps of 60–80°). After a 70–80° ice chimney, we arrived on the summit at 8:20 p.m. We bivouacked 50m below the top. With no sleeping bags or pads, it was a really cold and windy night.

Because we had underestimated the difficulties, we had brought only one 60m rope, and the next morning it was quicker to downclimb most of the route than to rappel. At 5 p.m. we reached our base camp and the following day descended to the car.

We called the mountain Pik Agamau—it is supposed to sound like a local name, though in fact it is the combination of the shortened names of our wives. The route was about 650m in height and had around 1,100m of climbing. The grade was D or Russian 3A/3B. [*Peak Buffy correction: The online version of this report corrects an error in the reported location and elevation of nearby Peak Buffy, first climbed by a British team in 2014.*] 📷

– JUDA TADEUSZ DZIĘGIELEWSKI, *POLAND*

Ak Baital Pass on the Pamir Highway and the climbers' means of transport from Poland. The glaciated north face of Pik Agamau, climbed in September 2019, is at far right. *Juda Tadeusz Dzięgielewski*

Rakaposhi (7,788m) from the southwest, showing (1) northwest ridge (1979), (2) southwest ridge (1958), and (3) south face and southeast ridge (2019). In the background, the major summits are (A) Pasu, (B) Shispare, (C) Bojohaghur Duanasir, (D) Ultar, and (E) Karun Koh. *Jon Bowles Photography*

RAKAPOSHI FROM THE SOUTH
HUGE NEW ROUTE UP PREVIOUSLY UNATTEMPTED FACE

BY KENRO NAKAJIMA, *JAPAN*

OUR PLANNED OBJECTIVE for 2019 was a new route on Tirich Mir, the highest peak in the Hindu Kush. However, by the time we arrived in Pakistan, Kazuya Hiraide and I still had not received a permit, and so we went to Gilgit to reconnoiter another objective while we awaited the final decision. Kazuya has made frequent visits to Hunza and holds a strong desire to climb peaks from that valley. One of the most outstanding is Rakaposhi (7,788m). The south side, although reconnoitered in the past, remained untouched.

The start of the valley of the Sulgin Glacier, leading to the south face, is only 40 minutes by jeep from Gilgit. Twenty kilometers of easy walking leads to the snout. Although low (3,660m), base camp could be no higher than the glacier snout. Our view of the south side of the mountain was not encouraging, boasting many treacherous seracs—there was only one feasible route.

We returned to Gilgit, and after two days there our agent told us a permit for Tirich Mir would not be forthcoming this year. We called back our Pakistani team, who were on standby in Chitral, and on June 16 we all headed to Rakaposhi with the necessary supplies. Ten days from our schedule had been lost.

For acclimatization, and to confirm the line, we spent three days negotiating the complex icefall and climbing the south face to 6,100m, with nights at 4,500m and 5,900m. After our return to base camp, the weather was bad for another six days.

After the weather improved, on June 27, Kazuya and I moved up to Camp 1 at 5,200m, carrying food and fuel for seven days but no rock gear. Next day we outflanked seracs and continued up a snow ridge and face. Our previous tracks had gone, and we struggled with the fresh snow. Even so, we managed to gain 1,000m to a camp at 6,200m, not far below the southeast ridge.

On the 29th we reached the southeast ridge, having climbed an ice wall just below the crest, using ice screw belays. The panorama to the northeast was magnificent, and the summit looked close. Unfortunately, the altimeter told us otherwise. Contrary to our expectations, there was no firm crust on the ridge crest, and we again struggled with deep, soft snow. We climbed 600m to a campsite at 6,800m, whereupon it snowed for the next two days and we remained in the tent.

On July 2 we decided our best chance of success was to try for the summit directly from this camp, an ascent of 1,000m. We left under a starlit sky at 4 a.m.

There were no technical difficulties and once the southeast ridge joined the final section of the southwest ridge (the route of Rakaposhi's first ascent in 1958), the snow conditions improved due to the westerly wind. We stood on top at noon, overwhelmed by the 360° panorama. Opposite stood Shispare, which the two of us had climbed the previous year.

We returned to camp, spent the night, and then descended our route all the way to base camp the following day. While the route had little technical difficulty, the height gain from base camp was more than 4,000m, and the weather remained unstable throughout the ascent. 📷

[Top] Kazuya Hiraide moves along a corniced section of the southeast ridge of Rakaposhi on summit day. Diran lies in shadow in the background, and distant left are the high peaks of the Hispar Glacier. [Bottom] The northwest side of Haramosh (7,397m) seen from Rakaposhi. The first ascent (Austrian, 1958) was via the left skyline (east ridge). *Kenro Nakajima (both photos)*

Tiphaine Duperier skiing the southeast face of an unnamed peak (ca 5,625 meters) above the Sgari-Byen Gang Glacier, having made the first ascent during acclimatization for Spantik. *Boris Langenstein*

SKIING SPANTIK AND NANGA PARBAT
TWO HIGH-ALTITUDE DESCENTS

BY TIPHAINE DUPERIER, *FRANCE*

As WITH EVERY trip, our month and a half of holiday in Pakistan begins with a long day of packing. It is not easy to find space for four pairs of skis, alpine climbing equipment, and massive amounts of food. A few days after leaving France, in mid-May, Boris Langenstein and I start from Arandu for the three-day trek to base camp for Spantik (7,027m), where we hope to make the first ski descent. We acclimatize by ascending two lower peaks, finding unstable snow on all exposures.

The normal route to Spantik is the southeast ridge, easy and safe to Camp 2. Between there and Camp 3, at 6,400m, things are more complicated: The ridge becomes a dome of deep snow, and we have to forge a route up the middle. We arrive at camp tired after a day of uncertain and changing conditions. On May 30, summit day, we find luck is on our side. Avoiding the ridge to the west, we find wind-compacted snow, with little risk of avalanche. At 1 p.m., in full sunshine and with no wind, we are on top. Our ski descent goes smoothly, with one more night in Camp 3 to aid our acclimatization for Nanga Parbat (8,125m).

On June 10, our first day above Diamir Base Camp, we head up toward Camp 2 on the standard route, climbing part of the Kinshofer Wall. After skiing down, we are forced to stay five days in base camp due to bad weather and Boris becoming ill.

On the 16th, in order to finish our acclimatization, we start up the Diama Face. Following a slightly different line to that taken by Elizabeth Revol and Tomasz Mackiewicz in the winter of 2018, we make three camps and on the 19th reach a high point of 7,450m, almost at the top of the Diama Face. We then ski down to base camp, with another night at our 6,600m camp. With this foray into the heart of the Diama Face, the trip, in our opinion, is already a success.

On the 26th we leave base camp at 4 a.m. Climbing with full gear and skis, we reach Camp 2 (5,900m) above the Kinshofer Wall on the standard route in 11 hours. On the 27th, breaking trail through deep snow, we reach Camp 3 at around 6,500m, and next day, at 7 p.m., we arrive at the normal site of Camp 4 at 7,250m.

Leaving at 5 a.m. on the 29th, we head for the summit. Making the trail requires determination. At around 6 p.m., in deteriorating weather, we decide to turn around: Boris at 8,040m, me at 7,989m. It takes nearly an hour to put on our skis, by which time it is nearly dark. Having forgotten headlamps, we make the descent using the lights on our smartphones. We reach our tent at 7,250m at 9 p.m., already thinking of our next attempt.

After a day in the tent, we take off again at 3:30 a.m. on July 1. Sadly, our previous tracks have vanished in the wind. Our pace is depressing and we swap leads often. A little after 1 p.m., at 7,800m, I have to stop. Something is wrong in my head and my balance is affected—later I'll discover I had a perforated eardrum. Boris is still strong, so I offer to wait while he continues. At 8,080m he leaves his skis 10m below the summit ridge, and continues up the crest, negotiating a few easy but unskiable rock steps, to the top. It is around 5.30 p.m. Returning to his skis, he starts down and we are reunited after a wait of 5.5 hours on my part. We both ski to Camp 4, reaching it at 8 p.m. after a magnificent sunset.

Next day we are slow to move, waiting for the warmth of the sun. We abandon the idea of a 200m ascent to connect with the Diama Face—four nights at 7,250m have exhausted us. Leaving at 1 p.m., we ski the Kinshofer Route, meeting other expeditions above Camp 3, and holding onto fixed ropes to pass a critical 100m section of thinly covered ice below this camp. We avoid the Kinshofer Wall by using the variation to the east first climbed by Norbert Joos and Erhard Loretan in 1982, and skied in 2008 by Luis Stitzinger (a German who skied the Diamir Face from Camp 3). This is the crux of the descent: 45° with difficult route-finding. By 3 p.m. we are skiing out onto the glacier at the foot of the face. 📷

MORE NANGA PARBAT SKIING: *Boris Langenstein's descent from 8,080m, using skis the entire way, and only safeguarded by holding onto fixed ropes for 100m, is most complete ski descent of Nanga Parbat recorded. Prior descents started from lower on the peak and/or downclimbed or rappelled significant sections. Two days after the French descent, Cala Cimenti (Italy) and Vitaly Lazo (Russia) skied from the same 8,080m high point. They also held the fixed ropes below Camp 3, and they downclimbed along fixed ropes on the Kinshofer Wall. Additional information for this report was provided by Rodolphe Popier, Chronique Alpine, FFCAM.*

Descending the Luis Stitzinger ski variant (first climbed by Norbert Joos and Erhard Loretan) to Nanga Parbat's Kinshofer Wall. *Boris Langenstein*

A SALTORO GIANT
FIRST CLIMB OF SHERPI KANGRI II IN THE EAST KARAKORAM

BY KURT ROSS, *USA*

SHERPI KANGRI II (ca 7,000m) lies on the Line of Control between the India- and Pakistan-controlled sectors of the East Karakoram. Prior to 2019, it had been attempted only once. In 1974, a Japanese expedition trying the east ridge of Sherpi Kangri I (7,380m) gave up and instead fixed around 1,000m of rope up the southeast ridge of Sherpi Kangri II, before retreating at 6,300m due to technical difficulty. On August 7, Matt Cornell, Jackson Marvel, and I (all USA) summited this peak via the southeast ridge in seven days round trip from base camp.

Porter shortages resulted in a significantly lower base camp than we had planned—at around 3,700m on the west bank of the Sherpi Gang Glacier, more or less level with the first icefall. This required establishing three additional camps several kilometers apart, ferrying loads through complicated terrain, to reach the glacier plateau below the peak. After investing

Looking north up the chaotic Sherpi Gang Glacier toward Sherpi Kangri I (7,380m). The approach to Sherpi Kangri II (hidden) was above the left side of the glacier. The first ascent of Sherpi Kangri I was by the left-hand (west) ridge in 1976. *Kurt Ross*

much time and energy on this approach, including portering some of our own loads to base camp, we did not have time to acclimatize as slowly as we would have liked for higher elevations. We therefore chose the seemingly nontechnical southeast ridge, so we could bail quickly if one of us began to show signs of acute altitude sickness.

We climbed to the summit from our highest glacier camp over two days, with one bivouac on the ridge. The terrain was largely classic AI3/4, and the height of the route around 1,100m. On the ridge we found some old Goldline rope and a couple of Japanese pins.

I'm proud of this ascent because I think we did a good job of restrategizing and working hard to summit our main objective, despite the logistical hang-ups encountered. We feel extremely grateful to tag a previously unclimbed 7,000m peak this late in the timeline of alpine climbing. 📷

HISTORICAL NOTES ON SHERPI KANGRI I: *One year after the Japanese expedition mentioned above, which reached 6,400m on the northeast ridge of Sherpi Kangri I, that peak was tried in 1975 by an experienced British team led by Dave Alcock. They attempted the peak from the south and gave up below 6,000m on realizing that the difficulties and distance were too great in their available time, and instead made first ascents of Pyramid Peak (6,500m), on the watershed ridge to the southeast, and Chorta Kangri (6,620m) on the ridge south of that, running toward Saltoro Kangri.*

Sherpi Kangri I was climbed the following year (1976) by Kazumasa Hirai's Japanese expedition, via the west ridge. Until 2019, this area had not been visited by climbers since the 1970s, because of military restrictions dating to the start of the Indo-Pakistan conflict in the early 1980s.

GESHOT PEAK, NORTHWEST SPUR AND WEST FACE

THE MOUNTAIN LOCALLY named Geshot Peak (a.k.a. Toshe III or Toshain III, 6,200m, 35°8'44.44"N, 74°24'14.92"E) lies about 20km southwest of the summit of Nanga Parbat. On June 29, I made the first ascent, starting from the Bunar Valley to the northwest.

My plan had been to climb the mountain together with my father Reinhold (Italy), Günther Göberl, and Robert Neumeyer (both from Austria). Difficult snow conditions, warm temperatures, and very unstable weather made this potentially dangerous for a party of four, so I decided to climb the mountain in a single push, solo, from an advanced base at 4,600m.

My aim was to climb fast to avoid incoming bad weather, and although I had to break trail for the entire ascent (sometimes up to the knees!), I reached the summit at 9:30 a.m., having taken 5.5 hours. The climbing was not difficult, but snow conditions were very bad, and I had to concentrate hard to avoid triggering an avalanche. Luckily everything went well on the descent, and I reached base camp the same day. This is a very glaciated mountain, and I have never seen so many seracs on a peak of this relatively low altitude.

Geshot Peak previously had been attempted unsuccessfully from the northwest by Polish expeditions (twice) and also Canadians. While trekking out from the mountain, locals in the Bunar Valley brought me wreaths and flowers to celebrate the ascent—what hospitality! 📷

– SIMON MESSNER, *ITALY*

THALO ZOM, SOUTH FACE AND SOUTHWEST RIDGE

THE MOUNTAIN WILDERNESS organization (*mountainwilderness.org*) strives not only to preserve the natural environment of the world's mountains and deserts, but also to maintain the quality of the experience for visitors to these extraordinary landscapes. The Swat Project of Mountain Wilderness International's Asian Desk is trying to encourage respectful tourism by discouraging the building of access roads, cable cars, hotels and mountain huts, and by encouraging the climbing of smaller summits, without using hundreds of porters, fixed ropes, and supplemental oxygen.

Supporting these principles, a team representing Mountain Wilderness left Kalam on August 19 with the aim of climbing Thalo Zom (5,990m GPS, 35°46'54.35"N, 72°16'54.49"E) on the

Thalo Zom seen from the Thalo Zom Glacier to the northwest. The 2019 expedition passed around the right side of the mountain to reach its south face. A 1971 Austrian expedition is believed to have crossed the snow col left of the mountain and climbed the south flank of the northeast ridge to make the first ascent. *Andrea Bollati*

Swat-Chitral border. From Kalam, we traveled by jeep, with our porters, along the Utrar road to the Kumrat Valley. The climbing party was Koki Gassiot (Catalonia), Massimo Marconi and I (both Italian), and Samiullah Ghaznavi, Sadam Hussain, and Abrar Saeed, three young local mountaineers trained by the Asian Desk and the Pakistani Chapter of Mountain Wilderness.

From a starting point of 2,700m in the Kumrat Valley, it took several days to cross Thalo Pass (4,220m) and establish base camp at 4,090m in the Thalo Gol. On August 23 we began working up the wide Thalo Zom Glacier, establishing camps at 4,750m and 5,100m, and a high camp below the south face of the mountain at 5,400m. From there, at 1 p.m. on the 29th, the entire team reached the summit via a 600m ice route up the south face and southwest ridge. We named it Guides' Way (D-, 60°).

At the time we thought this was the first ascent of the peak but later discovered it had been climbed on August 12, 1971, by a team from Graz, Austria, led by Herbert Zefferer. Looking at the available information, it seems most likely they ascended the Thalo Zom Glacier to the snow col at the foot of the northeast ridge, then climbed on the south flank of that ridge to the top, perhaps finishing up the southeast ridge. 📷 🔍

– ANDREA BOLLATI, *ITALY*

KARAKORAM / GHUJERAB MOUNTAINS

Jakub Bogdanski on the southeast face of Dih Sar. (A) Arman Sar (ca 6,000m), climbed from the far side in 2017. (B) Peak 5,970m. (C) Peak 5,883m. (D) Imtiaz Sar (5,930m), climbed from the far side in 2017. *Michal Ilczuk*

KARUN KOH SUBGROUP, MARIO SAR AND DIH SAR ATTEMPT

THE GHUJERAB MOUNTAINS form the northern Karakoram. This vast mountain area can be conveniently partitioned into four areas or subgroups: Khunjerab, Karun Koh, Tupopdan, and Shuijerab.

In 2018, Janusz Majer and I put together a comprehensive sketch map of the Tupopdan and Karun Koh groups at 1:100,000. This produced an immediate interest among Polish climbers. Two teams visited the Karun Koh group in 2019: one during August-September, and the other in September-October. The last team encountered the best conditions, although melting ice and snow after noon still presented problems.

Mariusz Samarak and Jacek Widera set up base camp in the Spesyngov Valley on September 7, having trekked from Shimshal via Boesam Pass and the Ghujerab River. This lies northeast of Karun Koh (reported as either 7,164m or 6,977m), the highest of the Ghujerab peaks and climbed only once, in 1984, by Austrians, via the southwest ridge. The goal of the 2019 expedition was to climb to Spesyngov Pass (5,400m) and try neighboring peaks.

On September 13, from a camp at 5,100m, the

pair reached the ridge north of the pass and followed it up to Peak 6,151m and from there northwest a short distance to Peak 6,210m, which they named Mario Sar (36°39'50.68"N, 75° 5'29.72"E). The terrain was snow and scree of 45° or less. On the descent, before reaching the pass, Saramak slipped on an icy section (his new light alloy crampons had blunted) and fell 300m toward their approach route. Fortunately, he was able to get back to camp unassisted and then reach the valley.

There are plenty of opportunities to be had in this immediate area, apart from the great northern flanks of Karun Koh, and it appears the second half of September is the best time for climbing here these days.

The second team to visit the Karun Koh mountains was Jakub Bogdanski and Michal Ilczuk. They arrived in Shimshal on September 11, and via the Boesam Pass and Ghujerab River reached the Dih Valley on the 16th. This is the last valley rising south from the Ghujerab River before reaching Spesyngov. The next day, not without difficulty, they established base camp at 4,700m, at the start of the Dih Glacier.

On the 20th they placed a high camp at 5,300m in the First Ice Flow, northeast of the main glacier, and below the southeast face of Dih Sar (reported as either 6,363m or 6,200m, 36°35'4.51"N, 75°17'36.66"E). On the 21st they tried to climb a gully on the right side of the face, but quickly had to move onto the bordering rock, which proved appalling. At 5,700m they decided it was too dangerous to continue.

On the 22nd they tried again, this time up the snow and ice in the center of the face, which at this point is 700–800m high. They simul-climbed the first 300m and then belayed eight pitches to a height of 5,950m, where, still four or five pitches from the summit ridge and with only two hours of daylight left, they opted to descend. 📷 🔍

– **JERZY WALA**, *POLAND, TRANSLATED BY MONIKA HARTMAN*

KHUNJERAB SUBGROUP, TWO-HEADED MASSIF, NORTH SUMMIT, AND OTHER ASCENTS

THE TWO-HEADED MASSIF lies to the east of Yawash Sar and northwest of the North Ghidims Glacier. When developing a sketch map of the Ghidims Valley, I bestowed the name Two-Headed Massif on a twin-summited peak almost entirely surrounded by glacier-filled valleys. The Chinese-Pakistani topographic border map defines the south top as 5,929m. I calculated the north top was around 5,900m. In 2014, a Polish-Italian expedition with the Pakistani guide Karim Hayat climbed halfway up a couloir leading to the summit ridge but retreated in bad weather.

In May 2018, a Polish Alpine Club expedition visited this area with seven members (Tomasz Hełka, Wiktor Jutrasz, Bogusław

Two-Headed Massif (ca 5,900m) and the route of ascent in late May 2018 to the north top, via the southeast couloir. *Detlef Seeling*

Magrel, Jan Pecka, Dawid Plewczyński, Monika Szławieniec-Reczuch, and Sławomir Wiktor), along with Karim Hayat and Rahmet Ullah Baig from Shimshal.

This team established base camp on May 26 at a place called Yakya (a.k.a. Dada Hakal Camp, 4,400m), and an advanced base on the North Ghidims Glacier at 4,900m. From there the team climbed Peak 5,531m (map height), lying on the Chinese border, and named it Polish Massif.

On the 31st, all but one team member climbed to the north summit of Two-Headed Massif. They followed the southeast couloir toward the gap between the two summits, then up the short southwest ridge to the top (PD+). This was the route attempted by the 2014 expedition. Once on top, they established that the south peak was higher.

On June 3 they left the area to head back to Shimshal. On the 5th, while in the vicinity of Boesum Pass, they made the first ascent of Lal Sirang Kateth (5,680m, PD+). This top lies along the ridge to the south of Boe Sar (first climbed in 2005 by Abdullah Bai and Francois Carrel; see AAJ 2006). The team climbed the west ridge toward the summit of Boe Sar, then slanted right to hit the north ridge of Lal Sirang Kateth, which they followed to the top. 📷 🔍

– JERZY WALA, *POLAND, TRANSLATED BY MONIKA HARTMAN, SUPPLIED BY JANUSZ MAJER*

The west face of unclimbed Yawash II with the route attempted by Krzysztof Wielicki and Jalal Uddin in 2018. Above the narrows, this face is around 850m high. *Karim Hayat*

KHUNJERAB SUBGROUP, YAWASH SAR II, WEST FACE, ATTEMPT

THE PEAKS OF Yawash Sar (I, 6,258m; II, 6,125m; and III, 6,060m) are the most prominent summits of the Khunjerab Group. The naming of these peaks, like the glaciers on their northern flanks, comes from the Yawash Jilga River, which appears on the 1986–1987 China-Pakistan boundary maps.

In 2018, Krzysztof Wielicki led an 11-member trekking group, mainly Polish, to the Ghidims Valley. During the acclimatization phase, Frank Gasser, who had twice visited this area (2012 and 2014) to attempt Yawash Sar I, made two solo attempts on that mountain, reaching 5,800m.

On August 20, from a camp below the west side of Yawash Sar II, Wielicki and Jalal Uddin, a high-altitude porter from Shimshal, made an attempt on the west face, with the idea to fix part of the route. They reached 5,800m but ran out of rope and decided to retreat, and everyone returned to Shimshal on the 24th. 🔍

– JERZY WALA, *POLAND, TRANSLATED BY MONIKA HARTMAN*

CHASHKIN I, SOUTHEAST FACE AND SKI DESCENT

IN JUNE I traveled to the Shimshal region, where, according to locals, I found the snowiest spring in memory. While the region's high but gentle peaks have a history of ski alpinism, I was most interested in the pointy ones, as long as there appeared to be a way to ski down (or partially ski down). The Chashkin Group seemed to fit the bill, especially Chashkin I (6,035m, 36°31'24.71"N, 75°29'46.90"E), which had a rock ridge and pinnacle with what looked like semi-casual snow to either side.

Most likely due to the 40km approach, Chashkin I and II both remained unclimbed, although Chashkin III (around 5,900m) has received three ascents. This was erroneously reported to have

(A) Chashkin III, (B) II, and (C) I from the south, showing the approximate lines of (1) Steeze Matters, the first ascent of the Chashkin I (6,035m), and (2) the subsequent ski descent from the summit. *Tico Gangulee*

been climbed first in 2010 by Samina Baig from Shimshal Village (*AAJ 2011*), but was in fact first climbed in the winter of 1997 by Shimshalis Qudrat Ali and Shaheen Baig; Chashkin III is sometimes referred to as Samina Peak after the woman who climbed it later (and who went on to become the first woman from Pakistan to climb Everest). With typical hubris, I planned on climbing all three Chashkins, with first ascents of I and II and ski descents of all three.

This was clearly not to be. Avalanche hazard and more difficult climbing than expected, along with daily snowfall and strong wind, ground my progress to a halt. On June 20, close to my last day in the area, I set out from advanced base at 5,000m for a shallow ridge line on the southeast face of Chashkin I, which seemed the safest place to be. I quickly found harder-than-expected mixed climbing, but thankfully never particularly sustained, with ledges or terraces every 30–40m. I brought gear for roped soling, but the cruxes were above ledges and felt like boulder problems, so I was comfortable free soling them in ski boots. (I hauled my pack and skis when it got steep.) The climbing was mostly moderate mixed, with cruxes either on slabs or with steep crimping, which I climbed barehanded. I named the ascent route Steeze Matters (900m, ED 5.11 (or V2) M4+ 85°).

The climb took about nine hours, and the daily storm hit as I was close to the summit. This made the ski descent harrowing, with a few wrong turns and re-ascents. There was a lot of standing around waiting for a view through the cloud, and I heard avalanches running. After 250m I was below the major cloud and able to make a break for the lower mountain on a more easterly aspect below the hanging glacier. Here, the skiing got pretty fun, but I was too tired to enjoy it. I would definitely return to the area for Chashkins II and III, but later in the season in the hope of getting more stable weather. 📷

– TICO GANGULEE, *USA*

SHUIJERAB SUBGROUP, GUNJ-E-DUR VALLEY, PETR KOH

JAN AND KRYSTIAN Kostecki and Sebastian Wolski (Poland) set up base camp in early July 2018 at 4,600m between the two streams coming down from the First and Second Gunj-e-Dur glaciers. Their porters refused to go any higher, so the three had to establish an advance base on the 9th at 5,165m, directly opposite Peak 5,913m (Peak 177 on Jerzy Wala's map of the Shuijerab mountain group).

On the 12th, Camp 1 was established at 5,440m near Gunj-e-Pir West Pass (5,622m). The next day the trio attempted the south ridge of Peak 6,047m (Peak 211 on the Wala map) via the west flank, but failed due to high temperatures and soft snow conditions.

On the 14th, the three made the first ascent of Peak 180/Peak 5,880m (GPS), to the west of Gunj-e-Pir Pass, via the northeast ridge. They named it Petr Koh. On the 19th, they had another go at Peak 6,047m but found conditions to be even worse, so they dismantled camp and returned to advanced base. On July 23 they tried Peak 5,913m, reaching the south ridge via an east-facing couloir directly above advanced base, but once the sun hit the conditions became dangerous and they retreated quickly.

There are many interesting unclimbed peaks in the Gunj-e-Dur Valley, particularly the main peak of Gunj-e-Sar (6,376m), but the middle of summer is not a favorable time for attempting them.

– JERZY WALA, *POLAND, TRANSLATED BY MONIKA HARTMAN AND SUPPLIED BY JANUSZ MAJER*

EARLIER POLISH GUNJ-E-DUR EXPEDITIONS: *In 2013, a Polish expedition from the Wrotnia Club placed a base camp at the entrance to the First East Gunj-e-Dur Glacier and from there climbed to the Gunj-e-Pir East Col, then south to a summit they named Snow Peak (5,730m). In 2016, a team from the same club established a base camp lower down the main valley, at 4,550m, and an advanced base at 5,157m a little way up the Northwest Gunj-e-Dur Glacier. From, there Andrzej Makaran, Grzegorz Mołczan, Agnieszka Garus-Saramak, and Mariusz Saramak climbed to Buspur Pass (5,642m) and continued north up the ridge make the first ascent of Mai Dur Sar (6,017m GPS).*

KARAKORAM / VIRJERAB MUZTAGH

KHUSHRUI SAR AND PEAK 6,099M, ATTEMPTS

IN AUGUST 2016, Bas Visscher and friends from the Netherlands had a permit to attempt Yawash Sar (6,258m) in the Ghujerab mountains, but on arrival in Pakistan they learned the army had closed this region in connection with arms smuggling. Instead they went to the Virjerab, where it

was far too warm: It rained at night at 5,000m, and there were frequent avalanches. The climbers attempted Khushrui Sar (5,900m), climbed by Poles in 2013 (*AAJ 2014*), and Peak 6,099m, which lies in the southeast corner of the Kut Glacier, a little to the east of Khushrui Sar. Bad weather ended both attempts.

The Dutch did come home with photos of impressive unclimbed objectives. Peaks in this area are likely to be better attempted in colder conditions, perhaps April-May or September-October.

– *INFORMATION PROVIDED BY* **BAS VISSCHER,**
NETHERLANDS

[Top] The north face of unclimbed Khurdopin Sar (6,310m) above the Spregh Yaz Glacier, a southern offshoot of the Virjerab Glacier. [Bottom] The serac-threatened north face of unclimbed Peak 6,316m (left) at the head of the First Virjerab Glacier. A passage of the obvious col would lead to the North Sekrwar Glacier and then southwest to the Khurdopin Glacier. *Bas Visscher (both photos)*

View southeast from the summit of Okheree Sar, over the upper Shim Dur Glacier, to Shim Dur Sar (6,495m, highest peak in center right) and other unclimbed peaks of the Insgaiti Mountains. *Justyna Markiewicz*

OKHEREE SAR, SOUTHWEST SLOPES

THE SHIM DUR (a.k.a. Shahim-i-Dur) Valley lies in the little-known Insgaiti or Wesm Mountains, which lie between the Braldu and the Shaksgam rivers. The main peak of this subrange is the Crown (7,295m).

In September 2017, Agnieszka Garus-Saramak, Andrzej Makaran, Justyna Markiewicz, and Mariusz Saramak (Poland) traveled by vehicle from Kasghar in China, via Khunjerab Pass and Sost, to Shimshal, then trekked over Shimshal Pass to the Braldu. They eventually established base camp at 4,520m below the snout of the Shim Dur Glacier.

By the 24th, they were all camped at 5,260m in a side glacier northeast of the Shim Dur. On the 27th, all four climbed snow slopes up to 45° to reach the summit of the peak at the head of this side glacier, which they named Okheree Sar (6,119m on the China-Pakistan border map; 6,132m indicated by two altimeters; 36°18'22.86"N, 75°57'19.34"E). The excellent panorama included the highest summit above the Shim Dur Glacier, which they named Shim Dur Sar (6,495m).

The party confirmed the best time for mountaineers to visit this area is late September and October. Conditions were relatively good; there were only three nights and one day of minor snowfall during their stay.

– JERZY WALA, *TRANSLATED BY MONIKA HARTMAN AND JANUSZ MAJER, POLAND*

BIACHERAHI NORTH TOWER, SKI DESCENT

IN APRIL 2018, a team of eight, mostly French, did a 150km ski tour up the Nobande Sobande Glacier, across the Skam La (5,600m), and down to Snow Lake and the Biafo Glacier. On April 24, Hélias Millerioux and Léo Taillefer (both from France) skied from the summit of Biacherahi North Tower (ca 5,880m), making one short rappel to enter the extremely steep east face. Yannick Graziani (France) and Zak Mills (USA) downclimbed from the summit to the rappel point, and then all four descended the east face, the three French on skis and Mills on a snowboard. The adventure was documented in an excellent film, *Zabardast,* available online.

– *INFORMATION FROM* HÉLIAS MILLERIOUX, *FRANCE*

TRANGO II, BASE CAMP SLABS, MANGO TANGO

CHILEANS NICO GUTIÉRREZ, Sebastián Rojas, Diego Saez, and Diego Señoret spent July at Trango Base Camp. They achieved their main goal, the first Chilean ascent of Eternal Flame on Trango Tower, and also climbed a probable new route on the Base Camp Slabs, the area of rock that lies directly behind the moraine lake and forms a lower feature of Trango II. Several routes climb this face, including the first, Oceano Trango (300m, 6a+, 2006), which has been repeated many times.

The four Chileans spent three days equipping the first eight pitches of their line before acclimatizing for and climbing Eternal Flame. Just prior to leaving the area, they added a further seven pitches to their Base Camp Slabs route for a total of 750m of climbing with difficulties up to 5.11b. They named it Mango Trango; it probably shares a little common ground with Piranski Zaliv (2006) in the upper section. ▣

– *INFORMATION PROVIDED BY* **DIEGO SAEZ**, *CHILE*

MUZTAGH TOWER, BLACK TOOTH, SOUTHEAST RIDGE AND TRAVERSE

PHILIPP BRUGGER, MARTIN Sieberer (both from Austria), and I trekked up the Baltoro Glacier in July with the intention of making the first ascent of Muztagh Tower's Black Tooth (6,719m). In 2016, two Germans attempted the ascent via the southeast ridge (*AAJ 2017*) but retreated in bad weather. Impressed, we thought we could at least give it a try.

We established base camp at 4,500m at the entrance to the Younghusband Glacier, and climbed to 5,200m on the lower part of the rocky southeast ridge. It became totally clear that our anticipated route along the crest was impossible. The rock was simply too loose—massive, detached boulders would have killed us. After a bivouac we returned to base camp. A new approach was required.

Although June in the Karakoram had atypically poor weather, with avalanches that killed pack animals and stranded porters, July had fantastic weather but with rapidly escalating temperatures. There was no time to lose! We set off on July 19 to find a way through the Dre Glacier below the south face, eventually following the far right side, the same route used by the French expedition that in 1956 made the second ascent of Muztagh Tower, via the upper southeast ridge, a route still unrepeated. A steep 20m pitch of black ice (WI5+) led to easy but crevassed terrain, which we followed to below the south face of the Tooth. On the way down from this reconnaissance, we left a rope fixed on the steep section.

Although not yet sufficiently acclimatized, we were prompted by a good forecast to take only one rest day and leave base camp on July 21, before the next spell of bad weather arrived. Regaining our high point, we continued up the south face, which, after the first steep snowfield, became more and more rocky (M4+). By midday, steep wet snow and the high temperature forced us to bivouac. Next day we went all the way down to base camp to reconsider.

The forecast was for increasing cloud over the next four days and then a long period of snowfall. Again, we rested only one day in base camp, then started back up, planning to climb at night and early morning, resting during the day. Philipp, who had not been to high altitudes previously, decided to remain behind.

At 1 a.m. on the 24th, we woke and had a meager breakfast. Climbing through the night, we made 1,200m of ascent to our previous bivouac spot, arriving at 8 a.m. We opted to stay here until it was light enough to see on the following morning.

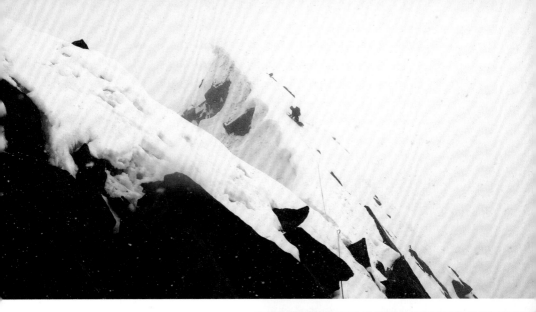

Starting out unroped on the 25th, we climbed mixed ground (M4+ maximum) and reached the upper snowfield at dawn. Damn! It was steeper than expected. With Martin in the lead, we continued simul-climbing for 250m up 55–60° ice of poor quality. We finally reached the upper ridge at 8:30 a.m., but we were too tired to continue. Also, we realized that our planned descent, rappelling the face from Abalakov anchors, was now out of the question, due to the unstable ice. We downclimbed the ridge for 60m to find a small but flat bivouac site. Realizing we would have to traverse the summit, we decided that next day we would abandon the tent and everything else we could spare, in order to save weight.

We began shortly after 4 a.m. on July 26. A steep section of M4+ led to a rock tower, which we climbed directly at M5. The angle eased, but the snow remained bad, and we had to pitch all the way to the summit, where we arrived at 1 p.m. By this time it had already been snowing several hours. We

[Top] **Climbing through bad weather on summit day on the Black Tooth.** [Bottom] **Muztagh Tower (7,284m, left) and its southeast ridge, showing the 2019 route up the Black Tooth (6,719m). To descend, Messner and Sieberer dropped to the hidden col between the Tooth and Muztagh Tower, descended to the right end of the conspicuous serac barrier, then continued down to the glacier. In 2016, Felix Berg and Matthias Konig reached the lower southeast ridge from the opposite side and climbed to the small tower (6,000m) visible at the top of the rock section.** *Simon Messner (both photos)*

traversed the summit slopes, then rappelled to the col between the Tooth and Muztagh Tower. From here we rappelled straight down the south face in thick mist. After the sixth rappel there was a brief clearing and we saw we were on the right route. [*From the col, the pair more or less descended the line of the original French route.*] Downclimbing and rappelling, ropes, gloves, and clothes now frozen, we reached a point at sunset where we had just one small rock peg left for an anchor. Martin drove it into a rock embedded in the snow. I was too tired to check its placement and just clipped myself in. The moment Martin started to rappel, I felt a hard pull on my harness.

The piton had pulled, nearly taking us both down. "Damn! We need to stay concentrated!" I said, knowing he was well aware of this.

We reached the foot of the face absolutely exhausted, and after melting snow to give our bodies much-needed liquid, we continued toward base camp, which we didn't reach until 3 a.m. the following morning. We had been lucky: The weather turned bad for days. On the morning of the 28th we left camp in the rain, all our gear still wet. But we were safe now—all we had to do was walk. 📷

– SIMON MESSNER, *ITALY*

GASHERBRUM VII, FIRST ASCENT AND SKI DESCENT

Foreshortened view of the northeast face of Gasherbrum VII (6,995m), seen from the upper southwest arm of the Gasherbrum Glacier, showing the ascent and ski descent route. *Cala Cimenti*

AFTER MY PARTIAL ski descent of Nanga Parbat in early July (*see p.273*), I traveled to Skardu to meet Francesco Cassardo. Our plan was to make the first ascent of Gasherbrum VII (6,955m) via the northeast face and then ski down. [*Editor's Note: Gasherbrum VII, formerly Gasherbrum V Northwest 2 or Corno d'Angolo, was the only unclimbed Gasherbrum. It sits on the ridge between Gasherbrums IV and V, at the head of the southwestern branch of the Gasherbrum Glacier.*]

Francesco and I arrived at the standard Gasherbrum base camp on July 16, and on the 19th left to establish Camp 1 at 6,100m, below the face. We agreed to try for the summit the next day. We set off in beautiful weather, with little wind, using skins to the first bergschrund, then carrying our skis. The slope was good névé [*reported to be nearly 60°*], and we climbed unroped—this part of the ski descent would be really exciting. I was faster than Francesco from the start, but we kept in sight.

After around 500m, I was level with the top of a large serac barrier to the left, and decided to traverse over the top of it to reach a couloir through the second bergschrund on the left side of the face. Before reaching the couloir, I decided to climb straight up a steep snow wall, but it wasn't the good snow I expected; there was only 1cm of snow over blue ice. I climbed around 20m of 70°, after which the angle eased and I was on skiable snow again. I shouted to Francesco to take the snow couloir to the left, which would be safer. It was now easy but tiring till just below the top, where a 50m tight, icy couloir led to the summit.

After 40 minutes on top, I started the descent on skis. The tight couloir was really scary, but once through the angle eased to about 50° or so, and the face opened up. I headed for the snow couloir through the second bergschrund, jumped it, and met Francesco. I had a talk with him about the upper part and suggested that if he was not 100 percent sure, he shouldn't try to ski, but instead downclimb with crampons. I continued down, skiing the relaxing traverse above the big serac and then turning right onto the 60° slope. Fortunately, it is wide and the snow was good. I was skiing better than ever in my life and was able to enjoy it, though there was no margin for error.

Back on the glacier, I turned to watch Francesco, who had not passed the bergschrund and was starting to ski down. When he made the first turn onto the 60° slope, he fell, lost his skis, and began to slide. He fell 500m, losing his rucksack and many of his clothes. He came to a halt at 6,300m. I expected the worst when I reached his motionless body, but amazingly he had survived. He was conscious but in a bad way. I used my satellite phone to call for an urgent rescue and then dug a snow cave, went back to Camp 1, and brought up sleeping bags.

The next morning, rescue helicopters were busy on a mission around Broad Peak, and by the time they were free, the weather had become too warm and unstable to reach us. Fortunately, in Gasherbrum base camp at the time were Janusz Adamski, Don Bowie, Denis Urubko, and Jaroslaw Zdanowich. They decided to take the matter into their own hands. By nightfall they had reached us. Deciding a helicopter evacuation would be

Looking down the upper northeast face of Gasherbrum VII during the ski descent. Far below is Francesco Cassardo, who is still climbing. *Cala Cimenti*

easier if we could get Francesco to a lower spot, we built a rudimentary stretcher and dragged him down to 6,100m. At this point we took a gamble and continued through the night, reaching Gasherbrum II's Camp 1 at around 5,900m. The following morning a helicopter took Francesco to Skardu Military Hospital. He had several fractures and damaged ligaments in one knee, as well as severe frostbite on the hands; he eventually lost the first phalanx from all fingers and thumbs. 📷

– CALA CIMENTI, *ITALY*

GASHERBRUM II, COMPLETE SOUTHWEST FACE

I HAD DREAMED about climbing this line since 2001. At that time I planned to climb the rock buttress to the left of the couloir: It would be more technical but would avoid the threat of serac fall. In 2019, moving quickly up the snow and ice of the couloir was more attractive. My girlfriend, Maria Cardell, would have been the perfect partner, but during the trek to base camp she fell, injured her back, and spent the next month and a half in great pain. I had to act alone.

The right equipment is crucial for a high altitude ascent—minimal yet workable. I took two axes, a harness, two ice screws, 20m of 4mm cord, two carabiners, a descender and carabiner, one carbon ski pole, headlamp, goggles, and rucksack. I had minimal clothing and took only two energy bars and four gels. I approached on snowshoes and left them near the foot of the normal route, to be collected during my descent.

I left Camp 1 (ca 5,900m) at 7 p.m. on July 31 and crossed the bergschrund (6,100m) below the couloir at 8:40 p.m. The sun hit the rock barrier below the seracs at around 4:30 a.m., just as I was approaching it. I was on the plateau below the upper triangular face at 11 a.m., then climbed more or less directly to reach the 8,034m summit at 8:40 p.m. I descended the normal route through the night, arriving back at Camp 1 at around 9 a.m. on the August 2. [*Urubko had already climbed the normal route 12 days earlier for acclimatization. In between, he had taken part in several rescues at altitude.*]

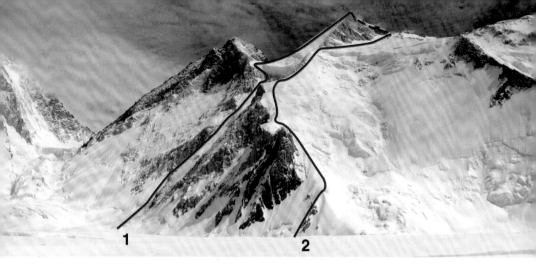

Gasherbrum II from the south showing the line of (1) Honeymoon (Urubko, solo, 2019, 1,935 meters of climbing above the bergschrund). (2) The normal route (southwest ridge, 1956). To the right is the summit of Gasherbrum II East, while to the left is Gasherbrum III and, farther left, the flank of Gasherbrum IV. *Denis Urubko*

The difficulties on this line centered around the sustained frontpointing on ice slopes and passing the rock barrier—120m of unroped climbing that I felt to be quite risky. Due to recent snowfall, there was much deep snow above 7,000m, and avalanche risk was real. It was hard work opening the trail: I lost a lot of power and spent a long time. I called the route Honeymoon (1,935m from the bergschrund, TD WI3 M6).

I did a number of interesting routes on 8,000m peaks during the period of my life when I lived in Kazakhstan, but then came emigration, work, troubles, and I found myself being influenced far too much by the opinions of other people. I was not able to concentrate completely on my own personal "art." Now I have managed to realize my idea of freedom with a new line on Gasherbrum II. It is possible to be true to oneself.

– DENIS URUBKO, *RUSSIA-POLAND*

KARAKORAM / MASHERBRUM MOUNTAINS

PEAK 6,410M (LILIGO PEAK), ATTEMPT AND TRAGEDY

IN JUNE A three-member Chinese team planned to make the first ascent of Peak 6,410m at the southeastern head of the Liligo Glacier. This sharp, attractive summit is sometimes called Liligo Peak, although several other mountains above the glacier also are referred to by this name. Success would have meant the first Chinese ascent of a virgin peak in Pakistan. (It is not known if this summit had been attempted prior to 2019.) Unfortunately, the two climbers who left to attempt the peak never returned.

While Ho Yui Keung remained in camp on the Liligo Glacier, Ng Ka-Kit and Li Haoxin appear to have climbed the north face of Peak 6,410m to reach the west-southwest ridge. They were in contact with base camp on June 14, their last reported position being at around 6,000m. The following morning they contacted Ho, who was in advanced base, and that afternoon they were spotted at between 5,800m and 5,900m.

When the two had not returned to base camp by the 17th, an alarm was issued through the Chinese embassy. Pakistan Army helicopters picked up the third climber, flew up the Liligo Glacier, and searched for the next two days without success. They did spot a sleeping bag (and possibly part of a tent) on the glacier at around 5,200m, which Ho confirmed belonged to one of his two missing friends. Avalanches then buried the site, preventing recovery until early August. 🗎 📷

– INFORMATION FROM **XIA ZHONGMING**, *GERMANY, AND* **SHAMYL SHARAFAT ALI**, *FRANCE*

HONBORO MASSIF, BONDIT PEAK, NORTHEAST SPUR ATTEMPT

BONDIT PEAK (A.K.A. Bondid) is a prominent mountain of a little less than 6,000m near the head of the Bondit Glacier, west of the Hushe Valley and southeast of Honboro (6,459m). Maps and satellite imagery of this region are poor, and there is very little information available. Irena Mrak reported briefly on Bondit in *AAJ 2010.* (Mrak referred to it as Muntin Peak.)

Elliot Bowie, Kadin Vincent (both New Zealand), Diarmuid Murphy (Ireland), and I attempted the northeast spur of Bondit from a base camp at around 4,400m on the last green meadow before the lower Bondit Glacier. Our first attempt was via the icefall, which proved too heavily crevassed. We than attempted to climb directly from the base of the north spur. While this may prove a feasible route, it is well-defended by numerous seracs. After August 10, when it started raining on the exact day our local friend Muhammed Ibrahim had predicted, any further attempts became suicidal. We switched our attention to a minor peak of around 5,600m further west, but serious avalanches forced us to abandon the attempt at around 5,300m.

The surrounding country offers several little-known glaciers and superb unclimbed peaks, many around 6,000m. Future parties would be wise to visit earlier—late June and July were recommended locally. 🗎 📷 🔍

– NATHAN DAHLBERG, NEW ZEALAND

KARAKORAM / TAGAS GROUP – KHANE VALLEY

HASHO PEAK II, TANGRA TOWER, AND THUMB SOUTH PEAK

IN MID-JULY, THE Russian team of Anton Ivanov, Konstantin Markevich, Nikolai Matyushin, Marina Popova, Denis Prokofiev, Valery Semenov, and Denis Sushko arrived in the Khane Valley, establishing base camp south of Tangra Tower at around 4,450m.

At first the whole team planned to make the first ascent of remote Hasho Peak II (6,080m), the highest peak in the valley, at the head of the Khane Glacier. Using this for acclimatization, they then planned to attempt lower technical climbs. However, once the three Krasnoyarsk climbers— Matyushin, Popova, and Prokofiev—saw their main goal, the unclimbed southeast face of Tangra Tower, they decided to get straight on it.

Base camp below the Khane Glacier, with stupendous Tangra Tower dominant to the northeast and the Thumb to its right. *Konstantin Markevich Collection*

The Krasnoyarsk Route on the southeast face of Tangra Tower (5,820 meters). The route is about 800 meters high. The couloir at far right was climbed to reach the southwest ridge of the Thumb, which was followed to the 5,780-meter south peak (off picture to the right). *Konstantin Markevich Collection*

The others headed up the Khane Glacier for Hasho Peak II, the approach to which took two days. There is a difficult icefall, and during acclimatization and reconnaissance the party outflanked this on a rock buttress, where they found difficulties up to 6b and A3, and fixed 100m of rope. They made camp on the upper glacier plateau at around 5,400m.

From there, on July 23, Ivanov, Markevich, and Sushko climbed snow slopes of 50–60° on the west flank of the mountain to reach the south-southeast ridge, which they followed to the summit. The ascent took four and a half hours, and the route was rated Russian 5A. (*See photo at right.*)

After this came a spell of poor weather, and Ivanov went home. It wasn't until August 5 that Markevich, Semenov, and Sushko achieved their second objective, the first ascent of the south peak (5,780m) of the Thumb. (The main summit of the Thumb is 5,811m). The three climbed the southeast couloir (50–60° snow) to reach a col on the southwest ridge at 5,550m. From there, seven long pitches of rock and mixed on the steep crest led to the summit. This section was climbed free at 6b+ and M6, and the overall grade of the 640m route was Russian 5B.

In the meantime, the Krasnoyarsk team had made the first ascent of Tangra Tower (5,820m), arriving on the summit on August 2. Matyushin, Popova, and Prokofiev started to the right of the line attempted by a British-Canadian team (*AAJ 2016*), crossed through it, then climbed well left of the large corner in the center of the face. (This corner was followed to about half height by the British-Canadian team.)

The three Russians ascended the 800m wall (1,200m of climbing) in three days, with a further day needed for the descent via their line. They used a portaledge, hauling the ledge to a new site each day as they moved continuously up the wall. The final stretch along the summit ridge was something of a trial, with deep loose snow (often to the waist) and even looser rock, which resulted in a fall onto a ledge, fortunately with only bad bruising. The difficulties had been sustained: 25 pitches, overall 6B, 6c+/7a A4. The team considers the wall to be the most attractive and biggest in the area. 📷 🔍

– *INFORMATION PROVIDED BY* **KONSTANTIN MARKEVICH**, *RUSSIA*

BRAKK NA BRAKK, BRAKK TRUC, AND RIDAKH RIDGE

Tomeu Rubí and Pep Roig (Spain), Derek Watson (U.K.), and I reached the our base camp at 4,470m, near the start of the Khane Glacier, in two days from Khane village, with a night at Boulder Camp (4,000m).

On August 4 and 5, we climbed a peak named Brakk Na Brakk (5,872m) according to some locals, though it was named Agil by Koreans in 2001 and has this name on Jerzy Wala's map of the area. It stands opposite Tangra Tower in the Second Khane Cwm.

On the first day we climbed to a bivouac on the southwest side of the peak, from which Tomeu and Derek climbed partway up a 300m rock wall leading to the upper glacier, leaving three ropes in place. Next day we left at 4:30 a.m., reached our high point, and continued for a few more pitches, one of which, the crux, was 6c A2. After 200m of easy but exposed mixed climbing, we reached a snow ramp leading to a sort of col, from which a gully on the

[Top] Brakk Na Brakk from base camp to the southwest. The first ascent climbed to the snowfield below steep walls on the left, then moved around right onto the south face, where a couloir led to the summit. *Tomeu Rubí* [Bottom] From upper First Khane Cwm: (1) The west face and south-southeast ridge of Hasho Peak II (Russian, 2019). (2) The southwest face and southeast ridge of Brakk Truc (Spanish-U.K., 2019). *Cati Lladó*

south face headed up to the gap between the north and south summits. Climbing this (up to 60°—we wished we'd brought a second axe), we could see the north top was higher, and we reached it at 4 p.m. We arrived back at our bivouac after midnight and a 20-hour day. The west face of this peak was attempted by Koreans from 2001 to 2003; we saw an old belay at the start of the headwall.

On the 8th, after having only one day's rest, as poor weather was predicted in just a few days, Tomeu, Derek, and I (Pep was ill) set off for the head of the glacier and the First Khane Cwm. Reaching the cwm was difficult, but a Russian team (*see report above*) had left fixed ropes on the rock buttress alongside the icefall, easing the way. Two peaks south of Hasho Peak II appeared straightforward, and we decided on the southerly one. We camped at 5,100m and set off before 5 a.m. The ascent was enjoyable: a 40° snow ramp on the southwest face to reach the southeast ridge, and a few easy meters of rock at the top. We called the peak Brakk Truc (5,672m), after the Spanish card game Truc. (It also means "six" in Balti.) It took only three hours from high camp.

During the approach to base camp, we had spotted a ridge on the right side of the north face of Peak 222.1 on the 2012 Wala map (*see AAJ 2016*). The peak is a subsidiary summit to the northwest of Grey Tower (Peak 222, 5,435m, climbed in 2012 by Bulgarians via the east ridge). The ridge we were eyeing exited onto the west ridge of Peak 222.1. Tomeu, Derek, and I left base camp at 5 a.m., descended 400m of the Khane Valley, and in around an hour were on the spur. Approximately 20 pitches later, we reached the characteristic "horns" on the west ridge and ended our climb there at 3:30 p.m. We made two rappels to reach a wide, steep couloir; the descent was infernal, with much loose rock. Sixteen hours after our departure, we regained base camp. We named the route Ridakh Ridge (1,000m, 6a+). 📷

– CATI LLADÓ, *SPAIN*

INDIA

IN A DAY, NEARLY ALL FREE
BOLD TACTICS ON BHAGIRATHI IV'S WEST FACE

BY MATTEO DELLA BORDELLA, *ITALY*

DESPITE THE MANY attempts to climb the west face of Bhagirathi IV (6,193m) in the Gangotri group of the Garhwal Himalaya, it was lack of good information that fueled my curiosity. In 2015, Luca Schiera, Matteo De Zaiacomo, and I made an attempt at the first ascent. It was a debacle. We quickly understood that a west face at 5,500m means -10°C until noon, and when the blood finally returned to our hands and feet, we were subjected to the intense whistle of stonefall. We were beaten after only two and a half pitches.

On our second attempt that year we tried a line 50m further right. This time we were allowed three full days of climbing, bivouacking in a portaledge for two nights, before starting up the final 200-meter-high schist band. We

Matteo Della Bordella on the 60m traverse that was the key to climbing the west face of Bhagirathi IV. Bhagirathi II is visible behind. *Matteo Della Bordella Collection*

Cavalli Bardati (800m, 7b A0), the first route up the west face of Bhagirathi IV, in icy condition. In 2015, the Italians attempted to climb directly above the first part of this line, stopping in the overhanging schist band. In 2019, they attempted a direct line on the left for three days but retreated at a blank corner. For their successful one-day ascent, the leftward traverse 10 pitches up the 2015 line proved to be the key. *Matteo Della Bordella*

had underestimated both the danger and difficulty of this section. Exhausted from fatigue and altitude, we bailed. However, during the descent we discovered a line that might just permit us to climb this wall: a long leftward traverse that would allow us to cross the schist band where it was much shorter. The weather then deteriorated, allowing no further attempts (*AAJ 2016*).

We decided to return in 2019. I wanted to see whether as alpinists we had made progress in the intervening years, or if our abilities had simply remained unchanged.

Our acclimatization consisted of bringing all our climbing equipment and the portaledge to the foot of the wall at 5,400m, then climbing Bhagirathi II (6,512m) via the standard route from the east. On September 3 we had moved up to advanced base camp at 5,000m, preparing for the climb. It was a hot day. We could not explain how four years earlier we had been so cold in this same spot. Suddenly a cry: "Look!" I rushed from the tent to see car-size blocks crashing down the line we proposed to start climbing the next day. Ten minutes later the show was repeated. With the lowest of moral, we returned to base camp.

Eleven days passed, during which we made a three-day attempt on a more direct, sheltered line, only to be brought to a halt by a totally blank corner. We carried down all our gear and declared the expedition over. Then an idea, possibly insane, crept into my mind. I asked the guys whether we could try a speed ascent, in one day, with only the basic gear. If we moved fast and chose a cold day, the rockfall risk would be minimized. It seemed impossible, but we decided to give it a try.

Leaving advanced base at midnight, we started up our 2015 line at 3 a.m. on the 14th, in temperatures of -10°C, with Luca in the lead. After six long pitches it was my turn. The climbing sucked: The beautiful, vertical to overhanging, 6c to 7a cracks were covered with dust and debris from the rockfall. After 10 pitches we left our old line and made the 60m leftward traverse (with a pendulum) that we had spotted in 2015. This took us outside the rockfall area into clean granite. Matteo followed fast with our one heavy sack, sacrificing himself for the team effort.

A few pitches above, I handed the lead to Luca for the icing on the cake: the last section of good granite before two pitches of friable schist. It was already dark as he climbed the second of these pitches. Then came the final snow slope, about 200m high. We had only carried one lightweight pair of crampons, so, in the lead, I made solid anchors so my friends could jumar. At 11 p.m. we reached the summit, so euphoric that we no longer felt tired. We rested a few hours in our sleeping bags before descending the east face.

We named our route Cavalli Bardati (800m, 7b A0). We aided past the 7b pitch that Luca had freed back in 2015 but otherwise used only two points of aid. No bolts were placed.

Rushad Nanavatty climbing across the east flank of the south ridge of Menthosa during the second day of a weeklong traverse of the mountain. *Spencer Gray*

MENTHOSA
FIRST ASCENT OF SOUTH RIDGE AND EIGHT-KILOMETER TRAVERSE

BY SPENCER GRAY, *USA*

RUSHAD NANAVATTY, ALEX Marine, and I (all from the USA) had come to India to climb an objective in Ladakh, within the state of Jammu and Kashmir. The day we landed in Delhi, the Indian government scrapped the state's special constitutional status, imposed a lockdown, and revoked our climbing permit. We were directed to find a new objective in another state. On the strength of a photograph of its impressive southeast pillar, a location near the outer limit of the monsoon, and a bedrock map that suggested the presence of granite along a large fault, we picked Menthosa (6,443m) in Himachal Pradesh.

Menthosa is downstream from the well-known granite walls of the Miyar Valley, which have received sustained attention from climbers for over 25 years. It was first climbed in 1970 via the east-northeast ridge, by a British military team, and is regularly guided via a variation of the first-ascent route. Our base camp (4,470m) was located in an alluvial side valley full of pink stalks of fleeceflower and mats of rock jasmine, blue forget-me-nots, and occasional spiny blue and violet poppies.

Upon arriving, we faced a week of unusually heavy monsoon storms that deposited a meter of wet snow on the upper mountain and snapped the poles of our cook tent. The Indian meteorology agency reported that, at lower elevations, this storm caused the highest recorded rainfall (36cm in one location) for a 24-hour period in the state of Himachal Pradesh. Landslides and floods killed scores of people and washed out hundreds of roads. Dorje, our cook, who comes from a long line of local farmers, spoke of how the changing climate had made Lahaul's summer

[Top] **Menthosa** from the east-southeast showing the American route up the south ridge. The route passes behind the prominent southeast pillar, partially hidden in clouds. The climbers' descent, and the standard route up the mountain, follows snow slopes on the right side of the image. [Bottom] **Rushad Nanavatty** traversing the west flank of Menthosa's upper south ridge during the first ascent of the ridge. *Spencer Gray*

weather increasingly wet and unpredictable. Throughout our expedition, snow stability and rockfall associated with snowmelt remained our biggest concerns.

Rushad and I left base camp early on August 22. (Unfortunately, Alex had experienced symptoms of serious altitude sickness and had already left the area.) We reached the base of the south ridge at dawn. A hot morning of wallowing uphill through deep snow and a jumbled icefall led to a campsite on a roomy saddle on the south ridge (5,600m).

Three days of tricky pitched-out mixed climbing followed, first on the east face under a series of prominent gendarmes, then traversing along the western aspect of the south ridge. On our third night we had an open, hanging bivouac at 6,220m, when fog obscured the way forward. The following evening, as we climbed perfect névé and ice to a bivouac spot just below the summit, a lightning storm in the foothills illuminated the glacier beneath us, flashing neon white between the Milky Way above and a cloud inversion below.

We summited on the morning of August 26, then spent another day on the summit ridge waiting for a white-out to clear. Next morning, the sunlit peaks of Zanskar and Kishtwar shone along the rim of a steely overcast sky as we started our descent, spending one long day navigating the glaciated east-northeast ridge route back to base camp. As far as we know, this was the first traverse (more than 8km) of the mountain.

Future parties may be drawn, like we were, to Menthosa's unclimbed southeast pillar, jutting out slightly east of the south ridge proper. This feature is cleaved diagonally by a dike across its south face, but this attractive weakness can only be accessed after crossing about 300 vertical meters of loose rock at its base. In the center of the pillar, the dike also crosses several sections of overhung flakes arranged like guillotines. The heavy snowfall and variable rock quality eliminated the southeast pillar as a reasonable objective for us, but it likely has sections of worthwhile granitic rock.

We thank the Indian Mountaineering Foundation, Aftab Kaushik, Chewang Motup, Fateh Singh Akoi, Harish Kapadia, Karan Singh, Kaushal Desai, Raj Kumar, and Yangdu Gombu for their assistance.

SUMMARY: *First ascent of south ridge of Menthosa (6,443m) and descent by the east-northeast ridge, August 22–27, 2019. The vertical gain was 1,350m, and the route was graded ED2 WI4 M6.* 🖸

EAST KARAKORAM

RONGDO VALLEY, PAST ASCENTS AND POTENTIAL

The beautiful Rongdo Valley is located in Nubra and administratively belongs to Ladakh (recently and controversially separated from the state of Jammu and Kashmir). Many of its mountains exceed 6,000m, but as Rongdo is close to the border with China, gaining approval from the Indian Mountaineering Foundation can be challenging. Until now, 12 expeditions have passed through or climbed in Rongdo, and 16 peaks have been climbed, but there are still many unclimbed peaks and even unexplored areas.

With several expedition leaders' input, I have prepared a 42-page historical report that collates all previous ascents and also identifies some interesting unclimbed peaks. It can be downloaded at the AAJ website: publications.americanalpineclub.org.

– KEITH GOFFIN, *GERMANY*

RONGDO VALLEY, SA'I LHAMO, NORTHWEST RIDGE

In the summer of 2016, Pascal Hottiaux, Alain Pozo, Cyril Renailler, and I visited the Rongdo Valley, which extends to the northeast of Rongdo village and the Shyok River. Our first problem was reconstructing the path into the valley, which had been washed away by flooding above the village. We acclimatized in the area called Thipti, where we did a lot of rock climbing and bouldering. The Rongdo Valley is home to many granite walls, where numerous routes could be opened (*see report below*).

On the northwest ridge of Sa'i Lhamo, with (A) Karpo Kangri (6,535m), (B) Argan Kangri (6,789m), (C) Peak 6,420m, and (D) Gazgazri (6,150m) in the back. *Cyril Renailler*

We established base camp at 4,850m above some hot springs and explored different valleys to find an aesthetic line that suited our abilities. The northwest ridge of Sa'i Lhamo ("Earth Goddess," 6,030m according to the first ascensionsts) fitted the criteria, and we set up advanced base at 5,250m on a grassy shoulder with sumptuous views of the upper Rongdo Valley and Sagtogpa Glacier.

We climbed the mountain on July 25 (Alain's 62nd birthday) in a 19-hour trip from advanced base. There were no real difficulties, but the distance was deceptive, as we had to travel around the entire mountain to reach the route. After gaining the 5,800m col at the start of the northwest ridge, we followed the crest—easy at first, then more exposed—to an airy passage beneath cornices on the east flank. A spectacular, elegant ridge then led to the summit, on which our altimeter recorded 6,038m. This is likely to be the first ascent of this route, as the original ascensionists, the 2013 Indian Air Force Expedition (*AAJ 2014*), climbed the southwest ridge.

– LAURENT LAFFORGUE, *FRANCE*

RONGDO VALLEY, ROCK CLIMBING

MOTIVATED BY JOIE Seagram's quote in *AAJ 2013* ("...we were once again astounded by solid-looking rock walls several hundred meters high on both sides of the valley—a rock climbers' paradise") and armed with great local information from Andy Selters, we visited the Rongdo Valley in July. The villagers in Rongdo were extremely friendly and helpful; it was a joy to spend time with them.

There is indeed a lot of granite in the central part of the valley, although closer inspection revealed large expanses of exfoliated arches and flakes, making climbing less than perfect. Trying to avoid said loose rock, we established two fine four-pitch routes up a solid wall on the right side of the canyon, left of a prominent waterfall, about 90 minutes' walk above the summer herding village of Daksa (a.k.a. Fatha, after the nearby gompa). Both routes were 5.10. We ended them partway up the cliff where we encountered steep, exfoliated rock.

– TODD AND DONETTE SWAIN, *USA*

LADAKH

CHOMOTANG, SOUTH-SOUTHWEST TOP, SOUTH FLANK

IN AUGUST 2006, Giulia Di Fiore, Betta Preziosi, Fabiano Ventura, and I made a 13-day trek from Padam to Lamayuru. Marked on our poor-quality map was an unnamed summit of over 6,000m. It was only a short detour from our planned itinerary, so we decided to make an attempt. We left the main trekking route toward Hanupata and followed the valley southwest, camping to the southeast of the mountain at 4,860m. On August 27, Betta, Fabiano, and I set off to climb the south face. We reached the south glacier at around 5,550m and kept to the right edge, climbing snow slopes up to 50° until they eased and led to the ridge. In late morning we reached a rocky top on the south-southwest shoulder of the mountain at 5,882m GPS. A snow ridge led toward the main summit, but we were quickly covered in cloud and didn't feel it was wise to continue. [*See this report at the AAJ website for useful historical and geographical background on the group.*]

– ANDREA BOLLATI, *ITALY*

The Chomotang Group from the southwest. (A) Thorchuk II. (B) Thorchuk I. (C) Chomotang III (Chomotang southwest). (D) Chomotang I. (E) Chomotang south-southwest top, reached in 2006 by the obvious glacier. (F) Chomotang II. *Laurent Lafforgue*

CHOMOTANG GROUP, VARIOUS ASCENTS

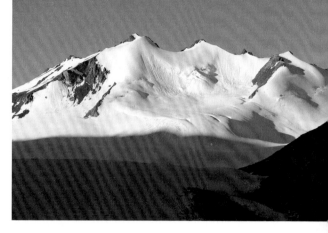

The north face of Sum Nomo Kangri. The French climbed near the left skyline to reach the west top. *Laurent Lafforgue*

THE COMBINATION OF a virtual tour on Google Earth, suggesting the existence of several straightforward summits, and the Chomotang report in AAJ 2016 showing the picture of a beautiful, unnamed snowy summit of 5,720m, led Fabrice le Bobinec and me to visit the Spang Nala in August. This is the valley that ascends southwest beneath the Chomotang Group from just west of the Sirsir La. Using the road from Hanupata, a vehicle dropped us near the bridge crossing the Spang Nala at 4,500m. From there we walked southwest up the valley, with the food and gear necessary for 15 days, to a base camp at 4,900m, where the valley divides into two glaciated arms. We chose to explore the western glacier, and on August 20 we climbed the most elegant summit, which we named Spang Nala Kangri (5,750m, 34°1'4.16"N, 76°41'32.81"E). It lies on the southern rim of the Spang Nala Glacier and offered little in the way of difficulties besides several seracs and large crevasses.

On August 22, we climbed the west face of the "5,720m" peak featured in AAJ 2016. It lies on the watershed ridge between the two Spang Nala glacier basins. We named it Spang Nala Dome, and the altimeter recorded 5,850m. Two days later we reached the western top (5,700m, approximately 34°1'45.47"N, 76°40'40.01"E) of an elegant peak that we named Sum Nomo Kangri ("Three Sisters" in Ladakhi). An east-west crossing of all three summits would be spectacular. Earlier in the season, Spang Nala Kangri and Spang Nala Dome would be perfect on skis.

In September, I returned to the Spang Nala with Amandine Gau and Camille Turries. We climbed the main summit of Chomotang (6,065m) by the glacier that rises below the northwest face of the mountain, then the west slope. [*This is likely different from the Australian route climbed in 2015.*] The direct exit to the summit, all on ice, was fairly sustained at 55–60°. For a more aesthetic and less exposed route, it would be preferable to continue up the glacier and climb the south ridge via Chomotang III.

On September 15, we ended our stay by climbing a small, unnamed summit, which we named Amloca Kangri (5,700m). It is located immediately east of the glacial lake in the eastern arm of the Spang Nala. 🖸

– LAURENT LAFFORGUE, *FRANCE*

NUN AND OTHER PEAKS, SKI DESCENTS

IN MAY 2017, the French skiers Tiphaine Duperier and Boris Langenstein made a very productive visit to the Nun-Kun region. The pair took a jeep from Kargil to Parkachik, where snow still blocked the road, and walked to the village of Tangol at 3,350m. From here they climbed and skied two peaks: a 5,550m summit that was probably a first ascent and a 5,900m peak that overlooks the normal site of camp 1 for Nun.

On the 18th, the pair packed food for a week and headed south up the Parkachik Glacier. On the true right of the glacier, they climbed an attractive peak of 6,050m by the northwest face, then skied the 1,800m face, taking a slightly different line to avoid 55° mixed terrain in the upper half.

On May 24, the two started up the northwest side of Nun (7,135m), encountering waist-deep snow as well as two pitches through a rock band. After nine hours of nonstop climbing, they reached the top, with clouds gathering. Soon after beginning their descent, in order to avoid the rock band they'd ascended, they dropped over a 55° step and then roped up for a 200m traverse to rejoin their ascent track. After barely two hours of descent, they regained their tent.

The first ski descent of Nun was made in by the Swiss skier Sylvain Saudan on June 26, 1977, after an unsuccessful attempt in 1976. These expeditions were part of his buildup to make the first ski descent of an 8,000m peak, which he did on Gasherbrum 1 (8,080m) in 1982. 📄 ⃞

– **DAMIEN GILDEA**, *WITH INFORMATION FROM* **TIPHAINE DUPERIER**, *FRANCE*

RANGTIK VALLEY, CHAREZE RI NORTH, EAST-NORTHEAST RIDGE

(A) Shawa Kangri (5,728m). (B) Chareze Ri and the line of Jullay Temù on the east-northeast ridge. The route reached the north top and continued toward the higher summit (hidden) but stopped about 200m short of it. (C) Peak 6,095m. *Anastasija Davidova*

FOR ABOUT A month starting in mid-August 2018, our Italian group explored the Rangtik Valley, inspired by the extremely useful report by Matija Jošt published in *AAJ 2017*. Our main goal was the first ascent of Peak 6,080m (H2 as designated on the Sakamoto sketch maps) toward the head of the valley.

After a period of acclimatization, Davide Limongi, Federico Martinelli, Enrico Mosetti, Federico Secchi, and I used the first good weather window to climb the obvious ridge bounding the left side of the northeast face. We spent August 30–31 on the route (one bivouac), at first in an ice couloir (70° maximum) and then on top-quality rock (V+ maximum) leading to the north summit at 5,959m.

We attempted to cross the very sharp connecting ridge to the main summit, but after six pitches we were stopped about 200m short when nightfall caught us on the top of a small tower, forcing a retreat down the northwest face and a series of adventurous rappels in the dark.

Our route was 1,000m or 25 pitches to the north top, with difficulties of V+ 70°; one piton was left in place. We named it Jullay Temù ("Hello Bear" in Ladakhi). A discrete family of Himalayan bears had visited the valley during our stay, leaving footprints and making suspicious noises at night. Our base camp staff, Lobsang and Sonam, would like to name the peak Chareze Ri, as this, they explained, is a type of stupa that resembled our summit.

Bad weather prevailed for the second half of our stay, preventing further attempts to reach the main top. Earlier in the trip, Limongi, Martinelli, and Secchi made the second ascent of Rolling Stones on Shawa Kangri (5,728m, Pellissa-Ricart, 2008). ⃞ 🔍

– **LUCA VALLATA**, *ITALY*

HIMACHAL PRADESH

SPITI VALLEY, NEW ICE CLIMBS

KARSTEN DELAP AND I spent the first two weeks of January 2019 ice climbing in the Indian Himalaya, just outside the village of Kaza in the Spiti Valley. The Spiti is a trans-Himalayan desert, near the border with China. It is extremely remote, with only a rudimentary road in and out. During our expedition, we observed snow leopards and a wealth of biodiversity.

The village of Kaza is located at approximately 12,500 feet. For centuries it has been cut off during the winter from the rest of the population of India and its neighbors. Many of the residents in the village of Kaza are forced to leave the region because of the lack of economic opportunity at this time of year.

Our expedition grew out of a chance bar meeting with Karn Kowshik at the Michigan Ice Festival. Karn, who lives in the Himalyan foothills, was one of the organizers of the planned Piti Dharr ice climbing festival in Spiti, and he invited me to participate. We had a mutual desire to help the emerging Indian climbing community in the region with badly needed gear and climbing education.

During our short visit, we established nine first ascents, including Snow Leopard (180m, HWI 7), north of Kaza near the village of Kibber, now the hardest water ice line in the Indian Himalaya. (The Himalayan Water Ice, or HWI, grade system was developed locally and does not correspond directly to Western water ice grades; it also takes into account the high elevation of the climbs.) With the local Spiti climber Bharat Bhushan, we also established Frozen Diesel (HWI 6+) near the village of Tabo. This route is a continuous 360m of ice, ending in a spectacular pillar that is fed by a mineral-rich spring,

Karsten Delap on the black ice of Frozen Diesel (HWI 6+). *Austin Schmitz*

giving the route an unusual black-ice aesthetic. Karn and I established Cowboys in the Mist (150m, HWI 5), and Karsten, Karn, and Prerna Dangi established Stairway to Something (380m, HWI 4).

As a part of our trip, Karsten and I also helped establish a safe teaching crag with bolted anchors, donated climbing equipment, and taught at the Piti Dharr festival.

We passed hundreds of potential new ice routes while traveling in the region and only scratched the surface. Perhaps the most significant accomplishment was helping this emerging climbing community with knowledge and badly needed equipment. Since our departure, the locals have established numerous new routes and held a second year of their ice climbing festival. With responsible practices and input from the local community, ice climbing can offer the people of Spiti Valley much-needed help in the winter months. 📷 ▶

– ARI NOVAK, *USA*

Foreshortened view of Raldang Spire (ca 4,900 meters) above the Baspa Valley. (1) Baba Ji (Austrian route, 2019). (2) American-Belgian-Italian route (2019). (3) American attempt (2015). *Much Mayr*

BASPA VALLEY, RAKCHAM PLATEAU, NEW ROUTES; RALDANG SPIRE, BABA JI

ON THE FIRST day of our 2018 trip to the Baspa Valley in Kinnaur district, Hansjörg Auer and I hiked to the base of Raldang's big wall, and then planned to come back the following year with the right equipment. Things changed tragically in April 2019 (see "In Memoriam," p.348).

In September, Alexander Blümel, Matthias Wurzer, and I returned as mentors for seven members of the Austrian Alpine Club's Young Alpinists Group: Domenic Barbist, Julian Gahbauer, Magdalena Hofinger, Tobias Holzknecht, Peter Mühlburger, Hannes Wechner, and Simon Wolsegger. With these young guns, we opened a few lines on unclimbed peaks above the Rakcham Plateau. These were largely non-glaciated granite peaks that gave good rock climbs.

Various members of the group climbed Tororang (4,770m) via the northeast flank (Austrian Direct, 6b); Hace and Charas (4,850m) via the north flank and west ridge (450m, UIAA VI A1); the Third Pillar of Ray Peak (about 12 pitches, 6b+); and Muppet Peak (5,000m) via Eagle Ridge. [*More details and photos are at the AAJ website.*]

From September 14–17, a six-member group, including myself, climbed the foresummit (ca 5,500m) of Shiva's Tooth, calling it Shiva's Milk Tooth. This involved crossing a pass from the Plateau, rappelling 60m to a glacier on the far side, and making a high camp at 5,000m. From there we climbed a southwest-facing ice slope (200m, 55°) to reach a glacier plateau, traversed this north to reach the 200m-high rocky west ridge, and climbed seven pitches of UIAA IV and V to the foresummit of the peak. We rappelled the route.

After this, we three mentors and Peter Mühlburger had a closer look at Raldang. With the help of locals and porters, we carried heavy loads in two trips—five days in total—to the base of the wall. [*This impressive granite wall, almost 1,000m high, terminates at around 5,250m on the southern flanks of Raldang (5,499m), and was climbed in 2010 by Sílvia Vidal; see AAJ 2011.*] The main wall looked too blank for free climbing, so we opted for a logical, aesthetic line on a spire on the lower left side of the face, which reached a height of around 4,900m. [*This spire is left of the line attempted in 2015 by Quinn Brett, Whitney Clark, and Crystal Davis-Robbins; see AAJ 2016.*]

For two days we fixed lines, returning to our portaledges to sleep. On the third day, October 11, we reached the top of the spire. Most of the anchors have one or two 8mm bolts. In addition to those, we placed three more bolts to protect pitches, and we left most pitons in place. The climbing varied from wide to thin cracks, plus technical face climbing. We named the route Baba Ji (500m, 17 pitches, 7b). 📷 🔍

– **MUCH MAYR,** *AUSTRIA*

BASPA VALLEY, RAKCHAM PLATEAU, VARIOUS ROUTES

A NORTH FACE team visited the Baspa Valley in the autumn, mostly operating from the plateau north of Rakcham village on relatively low granite peaks.

Eneko and Iker Pou (Spain) first climbed a previously virgin peak of 4,670m, which the brothers named Midi d'Ossau after the famous Pyrenean mountain. They summited this via a route named the Latin Brother (560m, 7c+), referring to Hansjörg Auer, with whom they shared two of their best expeditions. Their second route led to a 4,900m summit, Hace and Charas, climbed just 10 days previously by an Austrian team. The Spanish route climbed an elegant and spectacular ridge and was named Miquellink (600m, 6b, 12h), dedicated to the Mallorcean climber Miquel Riera, who is generally credited to have "invented" deep water soling and died while the brothers were in India.

The Pous' last route reached the previously unclimbed summit of a slender needle they named Gorbea (4,560m) after the highest mountain in the Spanish province of Alava. The route was Beti Alavés (340m, 6b+). These three routes were opened in a period of 10 days during October.

The other members of the team comprised Matty Hong (USA), Jacopo Larcher (Italy), and Siebe Vanhee (Belgium), plus photographer Matteo Mocellin. From October 10–13, these four climbed a new route on Raldang Spire: Toby's Shipwreck (450m, 7b). The first ascent of this spire had been made just two days earlier by the Austrian team (*reported above*). The American-Belgian-Italian route lies on the right flank of the pillar, left of the big corner system attempted in 2015 by Americans Quinn Brett, Whitney Clark, and Crystal Davis Robbins. They started one day later than the Austrians and avoided the first steep part of the pillar (approximately five pitches) by coming in from the right and then continuing up a prominent dihedral. 🖼️ ▶

– *INFORMATION PROVIDED BY* **ENEKO POU**, *SPAIN, AND RODOLPHE POPIER, LA CHRONIQUE, FFCAM*

WESTERN GARHWAL / GANGOTRI

BHAGIRATHI III, WEST FACE, ATTEMPT

As PART OF a larger Slovakian expedition to the Gangotri, Jan Smolen and I planned to climb a new route in alpine style on the left side of the west face of Bhagirathi III (6,454m). More specifically, we wanted to climb the wall between the Catalan Pillar and Seed of Madness (immediately right of Bhagirathi IV). We took no portaledge, tent, bolts, or ropes for fixing, just two half ropes, a 6mm tag line, standard climbing gear, bivouac bags, and food for five days. Worried about a change in the weather, we started up the face on September 18 after only a week of acclimatization.

Photos of the face in previous times show a snowfield on the first six pitches, but we only found dry, loose rock. Above, we followed a fine crack beneath an overhanging wall that protected us from rockfall. It was warm and we could climb free up to 7a. Our first bivouac was on a large ledge, where we slept comfortably.

Next morning was surprisingly cold. We tried to climb two hard pitches in rock shoes, but without the sun we were forced to use aid. After that we reached the mixed climbing and in the evening excavated a bivouac in steep ice and névé beneath the final headwall. That night it started to snow, and the wind strengthened. It turned into the worst night of my life.

In the morning, at first we wanted to begin a rappel retreat immediately, as the weather was so bad, but eventually we decided to try the headwall, which was ice and mixed climbing. Our last belay was around 15m below the top, above which there was only snow leading to

The west faces of Bhagirathi IV (left, see also p.292) and Bhagirathi III. (1) Huserka-Smolen attempt (2019). (2, yellow lines) Stairway to Heaven (2004). (3) Scottish Route (1982). *Ondrej Huserka*

the ridge between Bhagirathi IV and III. We almost started to celebrate, but within five minutes all hell broke loose, and we were nearly drowned by snow. Visibility was limited to one meter, and avalanches began to fall. In 15 minutes we were covered with snow and frozen to the bone. We realized that if we were not going to stay there forever, we needed to get down.

Rappelling to the first bivouac site seemed endless, and we barely found it in the mist. We shivered the whole night, but next day managed to rappel to the foot of the face. We had climbed 900m, reaching an altitude of 6,100m, with climbing difficulties to 7a C2 WI5+ M7.

Three other members of our expedition, Martin Krasnansky, Pavel Kratochvil, and Robert Luby, attempted the second ascent of Stairway to Heaven, the more direct variation to the classic Scottish Route on the southwest pillar. After four days, having also reached an altitude of 6,100m, they too were forced to retreat in bad weather. 📷

– ONDREJ HUSERKA, *SLOVAK REPUBLIC*

NOTES ON THE SOUTHWEST PILLAR: *Over the years, the line of the original Scottish Route (Bob Barton and Alan Fyffe, 1982) up the southwest pillar of Bhagirathi III has been increasingly misrepresented on photographs, giving the impression that it climbed much farther to the right from the crest of the pillar. For instance, in AAJ 2005, in which Bavarian Walter Holzer reports his ascent of Stairway to Heaven (1,300m, 7b A2), the two lines are mostly shown a long way apart. In fact there is little difference between the two, and Holzer and Pflugmacher added bolts to terrain that Barton and Fyffe climbed without. As Bob Barton notes, to climb out right as shown would have exposed them to dangerous rockfall, which is why they avoided doing so. The Bavarian team essentially repeated most of the 1982 route with a difficult five- to six-pitch direct variation in the central section.*

SIKKIM

CHOMBU, NORTHEAST SPUR, ATTEMPT

BY OCTOBER 10, Mick Fowler and I were running out of time. We had ruled out the east side (not accessible from our base camp), the west (too dangerous), and the south side (too long) of unclimbed Chombu (6,360m). We had already made one trip to northeast Sikkim, in the spring, hoping to climb the attractive west face, but had been shut down on the West Chombu Glacier by bad weather and unstable snow conditions. This left just the north face, by a line we had identified as the northeast spur. The face looked accessible from a glacier flowing to the Sebu Cho on the Lanchung Valley (east) side of Chombu. The question was whether we could reach this glacier from the west.

A short exploration in bad weather revealed an approach over moraines to a 400m couloir on the watershed ridge between the Lasha Chu valley (west) and Sebu Cho valley. What we could not know was if what we had dubbed the "Fowler Couloir" would give us access to the North Chombu Glacier or if, after climbing the couloir, we would be faced with a problematic descent to a glacier hidden from view.

On October 11, making a predawn start, we trekked up the moraines and boulder fields leading to the Fowler Couloir. We had run out of exploration time—this would be our one

Chombu from the North Chombu Glacier, with the northeast spur on the left and approximate 2019 high point marked (H). *Victor Saunders*

chance to get to grips with the mountain. We were in luck: At the top of the couloir, we stepped off the watershed ridge and onto the North Chombu Glacier. After waiting the next morning till sun burned off fog, we could see a good route through the long, wide crevasses that guard the base of the north face. The snow became deeper as we approached the face; the glacier, shaded from the sun, lacked the melt-freeze cycle necessary for a firm surface.

On day three the real climbing began. First there were bottomless snow flutings with no possibility of ice screws or other protection till we were in reach of the northeast spur. After that the climbing continued with deep, cold, unconsolidated snow over rock. While trying to traverse snow-covered slabs, I took a 20m fall. Fowler was persuaded to lead the next few pitches while I recovered composure. The bivouac was on a fine narrow ridge, belayed to a large boulder. With the change to good weather, the temperature also dropped, and it became very cold at night.

Day four was short but demanding. The crux of the route passed though steep, snow-covered buttresses before breaking out onto a relatively low-angle shoulder leading to the north summit of Chombu. Most pitches were physically exhausting, with the added psychological uncertainty of unconsolidated snow, sparse runners, and potentially big falls. Our bivouac at 6,107m was barely 250m of moderate climbing below the summit. In the snow conditions we were experiencing, and with the horizontal distance involved, we estimated it would take us another day and a half.

During that night we shared a package of dried food: "Beef Stroganoff with Noodles." It tasted strange, a bit like oxidized linseed oil, but we knew we would need the energy for the next day. This was a mistake. A bad mistake. By the morning we both had been so sick overnight there was no option but to descend. We were not able to eat again for two days.

Days five and six were spent reversing our route, the rappels revealing the seriousness of the climbing. We left base camp four days later, trekking out in heavy snow. The weather had been consistently poor for most of our time in the area, with rain and snow through much of the day. The monsoon didn't seem to leave until October 11, the day we started up, and the first winter snows arrived only one week later. It's not clear there is a "best" season to climb this mountain.

Sikkim weather is best summarized by a note from Julie-Ann Clyma, who visited the area in 2007: "Just how much uncertainty can you take?" 📄 📷

– **VICTOR SAUNDERS**, *FRANCE*

NEPAL

Unfinished Symphony on the east face of Jannu (7,711 meters). The route gained about 1,950 meters from the base of the icefall. The climbers descended the French route on the opposite side, without going to the summit. The upper part of the right skyline ridge is followed by the original route on Jannu's north face, climbed by Japanese in 1976. Part of unclimbed Jannu East is visible to the right. *Dmitry Golovchenko*

UNFINISHED SYMPHONY
THIRTEEN DAYS UP THE EAST FACE OF JANNU

BY DMITRY GOLOVCHENKO, *RUSSIA*

JANNU (KUMBHAKARNA, 7,711M) in the Kangchenjunga Himal has four established routes, but the east face remained unclimbed. Our expedition to attempt this face comprised Sergey Nilov (Russia), Marcin Tomaszewski (Poland), and me, together with a documentary film crew led by the Polish director Eliza Kubarska. The winter was very snowy, and after arriving in Ghunsa by helicopter, we had to use a much longer, alternative route to base camp on the Yalung Glacier. This cost us much time and a considerable part of our acclimatization period.

The day after arrival at base camp, we set off to find a way to the Jannu plateau (Jannu Southeast Glacier) below the face. We discovered the only safe route to be a 300m rock buttress and began fixing this on March 12. That day we climbed around nine pitches, most of which Marcin led. Next day Sergey and I added another three pitches and reached the plateau. When we returned to base camp, Marcin said that he'd decided to quit the attempt. Lack of acclimatization, his impression that the wall was in dangerous condition, and the fact that he didn't feel comfortable within the team were his main reasons. Both Marcin and Eliza offered their full support and helped us take gear to the plateau, where on the night of the 15th we enjoyed a nice meal together.

On the 16th, Sergey and I spent the whole day crossing the convoluted glacier with packs of 20kg each. We camped at 5,525m, near the base of the main east face. Next day we tried to work through the icefall. There was no easy way, and often we came to dead ends. Heavy snow began at 2 p.m., and as soon as we found a safe spot (at 6,100m) we stopped. It was at around this altitude that the only other expedition to attempt the face, a Korean team in 2011, retreated when one member fell into a crevasse and broke some ribs.

On the 18th, fresh snow in the icefall made conditions worse, and then it began to snow again in early afternoon. We stopped in another safe spot, sheltered by a huge ice block, at 6,316m. We missed the alarm on the 19th and didn't wake up until 6 a.m. It took three hours to leave, and again it started to snow at 1 p.m. We were now on our planned leftward-slanting line up the face toward the headwall, where we found a rock wall at 6,513m and spent three hours building a sheltered tent site below it. Next day there was snowfall from early morning on, but we managed around six pitches in poor visibility before making a ledge at 6,654m on which we could fit half the tent. That night it snowed a lot, and we had to dig from time to time.

The 21st dawned sunny, at last. One of our tent poles had broken, so while Sergey fixed it, I dried out our clothes and sleeping bags. Sergey did a great job leading that day: The angle was 60–70° and the rock was covered by fresh snow, requiring difficult mixed climbing. At 3 p.m. we found a small ledge at 6,771m and decided to stop. That night we used our last tea bag. We also decided not to climb the headwall to the right, directly toward the summit, but to follow the continuation of our line to the south ridge and then continue up the original 1962 French route to the top. The French route would provide our only descent, as reversing our route was now far too dangerous.

Next day we reached 6,923m. The morning had been sunny, but the ground was steeper. Then came the usual midday snowfall. We spent two or three hours preparing a ledge on a small snow ridge before erecting the tent.

The weather on the 23rd was great—sunny all day. The ridge felt close, so we climbed until late into the night, reaching 7,127m. We finally got to sleep at 2 a.m.

[Top] **Sergey Nilov during the first ascent of the east face of Jannu.** [Bottom] **Nilov mixed climbing on March 21, the first day of spring, at around 6,750 meters.** *Dmitry Golovchenko*

Over the next two days, the fresh snow, poor protection, and afternoon snowfall meant we progressed slowly. On the night of the 25th, at an altitude of 7,279m, the weather was awful, and the news from our radio contact with base camp was that it would get worse. We didn't move all day on the 26th, the biggest challenge being not eating, in order to preserve what food was left.

On the 27th we continued. The wall became very steep, an average angle of 80°. We still found fresh snow everywhere, and the ice was bad, full of holes like cheese. At dusk Sergey found a nice gap between rock and ice, and we set up a good bivouac inside. It was my 36th birthday, and base camp sang me celebratory Polish songs over the radio. It was at that point Sergey showed me his feet, with a few black dots, the first signs of frostbite. We needed a minimum of one more day to reach the ridge. The decision on what to do next was simple: We would forgo the summit and descend the French route.

On the 28th we could finally see the ridge above us. Sergey made a long traverse across a very steep snow face, climbed up another steep pitch, and we were there. The height was 7,412m, and after an hour's rest we started down, bivouacking that night at 7,380m. It had been 13

[Top Left] Sergey Nilov leading the last pitch of the day on March 27 at over 7,300 meters. *Dmitry Golovchenko* [Bottom Left] Very steep snow on the penultimate pitch of the east face, nearly two weeks after starting the climb. *Dmitry Golovchenko* [Above] Golovchenko looks back at the summit of Jannu from the Throne glacial plateau. The Russians topped out on the right-hand ridge just below the rocky summit cap and descended straight down the snow and ice face to reach the glacier. *Sergy Nilov*

days since we left Marcin and Elena at the plateau camp.

On the 29th, during a day of good weather, we descended straight down the other side of the south ridge to reach the large glacier plateau of the Throne, where we could camp in a luxurious crevasse at 6,995m. Eliza had moved around to the Yamatari Glacier to assist us, and on the 30th she tried to talk us down. We had to cross over some small peaks (the Dentelles Ridge and Tête du Butoir), then reach the Col des Jeunes, from where we could descend to the Jeunes Glacier. However, we were forced to stop at 6,508m, as it was snowing again and we couldn't see where to go. On the morning of the 31st, we ate our last pack of noodles, but this day managed to downclimb until 4 p.m., reaching an altitude of 6,050m before losing our way in the cloud and deciding to stop.

The following day was April Fools, but we were serious. We needed to get down that day. We found a way to the col, then down to the Jeunes Glacier, which would have been straightforward were it not for fresh snow and the fact we were far from fresh. Unfortunately, we were stopped by a big crevasse and had to spend the night at 5,884m.

The morning of the 2nd dawned fine. We quickly boiled water and ate a piece of chocolate we found at the bottom of the haul bag. Then we tried a way much farther right, made two rappels, and later two more, and found ourselves on easy terrain. We were now constantly in touch with Eliza and her team, telling them we were close. At 1 p.m. it began snowing, but we just kept going. We reached a rock barrier and were arranging an anchor when we heard voices. A 45m rappel and we were on the Yamatari Glacier, met by Eliza, her sound technician, and two Sherpa assistants. They had brought tomato soup, boiled eggs, fresh chapatis, tea, vitamins, and even a bottle of Coca-Cola. From the Jannu plateau, we had spent 18 days on the mountain.

The ca 1,950m route is Unfinished Symphony (ED, 80+°). ▣

Alan Rousseau on the upper crux of Release the Kraken, the ice hose at 6,700 meters, on the west face of Tengi Ragi Tau. *Tino Villanueva*

RELEASE THE KRAKEN
FIRST ASCENT OF THE WEST FACE OF TENGI RAGI TAU

BY TINO VILLANUEVA, *USA*

IN AUGUST, ONE week before departing for an expedition to India's Zanskar Range, Alan Rousseau and I were notified that our climbing permit had been canceled by the Indian government due to the volatile political situation in the state of Jammu and Kashmir.

Given the difficulty of finding a new objective in less than a week, it made sense to go somewhere familiar. In 2012 and 2014, Alan and I had embarked on expeditions to the Rolwaling Valley, with the ultimate goal of climbing Tengi Ragi Tau (6,938m). It was our first Himalayan objective, and over two expeditions to the mountain, we fell short of the summit.

In 2012, after a month of climbing in the Rolwaling, we made an eight-day, self-supported push to the summit of Langmoche Ri, a previously unclimbed peak that marks the start of the north ridge of Tengi Ragi Tau (*see AAJ 2013*). Returning to the village of Beding, we were struck by the west face of Tengi Ragi Tau, with its runnels through beautiful granite leading directly to the summit. In 2014, we returned with the west face in our sights, again spending nearly two months in Nepal and not seeing another climber in the Rolwaling. We retreated from the face only 400m from the summit and decided we would leave it be (*AAJ 2015*).

Now, however, we were fired up by the idea. Our familiarity with the Rolwaling, combined with experience gained in the five years since our last attempt, gave us a high level of confidence that we could not only plan a last-minute expedition to the area but also have a good chance of success. As it turned out, our unfinished route up Tengi Ragi Tau's west face had also garnered interest from other strong teams. In the autumn of 2019, teams from France and Spain, as well as our own, would descend upon the mountain. It was nerve-wracking knowing that others would

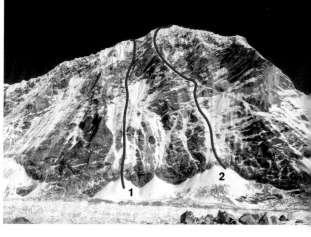

be vying for the same objective, especially given the relative isolation we had enjoyed on our last attempts.

After a three-day approach up the classic Everest Base Camp trail, a four-day acclimatization and conditions scouting foray, and a 16km, 2,000m vertical approach over Tesi Lapcha Pass, we were ready to go to work. However, before launching into the climbing, we tried to spend a restful day and night below the face. Just as the sun was setting, we took a rock through the tent wall. That night, which was spent patching the tent with Band-Aids and athletic tape, was decidedly not restful.

The west face of Tengi Ragi Tau (6,938m). (1) Trinité to north top (see report on p.321). (2) Release the Kraken to summit. Both routes were climbed in October 2019. *Tino Villanueva*

Our first day on the route, October 13, covered familiar terrain, albeit drier than our previous attempt. We had a few fun pitches of true M5 dry-tooling to get onto the snowy face, and then continued on steadily steepening snow and ice. Our bivouac ledge from 2014 was utilized again: protected, flat, and big enough to untie.

Day two continued into ever-steepening terrain, again with a smattering of steeper ice pitches, mixed moves, and snow flutings. It was on this ground that we had reached our high point in 2014, and had struggled to find a bivouac spot while battling high winds, falling debris, and fatigue. This time we managed to find a tight ledge, barely big enough for the tent. It was necessary to clip everything into a nine-piece anchor.

On day three, the high crux of the route, characterized by a multi-pitch ice hose at 6,700m, rose directly overhead. The climbing started with a huge sheet and then pinched to a hanging, chandeliered hose, giving incredible AI5 climbing at such a high altitude. After five pitches of ice, the route pulled into the upper reaches of the mountain, with terribly steep flutings of unprotectable snow. It was arduous, physical work questing up a maze of flutings, hoping the route would connect and that somewhere we would be able to find an anchor. After a handful of these pitches, the day was getting late, and while digging deeper and deeper for an anchor (which we never did get), we eventually created a bivouac platform. It was in such steep snow that the fluting overhung the tent and our feet overhung the edge on one side.

Summit morning was brutally cold: Our violently swinging appendages were comical, with both of us vigorously trying to pump blood into our frozen hands and feet. After five more pitches, we emerged onto the summit ridge, the end of the north ridge we had hoped to climb in 2012. The summit pinnacle was a short walk away. After tagging the top, we basked in the glory of the warm sunlight, soaking in an experience eight years in the making.

Soon, though, we began rappelling back down the face, stopping for one more night at 6,300m when it got too warm. The next day we rappelled to the glacier, climbed back over Tesi Lapcha Pass, and returned to Thame after a 14-hour day, our eighth day on the move. Our route, Release the Kraken, was the first alpine-style climb of the peak and only the second ascent of the mountain. 📷 ▶

Summary: *First ascent of the west face of Tengi Ragi Tau by the route Release the Kraken (1,600m, AI5 M5+), October 13–17, 2019.*

PHUPHARKA HIMAL, ARDANG, FIRST ASCENT

IN LATE AUTUMN, two teams attempted unclimbed Ardang (6,034m) in the Limi region: Bryce Brown and Sunny Twelker (Canada), and Mark Bielby and Emily Ward from the U.K. Ardang was officially opened for mountaineering in 2014, though it had been the main goal of Paulo Grobel's 2013 expedition (*AAJ 2014*).

Villagers of the Jang Valley/Limi Khola, which is traveled en route to the north side of Ardang (and also for a southern approach to the Takphu Himal), told the Canadians that Ardang was sacred and they could not set foot on the mountain. The Canadians were traveling with a Sherpa guide and friend, who was able to negotiate on their behalf; they eventually were given a blessing from the village in exchange for a "local tax" of $150, but were told the mountain could only be attempted from the northwest, as a snow leopard lived in the valley to the east and might be angered by the climbers. This is the third known incident in Limi of locals not recognizing permits issued by Nepal's central government.

Bielby and Ward arrived at base camp below the north side of Ardang on November 13, almost two weeks after the Canadians. On the following day, through a heavy blizzard, they heard Brown and Twelker's whoops as they descended the mountain, having summited Ardang at 2 p.m. the previous day in fine weather.

Brown and Twelker had established base camp on October 31 at around 4,200m, made Camp 1 on November 6 at 5,200m, below the big glacial ramp on the north face, and then on the 12th climbed the ramp and camped by the col at its top (5,650m). Next day they followed the mixed north-northwest ridge to the summit snowcap, then continued up this to the top. Slopes were heavily loaded on the ascent, and a good 60cm of fresh snow covered their tracks by the time they were making the descent.

The British pair decided to attempt the less avalanche-threatened but potentially more technical northeast ridge. They aborted at around 5,350m on the 20th when the snow became too dangerous to continue. ◙

– **LINDSAY GRIFFIN**, *WITH INFORMATION FROM EMILY WARD, ALPINE CLUB, U.K., AND RODOLPHE POPIER,*
LA CHRONIQUE, FFCAM

LIMI HIMAL, LORE PEAK, NORTH FACE AND WEST RIDGE

FROM EARLY AUGUST until the end of September 2017, a Japanese expedition led by Tetsuji Otsue visited West Nepal. Their original aim was Aichyn (6,055m, first climbed by another Japanese expedition in 2015), but after seeing the peaks were dry, they changed their objective and headed south to Nying Himal (6,140m) at the head of the Nying Glacier. From a base camp on the moraine, they tried to climb the west ridge of Nying Himal, but the rock was bad and the ice conditions dangerous. Instead they turned to Lore Peak, so named on French guide Paulo Grobel's Limi map. [*This mountain has no name or spot height on the HMG-Finn map. It lies immediately north of the Lore La, opposite (northeast) of Nyalu Lek, and immediately southwest of unnamed Peak 6,020m.*]

On September 5, from a high camp at 5,350m, Otsue, Kazumichi Nakagawa, Akio Kurita, Yasushi Maeda, Sadayuki Motoya, Kimio Tominaga, and Miyuki Yamamoto reached the summit of Lore Peak via the north flank of the northwest spur and the west ridge. Four climbing Sherpas (names not reported) assisted the team. There was much loose rock, and about 10m of climbing on the "hanging wall" above the col to gain the west ridge was grade III. The team recorded a summit altitude of 6,080m. They returned to camp after a round trip of 13 hours. 📷 🔍

– *INFORMATION SUPPLIED BY* **HIRO HAGIWARA,** *EDITOR, ROCK AND SNOW, JAPAN*

CHANGLA HIMAL, SOUTH LACHAMA GLACIER, EXPLORATION

FOLLOWING A SUGGESTION from Julian Freeman-Attwood, Drew Cook, Lorna Earl, Mike Fletcher, Nick King, Stephen Humphries, and I chose to explore the southern branch of the remote Lachama Glacier. Our expedition lasted from September 27–October 27. We flew from Kathmandu to the hilltop town of Simikot, and then made a five-day trek to our base camp at the junction of the north and south Lachama valleys.

An advance base was established just short of the terminal moraine of the South Lachama Glacier at 4,585m. From this camp, the team made exploratory forays both to the pass leading south, toward our primary objective of Peak 5,822m, and eastward in an attempt to access the glacial headwall and a secondary objective. During these forays, it became obvious that the photograph we had been given depicting Peak 5,822m (which we now called "False Peak 5,822m") was in fact a lesser summit estimated to be around 5,590m. We now believed the "True Peak 5,822m" was our secondary objective, at the head of the glacial cirque.

After time-consuming work to reach the glacier (the preferred route being the true right lateral moraine) and closer inspection of the icefall leading to True Peak 5,822m, we decided we did not have time to attempt this summit. Instead, we focused on establishing a camp near the 5,201m pass due south of advanced base camp and beneath False Peak 5,822m. Once there, we were unable to identify a reasonable route up the peak under the prevailing conditions. We attempted Peak 5,320m, a rocky outcrop on the ridge leading westward from the pass, but a steep, snow-plastered wall defeated our efforts just 20m below the summit. 📄📷

– **DEREK BUCKLE,** *U.K.*

Nick King at the high point just below Peak 5,320m, above the South Lachama Glacier. The prominent rock spire on the right is "False Peak 5,822m" (ca 5,590m). *Stephen Humphries*

DOLPO / GYAEKOCHEN HIMAL

KLANG HIMAL, NORTHEAST FACE, AND EXPLORATION

DOLPO IS CONSIDERED a land for trekkers, not a destination for mountaineers. However, there are beautiful peaks: not necessarily that high, but wild and remote. Gyaekochen (6,107m, 28°58'49.47"N, 83°10'51.57"E), the highest point of the small Gyaekochen Massif, has remained unknown, not even named on maps. It lies between the villages of Kakkot and Dho, due north of Putha Hiunchuli, and is not on the list of peaks authorized by the Ministry of Tourism. My objective was to document thoroughly its appeal and access, so that it might be opened to mountaineers.

On an expedition in 2018, we explored an approach to the north side of the massif, from the Tarap Khola to the west. We discovered a route up the mountain that is both elegant and reasonably straightforward, but bad visibility stopped us just 50m below the summit.

In the fall of 2019, we approached from Kakkot to the south, the idea being to open a new trekking route—the Gyaekochen Trek—to Dho over Gyaekochen Pass (5,318m). We made base camp at Ghadek Kharka (4,700m) to the southeast of the Gyaekochen Massif, then headed up toward the pass and camped at around 5,200m to the northeast of the three peaks that make up the massif: Gyaekochen, Dolpo Peak (6,075m), and Klang Himal (6,042m).

The Gyaekochen Massif from Puthi Hiunchuli to the south. (A) Gyaekochen. (B) Klang Himal. (C) Dolpo Peak. *Paulo Grobel*

On November 2, Bernard Meurin (France) and Dhan Magyar (Nepal) reached the summit of Klang Himal via the northeast face. Deep, unconsolidated snow made the going difficult, and they were the only members of the team to succeed. The route led to a large plateau-like pass from which any of the three peaks could be ascended. [*Editor's note: Additional information is at paulogrobel.com.*] 🖸

– PAULO GROBEL, *FRANCE*

DAMODAR HIMAL

SANO KAILASH I, NORTH FLANK AND NORTHEAST RIDGE

WHEN TREKKING FROM Mustang to Saribung Pass, the view to the south of the holy lakes of Damodar Kunda is dominated by the conspicuous north face of a mountain resembling Kailash in Tibet. The local name for the peak is Sano Kailash (Little Kailash). However, the rock and ice north wall belongs to the second-highest peak in the group, Peak 6,417m, which I call Sano Kailash II. The highest summit (6,457m) is hidden behind at 28.928885°N, 84.133329°E. The whole group comprises four peaks above 6,000m, and all were unclimbed before 2019.

Elisabeth Bartmann, Lawang Tamang, 14 camp staff, and I trekked to Damodar Khunda, arriving on the 22nd. On the 25th we crossed the Jampta Khola and established base camp at 5,400m in the Itiya Khola valley, not far from the lower end of the glacier. On the 26th, after a cumbersome approach over moraine, a tiring climb with serious rockfall danger led to the gentle northeast ridge of Sano Kailash at around 6,000m, where we cached equipment and descended.

Lawang and I left for the summit at 3 a.m. on the 28th. Above our cache, we continued easily up the ridge. The summit glacier was free of crevasses, so we left the rope and cramponed to the top, arriving at 8:30 a.m. in clear, windless weather. In descent we were able to follow a steep snow gully that started shortly below the summit and led quickly to the valley, regaining our base camp at 11:20 a.m. 🖹 🖸

– WOLFGANG DREXLER, *AUSTRIA*

AMOTSANG, SOUTH RIDGE

AMOTSANG (6,393m, 28°50'5.76"N, 84°10'13.19"E) was brought onto the permitted peak list in 2002. French guide Paulo Grobel reconnoitered the peak in 2003 but did not make an attempt. Instead, he climbed a 6,084m summit to the southwest of Amotsang that he named Thansunjiti. He later reached the col between Thansunjiti and Jomson Peak (6,335m, inaccurately named on the HMG-Finn map), and from there climbed the rocky south ridge of Peak 6,120m, traversed east below its summit to reach the west ridge of Jomson, and followed the crest to make the first ascent of Jomson.

Amotsang from the south in poor weather, showing part of the solo first-ascent route. *Jost Kobusch*

In 2009, an Australian team tried to access the glacier to the north of Amotsang for an attempt, but were foiled by bad weather. In 2012, the French guide Lionel Chatain made the first of two unsuccessful trips to Amotsang, aiming for the west ridge, approaching from the north. He reached the crest west of Jomson Peak and climbed to 6,220m on that peak before retreating in poor snow. As a consolation prize, Chatain and clients made the first ascent of Peak 6,305m, on the ridge north of Jomson Peak, naming it Margot Peak. Chatain returned in 2017 but failed to climb Amotsang.

In 2018, Grobel was back, planning to reach the 6,147m col (dubbed Sasurali Pass) at the head of the glacier on the north side of Amotsang, then traverse Margot Himal and Jomson Peak, and finish up the west ridge of Amotsang. However, the team retreated from 6,200m on the northeast ridge of Margot Peak.

Thus, after many attempts, Amotsang remained unclimbed.

On October 18, 2019, as a preparation for a solo winter attempt on Everest, the German Jost Kobusch arrived with two porters on the south side of Amotsang and set up base camp at around 4,700m. The last day of the approach had been a 12-hour hike from the village of Nar, and after the porters dropped their loads, they immediately set off at a run back to the village, leaving Kobusch alone.

Kobusch's plan had been to attempt the southwest face, but he quickly found he couldn't reach this face alone. He then inspected an approach to the southeast face, establishing a second camp on the 21st at 5,600m, close to the start of the glacier. On the 22nd he checked out the route through the icefall.

After a rest day, at 4 a.m. on the 24th, Kobusch set out to climb the southeast face directly. Although he saw good ice runnels that would be fine for a solo climber, the initial 50m rock wall was highly shattered and looked too difficult to attempt on his own. From his vantage, the south ridge now looked like the best option. But as he moved up the ridge, it too had a few surprises, in the form of serac walls, steep sections of ice, and deep snow. The ascent therefore took longer than expected, and he only reached the summit at around 5 p.m.

As he started down, the sun began to set. One hour in twilight and another three in the dark brought him back to camp. Once in base camp, he packed up and walked out alone to Nar.

Kobusch later spent the winter attempting Everest, solo and without bottled oxygen, by the West Ridge route, accessed via the Lho La. Late in the season, he reached a high point of 7,366m on the West Shoulder. 🖻 🔍

– **LINDSAY GRIFFIN,** *WITH INFORMATION PROVIDED BY* **JOST KOBUSCH,** *GERMANY*

LUGULA, NORTHWEST RIDGE OVER BHRIKUTI SHAIL; SELKA KANGRI, EAST RIDGE

LUGULA (6,899M) IS a beautiful summit on the Nepal-Tibet border between Phu Valley and Mustang. We had planned to climb it from Mustang and the Damodar Kunda Lakes to the north and then continue with a crossing of Bhrikuti Shail. However, the Nepalese government decided otherwise.

In mid-August, a friend informed me that the regulations in Restricted Area Zones (such as Upper Mustang or Upper Dolpo) had changed, requiring the additional expense of a TIMS trekking permit for each team member. We had to think again.

Keeping our main objective as Lugula, we approached from Phu to the south and established ourselves at Bhrikuti Shail base camp (5,015m). From there we established Camp 1 on the south ridge of Bhrikuti Shail at 5,650m. On October 1, after a period of bad weather, we made Camp 2 on the Tirhawa La (ca 6,200m), west of Bhrikuti Shail. This was the same route I had climbed in 2005 while making the first ascent of Bhrikuti Shail.

[Top] Camp 2 at around 6,200m on Tirhawa La. Up to the right is the east ridge of Julie Himal; a party can just be seen returning to camp from the peak. The flat-topped mountain at the head of the small glacier on the left is Chhiv Himal (6,650m), while the taller peak in the center is Khumjungar (Khamjung, 6,759m). [Bottom] Traversing Bhrikuti Shail toward Lugula. The two routes on the west flank of Lugula are marked: (1) the Dutch-French route of 2019 and (2) the French route of 2010, repeated in 2014 by Koreans. *Paulo Grobel (both photos)*

From this high camp, we were able to traverse Bhrikuti Shail (6,361m) to the east and reach the broad, gentle Minerva Snowfield on the west flank of Lugula. [*This snowfield, named later by Korean climbers, was first reached in October 2010 by Renaud Guillaume from a French expedition that climbed Bhrikuti Shail; he followed the snowfield's south side until able to climb onto the upper west ridge of Lugula and continue to the summit, making the peak's first ascent.*] After establishing Camp 3 at 6,350m on the snowfield, our Dutch-French team slanted north to gain the northwest ridge and followed it to Lugula's summit. The overall grade was PD. Six members summited on October 5 and 11 more the next day.

Previously, on the 2nd, five of us had headed west from Camp 2 to the summit of Julie Himal (6,337m, first climbed and named in 2010 by Guillaume and his girlfriend Julie Vesz, the day before Guillaume's solo of Lugula). On the 4th, this was repeated by Sergio di Léo and Karma Sherpa, who then continued west to make the first ascent of Selka (Shelka) Kangri (6,358m).

Lugula is a particularly interesting summit belonging to the "almost 7,000m" category—a category of peaks that has much interest for mountaineers able to distance themselves from the ego associated with attaining 7,000m. We were completely alone at base camp, while 15 expeditions crowded into nearby Himlung base camp. There is still plenty of space in Nepal to enjoy an intimate adventure. 🔲

– PAULO GROBEL, *FRANCE*

Seen from Manaslu Base Camp, Panpoche I is the triangular rock peak in upper left; the northeast ridge is just behind the left skyline. Panpoche II is the snowier peak to its right; the Georgian climb started on the southwest ridge, more or less pointing toward the camera, then moved right to finish. *Mingma David Sherpa*

PANPOCHE II AND PANPOCHE I, FIRST ASCENTS

"THOSE MOUNTAINS ARE so beautiful!" Giorgi Tepnadze, Baqar Gelashvili, and I all said the same thing while gazing eastward to the horizon from the summit of Larkya Peak (*AAJ 2018*). The mountains in question were the unclimbed Panpoche brothers: Panpoche I (a.k.a. Kutang Himal, 6,620m) and Panpoche II (6,504m). The higher Panpoche had been attempted in 2009 by Japanese, via the northeast ridge, and again by Norwegians on the same route in 2012. It appeared Panpoche II had never been attempted.

We arrived in Kathmandu on September 10 and heard that an Italian-Swiss expedition was also due to attempt Panpoche I (*see editor's note below*). Giorgi, Baqar, and I trekked over the Larkya La toward Samagaon village and reached base camp below Panpoche at 3,880m.

On the 20th we started up the southwest ridge of Panpoche II. After 600m we were able to see the whole of the mountain, and it looked possible to climb it in two or three days, so we left some equipment and food, and continued light and fast. Fast seemed a good idea, as the forecast was not promising and the weather was unpredictable throughout our stay, with rain or snow almost every day.

We continued up the ridge, which proved extremely loose, sharp, and unprotectable. However, our long-term experience on loose terrain gave us courage. After a total of 1,900m, we reached the only spot on the ridge that would take a tent. There began a long spell of snowfall.

Next morning we set out in very poor visibility, and after a difficult, near vertical pitch we realized this was not the way. To the right, the funnel-shaped south-southwest face looked to provide a better option. We crawled inside the tent and remained there until the following morning, when snowfall decreased and we decided to make a summit push.

We traversed right, then down, to reach the snow funnel. The snow cover was relatively thin over sloping rock barriers. We simul-climbed the 900m face as calmly as we could, overcoming long stretches of 60° and sections up to 80°. At 5 p.m. on September 22, we gathered on top and briefly enjoyed a clear view of the surrounding mountains. We became thoughtful. Envisioning a descent of the poorly protected sections in the dark took our smiles away—yes, even from cheerful Georgians.

After six hours, four rappels, and much downclimbing, we reached our bivouac gear, which

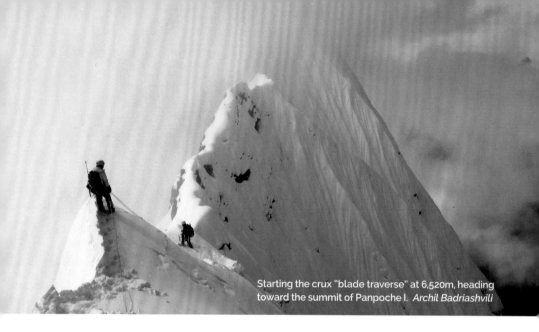

Starting the crux "blade traverse" at 6,520m, heading toward the summit of Panpoche I. *Archil Badriashvili*

we had cached at the start of the funnel at around 5,720m. Dehydrated, we dug a bivouac site, had a three-hour nap, and woke to sunshine in an exceptionally good mood. We opted to continue straight down the central couloir on the face, and by evening we had regained base camp. From where we started climbing, our route was 1,700m, ED 80°; from base camp it was around 2,600m.

We now moved our base camp to 4,300m in the uninhabited Samdo Valley for an attempt on the northeast ridge of Panpoche I. The Japanese had spent many days on this route in 2009 in expedition style, retreating from the blade-like corniced summit ridge at 6,500m. We had seen part of this from Panpoche II and knew it would be the crux.

On September 30, after another intense bout of bad weather, we set off with relatively light packs, breaking trail on the snow-loaded Sonam Glacier to a col at 5,580m on the northeast ridge (the border with Tibet). Another day in strengthening wind brought us to our second bivouac on the ridge at 5,860m. On the third day route finding was trickier and slopes heavily loaded. We had a grueling time before reaching the pinnacle at Point 6,335m. [*This point was given the name Samdo and was climbed in 2009 by the Japanese.*] That day we had almost voted to retreat due to avalanche hazard, but decided to continue, although it still seemed a long way to the top.

On October 3 we started our summit push. The weather was cold and clear, and after five hours we had reached the start of the "blade." We sent avalanches down to the right and loose rock to the left. The only protection if someone fell off was to jump down the other side. We therefore climbed slowly! After three hours of difficult work, we each went up to the narrow summit one by one.

After such stressful work we had great emotions (and a small sip of cognac), but then we had to go down. Before sunset we had reached our last bivouac, and the following day reversed our route to base camp. Our 2,300m route from base camp was ED 70° in numbers and symbols, but so much more in reality. Both ascents had required a coordinated team with extremely focused attention in order to deal with complex route-finding, weather conditions, and our mood swings. 📷

– **ARCHIL BADRIASHVILI**, *GEORGIA*

PANPOCHE I ATTEMPT: *After an ascent of nearby Manaslu in the autumn season, Marco Camandona, François Cazzanelli, Emrik Favre, Francesco Ratti (all from Italy), and Andreas Steindl (Switzerland) attempted the west-northwest ridge of Panpoche I, which eventually gains the north ridge before the start of the "blade." They retreated at 5,800m.*

LANGSHISHA RI GROUP, PEAK 6,130M, WEST RIDGE

Taking a permit for Langshisha Ri (6,412m), the French guide Pierre Rizzardo and two clients, Karl Grigulis and Sandra Lavorel, established base camp at 4,450m on the true right (northern) bank of the Langshisha Glacier. From here they climbed the huge scree slope to the northeast that leads to a pass at 5,481m and gives access to the glacier on the south side of Langshisha Ri, above its difficult icefall. From a camp on the pass, they could see that the southern slopes of the mountains were very dry, so they changed their objective to an "all white" summit to the east. This is immediately to the west of Peak 6,152m, as marked on the HMG-Finn map.

On October 16, the French team climbed on the left flank of the west ridge, zigzagging between crevasses and short, steep snow steps. The grade was PD and their GPS read 6,130m on the summit. While it is well known that much unauthorized climbing has taken place in the Langtang, no recorded ascent of this top has been found. 🖸

– *INFORMATION PROVIDED BY* RODOLPHE POPIER, *HIMALAYAN DATABASE, FRANCE*

JUGAL HIMAL

GYALSTEN, SOUTH-SOUTHEAST FACE

In 1955, Evelyn Camrass, Monica Jackson, and Elizabeth Stark (U.K.) launched the first all-female mountaineering expedition to the Himalaya (albeit with male Sherpa support). By completing the first ascent of a high Nepalese peak, they proved to many that women mountaineers could hold their own in a male-dominated activity.

After exploring the Jugal Himal and what is now named the Jugal Glacier, Jackson, Stark, Mingma Gyalgen Sherpa, and Ang Temba Sherpa climbed to the head of the Jugal Glacier and then up the south face and upper southwest ridge of a "22,000-foot" (6,705m) peak on the Tibetan frontier, which they named Gyalgen Peak after their sirdar. This peak was climbed subsequently by two Japanese expeditions in the early 1960s.

Fast-forward around 50 years to the creation of the "official" HMG-Finn maps for Nepal. The old Gyalgen Peak is now

Gyalsten (6,151 meters), as defined by the HMG-Finn map, seen from the Jugal Glacier above advanced base. The line followed on the first ascent, via the south-southeast face, is marked. A col on the frontier ridge off picture to the right was reached in 1955 by a British women's expedition. *Tul Singh Gurung*

named Leonpo Gang East and given 6,733m (though the map mistakenly names it "west"), and the map positions Gyalgen, now written as Gyalsten, as a 6,151m frontier peak some distance to the southeast. The 1955 expedition referred to this mountain as Ladies Peak, and though they did not attempt it, they reached a col on the frontier ridge just to the south during their explorations.

The mistakes on the map were discovered in 2005 when Camrass joined a primarily American expedition that planned to attempt the "new Gyalsten" but spent too much time determining which peak was which to mount an attempt (*see AAJ 2006*).

Gyalsten finally was climbed in the spring of 2019. Maya Gurung's all-Nepalese expedition of six amateur members (two women and four men) and four professional Nepalese guides (lead guide Tul Singh Gurung) visited the Jugal Glacier and established base camp at 4,470m on April 3. They avoided the lower icefall of the glacier on the right by technical ground, and placed an advanced base at a site named Nyang Kharka (4,724m). They were stuck at that camp for several days in bad weather, and when it cleared one member was evacuated by helicopter and more food was delivered.

On the 9th, an advanced team continued up the Jugal Glacier and set up Camp 1 at 5,180m; the rest left at 10 p.m. and rested at Camp 1 briefly, and then, at 12:30 a.m. on the 10th, the climbers all left Camp 1 to head for the summit. Guides Nar Bahadur Asthani, Ash Bahadur Gurung, and Tul Singh Gurung broke trail up the glacial arm below the peak and then fixed ropes up its steep south-southeast face. The last 200m were reported to be 50–70°. These three reached the summit at 5:30 a.m., then descended so they could escort the others to the top. At 11:30 a.m., the three previously named guides plus guide Samir Gurung and three climbing members—Maya Gurung, Milan Bahadur Tamang, and Sharmila Thapa—stood on the summit. They regained Camp 1 at 5 p.m.

– LINDSAY GRIFFIN, *WITH INFORMATION FROM TUL SINGH GURUNG, NEPAL, AND RODOLPHE POPIER, LA CHRONIQUE, FFCAM*

ROLWALING HIMAL

View along the south ridge of Chhopa Bamare from near the summit. The high point along the ridge is an unnamed subsummit of the Chhopa Bamare massif. *Benjamin Billet*

CHHOPA BAMARE, FIRST ASCENT BY SOUTHEAST FACE AND SOUTH RIDGE

IN FEBRUARY, John Kelley (USA) and I were in the northwestern Rolwaling to attempt the first ascent of Chhopa Bamare (6,109m), the highest of a group of peaks on the Tibetan border northwest of Lamabagar village. [*Editor's note: During the previous winter, Kelley had attempted the same mountain alone via the east ridge. He traversed the previously unclimbed eastern summit, but then found difficult snow-covered rock on the final section to the main summit, and he retreated. That same season, Kelley also made an impressive solo attempt on the unclimbed southeast ridge of Omi Tso Go, retreating a few hundred meters from the top.*] This was reportedly the snowiest winter for 25 years in this area, and it took seven days from Kathmandu to reach base camp instead of our anticipated three. Two of our three porters would not continue as soon as they saw a few centimeters of snow on the trail, forcing us to ferry all the food and gear for a 30-day expedition. From base camp, we only took the minimum gear to high camp, but this still took us three more days.

We started our climb at 2 a.m. on February 22. The weather forecast told of a few days of clear weather and no snowfall, but it was completely wrong. We began up a rocky buttress, following a snow gully and then some mixed climbing (M4), before reaching and traversing a glacier to the base of the southeast face. We arrived here at 6:30 a.m., just before sunrise.

Hundreds of meters of WI3 followed, and we simul-climbed all of this. Around 4 p.m., light snow started to fall. We kept climbing until 5:30 p.m., when snowfall became too intense to continue. Small avalanches came down the face, and with nowhere to bivouac, we cut a very small ledge (only just enough to stand on), attached ourselves to an anchor, and arranged the tent as a bivouac bag over our heads. Standing up in the cold, with spindrift rolling overhead, made for a long and sleepless night. Quite exhausted the next morning, we could only do a few pitches before snow began to fall again and we bivouacked once more on the face, this time on a larger ledge.

John Kelley during the rappel descent of the southeast face of Chhopa Bamare, eight days after starting the climb. *Benjamin Billet*

On the third day, John made a very long lead of M3/M3+, over rocks covered by 50cm of unconsolidated snow. This led us to the top of the southeast face, where at last we could see the summit. We moved along the ridge and put up the tent around 150m below the top, thinking we could make an attempt the following day.

However, the weather turned bad, with heavy snow and strong winds. We were stuck on the ridge at almost 6,000m for three nights, unable to leave the tent. On the following morning, almost out of gas and food, we were readying to descend when the sun started to shine. We rushed up to the summit, reaching it after a few hours of climbing. It was February 28, the last day of the Nepalese Himalayan winter season.

The next day we made 18 rappels down the southeast face and reached our high camp. We dug through one and a half meters of new snow to find the rucksack we had left with food and gas. On our way down to base camp we discovered the entire valley had been hit by avalanches. When we arrived at our campsite, there was no trace of the tent, sleeping bags, or any other gear. The following day we ran down to the nearest yak herders' encampment. They welcomed us in typical Nepali style and fed us plenty of dal bhat.

We named the route Seto Hi'um (1,100m, TD M4 WI4), which means "white snow." There are still a number of potential new lines to be climbed on this face, as long as conditions are conducive. 📷

– BENJAMIN BILLET, *FRANCE*

PEAK 5,976M, SOUTH RIDGE, ATTEMPT AND RESCUE

DURING NOVEMBER, a British expedition comprising Connor Holdsworth, Ken Hopper, Rich Lade, Simon Tietjen, and me established base camp on the Ripimo Shar (a.k.a. Rolwaling) Glacier, with the intention of climbing the north ridge of Drangnag Ri (6,757m). Difficult snow conditions following a heavy monsoon forced us to abandon these plans after climbing to a col at 6,100m below the north ridge.

We turned to a smaller peak north of our base camp: Peak 5,976m (HMG-Finn map), which lies between the Ripimo Shar and Ripimo Nup glaciers. [*While it seems likely this peak has been climbed in the past, and it was attempted in 2017 by an Italian team, there are no confirmed ascents.*] Based on the snow conditions, we opted for the south ridge.

Connor and I left base camp at 3 a.m. on November 21. There was a lot of broken ground and some finer easy climbing as the rock ridge grew steeper and narrower. As Connor was attempting to traverse a pinnacle that barred access to the upper ridge, the rock collapsed under his feet, and the resulting fall onto a ledge broke his leg badly. I was able to splint his legs together, and with difficulty we rappelled 300m of loose ground on the east flank to reach scree slopes, where we were met by other team members. A helicopter evacuated Connor in the morning. 📷

– WILL ROWLAND, *U.K.*

CHUGIMAGO, WEST FACE, VIA DEL TRONKO AND TRAGEDY

IN MID-OCTOBER, David Suela and Felipe "Tronko" Valverde from Spain climbed a hard new ice and mixed line on the west face of Chugimago (Chukyima Go, 6,258m), between the 2014 Hennessey-Kastelic line (the original route on the west face) and the 2015 Mucic-Strazar route.

The Spanish pair made one bivouac at the foot of the face, a second above two-thirds height, and the third on the summit ridge at an altitude of around 6,150m. Next day, October 19, they tried to climb the sharp crest southward to the summit, but snow conditions were so poor that they retreated to where they had topped out the face and prepared to rappel. Finding a suitable anchor on the ridge was difficult. The pair cut a large snow bollard, and at around 10 a.m., Valverde set off first. The anchor failed and he fell the full length of the 800m face, taking the ropes with him.

Suela was now stranded on the crest of the ridge. He still had the bivouac tent and a little climbing gear, but without ropes and a partner he couldn't move.

Also operating in the Rolwaling at the same time were the experienced Spanish climbers Sonia Casas Torcida and Mikel Zabalza. They had given a radio to the pair climbing Chugimago and agreed to rendezvous with them at 5 p.m. that day. Very fortunately, it was Suela who was carrying the radio. Casas and Zabalza were able to instigate a rescue, and in worsening weather the next morning, a helicopter was able to retrieve Suela from the ridge with a long line—a fine display of flying by the Nepalese pilot. Within minutes after the rescue, the mountain was covered in cloud.

The route has been named Via del Tronko in memory of Valverde, and has fairly sustained difficulties, with around 18 pitches up to M6 85°.

The new Spanish route Via del Tronko on the west face of Chugimago, ending on the summit ridge. Earlier routes on the face are not shown. *Mark Pugliese*

– LINDSAY GRIFFIN

TENGI RAGI TAU, NORTH TOP, WEST FACE, TRINITÉ

CLIMBING THE WEST face of Tengi Ragi Tau was my idea, but it soon became a joint dream. Charles Noirot and I had already shared great adventures in the mountains, as we were both members of the Young French Alpinists team. Silvan Schüpbach is the coach of the Swiss ice climbing team, and we'd seen each other several times at competitions. What brought us together was our common taste for adventurous climbs.

We established base camp on October 8 at 4,700m beside the Drolambo Glacier. We then spent over a week, until October 16, acclimatizing. During this period we witnessed Alan Rousseau and Tino Villanueva complete the first ascent of the west face (*see report and route photo on p.309.*) We decided to go for another line farther left on the same wall, finishing on the lower north top (ca 6,820m GPS). Sadly, at this point, Charles got very sick and was unable to climb for the rest of the expedition.

Symon Welfringer at around 6,500m on the west face of Tengi Ragi Tau, where the climbing became very steep and run-out. See route line on p.309. *Silvan Schüpbach*

Silvan and my first attempt ended in retreat, due to snowfall and strong winds. We made our second attempt around one week later, starting on October 26. Our first day included two pitches of steep ice, followed by moderate snow and ice slopes up to 60° to a small ledge at 6,100m, where we bivouacked. Wind and spindrift had made it cold. The next day the weather improved, but the angle steepened, the climbing became more technical, and the air thinner. We succeeded in finding a bivouac spot at dusk. The altitude was around 6,450m, and we knew that the next 300m would be the hardest.

We progressed up very steep ground the following day, the ice becoming rarer, as did the protection. On the hardest pitches, around M6, the leader hauled his pack. Climbing pitches like these above 6,500m was one of the most exhausting undertakings I have experienced. Especially the last pitch: After many meters of ice flutes, the summit looked close, but one final rock wall stood in the way. This pitch will be forever engraved on my mind as the toughest I've managed to lead.

We rappelled to our top bivouac in four hours, using headlamps, then the next day rappelled the remaining 1,000m to the base of the wall. We named the route Trinité (1,500m, AI5 M6): Although we climbed as a pair, the route we established came from the strength of all three minds. ▣

– SYMON WELFRINGER, *FRANCE*

PARCHAMO, WEST FACE OF NORTH RIDGE (HISTORICAL ASCENT)

IN NOVEMBER 1996, Kili Sherpa and I climbed a line on the far left side of the west face of Parchamo (6,273m) to reach the shoulder on the north ridge at around 5,950m. We began the route at a rock band of excellent granite, split by obvious cracks that led to good climbing on a mix of snow and rock. This was followed by steep névé. Fifteen pitches brought us to the normal route on the north ridge. We descended from there, reaching our tents on Tesi Lapcha Pass (5,755m) by midnight. This line is well to the left of the direct route climbed in 2014 by Alan Rousseau and Tino Villanueva (USA), and the face had much more snow and less menacing seracs in 1996. ▣

– TAD WELCH, *USA*

Quentin Roberts negotiates tricky mixed ground on the north pillar of Tengkangpoche. The 300-meter headwall required free climbing in rock shoes, aid, and traditional mixed. *Juho Knuuttila*

TENGKANGPOCHE, NORTH PILLAR, ATTEMPT

TIM BANFIELD, Quentin Roberts (both Canada), and I arrived in Nepal in mid-September after a hectic time picking an objective. Our first plan had been to try the north face of Chamlang, but that was climbed in the spring (*see p.36*). Our second idea, climbing in Kashmir, was politically impractical, so our third plan was the unclimbed north pillar of Tengkangpoche (6,487m).

We spent a few weeks acclimatizing in the Khumbu, but a long monsoon and, in my case, a weeklong fever allowed little climbing. Quentin and Tim got to 6,100m on Cholatse, whereas I spent only one night at 5,600m before descending. After recuperating in Namche, we moved to the beautiful village of Thengpo (4,350m), opposite the north face of Tengkangpoche.

Early in the morning of October 11, Quentin and I approached the foot of a ramp that had been spotted by Alan Rousseau and Tino Villanueva, two friendly Americans climbing nearby Tengi Ragi Tau. The ramp skipped the moss-covered and snow-free lower part of the pillar, slanting left from a point below the smooth pillar where the Anthamatten-Steck route (Checkmate, 2008) slants right. We carried food for seven days and gas for nine in our two 45-liter packs. Following the ramp route, we passed our planned bivouac spot early and continued until 2 p.m., when we reached something better at an altitude of 5,400m.

Our second day gained only 150m, diagonaling left to the base of the headwall at 5,550m. The climbing was similar to the north face of the Grandes Jorasses, with thin ice ramps and tricky mixed slabs offering plenty of action. The second carried a bigger pack but still climbed everything free.

When the morning sun hit the headwall next day, we launched. This was definitely Quentin's terrain. He fluently free climbed, aided, and climbed mixed ground, sometimes all in the same pitch. The sunlight quickly disappeared from the face, but Quentin kept rock shoes on for a long time after. We passed the 2006 high point of Canadians John Furneaux and Matt Maddaloni at around 5,600m, the highest rap anchor we found. They had spent nine days reaching this point more directly—we had spent two and a half days on our line.

Soon, the cracks were filled with ice and took a long time to climb. We hauled both packs, and I jumared. It got dark at the top of the seventh pitch on the headwall, and when I reached Quentin, belaying under a small overhang, he suggested bivouacking. We sat, our legs hanging free, the tent covering our bodies while spindrift poured all around.

Next morning it was my turn. The angle kicked back and the ice was finally climbable. At 5,880m we cut a poor tent platform on a snow ridge, and the next day we rested. The night on the headwall had taken a lot out of us, and we thought that staying still, eating, and rehydrating would help. It did, but it also took away some of our motivation after so many days on the wall.

In the afternoon, Quentin climbed a 50m pitch and fixed a rope, battling the hardest, most bizarre pitch so far. It was scary to watch. The next day we would try for the summit ridge, and the top the day after.

Day six, October 16, dawned cold. Above our high point, Quentin tackled a snow ramp, hoping to find features or ice

The north pillar of Tengkangpoche (6,487m). (1) Approximate line of 2006 Furneaux–Maddaloni attempt (5.11 A1 WI6 M8). (2) The 2019 Knuutilla-Roberts attempt (5.11 A3 M7), reaching 5,930m. (3) Part of Checkmate (1,700m, UIAA VI A0 M7+ WI5, Anthamatten-Steck, 2008). *Juho Knuuttila*

that would lead to the next snow ramp. There was nothing. What we had seen from the village as ice had probably just been snow, now blown away by the wind. The altitude was 5,930m and the rock ahead completely devoid of cracks and unclimbable by pure means. Maybe sometimes there is ice, maybe not. Maybe there is another way, maybe not. The crux turned out to be right at the top of the pillar. Thus far, we had encountered difficulties up to 5.11 A3 M7. We truly hope that future parties respect the mountain and also climb in alpine style, without a drill or bolts.

Our expedition received financial support from the Austrian Alpine Club and with a John Lauchlan Award and Finnish Alpine Award. [*An interview with Quentin Roberts was featured in episode 26 of the AAJ's Cutting Edge podcast.*] 📷

– JUHO KNUUTTILA, *FINLAND*

MAHALANGUR HIMAL / KHUMBU SECTION

KYAJO RI, WEST FACE, WAY OF THE DRAGON

FROM OCTOBER 2 to 9, Russian climbers Ivan Osipov, Dmitry Rybalchenko, Vitaly Shipilov, and Andrey Vasiliev, on their first trip to Nepal, made the first ascent of the true west face of Kyajo Ri (6,186m). This face had been the goal of several expeditions, including a Slovenian team in 2008 who attempted the central couloir with the aim of passing the headwall to the right. None had made much progress.

Bad weather prevented a flight to Lukla, so the four Russians traveled by jeep to a point 8km past Phaphlu, and then, in three days, carrying all their own food and equipment, walked the remaining 75km to Lunghden (a.k.a. Landen, 4,360m) on the west side of Kyajo Ri. They established base camp there on September 19.

The next few days were spent carrying gear to an advanced base at 5,000m, below the west face, and attempting to study the wall in the brief windows that appeared through rain and mist. The locals told them that in 2014 a large section of the headwall had fallen off, the largest section being 150m by 150m. However, the team thinks most of the visible scarring was due to a more recent event, as it was evident a considerable amount of rock had fallen since spring 2018, when Marek Holeček and Zdenek Hák, who climbed the west flank of the north ridge, photographed the west face headwall (see AAJ 2019). Continuing stone-fall was evident, but the Russians were convinced a line on the right side would be safe enough.

On October 2, after the weather had improved, they reached the foot of the face at 5,200m and started climbing, hoping to top the first 200m steep wall. They did not carry portaledges, so were relying on finding ledges big enough to take tents. However, they were unable to make it, so instead fixed three ropes and went down to advanced base for the night. The climbing had been mainly A2–A3.

Over the next three days, they continued up to the base of the headwall crowning the west face, finding a mix of short vertical steps (some requiring aid) and difficult mixed climbing over compact, thinly snow-covered slabs set at 60–70°. There were no real tent ledges on the entire route, so each night's site had to be excavated in snow patches lying on slabs.

On October 6, the team chose to try a more difficult and aesthetic line than planned, directly up the headwall. The rock was poor, with many loose

[Top] Negotiating steep, powder-covered rock on Kyajo Ri during the first ascent of the main west face. [Bottom] The west face of Kyajo Ri. Huge recent rockfall scars are clearly visible on the left side of the triangular headwall. *Dmitry Rybalchenko (both)*

blocks and few protection points. Eventually, they decided to bail, leaving one piton, and instead headed up right for two pitches on hard mixed and dry tooling, finishing with an A2/A3 corner. They returned for a second night to the 5,700m bivouac.

The next two days gave the hardest climbing: A3/A3+ followed by easy mixed to a bivouac at 5,830m, then big cracks and loose rock (5c A3+) to their final bivouac at 6,050m, the top of pitch 27 of the route.

On the 9th they climbed easy snow for 200m to the summit, reaching it at 9 a.m. They descended the peak's normal route to the Kyajo Glacier, where they slept on the moraine. The route had required the full gamut of climbing techniques, including the use of rock shoes at 6,000m. They named the route Way of the Dragon (950m, ED2/3, 5c A3+ and mixed). 📷

- INFORMATION SUPPLIED BY **ANNA PIUNOVA**, *MOUNTAIN.RU, RUSSIA, AND* **RODOLPHE POPIER**,
HIMALAYAN DATABASE

PEAK 6,065M, NORTHEAST COULOIR AND NORTHWEST RIDGE

NOT LONG AFTER passing through the village of Lobuche, and at an altitude of 4,900m, a left turn brings you into the valley of the Khangri Nup Glacier. This is rarely traveled, and there is good potential for climbing peaks and virgin walls. However, the approach is long and hard, with a lot of moraine. In early May, Ana Gracia, Ruben Gomez, and I managed it without help, establishing base camp at around 5,300m.

After carrying one load to this camp, we returned two days later, arriving at 1 p.m., then rested until midnight. We left camp carrying minimal equipment and two liters of water per person, aiming for unnamed Peak 6,065m, between Nirekha (6,159m) and the 6,010m northwest summit of Lobuche.

With only 100m of altitude gain, we reached the start of the northeast couloir, where we found soft snow, even during the night. There

Peak 6,065m and the line of the Spanish ascent to within 10m of the summit. The peak on the right is the southeast top of Nirekha. *Angel Salamanca*

was a short section of M4 through rotten rock and a section of 80° ice covered by a thin snow layer. When we reached the col on the northwest ridge, at around 5,900m, we found an old snow stake; there was no other evidence of this party on our climb.

From here to the top was a mixture of good and bad granite; it was so warm it was possible to climb without gloves. There was a step or two of 6a, and the final section was quite exposed. Ten meters below the top, we were stopped by a completely smooth gendarme of black rock forming the summit. Our altimeter read 6,090m. We turned back from this point at 9 a.m. on May 10, reversed our route of ascent, and regained base camp at 3 p.m.

The north face of Lobuche West was our original plan, but it looked very dry. It is worth noting that during the last three years all the peaks of around 6,000m that I've seen in this region have appeared very dry. 📷

- ANGEL SALAMANCA, *SPAIN*

LOBUCHE EAST, EAST FACE, THE GOLDEN FRIENDS (HISTORICAL ASCENT)

DURING THE 1990s, the French Federation of Mountaineering and Climbing (FFME) developed a training program for groups of elite young alpinists—the Jeunes Alpinistes de Haut Niveau. The final session was often an expedition. In 1994, chief coach Jean-François Hagenmuller (sadly killed on the Rochefort Ridge near Chamonix in 2016) and Alexis Mallon, both instructors at the prestigious École Nationale de Ski et d'Alpinisme (ENSA), took young alpinists Jean-François Mercier, Bruno Ravanat, Benoît Robert, and Jérôme Thinières to the Khumbu to attempt new routes on Lobuche East and Kwangde.

On October 14 and 15, Hagenmuller, Mallon, and Ravanat tried a line toward the right side of the east face of Lobuche East (6,090m) but retreated due to serious and repeated rockfall. In 2014 this line would become Two Arrows Flight (*see AAJ 2015*), where the Ukrainian first ascensionists found some remnants of the attempt 20 years earlier.

Mercier, Robert, and Thinières, meanwhile, wanted to open a "modern" route up the compact rock in the center of the face. Starting in the vicinity of the 1990 route Ave Maria (Czech, UIAA VIII-), they moved right, into the middle of the face, where they found excellent sculptured rock that surprisingly allowed them to place adequate protection. (They left only five bolts left on the route.) Near the top they outflanked a 100m band of rotten schist by climbing to its left, crossing through the 1992 Korean route and finishing up the last meters of Ave Maria.

This team spent October 14 and 15 preparing the lower section of their line, then climbed the 900m wall (the last 100m in snow to the ridge) from October 16 to 19, using a portaledge. Difficulties were up to 7a (6c+ obligatory), and Robert considered it a "very pleasant climb, though rather committing." They would later name the route the Golden Friends, in homage to Thinieres, who died in the Pyrenees during the winter of 2004. 📷 🔍

– LINDSAY GRIFFIN, *FROM INFORMATION PROVIDED BY BENOÎT ROBERT AND RODOLPHE POPIER, LA CHRONIQUE, FFCAM*

AMA DABLAM–OMBIGAICHEN RIDGE, NORTHEAST COULOIR

WHILE ACCLIMATIZING BEFORE unsuccessful attempts on the south face of Nuptse and south face of Lhotse Shar in the spring, Jordi Corominas and Jordi Tozas (Spain) climbed a steep ice couloir on the northeast flank of Ama Dablam's southeast ridge. This is the ridge (Georges-Hubert, 1983) that connects with Ombigaichen. Starting from what little remains of the upper Ama Dablam (Chhukhung) Glacier on April 26, the pair climbed a steep snow slope into the obvious right-slanting couloir and followed it to the col (850m, WI4+). They descended the same way.

– *INFORMATION PROVIDED BY* RODOLPHE POPIER, *LA CHRONIQUE, FFCAM*

PEAK 41, NORTHEAST FACE

PREVIOUSLY UNREPORTED WAS the first ascent of the northeast face of Peak 41 (6,648m) by a Korean team in 2016. The ascent remained under the radar, even in Korea, likely because of the use of a helicopter for descent.

The climbers arrived at their 4,800m base camp on October 10. Two of the team's four climbing members—climbing leader Koo Eun-soo and Choi Ji-won—had attempted the left side of the face in 2014 (see *AAJ 2016*). They had found much snow high up, and feeling this line might be too difficult to climb, they opted in 2016 for another route toward the far right side of the face.

The climbing on this appears to be steep, sustained, and technical.

On October 17 the team reached an advanced base at 5,027m, and then bivouacked two nights on the face at 5,400m, two nights at 5,577m, then again at 5,909m. At some stage Choi gave up due to altitude sickness, leaving Koo, Han Dong-ik, and Yoo Hak-jae to continue. At 6,244m they were forced to spend three nights before continuing over the north summit and down to a bivouac in a snow cave on the ridge at 6,405m, their first comfortable, warm site.

The northeast face of Peak 41. (1) Geldard-Greenwood, 2012 attempt. (2) Choi-Kim-Koo-Wang, 2014 attempt. (3) Korean Route (Koo-Yoo, 2016). *Rob Greenwood*

Next day, October 27, with all their fuel now gone, Han decided to stay put while Koo and Yoo continued along the sharp summit ridge to the main top. At times the snow was almost one meter deep. The two reached the summit that morning and returned to the cave, only to be told that their non-climbing expedition leader, fearing the risk of avalanches during the descent—and with an approaching return date to Korea—had initiated a helicopter rescue. That same day the three climbers were lifted from site of the snow cave.

The almost 1,700m line had rock difficulties of 5.9 A1. 🔳

– LINDSAY GRIFFIN, *FROM INFORMATION SUPPLIED BY RODOLPHE POPIER, LA CHRONIQUE, FFCAM, AND KIM DONG-SOO, KOREA*

MAHALANGUR HIMAL / BARUN SECTION

HONGU, FIRST RECORDED ASCENT OF NORTHEAST FACE

ON OCTOBER 25, Pemba Sherpa (Nepal) and Hiroki Nakayama (Japan) made the first documented ascent of Hongu (6,764m, a.k.a. Hongku, Honku, or Sura Peak) via the northeast face. From Baruntse base camp, the pair crossed the West Col, south of Baruntse, descended the top section of the West Barun Glacier (a.k.a. Lower Barun Glacier), entered the glacier bay on the right, and made their third camp at around 6,360m, immediately below the northeast face of Hongu. The final 350m of this face is a steep snow and ice wall with serac barriers. The pair climbed nine pitches with a 70m rope, reaching the top at 3:15 p.m. Their rappel descent used mostly snow stakes for anchors, but they were forced to sacrifice one of Nakayama's ice tools when the stakes ran out. They regained camp at 8:30 p.m.

The history of climbing on Hongu is not clear, as most ascents have been made by parties without a permit for the peak. The most logical way to climb the mountain in good conditions would be the northeast face, but the first known ascent was in October 1983 by Sepp Egarter and Volker Klammer, who climbed the southwest ridge (D, 1,200m). The mountain was brought onto the permitted list in 2003; it should not be confused with Hongu Chuli (6,833m, originally known as Pyramid Peak) to the east. 🔳

– LINDSAY GRIFFIN, *FROM INFORMATION PROVIDED BY HIROKI NAKAYAMA, JAPAN*

CHINA

THE GREAT ARCH
VALHALLA: A 14-PITCH 5.15 CROSSING A 300-METER ROOF

BY KAREL DOWNSBROUGH, *WITH INFORMATION FROM* EDU MARIN, *SPAIN*

"I NEED TO bolt a line there!" That was Edu Marin's reaction after seeing photos of Corazon de Ensueño (240m, 8c, Dani Andrada) in Getu's Great Arch back in 2011. Getu is a quiet village in China's southern Guizhou Province that became known to climbers after the 2011 Petzl RocTrip video hit the internet. At its narrowest point the Getu Arch spans 70m, and the minimum height above the floor is around 120m. Locals have been free soloing up the lower arch for centuries to collect bird's nests, but it wasn't until June 2008 that Chamonix guide Olivier Balma and students from the CMDI (China Mountain Development Institute) bolted the first sport routes in Getu.

Since ending his competition career several years ago, Edu has focused on ticking very difficult and long rock climbs, often with the support of his 68-year-old father, Francisco "Novato" Marin. At Getu's Great Arch, he imagined establishing the longest and hardest roof climb in the world.

In March 2018, Edu and his brother Alex left Barcelona with 300 bolts, hundreds of quick-draws, and a lot of rope. After spending hours examining the arch through binoculars to find a climbable line, they decided to start on the right side of the cave, where four pitches (7b+, 7a, 8a+, and 7c+) gave access to the roof. Then the real work started. They dangled fixed lines from the roof so they could jumar up to access each section more efficiently. Over the course of the next month, they bolted seven pitches through the roof to the exit of the arch, from which three more pitches led to the top. The horizontal section of the line spans about 300m.

With a little time left before their return to Spain, Edu was able to try the pitches and quickly realized this might be a tougher project than he had imagined. The first roof pitch (fifth overall) is called Odin's Crack and would go at 9a+. From there to the final anchor, there are nine more pitches of 8a or harder (including two 8c+ pitches). After spending two months in Getu, Edu returned to Spain to train. His goal was to free all 14 pitches in succession and in a single day.

Edu returned to Getu in the fall of 2018, along with his brother and father, and spent a few months working the route. Alex returned to Spain after about a month, while Novato stayed on to support his son. The two took a week off to rest in Cambodia in January. In February, conditions were perfect, and Edu managed to send all the pitches separately, finally ticking Odin's Crack on February 19. It was time to attempt a free ascent from the ground up.

On his third attempt on a one-day ascent, he had made it through the entire roof without a mistake. There was one hard pitch left, Thor's Hammer (8c+), before the final two relatively easy 8a pitches. "I named it Thor's Hammer, because after getting there with the whole roof behind you, it feels like you're being knocked down on every move," Edu had explained. He was about to enter the last hard moves when a crimp hold snapped and he fell.

After a week of recuperation, he was back on the route on March 20, 2019, starting at 7 a.m. The first four pitches went smoothly, and he climbed through Odin's Crack without a problem. He cruised through the rest of the roof and got to the last hard pitch. "*Ahora sí!*" ("Now, yes!") Novato yelled as Edu climbed through Thor's Hammer and then, finally, to the top of Valhalla. After almost six months in Getu, Edu had freed Valhalla (450m, 9a+) in nine hours. 📖

Edu Marin dangles from the Great Arch, high above the Getu River. Half of Valhalla's 14 pitches cross the roof, totaling 300 meters of climbing. [Inset] Edu and Francisco celebrate. *Karel Downsbrough (both photos)*

WESTERN KOKSHAAL-TOO, KYZYL ASKER, SOUTH PILLAR

Kyzyl Asker (5,842m) showing the 2018 route up the south pillar. The 2016 ice route Lost in China (Lindič-Papert) is just to the right. See AAJ 2017 for other lines on this face, which is over 1,000 meters high. *Evgeny Murin*

From July 24–30, 2018, Evgeny Murin and Ilya Penyaev (both from Russia) climbed the south pillar of Kyzyl Asker (5,842m). Their new route follows the obvious ridge line to the left of the 2016 Lindič-Papert ice couloir, Lost in China, probably joining that route for the last six pitches to the summit ridge, where the Russian route appears to terminate.

The pair approached from the Kyrgyzstan side (snowshoes were used) and placed base camp on the unnamed glacier below the face at 3,800m. They south pillar is broad and has no clear crest, which made route-finding complex. After the first two days of sunshine, they experienced mixed weather (one day was spent waiting out bad weather in their tent near the top of the pillar). They completed the 1,170m route in 31 pitches at 6B (ED2 7a+ A2 M5). Around a dozen pitches involved aid, and 33 drilled placements were used. They descended the route in 28 rappels over one and a half days and were back at base camp on August 1. 📷

– INFORMATION FROM **ELENA DMITRENKO,** *RISK.RU, RUSSIA*

BOGDA OLA RANGE, BOGDA V (5,216M), NORTHWEST FACE

Dili Xiati and Li Zongli made their first attempt on the northwest face of Bogda V in 2010. [*Bogda V is here defined as the summit at the western end of the Bogda Ola chain. At 5,216m, it is the fifth-highest summit of the Bogda group and lies a little over 2km southwest of the main summit. It was first climbed by Ryohei Uchida's Japanese expedition in 1981, via the north ridge.*] This was a couple of years after they had graduated from the Chinese Mountaineering Development Institute (CMDI) program. The two retreated after four pitches in 2010 due to a sudden storm.

In 2012 they made a second attempt, this time accompanied by Kang Hua, a Chinese guide who had been co-instructor on the first CMDI program. After climbing 900m of the ice face, they dropped their stove and, faced with several days without drinking water, they descended.

In 2013 all three tried again and this time bailed not far from the summit. During the descent, Li Zongli was fortunate to escape with his life, when he fell 600m. Descending in the dark, Dili Xiati and Kang Hua lost their way. Luckily, there was a mountain guide course in the massif at the time, and the participants were able to assist with the rescue of the injured Li Zongli and the others.

Starting in 2016, Li Zongli was busy trying to climb Minya Konka, which he succeeded in doing in 2018 (*see AAJ 2019*), but Bogda V was never far from his mind.

In late August of 2019 the same trio tried again. From base camp to Camp 1 was just two hours; the climbers were quite familiar with the route. The climbing from Camp 1 to Camp 2, near a crevasse close to the upper ridge, had been all on névé on previous attempts but was now hard ice. From Camp 2 they made their summit bid on August 28. After climbing along the snow ridge for 100m, they found hard ice. They traversed one pitch to the start of a 30m ice couloir, where the ice was so thin and hard that Li Zongli belayed only half-way up, at around the same height he had fallen in 2013. After climbing a slab they reached the crux of the route, a steep chimney, where a fixed rope and metal ladder are still in place from the Japanese ascent in 1981. A traverse on very exposed mixed terrain (the point from which the trio had retreated in 2013), two more pitches, and a final snow arête brought them to the top. It was a little before 6 p.m.

The northwest face of Bogda V (5,216 meters). The difficult final ridge to the summit is not visible. A Chinese trio succeeded after four attempts spanning a decade. *Li Zongli*

The descent to Camp 2 took until midnight, and the following day the climbers descended to base camp, largely by Abalakov anchors, reaching camp at 10 p.m. The new route was 1,300m, TD+ 5.10+ AI3+ M5 75°.

– LI ZONGLI, *CHINA, TRANSLATED BY* XIA ZHONGMING, *GERMANY*

TIBET / MAHALANGUR HIMAL

HISTORICAL NOTES ON PALUNG RI AND CHO OYU

MANY SOURCES (including the AAJ) have credited the first ascent of Palung Ri (7,012m) to Slovenians Andrej and Marija Štremfelj, who climbed the south-southeast ridge in 1995 as acclimatization for Cho Oyu. Palung Ri lies just north of the Palung La, a 6,500m pass at the foot of Cho Oyu's north ridge. To be fair, the Slovenian couple never claimed the first ascent—it was bestowed upon them.

Correspondence with Martin Lutterjohann, a member of the Academic Alpine Club of Munich, who climbed the south-southeast ridge of Palung Ri from the Palung La in 1992, led to further research and the conclusion that the true first ascent of the peak was by Edmund Hillary and George Lowe from Eric Shipton's Cho Oyu expedition in 1952. On May 14, the two climbed the west-northwest ridge from a 6,390m col, which they approached via the Gyabrag Glacier to the south.

The peak, which was not called Palung Ri at the time, was climbed again on May 16, 1955, by Erwin Schneider and Ernst Senn, during the early days of Norman Dyhrenfurth's extended expedition to attempt Lhotse. These two took the same route and climbed to over 6,800m on skis. It was climbed again in 1987, but the route followed is not certain. Then, in May 1992, Lutterjohann and Michael Kinne made the first documented ascent of the south-southeast ridge—the one credited to the Štremfelj pair.

Members of this same German expedition also made a strong attempt on the first ascent of the north-northwest ridge of Cho Oyu (8,188m), with Uwe Koblitz and Christoph Zuleger reaching 7,300m. More details on this attempt and on Palung Ri's history are at the AAJ website.

– LINDSAY GRIFFIN, *INFORMATION SUPPLIED BY* MARTIN LUTTERJOHANN, *GERMANY*

MT. GROSVENOR, WEST FACE, TCHEU C'TE PANTHÈRE

PIERRICK FINE, JORDI Noguere, and I landed in Chengdu on October 9 and immediately started our journey to Garze, the northern gateway to the Minya Konka Range. On the 11th we established base camp at 4,350m, after two days of approach. The weather was quite unstable, with a lot of snow and wind.

After five days of acclimatization we descended to base camp to rest and prepare for the next reasonable weather window. During this time we stashed gear below the west face of Mt. Grosvenor (a.k.a. Riwuqie Feng, 6,376m), four hours from base camp over burly moraine. Early on the 23rd, from a high camp, we started up the left side of the west face, well left of the central couloir climbed in 2010 by Kyle Dempster and Bruce Normand. In steep gullies, four pitches of AI5+ to 6 led to less difficult terrain. Above this, three steep pitches led to the north-northwest ridge, just as the sun was setting. After two mixed pitches up the crest, we dug a tent platform in the snow. A long section of snow on the following day got us to the summit at 1 p.m.

[Top] Ice gully on Tcheu c'te Panthère, west face of Mt. Grosvenor (6,376m). *Etienne Journet* [Bottom] Grosvenor from the northwest. (1) Tcheu c'te Panthère (2019). (2) Central Couloir (2010). (3) Black Wolves and Blue Poppies (2011). (4) French and Slovenian attempts. (5, right skyline) Southwest ridge (2003). *Jan Kreisinger*

All in all, conditions on the route had been good. However, the ice was quite thin, sometimes of poor quality, and sometimes covered with loose snow. The rock had been very compact and mostly hard to protect. We had planned to take three days for the ascent, with two bivouacs, but constantly changing weather and strong wind forced us to push hard on the first day to reach our second proposed bivouac site.

We descended the southwest ridge (the route of the peak's first ascent, in 2003, by Julie Ann Clyma and Roger Payne) in thick mist and cold. On the shoulder below the summit, as it narrows into the southwest ridge, all three of us, roped together, fell over a 6m to 7m ice wall formed by a wind scoop, which we had been unable to distinguish in zero visibility. Fortunately, there was a flat snow slope on the far side; unfortunately, Jordi, who was last on the rope and therefore was whipped faster over the icefall, broke some ribs.

At around 6,000m we set off down the west flank, making 14 rappels to reach the glacier. It then took some time to get back to our tent below the face, because the glacier proved highly crevassed. We spent a night here and next day descended to base camp, soon returning to France because Jordi's ribs were very painful.

Because of snow leopard tracks we saw during our acclimatization, we named the route Tcheu c'te Panthère (1,300m, ED). 📷

– ETIENNE JOURNET, *FRANCE*

TATSIENLU MASSIF, LAMO-SHE AND OTHER ASCENTS

In recent times I have realized that what really makes me happy is visiting new areas, particularly if they are little explored. My latest adventure was perhaps more intense than usual, but the mountain didn't let me down, the ascent giving me great satisfaction.

The east side of Lamo-she (6,070m, 29°56'57.97"N, 102°3'2.26"E) had only been visited by local herb collectors. Pietro Picco and I found little information beforehand, and, to complicate things, the weather was bad when we arrived. We established base camp at 3,400m, then managed to make a

Tomas Franchini in front of Lamo-she (6,070m). His solo ascent of the peak followed the diagonal ice line over his right shoulder to the northeast ridge and then the summit at far left. The new route gained about 1,500 meters. *Tomas Franchini*

gear cache at 4,400m and identify a line on the southeast face. We then waited days for good weather, until Pietro, with whom I got on very well, gave up and decided to head home.

I found myself alone in the middle of nowhere, isolated and totally wild. However, that same day, May 14, it was sunny and I set off to seek a more direct route to the start of the face. Having found it, I now had a difficult decision: After some thought I decided to continue immediately, but to go light and climb as fast as possible. I took axes and crampons and a light down jacket but left the rest of my gear, including harness and rope, at the foot of the face.

I started climbing the southeast face of Lamo-she a little after midday, reached the crest of the northeast ridge, and followed this to the summit, arriving at 7 p.m. The ascent had not been easy, and it had been long: maybe 1,500m of height gain. I reversed my route, getting lost near the bottom of the wall when mist arrived. I rested a few hours and regained base camp 21 hours after leaving. I named the route Wild Blood (1,500m, WI5 M5+ V 90°). [*The only previous known ascent of Lamo-she took place in 1993, when an American team came up the glacier below the northwest face, then followed the steep west-northwest ridge to the top (AAJ 1994).*]

Over subsequent days I made two ascents of unclimbed peaks on subsidiary spurs off the long northeast ridge Lamo-she. On May 17, I climbed the southeast ridge of a rocky 5,000m peak that I named Pietro's Picco, after my climbing partner. (Without his help in the early stages, I couldn't have achieved any of my climbs.) The ascent was around 600m with difficulties to VI. Then, on the 25th, I climbed the north face of a smaller rock peak, which I named Jiyue Shan (4,200m), after my friend and agent, Jiyue Zhang, who helped organize the expedition. The route was 400m high and D+. 🔘

— TOMAS FRANCHINI, *ITALY*

ABI, SOUTH FACE AND SOUTHEAST RIDGE, BREAKTHROUGH

At 5 a.m. on October 12, Wang Yongpeng and Xiang Shuxiang set out from their base camp at 4,680m in the upper Shuangqiao Valley for the south face of Abi (5,694m). It took them 1.5 hours to cross the glacier to the foot of the face at 4,850m, where they started climbing left of Graduation Exam (5.9 M4 AI2+ 50°, Liu Zhixiong, *AAJ 2015*).

The mountain was in very snowy condition, and the first 240m were mostly loose rock covered by fresh snow. It was hard to find protection and belays, and the maximum difficulties were M5. The next 150m gave steep mixed climbing up a stepped rock wall. Above this, another 240m of slightly steeper climbing led to the southeast ridge. They had wanted to climb a more direct route toward the summit, but were forced by the difficult terrain to veer right.

A final 220m of climbing along the ridge led to the summit—almost. Initially, this section was not particularly difficult, and they moved together in deteriorating weather until reaching a steep corner. This was compact and wet, and they saw no possibility of getting up it. They traversed right to a second corner with a few pegs from previous ascents. Xiang led it but somehow lost a crampon in the process. At the top of the corner, the summit was only one rope length higher.

The two continued in a full blizzard to a final rock wall, about 10m below the summit. Frozen, they decided not to climb this final step and began a rappel descent, west of their line of ascent. They reached the glacier at 1 a.m. The climb is Breakthrough (850m, 700m of new climbing, D 70°). 📷

– XIA ZHONGMING, *GERMANY*

The west face of Abi in the northwest Siguniang Range. (1) Chen-Hua-Tong Route (2019). (2) Shivering (Yan-Zhao, 2010). *Supplied by Xia Zhongming*

ABI, WEST FACE, NEW ROUTE

UNTIL 2019 THERE was only one route on the west face of Abi (5,694m): Shivering (5.7 M3 AI2, Li-Yan-Zhao, 2010*)*. Chen Chujun, Hua Feng, and Tong Haijun planned to open a second route to its left.

On September 12 they established camp above the Jiesigou (valley) at 4,500m. It rained next day, but on the 14th they were able to make a reconnaissance, climbing increasingly steep, smooth, rocky terrain (up to 5.7) to reach the foot of the hanging glacier. Throughout this section, the huge serac walls of the face loomed directly above. [*Since the two ascents of Shivering, in 2010 and '11, the structure of the hanging glacier has changed substantially.*] The three climbers scoped a direct line up the left side of the glacier and then descended to camp.

Next day they established a bivouac on a flat gravel slope at 4,900m and then, starting at around 4 a.m. on the 16th, simul-climbed 100m of loose rock to reach the start of the glacier, which provided the first crux. The ice here was separated from the rock beneath, with water flowing between the two. Hua Feng led this pitch, which finished with a couple of meters of 95° ice at the top. Above, the terrain was AI3. After two pitches of AI2, followed by a more or less horizontal section, they encountered a 60–70° ice step. Above this, steep mixed with rotten rock (difficult to protect, with only one or two runners per pitch) led to the summit.

They arrived on the highest point at 3:30 p.m. in poor visibility, their GPS recording 5,687m. The three then downclimbed and rappelled the face, arriving back at their bivouac at 9 p.m. The ascent took 12 hours, the descent five hours, and the 800m route, climbed mostly in poor weather and mist, was graded AD+ 5.8 AI3+ M4 60°.

– XIA ZHONGMING, *GERMANY*

Tom Grant in the upper half of the descent, above the huge serac bands. *Enrico Mosetti*

SKIING THE CAROLINE FACE
THE FIRST DESCENT OF AORAKI/MT. COOK'S GIANT SOUTHEAST FACE

BY TOM GRANT, *U.K.*

This historic descent was made in October 2017 but was not previously reported in the AAJ. This is a first-person account from one of the skiers.

THE CAROLINE FACE, the huge, steep, serac-laden southeast face of Aoraki/Mt. Cook, New Zealand's highest peak (3,724m), had been in the consciousness of small groups of dedicated steep skiers for some time. There had been several attempts by high-profile teams, and it was widely publicized in a 2010 article for ESPN featuring the biggest, gnarliest unskied faces around the world.

Ross Hewitt and I went for a first attempt in 2015 after our busy summer guiding season in Chamonix was over. Conditions were good that year, and the Caroline looked very white. However, the steep and crumbling middle serac band deterred us from making an attempt. It was only after studying aerial photos that we spotted a potential line, traversing the face far to lookers' right and bypassing the middle seracs by taking a couloir and face much closer to the east ridge. By the time we envisaged this as an option, we ran short of time and weather.

Ross and I were eager to return. The trip was an easy sell to fellow Brit Ben Briggs and Italian Enrico Mosetti, two of the strongest and most enthusiastic steep skiers I know. Unfortunately, Ross had to pull out due to a back injury. When Ben, Enrico, and I arrived in Aoraki/Mt. Cook Village, Cam Mulvey, the guardian at the Wyn Irwin Lodge, showed us a recent photo of the Caroline in which we spotted a weakness in the middle serac band that hadn't been there in 2015. It appeared

Aerial view of the ski line on the Caroline Face. The team made three rappels (R) totaling 140 meters on the 1,650-meter descent. *Ben Briggs*

there was some sort of ramp breaking through it. This was confirmed when we flew past the face, en route to the Plateau Hut, and zoomed in on our photos.

We set our alarms for midnight on October 27. Leaving the hut just after 1 a.m., we set out toward the east ridge, skinning under the east face to join the ridge as high as we could. On the face we encountered chest-deep breakable crust, and this, combined with a minor route-finding error, cost us some time. Nevertheless, in the absence of a compelling reason for turning back, we toiled on and upward. Reaching the east ridge, we broke trail on some delicate knife-edge arêtes loaded with fresh snow. On a section of exposed ice near the top, we got the rope out and moved together for the last 100m, topping out just before 9 a.m.

Our descent began from Porter Col, at about 3,550m, between the Low and Middle peaks of Aoraki/Mt. Cook. Setting up V-thread anchors, we made two abseils over unskiable 60–80° ice, totaling about 100m. As soon as our team touched down on the face, we were delighted to find cold, compact, and stable powder snow on the sustained 50° face. The skiing was consistent and open on beautiful pitches all the way down to the middle serac band. The three of us have skied substantially steeper runs in the Alps, so the skiing itself was not the crux—we had to nail the route-finding to ski the face safely and in good time. What looked obvious from below was not always obvious when on the face itself. Skiing into the ramp that we'd spotted on the middle serac band, I set up our final abseil on another V-thread anchor. Only 40m later, we reached the lower slopes.

For the first time we were now fully exposed to the active seracs overhead. The snow got a bit wet but remained very skiable, and we skied a long and fast, leg-burning pitch, trending leftward toward the exit we had scouted, the only feasible way off the face. Ben spotted the crumbling serac cave that we had earmarked as our reference point. An hour and a half after leaving Porter Col, we were safely off the face. We exited at around 1,900m, having skied approximately 1,650 vertical meters.

The Caroline is the biggest face the three of us have ever skied, and it rightly deserves its mythical status within New Zealand mountaineering. However, the last couple of very warm summers have drastically altered the middle serac band, making it a lot less appealing for ski descents. The three of us couldn't have been happier to succeed when we did, knowing that we had skied it with what felt like a solid margin of safety. 📷

More Aoraki/Mt. Cook Ski Descents: *In November 2019, Ross Hewitt and Dave Searle skied a possible new line on the lower Caroline Face, dropping in from the east ridge for a 650m descent. The two also made the second known descent of the Bowie Couloir on the north face. The latter was first skied by Andreas Fransson and Magnus Kastengren (Sweden) in 2013. Shortly afterward, Kastengren took a fatal fall from near the summit of Aoraki/Mt. Cook as he and Fransson began an attempt to ski the Caroline Face.*

NEW ZEALAND ALPINE HIGHLIGHTS

THE SUMMER SEASON in New Zealand was highlighted by several significant repeats in Aoraki/Mt. Cook National Park. During a settled period of weather in mid-December 2018, Sooji Clarkson and James Warren ventured onto the upper Balfour Glacier to check out the alpine rock faces of Mt. Drake (2,960m) and Mt. Magellan (3,049m). Here they managed ascents of Astrolabe (Defourneaux-Dickson-McDermott, 1988) and Shogun (Aubrey-Pears, 1981) on the northwest face of Drake and Anyone Can Play Guitar (Flyvbjerg-Palman, 1995) on the west face of Magellan.

Warren then teamed up with Evan Davies in January to climb the Hillary (South) Ridge on Aoraki/Mt. Cook (3,724m). This was the first ascent of the ridge following a 2014 rockfall event.

In March, Richie Jacomb and Asher March ventured to the upper Bonney Glacier, where they climbed a new alpine rock route on the north face of Malte Brun (3,198m). Called Multi-Sport (700m, V, 5, 18/5.10a), the route follows a prominent rib up the center of the face to top out high on the northeast ridge.

Ben Sanford reaching the summit ridge of Mt. Haast after the first ascent of Hotline. *Gavin Lang*

Down in the Darran Mountains, further development occurred on the Sinbad Gully Wall (*see AAJ 2019*). Jimmy Finlayson and Helen Sinclair climbed four new pitches from the end of Welcome to Sinbad (Jefferies-Rogers, 2003) to establish Drop Zone (grade 24/5.11c, A1), while Camille Berthoux, Tom Hoyle, Paul Rogers, and Karl "Merry" Schimanski combined to put up Rainmaker (300m, 23/5.11b).

Despite some early season promise, the winter of 2019 will be remembered as being unsettled and uncharacteristically warm. After a cold snap in late May, Ben Dare soloed a new line on the west face of the Dasler Pinnacles (2,315m) in June, following a prominent gully on the right side of the face, parallel to and just right of White Strike, with difficulties of WI3 and M4. In the Remarkables, Craig Jefferies, Stephen Skelton, and Kyle Walter established a multi-pitch mixed climb on the southwest face of Single Cone (2,319m): Gone Rogue (M5).

The arrival of spring saw a flurry of activity on peaks above the West Coast Neves, the huge snowfields feeding the Fox and Franz Josef glaciers. Gavin Lang and Ben Sanford took advantage of good rime on the east face of Mt. Haast (3,114m) to claim the first ascent of Hotline (IV, 5+, M5), which ascends 450m up the third spur between the High and Middle Peaks. Milo Gilmour and Llewellyn Murdoch teamed up to climb Bottlenosed Dolphin (IV, 5+) on the west face of Lendenfeld Peak (3,194m). This ice and mixed route follows the second gully to the left of the Mutant (McCartney-McFarlane, 1995) for 400m before following the upper Northwest Rib to the summit. The pair quickly followed this up on the south face of Mt. Barnicoat (2,800m), where they climbed six pitches of steep ice in the vicinity of the 2010 rockfall scar: Make My Day (III, 6).

In September, Reg Measures and Rose Pearson made the long trek up the Hooker Valley to the Sheila Face of Aoraki/Mt. Cook, where great ice conditions helped them make the second ascent of Pilgrim (VI, 7, M6, WI5, Jennings-Ladiges, 2018). In early January 2020, Pearson returned to the Hooker Valley with Alastair McDowell, starting at midnight to make a rare sub-24-hour, car-to-car Grand Traverse of Aoraki/Mt. Cook. 🖹 🅾

– BEN DARE, *NEW ZEALAND*

BOOK REVIEWS

EDITED BY **DAVID STEVENSON**

THE ADVENTURER'S SON

Roman Dial. William Morrow, 2020. Hardcover, 351 pages, $28.99.

IN THIS HEART-WRENCHING memoir, Roman Dial walks the reader through that most horrific of losses, the death of one's child. On July 10, 2014, Cody Roman Dial began a risky and illegal crossing of Corcovado National Park in Costa Rica, a complex wilderness of trackless rainforest, its bewildering arroyos choked with fallen trees and tangled vines, each step bedeviled by the possibility of a deadly snakebite or a twisted ankle. Roman—he'd gone by his father's name since age six, when the two had done a 60-mile crossing of Umnak in the Aleutian Islands—was in the middle of a months-long solo journey through Central and South America. Seasoned and mature at 27, he was well-equipped for the challenge. "He'd been raised on trips of independent discovery where we used our wits, knowledge, and experience to explore the natural world," Dial writes of his family's travels in Australia, Borneo, and Puerto Rico, as well as close to home in the Alaska wilderness. "It was good to see him continuing those kinds of adventures on his own."

On July 23, concerned that he hadn't heard from his son, Dial reads his last email more thoroughly and discovers that Roman is now ten days overdue. He realizes in that instant that something is seriously amiss. "Shock washed over me," Dial writes. "Then guilt. Guilt over the fact that…I hadn't given him the attention he deserved…[and] spent too much time on my own trips, on my own interests." He leaves the next day for Costa Rica and begins a two-year search for Roman, replete with numerous dashed hopes, corrupt and uncaring officials, a devious and manipulative TV producer, yet also many kind souls who help in ways large and small. In the end, a few days before the airing of the made-for-television reality show *Missing Dial*, which reached the conclusion that Roman had been murdered, Dial and his wife Peggy get word that human remains and camping gear had been found by a remote creek in Corcovado. Emailed photos confirm the dreadful news. Further investigation reveals that Roman had likely been bitten by a poisonous snake or crushed by a falling tree. "He had probably died before any of us knew he was in trouble," Dial concludes. "Before I had even read his last words: 'It should be difficult to get lost forever.'"

Far more than just a grim chronicle of uncertainty and grief, though, *The Adventurer's Son* is an honest and hopeful celebration of lives lived to the fullest, of the powerful experiences and connections that nature and adventure provide to Dial and his family. As a grad student at Stanford, he moves to Puerto Rico with Peggy and two young kids (Jasper, their daughter, is just a year old) to study "complex food webs in tropical rainforests," the subject of his Ph.D. "Like every three-year-old, our boy asked a barrel of questions," he recalls of their first jungle visits. "Why do lizards lose their tails? Why do birds sing? Why are flowers bright? I tried hard to nourish this insatiable curiosity on a trip that initiated our shared explorations across five continents and two decades." Dial clearly has been successful in this quest, yet he is also brutally honest in revealing his own flaws. In particular he explores the tension between holding onto the child he nurtures and protects, and letting go of the adult Roman becomes as he discovers his place in the world. "For miles, we each stammered in frustration as emotion eclipsed logic," Dial writes, describing an argument with his son during a scientific trip to Bhutan in 2012. "All fathers readily see their foibles reflected in their sons, and there, plain as day, were mine." This reader is thankful for Dial's willingness to share the unique joys and challenges of his life. You will be too.

– MICHAEL KENNEDY

BLACK CAR BURNING

HELEN MORT. Chatto & Windus (U.K.), 2019. Hardcover, 336 pages, £14.99.

A CROWDED SOCCER stadium in 1989, a throng of fans so large that nearly 100 of them are crushed to death. The modern-day crag outside the northern English city that bills itself as the climbing capital of the U.K. Poet Helen Mort sees the ties between the two, linked by the complex tether of trust that links one person to another. In a debut novel that jumps between three residents of Sheffield, a midsize metropolis in Yorkshire, Mort untangles those ties. Climbing, for all its introspection, is not a solo sport; neither is life.

Black Car Burning is named for a route at the Stanage Edge in the Peak District, a miles-long lip of grindstone most famous for climbing routes (plus a cameo in a big-budget Jane Austen movie). But Mort is less concerned with the route and the climber who chases it, a charismatic young woman named Caron, than the complex web around her: Caron's polyamorous relationship with Alexa, a police community officer who doesn't climb; her budding connection with Leigh, who works in a climbing shop and feels unanchored to the world unless she's climbing; and, even farther removed from Black Car Burning's E7 moves, there's Pete, haunted by Sheffield's real-life sports tragedy known as the Hillsborough Disaster.

As chapters bounce between points of view, interstitial passages speak in first-person from geographic locations. Not just the windswept bluffs and tiny crag caves littered with trash, but Sheffield's crowded streets. Alexa patrols Page Hall, a city district simmering with racial discord between Slovakian Roma and British Pakistani populations; Mort captures the heaving discontent of a neighborhood with no clear way forward. Lyric passages bequeath paved car parks with humanity, and trauma echoes from one generation to the next.

Characters relieve tension on rock, with a refreshing perspective on Sheffield's signature sport. Mort comes at the crag by way of queer women, plus a husband whose wife's skill surpasses his. In brief scenes she sketches familiar one-upmanship and macho attitudes, the hierarchies of bold youngsters and dirtbag seniors. The vague hero-worship for what a climber had done, or said he'd done, or been thought capable of—no one's quite sure. How a petite woman is first dismissed and then refused even acknowledgment when she outdoes her male partners. The scenes are rendered with such specificity, folded into the fabric of her characters, as to blend into the greater milieu of modern sport.

There's nothing clichéd about Mort's community of climbers (unless it's the rickety van that smells of feet, which must be given a pass as a primal archetype). Her characters don't dance on rock, they're martial artists. And a belay is not simply an act of protection, not a lifeline. It's also an act of disappearing, of becoming "a sign you only notice when it's gone. Like a relative." Leigh explains how some measure of disinterest is key, and she can't keep belaying coworker Pete once she cares too much about his survival.

Trust, argues Mort, is not the same as love. It's more basic than that. A stable foothold is less about skill or strength than it is about belief in the rock itself. Her characters dig into the lost bonds between community and police, between romantic partners, between parents and children, to finally unearth the bedrock of connection and build anew.

– ALLISON WILLIAMS

THE IMPOSSIBLE CLIMB: ALEX HONNOLD, EL CAPITAN, AND THE CLIMBING LIFE

Mark Synnott. Dutton, 2019. 416 pages, hardcover $28, paperback $18.

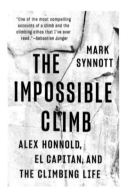

IF THE QUALITY of Mark Synnott's book, *The Impossible Climb*, were on trial, I would be struck from the jury. I have too much prior knowledge, too many opinions and prejudices. Like most climbers, I've been so inundated over the past year with media about Alex Honnold's Freerider solo that I was already sick of it by the time I picked up Synnott's book. Kind of like how you feel after an underground band you have loved forever releases a single that goes big, the posers and wannabes catch on, and you can't stop rolling your eyes and saying, "Dude, that's not even their best song."

The Impossible Climb, as I assume most people reading this will know, recounts Honnold's free solo of El Capitan on June 3, 2017. But it's also equal parts coming of age story for the sport itself and memoir of the author. It was my interest in Synnott's story that most drew me to this book, along with John Long's quote on the dust jacket comparing it to surf journalist William Finnegan's *Barbarian Days*, which I devoured a few years ago. In fact, ever since I finished *Barbarian Days*, I've been wondering who would write the climbing version and when.

Unfortunately, I don't think the comparison holds water, mostly because there's no singular event in Finnegan's book—one big, crazy wave, for example—which all the drama leads up to. If Honnold's climb were a footnote instead of the main event, the analogy would be more apt. But that's not the book Synnott wrote, and, as it stands, the parts of the narrative that do read like *Barbarian Days* sometimes feel cobbled—even shoehorned—in there. There were moments when I felt like I was watching a mashup of all the popular climbing films of late: *Valley Uprising*, *The Dawn Wall*, and of course, *Free Solo*. I thought the book would have been better without some of those diversions, but I doubt Synnott is to blame for them. I wouldn't be surprised to learn that a non-climbing editor thought it imperative to cover all the times in recent memory that climbing made a blip in the mainstream media.

That said, the deeper I got into *The Impossible Climb* the more engrossed I became. Synnott's storytelling was compelling, his pacing was perfect, and his ability to walk the fine line between explaining too much and too little was uncanny. I'd as readily gift the book to a climbing devotee of 20 years or that veteran's "climbing curious" relative. After the first 70 pages, I stopped making silly notes about how Synnott might have done things differently, and just started enjoying what he did. I read the last few chapters in bed in one long headlamp-lit vigil during which I could not put the book down, surprisingly rapt by a story whose ending I already knew.

There's a moment where Synnott describes Honnold looking stiff and awkward at the start of his historic climb, but eventually finding his rhythm. That's how I felt about Synnott's writing. *The*

Impossible Climb seemed to me to start off a bit shaky, but by the end it was tight, composed, and deeply impressive. It isn't *Barbarian Days*. But maybe it's not meant to be. Maybe that's Synnott's next book. I sure hope so. If it is, I'll be first in line to buy it.

– CHRIS KALMAN

PAUL PREUSS: LORD OF THE ABYSS.

David Smart. Rocky Mountain Books (Canada), 2019. Hardcover, 247 pages, CAN $32.

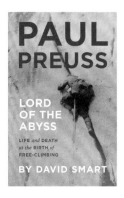

In 2014, as Alex Honnold and I were working on his memoir, *Alone on the Wall*, I laid a little trap for him. "So, Alex," I said earnestly, "I'm sure Paul Preuss is one of your heroes."

I got the blank look I expected. "Who?"

"Alex! Preuss invented free soloing!"

To tell the truth, I knew only the bare outlines of the meteoric career of Paul Preuss, who died in 1913 at the age of 27 on an unwitnessed fall from the daunting north ridge of the Mandlkogel. Somewhere along the way I had come across the scenario of Preuss's demise that David Smart calls "the knife theory." In *Alone on the Wall*, instead of giving me a blank look, Alex ruefully empathized with the Austrian prodigy's final moments. "I can just picture it," he wrote. "Preuss stops for a lunch break. He takes out his knife, maybe to cut an apple or a hunk of cheese. The knife slips out of his hand, so he lunges forward to grab it, forgetting for the instant where he is. Goes off the edge, tries to grab something, and misses. Talk about the worst four seconds of his life!"

Even today, outside of Austria and perhaps Germany, Paul Preuss remains little known and less understood. We can hope that David Smart's deeply insightful biography (the first in English, though Reinhold Messner has written two lives of Preuss in German) may rectify that neglect. Smart's command of the primary sources, including Preuss' startling polemic "Künstliche Hilfsmittel auf Hochtouren" ("Artificial Aids on Alpine Routes")—reminiscent of nothing so much as Messner's own "The Murder of the Impossible"—allows him to paint a nuanced portrait of a man who was half mad genius, half insecure striver. As a Jew, Preuss was excluded from many Austrian and German climbing clubs and circles (he would convert to Protestant Christianity at 22, though for spiritual and aesthetic rather than political reasons.) For all his competitiveness, he so enjoyed roping up with women (including Anna Freud, Sigmund's daughter) that he felt the need to write two articles explaining this apparent aberration to his misogynistic peers.

In his short life as a climber, Preuss dazzled his contemporaries. Tita Piaz, his only equal in the Dolomites, hailed him as "the most fantastic knight of the mountains of all times and all nations." Hans Dülfer called Preuss "the complete master." Later climbers, including Emilio Comici, Giusto Gervasutti, and Willo Welzenbach, were in awe of the climber that Gervasutti saluted as "unsurpassed and unsurpassable."

Preuss' soloing ethic makes even Alex Honnold's style look half-hearted. To Preuss' way of thinking, not only was the use of pitons an abomination, but relying on the rope to rappel, except in an emergency, was arrant cheating. "If you cannot climb down," Preuss declared, "you should not climb up." Yet the romantic image of a soloist confronting the most dangerous walls in the Alps only "by fair means" is undercut by Smart's shrewd analysis of the nakedly ambitious youth whose drive "was fueled by a relentless need to prove himself."

It came as a complete surprise to me that in his mid-20s Preuss made his living by writing articles and giving lectures for which he was handsomely paid. According to one source, Preuss delivered no fewer than 100 talks during the last three years of his life.

If we come away from Smart's evocation of Paul Preuss puzzled by the man's contradictions and confused about his legacy—is Alex Honnold really the perfectionist heir of Preuss' radical vision or something else entirely?—we must stand in admiration of one of the finest biographies of a climber ever written.

– DAVID ROBERTS

RISING: BECOMING THE FIRST NORTH AMERICAN WOMAN ON EVEREST

SHARON WOOD. *Mountaineers Books, 2019. Hardcover, 272 pages, $19.95.*

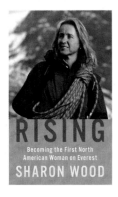

IN 1986, CANADIAN alpinist and mountain guide Sharon Wood became the first North American woman to summit Everest. Now, more than 30 years later, she's sharing her story.

Rising is a detailed, specific, focused account of the 70 days Wood and her teammates spent climbing the challenging west ridge of Everest. Of the team of ten climbers, only Wood and her partner Dwayne Congdon reached the top, and their successful summit route via a new variation—and without Sherpa support—has never been repeated.

This book reads like a thoughtful real-time expedition log: The team arrives at base camp, starts moving up the mountain, and addresses each challenge as it comes. While most books about Everest involve extensive history, science, logistics, route beta, weather, and/or other background information, *Rising* is strikingly devoid of details that aren't relevant to Wood's specific tale. "As overbearing friends can be, Everest wanted this book to be about it," she writes. "But the mountain merely serves as a stage and a timeline for the real story."

What, then, is the real story? The media had one suggestion, pitting Wood against the other female climber—her ex-lover's new girlfriend—who was part of an American team attempting a similar climb. But to a discerning reader, there are other narratives: Wood's training with Outward Bound and early mentorship with other climbers and guides; her experience as a woman on a Himalayan expedition in the 1980s; her references to substance abuse, depression, and other mental health challenges; and, perhaps most of all, the whiplash of her experience upon returning from the climb. Front and center, though, are Wood's personal interactions: with her teammates, with her family, and, inevitably, with the mountain itself. She states it concisely in the introduction: "Everest taught me…the value of relationships: my relationship with myself, with some remarkable people, and with the world around me."

Despite the refreshing humility in Wood's writing, it's very clear she was a spectacularly strong and motivated climber, both mentally and physically. That strength is reflected in this book: Just as it takes a concentrated, almost obsessively single-minded effort to climb Everest, this tale firmly avoids wandering off scene. I deeply respect Sharon Wood, and would have liked a more substantial peek behind the curtain of her story—what it took to combat the sexism she faced, what challenges she met at other times in her life, what else she learned in her career as a climber and a guide—but I understand her decision to keep *Rising* focused on the climb, and I respect that, too.

– CHARLOTTE AUSTIN

HANGDOG DAYS: CONFLICT, CHANGE, AND THE RACE FOR 5.14

Jeff Smoot. Mountaineers Books, 2019. Paperback, 320 pages, $21.95.

ONE OF THE enduring phenomena in American climbing history has been clashes between the old guard and the new. While not entirely absent in European countries, I think it's safe to say the most influential and dramatic episode of bolt chopping happened on El Capitan on the Warren Harding route known as the Wall of the Early Morning Light. This episode in 1971 would have a huge impact on the future of American climbing in ways its perpetrators could not have entirely foreseen. In their quest for an ethically pure climbing style, Royal Robbins and other Yosemite locals had failed to reckon with the impact of another giant in American climbing, John Gill, who was redefining climbing away from following protectable features on big walls and toward exploration of physical difficulties untethered to natural protection. Robbins and his Yosemite followers were caught in a vision of climbing that ultimately was antithetical to Gill's vision and indeed hostile to the future of climbing as it was shaping up elsewhere in the world. This situation is where Jeff Smoot's book *Hangdog Days* essentially places its reader.

Hangdog Days explores the conflicts and controversies surrounding changes in climbing practice in the early 80s into the mid-1990s. Now that sport climbing on preplaced bolts has become the dominant mode for most roped climbers, it's almost impossible to comprehend that there were numerous incidents of route chopping, physical attacks on climbers, and of course countless words exchanged as each side argued its side. Even now, some members of the old guard rail against the sea change that overtook climbing in this era, but few contemporary climbers will understand the source of their angst. Reading this book will help them understand what it took to get climbing to the place we see it now.

Jeff Smoot has personal insight into two key players from this period: Todd Skinner of Pinedale, Wyoming, and Alan Watts from Madras, Oregon. They adopted the Gill vision of climbing from the boulders to bigger cliffs. Both were from relatively obscure locations and were pushed, in a sense, to make the most of those places by using tactics that other climbers viewed as suspect. However, much as Gill had explored off-the-map boulders for years and made some of them iconic locales, these efforts would also bear significant fruit. Most readers of this review will be very familiar with Todd Skinner (who sadly died in a rappelling accident in 2006), as Skinner was a very outgoing personality and one of the country's earliest professional climbers. Alan Watts never sought or gained that status but in his time was among the very best climbers in the world. It's nice to see him given ample space in this account, as he proved very influential in creating Smith Rocks as a world-class climbing area and legitimizing hard sport climbing in America and even around the world.

The account of Skinner really stands out in this book, and at times the narrative feels like a welding of climbing history and quasi-biographical memoir as Smoot vividly evokes the personalities and recreates the conversations of the major players of the day. History is full of irony, as any reader of it will know, and this is well illustrated when Alan Watts proposes near the end of the book that "the sport climbers didn't win. The trad climbers didn't win. Instead climbing won." I think this is a valid take on the outcome, as the hardest "trad climbs" today are done by people with deep sport climbing backgrounds. It's unfortunate that this took so long and consumed so many in fruitless controversies.

– PETER BEAL

END OF THE ROPE: MOUNTAINS, MARRIAGE, AND MOTHERHOOD

JAN REDFORD. Random House (Canada), 2018. Hardcover, 302 pages, $26; paperback, $16.95.

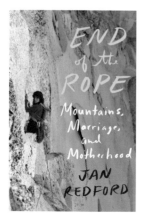

MY TWO LONGSTANDING criteria for measuring a written work's effectiveness are: When I get to the end of the book, can I say, "Wow, I never read anything like that before," and, after I'm finished reading, how long does the work linger in my imagination? Jan Redford's memoir easily clears these bars. It's also utterly compelling. Its title speaks to a sense of desperation the author feels for much of the story, trapped in a co-dependent marriage. Its subtitle *Mountains, Marriage, and Motherhood*, lays out the book's themes. It's true that "mountains" probably only take up about a third of the pages here, but make no mistake, this is a climber's memoir.

The book starts off typically enough: a longing for the mountains after the family moves across Canada to Ontario, an unhappy home life, a first rock climb—"a five-foot-nothing, 110-pound, flat-chested Anglophone tomboy from Munster Hamlet," unroped and alone in the Laurentians on a family vacation. From the first chapter she is particularly good at describing the inner fears and exhilaration climbing affords us. Rarely does she describe the degree of difficulty of a particular route; instead we're right there in her head.

We follow her into the mountain life, working in the male-dominated world of 1980s North American climbing culture as a diminutive, tobacco-chewing young woman with a terrific knack for cursing. After a series of unsatisfying trysts, she finds love, real love, with Dan Guthrie and then loses him to an avalanche on Mt. Foraker. She describes this loss and its attendant grief and anger with a clarity perhaps afforded her by the passage of time. Unfortunately, it won't be the only occasion of deadly climbing accidents among her circle of friends. Reading these felt achingly familiar and gave me pause to consider how much we have normalized (for lack of a better word) loss in our community.

Much of the book reports on what happened next: Reeling from the loss of Dan, she takes up with one of their circle, on the rebound; he is also an elite alpinist. They endure what appears a pretty typical co-dependent relationship, during which he suffers from a kind of split personality: "happy climber/unhappy logger." He wants a traditional homemaker for a spouse; she wants to go to school. It takes her a long time to disentangle and follow her dream of a college education. I read their relationship as a kind of climbing story, too, showing the particular difficulties of balancing the climbing/career/family needs of both partners.

Most climbers' memoirs, unsurprisingly, stick strictly to the climbing, as if their days away from the heights don't exist. Here, Redford tells the story of a whole life, one that's interchangeable with no other. You won't find these lines in another climber's memoir: "Jenna (her infant daughter, born days after her husband returns from a nearly disastrous attempt on Nanga Parbat) started to mewl like a kitten. My nipples were cracked, so nursing was like clamping them in a vise."

We still need more women's voices in our community, and what we really need are the stories we haven't heard before. Redford has delivered both here, served with an unflinching eye, a big heart, and an enormous rucksack of perseverance.

– DAVID STEVENSON

STARVATION SHORE: A NOVEL

Laura Waterman. The University of Wisconsin Press, 2019. Hardcover, 416 pages, $27.95.

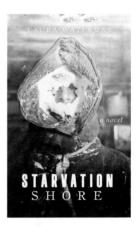

In *Starvation Shore*, Laura Waterman (no relation to reviewer) has turned her scholarly pen to a forgotten Arctic tragedy. In 1881, 25 men led by Adolphus Greely of the U.S. Army were dropped off on Canada's Ellesmere Island to establish a scientific research fort. Greeley's men methodically logged weather observations, traversed Ellesmere Island, and attained "Furthest North" toward the North Pole, a grail for explorers until the present day.

But over the next two years, resupply teams failed to reach Greely's Fort Conger. Unwisely abandoning their post and heading south on meager rations, they eventually encamped on Cape Sabine. This grim yet fascinating story of inept leadership includes a shipwreck, drowning, hypothermia, mutiny, suicide, execution, scurvy, and starvation. By the time a rescue ship finally arrived, only seven of the 25 men had survived. Over more than a century, beginning with Greely's *Three Years of Arctic Service* in 1886, several authors have tried to resurrect the saga.

In previous books, let alone the extant explorer diaries, an essential detail has been left out: how and why the men resorted to cannibalism. Waterman realized she had to find a new framework for presenting their story, so that she (and ultimately her readers) could understand what really drove Greely and company. She began reading and transcribing Sgt. David Brainard's diary (available online at the Dartmouth Library), limiting herself to two entries a day in her quest to figure out what these men were made of. The research and writing of her book would take a full decade.

So, seven men survived by eating the flesh of their dead companions—like the Donner Party in California. Yet none of the Arctic survivors would ever cop to this cannibalism. Back in the day, the feds tried to suppress the news. However, even though the bodies were brought home in sealed caskets, eventually a reporter got a look inside—at least ten had been cut into for food, and the media blew this up to sensational proportions.

Waterman, after writing a dozen drafts, discovered that to make these men real and "slide my sleeping bag in next to theirs," she had to reimagine parts of their story and fictionalize what may have driven them to such desperate ends. As a winter mountaineer, she drew on a her knowledge of cold, of wind-driven ice and snow, and of the breathtaking, often frightening beauty to be found in remote landscapes in order to fully flesh out their story.

She prompts us to consider what's it like to starve to death, as these explorers' bodies began to feed on themselves for sustenance. This would have been followed by starvation, edema, diarrhea, and extreme dehydration. Yet along the way, particularly in the last days, as, "the extreme craving for food" stops, death often comes peacefully as victims drift into euphoria.

In *Starvation Shore*, Waterman fills in the blanks between the lines of the surviving diaries and letters, and shows us what likely transpired in the minds of these desperate men. The author continually asked herself, *What would I have done in these circumstances*?

Waterman delivers her climax with compassion and empathy, and brings the reader into the thoughts of these frantic men as no book has done before. In her hands, this tale of explorers pushed to their limits stands as a parable for the character of the human soul.

– JONATHAN WATERMAN

THE SHARP END OF LIFE: A MOTHER'S STORY

Dierdre Wolownick. Mountaineers Books, 2019. Hardcover, 256 pages, $24.95.

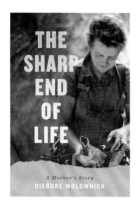

In Dierdre Wolownick's inspirational memoir, the journey from frazzled mother struggling through an emotionally abusive marriage to being the oldest woman to climb El Capitan is motivational without ever feeling overbearing. Wolownick is up-front about her identity: It's right there in the title—she's a mother. She smartly doesn't shy away from what to most readers is her most defining characteristic, being Alex Honnold's mom. Die-hard Honnold followers will be able to glean minute insights into the legendary climber's upbringing and temperament. But, happily, Wolownick has her own story of perseverance that led her to scaling El Cap and other big-wall routes, and it's Dierdre Wolownick's story, not mom-of-Alex-Honnold's, that readers will find most compelling.

Wolownick's early and midlife will feel familiar to many readers. She was raised in a traditional home that taught her girls are supposed to be efficacious homemakers and obedient to their elders and husbands. She married an emotionally neglectful man and stuck out the marriage so her children would have a stable home life. As Alex and his sister Stasia grew up, Wolownick struggled to make the best life possible for her children. Wolownick's spare, direct prose achingly conveys her growing frustration with her husband and her desperation for a different life.

Driven by a desire to understand her children's worlds, Wolownick takes up climbing and running in her 50s, and here her stark prose flourishes, revealing the vulnerability she feels so keenly as an older woman, and also her incredible tenacity. Her physical weaknesses are overcome by the sheer force of her stubbornness and commitment. This section holds the memoir's best writing, as Wolownick wrestles with how to find satisfaction in her climbing achievements when her son is among the world's best climbers. Though the inevitable triumphant conclusion is perhaps too easy to predict, based on Wolownick's inability to accept failure, she includes enough highs and lows throughout her journey to make her account of scaling El Capitan engaging, nevertheless. *The Sharp End of Life* illuminates the incredible within the everyday struggles and successes of one climber and mother.

– REBECCA YOUNG

SOME STORIES: LESSONS FROM THE EDGE OF BUSINESS AND SPORT

Yvon Chouinard. Patagonia Books, 2019. Hardcover, 464 pages, $45.

Sometimes a former ropemate makes good so spectacularly that all you can do is rock back on your heels and say, *Thanks!* Of course we all recognize Yvon Chouinard for his breakthrough climbing. And we might tease his business as Pata*gucci*. No matter. Building great outdoor gear has given my old friend huge leverage to fight the good fight for our suffering environment. Patagonia's latest catalog has hardly any gear for sale. Instead there is page after page of effective activism, starting with an inspired teenager on the cover. Flip it over and the walk-off line is "See You at the Strikes!"

How did that come about? The answer—and a lot of great reading—is found in Chouinard's new book, *Some Stories: Lessons From The Edge Of Business And Sport.* He had already changed the world before we met, by joining Royal Robbins, Chuck Pratt, and Tom Frost as one of Yosemite's "Fab Four," the quartet of visionaries that forged ever more committed lines during the Golden Age of big-wall climbing. Fewer will remember that in 1963 Chouinard spearheaded turning this journal, and the American Alpine Club behind it, toward the future with his seminal article "Modern Yosemite Climbing." It's in here, and it's still an inspiring read.

By his own count, Chouinard has taken part in seven golden ages, so there's a lot of surfing and fly-fishing in here, as well as the ice climbing revolution. The guy's life has had an amazingly broad reach, and he has written grippingly about each of its facets. Extremely poignant is his farewell to Doug Tompkins, "We Lost a Chief." Under the banner "Viva los Fun Hogs," they had rocked Patagonia (the place) by pioneering, with Dick Dorworth, Chris Jones, and Lito Teja-Flores, the California Route on Fitz Roy in 1968. Later, Tompkins spearheaded the hustling of over two million acres of greater Patagonia into new parks, only to die in a kayaking accident that Chouinard survived.

Many of my favorite stories here are previously unpublished tales of growing up in SoCal in the 1950s and starting Chouinard Equipment by forging pitons in "a chicken coop in my parent's backyard in Burbank"—before moving to the iconic Tin Shed, blocks from the Ventura surf. In those years, he writes, "I'd often climb for half a day at Stoney Point in Chatsworth, then go up to Rincon [to surf] the evening glass, and after I'd free dive for lobsters and abalone on the coast between Zuma and the county line. I almost always got my limit of ten lobsters and five abalone."

Reflecting back, Chouinard shows a powerful ability to see, and personalize, the grand sweep of cultural history. "The '50s were the easy years in California. With full employment from the Korean War, we were enjoying all the fruits of the fossil fuel culture. Gas was a quarter a gallon, used cars could be bought for twenty-five dollars, campgrounds were free, and you could easily live off the excess fat of society. Those of us in the counter-cultures of climbing and surfing were, as climber Pete Sinclair said, 'the last free Americans.'"

I don't know whether to thank Chouinard more for the great stories, the advances in so many sports, or for crucial work to help save the planet. And he's not done yet.

– DOUG ROBINSON

IN BRIEF

THE 1993 CLASSIC *Yankee Rock & Ice: A History of Climbing in the Northeastern United States* (Stackpole, $19.95), by Laura and Guy Waterman, was published in a new edition in 2018, with four new chapters by Michael Wejchert and a foreword by Sarah Garlick. *Stories Behind the Images: Lessons from a Life in Adventure Photography* (*Mountaineers Books, $29.95*) is an autobiographical look back at memorable photos by Corey Rich, a climber and photographer whose work has graced over 100 magazine covers. Philosopher and '60s Yosemite climber Michael P. Cohen's *Granite and Grace: Seeking the Heart of Yosemite* describes his decades-long love affair with Tuolumne granite (University of Nevada Press, $21.95). Look for John P. O'Grady's full review of *Granite and Grace* at the AAJ website: publications.americanalpineclub.org.

– DAVID STEVENSON

IN MEMORIAM

Some of these tributes have been edited for length; the complete versions are at the AAJ website: publications.americanalpineclub.org. Here, readers also will find tributes to some other climbers who passed recently, including Martin Moran and Dr. Robert Rockwell.

HANSJÖRG AUER, 1984 – 2019

HANSJÖRG AUER WAS born February 18, 1984, and was raised on his family's alpine farm in the Ötztal valley of Tirol, Austria. He grew up in an environment where climbing came naturally. Before he'd even reached the age of ten, he'd already summited a 3,000m peak in winter with his older brother and regular climbing partner, Matthias. In 2006, Hansjörg free soloed the classic Tempi Moderni ("Modern Times"), a 6c+ (5.11c) route of 27 pitches on the Marmolada's south face, in Italy's Dolomites. Hansjörg kept the feat largely to himself, for fear of scorn from his family and friends, but slowly word got out and his mythical status began to unfold.

The following year, 2007, Hansjörg redefined free soloing in the Alps when he climbed Via Attraverso il Pesce, commonly known as "The Fish," also on the Marmolada's south Face. The 37-pitch route, named after a large fish-shaped pocket on the 20th pitch, is graded 7b+ (5.12c). From this point forward, Hansjörg was no longer an undercover hardman. Adding to the audacity was the fact that Hansjörg hadn't previously climbed the route cleanly on a rope prior to his free solo.

Up to this point, Hansjörg was a certified UIAGM guide who had studied to become an elementary school teacher. It wasn't always easy for him to admit, but deep down he had always wanted to climb for a living. His free solo of the Fish solidified that opportunity.

Hansjörg had a talent for just about every style of climbing. Shortly after turning to climbing full-time, he climbed his first 5.14c sport route, and with his younger brother Vitus he managed a first ascent of his own on the Marmolada, an 8b (5.13d) they named Bruderliebe ("Brotherly Love").

In 2012, together with Michael "Much" Mayr, Hansjörg again turned his attention to the Marmolada, where the two of them made the first free ascent of the bolt-less L'ultimo Dei Paracadutisti, which weighs in at 8b+ (5.14a) and is still unrepeated. Right up until Hansjörg's untimely passing, Much and Hansjörg forged a collection of diverse first ascents across five continents, the majority of which are unrepeated.

In remembering Hansjörg, one also has to mention his achievements in the Himalaya and Karakoram, starting in 2013 with the first ascent of Kunyang Chhish East, carried out with the Swiss ace Simon Anthamatten and Matthias Auer. The three tackled the southwest face of this 7,000-meter peak with technical difficulties up to M5. The ascent was followed by a 2017 first ascent of Gimmigela East (7,005 meters) with a fellow Austrian, Alex Blümel, and a solo first ascent of Lupghar Sar West (7,157 meters) in 2018. For the latter, Hansjörg won a Piolet d'Or in 2019, posthumously.

Heiko Wilhelm

Hansjörg lived and climbed with an unmeasurable amount of optimistic stubbornness, sweet irreverence, courage, and love. He never held back, and he never disguised or feared his own vulnerabilities. Hansjörg is mourned by his partner, Tatjana, his family and friends, and the people of the Ötztal valley where he was raised and rests.

– CODY ROTH

Megan Bond

HELMY BECKEY, 1925 – 2019

HELMUT FRITZ BECKEY, known as Helmy, was born in Seattle and died in Munich, Germany, at age 93. In his youth, he established first ascents and new routes throughout the Cascades and elsewhere.

Helmy learned the basics of climbing as a member of the Mountaineers, where his aptitude was recognized early. In 1940, he and his brother Fred, who was two years older, made two extensive excursions into the Picket Range. The teenagers climbed the west ridge of Mt. Thompson and made the first ascents of Forbidden Peak, Phantom Peak, Whatcom Peak, Mt. Challenger, Crooked Thumb, Luna Peak, Mt. Fury's East Peak, McMillan Spire's West Spire, and Inspiration Peak.

In 1941, along with the numerous first ascents and new routes in the North Cascades he did with Fred, Helmy joined Lloyd Anderson, Lyman Boyer, and Tom Campbell in the Bugaboos of British Columbia, where they completed the first ascent of the South Tower of Howser Spire.

In the summer of 1942, Helmy and Fred embarked on a six-week expedition into the Coast Mountains of British Columbia. Here, the teenage brothers famously climbed the remote and challenging Mt. Waddington. It was only the second ascent of the peak, which had repelled a multitude of summit attempts.

Fred Beckey wrote in the 1943 AAJ about the descent: "Helmy was hit on the knee by one of a flurry of rocks that sped down the mountain side. All hope of reaching camp that night was gone because of a heavily bleeding cut. This was Helmy's 17th birthday present, donated by Mt. Waddington." The trauma Helmy sustained to his leg on Waddington necessitated several surgeries, which kept him out of World War II. The injury plagued him the remainder of his life.

The two brothers continued doing new routes in the Cascades for some years. Meanwhile, Helmy became the first paid employee of the Recreational Equipment Cooperative (REI). As a teenager, he worked in a tiny attic space in the home of Lloyd and Mary Anderson, the co-op's founders, filling orders for, in his words, "climbing odds and ends". He also translated documents written in German that came with shipments of climbing equipment from Europe.

Helmy was valedictorian of his high school class at West Seattle High School. He entered the University of Washington, where he intended to study medicine like his father. However, after a year at the university, he decided to pursue opera instead of medicine, and he moved to California in 1945. He had been advised that the opera program at the University of Southern California was the best on the West Coast at that time. He also was a competitive skier and loved to swim.

Committed to the care of his mother, he quit his university studies early to find full-time employment, in order to help her financially. He moved her to California in the 1940s to live with him, and this freed his brother Fred to climb and pursue his passions. For many years, he worked as a pharmaceutical salesman for Pfizer in the Los Angeles area. In 1974, Helmy took his savings and emigrated to Germany to finally follow his dreams and pursue an opera career full-time. He sang in opera houses in the Munich area; he was considered a "heroic baritone."

Although the Beckey brothers were known to bicker, they remained fiercely close, loyal, and protective of one another through their lives; they wrote or phoned each other monthly, even when they lived on separate continents. Fred made many trips to Germany to visit Helmy, the most recent in 2015. (Fred Beckey died in 2017.)

"Looking back on my life," Helmy wrote to Fred in 1980, "I find that the happiest times I had was when I was climbing with you. Such adventures like the North Pickets, the South Pickets, Twin Spires, and Mt. Waddington were really remarkable, especially because of our youth."

– MEGAN BOND

JOHN EVANS, 1938 – 2020

Evans Family Collection

"YOU SHOULD COME have dinner with my brother, John. He's done some climbing," Rick Evans said in a meeting one day. My brain didn't make the connection between this guy who had "done some climbing" and the John Evans who was a hero of mine since childhood—the Evans of Everest, Tyree, Logan, the Pamirs, Nanda Devi, and more.

Upon arrival at the Evans family home in the foothills above Denver, we ambled past images of the high mountains, deep canyons, and dazzling rivers. It began to click: This John Evans was *that* John Evans. To say I was nervous is an understatement. However, John's kind, humble, inquisitive nature quickly put me at ease.

That is a remarkable character trait for anyone, but especially someone with such a long list of brag-worthy accomplishments. Adventure and doing things differently were in his blood early: To help pay tuition at University of Minnesota, John spent summers wrestling alligators in South Dakota. A climb of Gannett Peak in the Wind Rivers opened up the mountains to the Ohio native, and the passion never ebbed.

An early Yosemite climber, John made the fourth ascent of the Nose in 1965 (with Dick McCracken and Gary Colliver) just days before departing for the Yukon and Mt. Logan's Hummingbird Ridge. The climb, done with teammates Allen Steck, Dick Long, Frank Coale, Jim Wilson, and Paul Bacon, is one of legend: Despite many subsequent attempts on the Hummingbird, the original route has yet to be repeated. I remember John recounting the legendary and harrowing Shovel Traverse in his usual modest fashion: "It wasn't so much that we had great skill," he said. "We just knew we couldn't go back the way we came, so we figured we just had to keep going forward."

John had worked in the Ellsworth Mountains of Antarctica as a geology student, so he was a natural pick for the 1966-67 American Antarctic Mountaineering Expedition, led by Nick Clinch. The team made first ascents of Mt. Vinson and Mt. Shinn, and John and the late Barry Corbet made the first—and only—ascent of the northwest ridge of Mt. Tyree, the continent's second-highest peak. Describing the climb at the time, John wrote in his journal: "The uncertainties in the outcome include a mile of horribly serrated ridge starting at about 14,000 feet or so and culminating at the summit of Tyree…. Temperatures probably around -30°F, scanty food supplies, and, most of all, the weather…. How's that for an exhilarating bunch of uncertainties? Fortunately, Barry is a splendid climber and companion, and even if we get no further than today, morale is high and the conversation stimulating."

After Antarctica, John continued to push boundaries on big mountains, attempting Everest's unclimbed southwest face in 1971, climbing as part of the U.S. delegation to the Pamirs in 1974 and on Nanda Devi in 1976, and leading the 1981 American expedition to Everest, which conducted groundbreaking research on high-altitude physiology. After working as a banker for years, he was given the chance to manage the U.S. part of Ice Station Weddell in Antarctica, which he parlayed into a full-time job running logistics for the U.S. Antarctic program, a role he filled until his retirement in 2012. He was devoted to his family, including Loie, his wife of 52 years (and a stalwart adventurer herself), a daughter, Lynne, son-in-law Mark, and two granddaughters, Zoe and Spencer.

John lived a life most can only dream of, but he never succumbed to braggadocio. His climbs were not motivated by clicks and likes, but by the pure, unadulterated love of adventure. Like many of his generation, John was afraid less of death than of not living life fully, with love, heart, passion, and compassion.

– JAKE NORTON

EDITOR'S NOTE: *A collection of photographs and journals from Evans' expeditions is available at johnevansclimbing.com.*

Samuel Crossley

BRAD GOBRIGHT, 1988 – 2019

BRAD GOBRIGHT GREW up in Orange County, California, along with his sister, Jill, three years his junior. His parents, Pam and Jim, who are avid hikers, brought the family to Lone Pine Lake in the Sierra Nevada when Gobright was 4, cementing his love for the outdoors. At age 8, Gobright summited Mt. Whitney with his father. "He was the youngest kid to sign the book at the top that year," Pam says. "When he came down, he was like a changed kid. From then on, it wasn't about being at school for him. It was about being outdoors and getting to the mountains."

Gobright started frequenting the Rockcreation climbing gym in Los Angeles, and over the next few years attended climbing competitions in Colorado and Virginia. When Gobright was 8, he went to Mt. Woodson, outside San Diego, to crack climb. Despite his ability to tackle difficult climbs or maybe because of his obsession with them, Gobright struggled with school. When he finished high school, he enrolled in community college, but after a miserable semester realized school wasn't for him.

"I think you need to go to Yosemite and try to get work there for the summer," Pam told her son. "You should spend a summer away from us, finding your way." Gobright took a job as a housekeeper at Yosemite's Ahwahnee Hotel for two six-month seasons. "The joke is that he just never really came back," Pam says.

From 2013 to 2016, Gobright lived seasonally in Boulder, Colorado, climbing extensively in Eldorado Canyon, where he free soloed the Naked Edge (5.11b), Doub-Griffith (5.11c), and Hairstyles and Attitude (5.12b/c). He climbed obsessively, sending routes like Musta Been High (5.13c R) but forgetting to bring shorts to wear under his kneepads, and thus redpointing the climb in his underwear. It was also in Boulder that Gobright began setting speed records, climbing the Naked Edge around 20 times with Scott Bennett until they whittled their time down to 24 minutes, 57 seconds, bridge to bridge, in October 2014.

In 2013, Gobright and Bennett free climbed four walls in Zion National Park in just 19 hours. "Watching him go up that dihedral," Bennett says of belaying Gobright on the crux 5.12+ corner pitch of Moonlight Buttress, "he didn't stop. [It was] how you would imagine a robot climbing—just unstoppable."

At the exact moment he turned 30, in June 2018, Gobright was on the Boot Flake (5.10c) of the Nose of El Capitan completing the Triple: climbing the Nose, the South Face of Mount Watkins, and the Regular Northwest Face on Half Dome in a day with Jim Reynolds. "It was really fun climbing with Brad because I could climb things that I couldn't climb with anyone else," says Reynolds. In 2017, Gobright and Reynolds set a Nose speed record of 2:19:44. "I could also trust Brad in the sense that he never let go," Reynolds says. "The partnership we had allowed both of us to imagine great things and be able to go for them."

Gobright loved climbing too much to maintain a steady job, though in recent years he enjoyed spending summers helping with a kids' climbing course at the Sender One gym in Los Angeles. "I'm getting paid to go to camp, and afterward there's nothing better to do than jump on the hangboard and train," Gobright wrote in July 2018. He'd also taken an AMGA course and started to guide a little, and was finding some stability as a professional climber sponsored by Gramicci, Evolv, Friction Labs, Blue Water Ropes, and Metolius. His roles in Reel Rock 12's *Safety Third* and Reel Rock 14's *The Nose Speed Record* solidified his ability to be a full-time pro.

Gobright also was known for his antic sense of humor. "Bawk. Bawk. Ba-kaw!" Gobright would call from the bushes in Yosemite. He would then hop out to the trail, asking befuddled tourists if they'd heard the rare Yosemite chickens. For three years, he dated the climber Taleen Kennedy, and one day the pair went to the Virgin River Gorge, Arizona. They parked on the side of the highway, next to a blasted-out roadcut—a short walk from the actual climbing. "This is it!" he told Kennedy, pointing up at the chossy wall. It wasn't until Kennedy had flaked out the rope and put on her shoes that he said, "I'm kidding. The crag's up the hill."

Gobright had begun free climbing harder in recent years, putting emphasis on being more calculated and safer. At Indian Creek, in March 2018, he sent Carbondale Shortbus (5.14-), which has a notoriously difficult beginning protected by thin gear. He also began to focus more on El Capitan free climbing. In the spring of 2019 he did three one-day free ascents in a single season: Pineapple Express, The Shaft, and Golden Gate. Gobright had arrived in Yosemite a round-faced boy with a predilection for donuts and had developed into a thoughtful and funny man—and a fearsomely accomplished free climber.

On November 27, 2019, Gobright died in a rappelling accident on the 1,500-foot El Sendero Luminoso (5.12d) in El Portrero Chico, Mexico. The world is a darker and far less entertaining place for Brad Gobright's absence. He shared his light and bottomless passion for climbing with all who met him. If there is one thing we can do like Brad, it is to go brightly.

– JAMES LUCAS

EDITOR'S NOTE: *This tribute is adapted from a long piece by James Lucas for Climbing magazine, available at Climbing.com.*

DAVID LAMA, 1990 – 2019

FOR THE MILLENNIAL generation, those born between 1981 and 1996, there is no climber that systematically challenged and defined the standards and disciplines of mountain sports as David Lama did. When we lose exceptional people at much too young an age, we weep with empathy for the family and feel the loss of potential. Time heals loss slowly, and understanding and appreciating our friend's personality through their accomplishments helps us bring balance.

David was born on August 4, 1990, in Innsbruck, Austria, to Claudia and Rinzi Lama. Nestled in the eastern Alps, Innsbruck is one of the epicenters of global climbing. Claudia, an avid climber, was part of an all-women's expedition in 1988 to Langtang, Nepal, where she met Rinzi, who was from the Phaphlu/Taksindu area of the Solu Khumbu. Rinzi was her true love, as he was for her. They moved to Austria, had their son, and introduced him to the mountains. When David was five years old, Peter Habeler, an icon of Austrian climbing, recognized his ability to move over rock, without much apparent effort and with preternatural grace.

David, at the intersection of two mountain cultures, entered climbing as competitions were starting to gain momentum and become recognized as part of the growth of mountain sports. Reinhold Scherer and the Kletterzentrum Innsbruck incubated his nascent ability through mentorship, training, and coaching. David won international lead, bouldering, and ice competitions between the years of 2007 and 2009.

The pursuit of difficulty led David from the crags to mountains. He focused his efforts on the alpine, where the environment and weather create a more variable and demanding experience. He found this passion in the Greater Ranges with trips to the Karakorum and Patagonia, some successful, some not. One constant was that they were always bold and ambitious. David spent three seasons getting humbled by Cerro Torre in his quest to free climb the southeast ridge. On the 19th of January, 2012, he succeeded in his goal. Controversy surrounded the climb, as filming on the first attempt interfered with the style, ethics, and heritage of Cerro Torre. In an ironic twist to the bolts added by the film team in 2009, David and Peter Oertner completed their free climb after Hayden Kennedy and Jason Kruk removed the route's original Maestri bolts. This ascent was emblematic of the direction in which climbing—and specifically alpine climbing—was heading.

Being a professional climber in this day and age requires a keen sense of marketing and self worth. David understood at a young age that climbing was his career, and he had deep partnerships with Mammut and Red Bull, the Austrian energy drink. In working with Florian Schulz, his climbing partner and adviser, he was able to motivate climbers around the world with his personality and ability. We met four years to the month prior to his passing, climbing a route together in Zion. That fall we visited the Khumbu on the first of two trips to Lunag Ri, an unclimbed peak of around 7,000 meters on the border of Tibet and Nepal. On our second attempt he saved my life. I began to understand the true measure of who he was. Thank you, David. The eventual solo ascent of Lunag Ri in October 2018 was the peak of his dreams. It was the highest unclimbed peak in Nepal, the country of his father, and he climbed in an uncompromising style. Through these years, he found a second family with the North Face climbing team, and it was with his North Face partners Hansjörg Auer and Jess Roskelley that he lost his life in the Canadian Rockies on April 16, 2019.

Climbers around the world are at loss following the accident that befell these three young men. The depth of sorrow for the families is something we approach with deep empathy and compassion. As strength and ability turn what was once large into the new standard, we're always reminded that the mountains have the ultimate strength. That is why we go to them. The mountains expose our weaknesses and this makes us better. We miss you David. We will ascend our next summit with you in mind.

– CONRAD ANKER

Dick Long (Merry Collection)

WAYNE MERRY, 1931 – 2019

WAYNE PROCTER MERRY passed away at home in Atlin, British Columbia, on October 30, 2019. He was 88. Wayne lived a consequential and deeply satisfying life as a trailblazer in a variety of arenas: big-wall climbing, national park administration, search and rescue, mountain guiding, wilderness first response, experiential education, and conservation.

He was born in California, and his family moved frequently in his youth. All the way through school, Wayne was free to roam in the nearby woods in search of adventure with his younger brother Bill, who belayed him on his first climb in the St. Helena Palisades. He briefly attended Stockton College, where he pursued an interest in music as he played both trumpet and baritone trombone. With the outbreak of the Korean War, Wayne enlisted in the Navy, a move that ended up advancing his climbing career. While stationed in San Diego as a dental technician, he joined the local Rock Climbing Section of the Sierra Club and paired up with the likes of Jerry Gallwas, Gary Hemming, George Schlief, and Barbara Lilley to climb at Mission Gorge, Tahquitz, Joshua Tree, and eventually Yosemite Valley.

Wayne was drafted for the final push on the first ascent of the Nose of El Capitan, his most famous climb, during a summer in Alaska working with Dr. Dick Long on a three-man glacier-survey crew. "At the end of that summer, Harding contacted me to climb the Nose," Long recalled. "I was married with two kids and my 'job' started the same week, so Wayne took my place."

After narrowly missing out on the first ascent of the northwest face of Half Dome, Harding and friends started up the Nose on July 5, 1957. They pushed the route higher over a total of 45 days spread across two seasons. By the time Wayne joined the effort in September 1958, ropes were fixed to the halfway point atop Boot Flake.

Team members working on the Nose were forced to climb outside of peak tourist season because of the logistical problems caused by the spectacle they created. Under pressure from the Park Service to complete the project, Warren, Wayne, George Whitmore, and Rich Calderwood left the ground on November 1 for a final 10-day effort. On November 12, Harding drilled through the night by headlamp to overcome the summit overhangs and the Nose had been climbed.

When I asked Wayne to reflect on the Nose in 2017, he said, "It is a great thing to look back at from a great distance. No matter how clumsily it was done by comparison to modern techniques, there is only one first. It feels pretty good to have made that particular one. It is a beautiful climb and recognized as one of the most famous in the world, and I am happy with that."

While he was on the Nose, Wayne wrote letters to Cindy Barrison, with whom he had fallen in love. He tossed the notes to the ground in cans with small streamers, and the ground support team added a stamp to each letter and sent them to Santa Monica where she lived. They were married not long afterward.

The National Park Service hired Wayne as a Yosemite interpretive ranger in 1959. After a few years in Yosemite, Wayne and Cindy had their first child. In 1964 the family was transferred to Olympic National Park. A year later, they moved to Wonder Lake in Denali National Park, where Wayne was assigned as a mountaineering ranger.

The Wilcox Expedition tragedy on Denali in 1967, in which seven climbers died, marked a turning point for Wayne's career. He was so frustrated by what he and some others saw as a deficient rescue attempt by the Park Service that he threatened to resign unless he was promoted to chief ranger. He got the job. Wayne quickly developed an aversion for the politics involved in upper level Park Service administration, so he accepted an offer from the Yosemite Park and Curry Company in 1969 to establish a mountaineering guide service. This effort earned quick success and also helped establish some mutual respect between the climbing community, the rangers, and the concessionaires, who often viewed climbers as "somewhere between hippies and bears," in Wayne's humorous estimation.

During the 1960s, as visitors to Yosemite greatly increased, rescues and injury-related evacuations became an almost daily occurrence in peak season. After enlisting Jim Bridwell to act as spokesperson for climbers, Wayne approached Assistant Superintendent Keith Neilson with a sensible proposition: "Look, you have some of the best climbers in the world over in Camp 4. Why don't you take a select group and give them unlimited camping privileges so long as 50 percent of them are available at any one time to be teamed up with you on rescue.... I was so happy that Keith had the foresight to go along with that proposal." This was the beginning of YOSAR.

Wayne next set up the Mountain Shop in Yosemite Valley for the Curry Company and also founded Yosemite's Nordic ski school. As part of the school's promotions, Wayne, Ned Gillette, Jack Miller, and Jed Williamson skied across the Brooks Range on wooden skis, with no climbing skins or sleds, starting with 80-pound packs for the 30-day outing.

During a summer break, a friend who lived in Atlin, British Columbia, invited them to visit and Wayne immediately fell in love with the place. In 1974 he and Cindy bought a house in the town of 400 and set about making a living. Wayne organized a volunteer ambulance service and fire brigade along with search and rescue training seminars, while Cindy taught school part-time. In the late 1970s they started Nortreks, a company that outfitted and conducted wilderness excursions. In the 1980s, they lived on Baffin Island for a time, doing a variety of first-responder and educational work. After moving back to Atlin in 1990, they founded Context North and wrote a series of area-specific search and rescue manuals, which were then combined into a single publication covering all of Canada.

Wayne felt a deep satisfaction from having saved many lives and contributed to the wellbeing of his home and wider community. In assessing Wayne's life and character, a mutual friend and admirer, David Harris, reflected "the world would be a perfect place if it were filled with people like Wayne Merry."

– STEVE GROSSMAN

EDITOR'S NOTE: *This tribute is adapted from a longer article originally written for Alpinist magazine (available at Alpinist.com).*

DEE MOLENAAR, 1918 – 2020

DEE MOLENAAR, AN international mountaineering legend, geologist, and artist, passed away on January 19, 2020. He was 101.

Throughout his life, Dee demonstrated great generosity, getting as much satisfaction from helping others achieve their mountain goals as he did from achieving his own. His bravery and selflessness were legendary. Dee's résumé included pioneering routes on Mt. Rainier, completing the first ascent of Canadian peak Mt. Kennedy with Senator Robert Kennedy, and sharing a microphone with Sir Edmund Hillary during a radio broadcast. He also served the mountaineering community for many years as a climbing ranger at Mt. Rainier National Park. His dedication to sharing his love of "The Mountain" with others is reflected in his book, *The Challenge of Rainier*, considered the definitive climbing history of the peak.

Born to Dutch immigrants in June 1918, Dee spent much of his youth discovering the mountains of Southern California. He ventured northward to explore the glaciated peaks of the Pacific Northwest, where he served as a park ranger and guide at Mt. Rainier National Park.

During World War II, Dee served in the U.S. Coast Guard in the Aleutians and Western Pacific. In 1950 he earned a degree in geology at the University of Washington and served as civilian adviser in the Army's Mountain & Cold Weather Training Command at Camp Hale, Colorado. His career in geology took him across the western U.S.; he retired from the U.S. Geological Survey in 1983.

Dee climbed peaks throughout the western U.S., Canada, Alaska, Himalayas, New Zealand, and Antarctica. He participated in major expeditions to Mt. St. Elias in Alaska in 1946, Mt. Kennedy in the Yukon, and in the 1953 American expedition to K2 in the Karakoram Himalaya. Dee was the last surviving American member of the K2 expedition—he was one of the six men saved by "The Belay," when one climber slipped at nearly 25,000 feet and pulled off the others, all of whom were held by an ice axe belay manned by Pete Schoening. Many years later, in a letter to Charles Houston, leader of the expedition, Dee wrote, "K2 1953 was the high point of my life in so many ways, and nothing will equal it."

Dee was also a member of the Mountain Rescue and Safety Council, a group formed by members of the Mountaineers that eventually grew into the national Mountain Rescue Association.

An essential item in Dee's pack was a box of watercolor paints. He painted mountain landscapes from Death Valley to Mt. Rainier. While hunkered down by a severe storm on K2 in 1953, he painted the highest watercolor in history, spending 10 days painting the peak from memory. With precious fuel for melting snow running low, his teammates made him drink the remaining water colored with pigments.

His artwork and maps have appeared in books, exhibits, and art shows all over the world, and some of his sketches appeared in the first edition of *Mountaineering: Freedom of the Hills*, published in 1960.

Dee was an Honorary Member of the American Alpine Club, and in 2017 he as bestowed with the Mountaineers' Lifetime Achievement Award. Tom Hornbein, a longtime climbing partner of

Scott Terrell / Mountaineers Books

Dee's, spoked at the Mountaineers' ceremony about their friendship and the influence Dee had on his life. The very morning of the gala, Dee inspired Tom to climb nearby Tiger Mountain in the rain. As he was hiking, Tom thought, "What kind of an idiot does this?" When he got to the top, Tom found he was "in the company of a whole lot of idiots!" Dee loved that story. As history has shown, a life spent in the outdoors is a life well-lived.

– KRISTINA CIARI *AND* MARY HSUE

Clint Helander

JESS ROSKELLEY, 1982 – 2019

JESS FENTON ROSKELLEY was born in Spokane, Washington, on July 13, 1982. He graduated from Mt. Spokane High School in 2001 and attended the University of Montana for two years before embarking on an expedition to climb Everest with his father, John, in 2003. Jess became the youngest American to climb the peak at the time, a defining moment in his career as a professional alpinist.

Jess lived by Ernest Shackleton's family motto, Fortitudine Vincimus: "By Endurance We Conquer." He was considered by his peers and partners to be an exceptional and safe alpinist. He spent the better part of his life climbing around the world and made first ascents across South America, Alaska, Asia, and the Canadian Rockies. Between climbing expeditions, Jess worked as a certified welding inspector, specializing in very technical, high-angle rope-access jobs. He spent seven years working in Prudhoe Bay on the north slope of Alaska as a mechanic and welder. He also guided for RMI on Mt. Rainier for three seasons and was the first snowboard patroller on Mt. Spokane.

Jess had a kind soul, a sense of humor that rivaled Jim Carrey, and a heart as big as the mountains he climbed. His integrity was unparalleled, and his loyalty to his family and his climbing partners was unmatched. His love for the mountains was only rivaled by the love he had for his wife, Allison, his immediate family, and his English bulldog, Mugs.

Jess had one obsession that cannot be denied: lifted, monster-tire trucks, which he used to his advantage when visiting his favorite "topless" coffee stand in Spokane, for which he coined the nickname "Naugh-tay Latte." (He always said they had the best chai latte—sure, Jess!) The Dave Smith Motors dealership for Dodge Rams in Kellogg, Idaho, where Jess tricked out his trucks to the delight of the salesmen, had his name on speed-dial.

Jess' life came to an end during a tragic climbing accident on Howse Peak in the Canadian Rockies on April 16, 2019. Jess and Austrian alpinists Hansjörg Auer and David Lama, all elite members of the North Face athlete team, had reached the summit via a new route in record time. The three were caught in an avalanche that afternoon while descending (see p.150.)

The way in which Jess felt about climbing is best conveyed in his own words: "Mountains help me navigate what is most important to me. They balance the chaos that is regular life. Balance is what I strive to accomplish with climbing—a balance of life, love, and mountains. Alpine climbing is a lifelong commitment. I live and breathe it."

– ALLI ROSKELLEY AND FAMILY

BOB SWIFT, 1930 – 2019

BOB SWIFT BEGAN backpacking in the Boy Scouts and took up climbing with the Sierra Club as a teenager. There were practice climbs at Berkeley's Cragmont and Indian Rocks, learning from the likes of David Brower and Richard Leonard, who had been cutting-edge Sierra climbers in the 1930s. Afterward, Brower would invite them over for a spaghetti feed and cheap red wine.

As soon as World War II was over, gear from the 10th Mountain Division troops showed up as Army surplus. Baggy khaki pants with a cargo pocket on the thigh became Bob's climbing fashion. The biggest prize, though, was nylon ropes. Fraying hemp was out—falls could actually be held!

Climbs like the 1950 Steck-Salathé Route in Yosemite Valley set a world-class standard, and Bob Swift was ready. In 1952, he teamed up with Allen Steck for the first ascent of El Cap Tree, the first-ever foray onto the Valley's greatest monolith. Steck became his favorite climbing partner. That same year they made the first ascent of Yosemite Point Buttress. Then Bob joined Warren Harding for the second ascent of the Lost Arrow Chimney (1954) and the first ascent of the East Buttress of Middle Cathedral Rock (1955), one of the "Fifty Classic Climbs of North America." Along the way he got a degree in geology from UC Berkeley and began teaching high school science.

In 1956, Bob turned to expedition climbing in Pakistan, attempting 25,551-foot Rakaposhi. "We got higher than any other team," Bob said, "but we ran out of time and weather at 23,000 feet."

He had caught the expedition bug and joined a 1958 trip that succeeded in making the only American first ascent of an 8,000-meter peak: Hidden Peak (Gasherbrum I) in the Baltoro region of the Karakoram. "We got two people on top and we all came down alive," he said. "We made the climbing journals and all that. It made a big splash." Bob created a fine film of their expedition in preparation for the 50th anniversary, *Remembering Gasherbrum I*, which debuted at the Mountain Film Festival in Graz, Austria.

Bob returned to teaching and became chief guide at California's first climbing school, the Palisade School of Mountaineering. Later he took to the sea, sailing four months to the Galapagos and then frequenting the Inland Passage from Seattle toward Alaska. Eventually, he moved to Arizona, where he became an adjunct professor at Northern Arizona University in Flagstaff. A cherished project was his trailer full of computers and telescopes, with which he would travel hundreds of miles bringing outreach to remote Navajo and Hopi communities.

Why climb? "It is all-encompassing…there's a joy of moving smoothly over steep rock," he said, adding, "I think that the kinesthetic feeling of climbing fills that depth for me, the muscular part of it."

Muscular to the end, Bob clocked 5,000 miles on a recumbent bicycle before lymphoma became overwhelming. He bought himself a plot and shared in his own wake ("Hey, I want to be there—a wide awake!") with his long-ago students Jan Tiura and Joe Brennan, who had become friends, then fellow guides and sailing buddies, and finally offered Bob sanctuary in their home. The next morning he quietly, and quite legally, took his own life.

– DOUG ROBINSON

STEVE WUNSCH, 1947 – 2019

WHEN I HEARD that Steve Wunsch had died, and how he had, until the end, kept his cancer private, an Irish song, "Johnny, I Hardly Knew Ye" came to mind, and I realized that during all the time we traveled together, the climbs, the successes, the failures we shared, I never really knew Steve.

Steve's contribution to climbing is more than a list of free ascents, though the list is certainly important: Psycho and Jules Verne in Eldorado Canyon; Open Cockpit, Yellow Wall, and of course Super Crack in the Gunks. Steve was a quiet innovator of technique. Rather than strength, he emphasized flexibility. He was the first person I saw do a heel hook—perhaps the first ever. I was not there for his lead of Super Crack (free climbed in 1974 and now rated 5.12+), but I watched him develop the strange finger stack that ultimately proved to be the key.

Bragg Collection

Steve made things look easy. He climbed with an exceptional poise. A poise not gained naturally, but created by fierce, intense control. Never a struggle, a shake, a tremor. Focus. Intensity. There was a certain way you did things. Ground up. Always. No inspection of any kind. You fall, you come down and start over. We climbed with a small rack of RPs, Stoppers, perhaps a hex or two. Steve was a master at creating protection where it seemed none would be found.

Steve led the first ascent of Orangutan Arch in Yosemite—an awkward climb, to say the least—with a precision that made it look like a face climb. I remember him laughing as I floundered and struggled and arrived at the belay bloodied and bruised. I remember watching with horror as he freed Psycho and I realized I was going to have to try to follow it.

More memories: a rainy morning in the Plaza Diner in New Paltz, Steve reading *The Wall Street Journal* cover to cover; a tent on Guide's Hill in the Tetons, Steve practicing classical guitar; in my van parked on Underhill Road, Steve explaining in detail the correct method of spreading cashew butter on a rice cake.

Memory: Steve exploring the unknown expanse of rock on Jules Verne, one move at a time. Downclimbing, returning to the ledge. Steve's was a boldness born of the careful acquisition of knowledge.

Many years later, a Gunks reunion: I was preparing to struggle my way up Double Crack. Steve and Marcia, his wife, walked by. "You're sure you're going to be safe up there?" Steve said with a laugh. When I suggested he tie on, he demurred. "I'm done climbing. Too out of shape." That too was Steve: self-deprecating, but also, when he could no longer climb to his exacting standards, he moved on. Steve devoted himself to a career in finance (he became famous as founder of the first automated stock exchange) and to the guitar, with the same discipline, the same pursuit of excellence.

Rich Romano tells this story: Segovia was 94 when Steve, 44 at the time, was working on Segovia's transcription of a fugue by Bach. It's a three-movement piece that begins with a prelude. Steve had that wired. Then comes the fugue. It is long and complicated, with many twists and turns, and it inspired Steve to say, "Segovia is 94—that means I have 50 years to get it right!"

When I think of Steve Wunsch, he is in the Gunks. It is autumn; it is always autumn. I can see him in his long corduroy shorts held up by suspenders, surrounded by the glorious colors of the season, laughing, walking the carriage road on the way to another adventure.

– JOHN BRAGG

INDEX

COMPILED BY **EVE TALLMAN & RALPH FERRARA**

Mountains are listed by their official names. Ranges, geographic locations, and maps are also indexed. Unnamed peaks (e.g. Peak 2,340m) are listed under P. Abbreviations are used for some geographic locations and the following: Cordillera: C.; Mountains: Mts.; National Park: Nat'l. Park; Obituary: obit. Indexed photographs are listed in bold type.

AAJ

INTERNATIONAL GRADE COMPARISON CHART

SERIOUSNESS RATINGS

These often modify technical grades when protection is difficult

PG-13: Difficult or insecure protection or loose rock, with some injury potential

R: Poor protection with high potential for injury

X: A fall would likely result in serious injury or death

YDS=Yosemite Decimal System
UIAA=Union Internationale des Associations D'Alpinisme
FR=France/Sport
AUS=Australia
SAX=Saxony
CIS=Commonwealth of Independent States/Russia
SCA=Scandinavia
BRA=Brazil
UK=United Kingdom

Note: *All conversions are approximate. Search "International Grade Comparison Chart" at the AAJ website for further explanation of commitment grades and waterfall Ice/ mixed grades.*

YDS	UIAA	FR	AUS	SAX	CIS	SCA	BRA	UK	
5.2	II	1	10	II	III	3			D
5.3	III	2	11	III	III+	3+			
5.4	IV- / IV	3	12		IV-	4			VD
5.5	IV+		13		IV	4+			S
5.6	V-	4	14		IV+	5-	4a	4a	HS
5.7	V		15	VIIa		5		4b	VS
5.8	V+	5a	16	VIIb	V-	5+	4 / 4+	4c	HVS
5.9	VI-	5b	17	VIIc		6-	5 / 5+	5a	E1
5.10a	VI	5c	18	VIIIa	V	6	6a	5b	
5.10b	VI+	6a		VIIIb			6a		E2
5.10c	VII-	6a+	19			6+	6b		
5.10d	VII	6b	20	VIIIc	V+	7-	6c		E3
5.11a	VII+	6b+		IXa			7a	5c	
5.11b		6c	21	IXb		7	7b		
5.11c	VIII-	6c+	22		VI-	7+	7c		E4
5.11d	VIII	7a	23	IXc				6a	
5.12a	VIII+	7a+	24				8a		E5
5.12b	IX-	7b	25	Xa	VI	8- / 8	8b		
5.12c		7b+	26	Xb		8+	8c		
5.12d	IX	7c	27				9a	6b	E6
5.13a	IX+	7c+	28	Xc		9-	9b		
5.13b		8a	29				9c		
5.13c	X-	8a+	30			9	10a		E7
5.13d	X	8b	31	XIa	VI+		10b		
5.14a	X+	8b+	32	XIb		9+	10c	7a	E8
5.14b	XI-	8c	33				11a		
5.14c	XI	8c+	34	XIc			11b	7b	E9
5.14d	XI+	9a	35				11c		E10
5.15a	XII-	9a+	36	XIIa		10	12a		
5.15b	XII	9b	37		VII		12b		E11
5.15c		9b+	38	XIIb			12c		
5.15d	XII+	9c	39						